I0129360

A
Boggs/Garringer
Family History

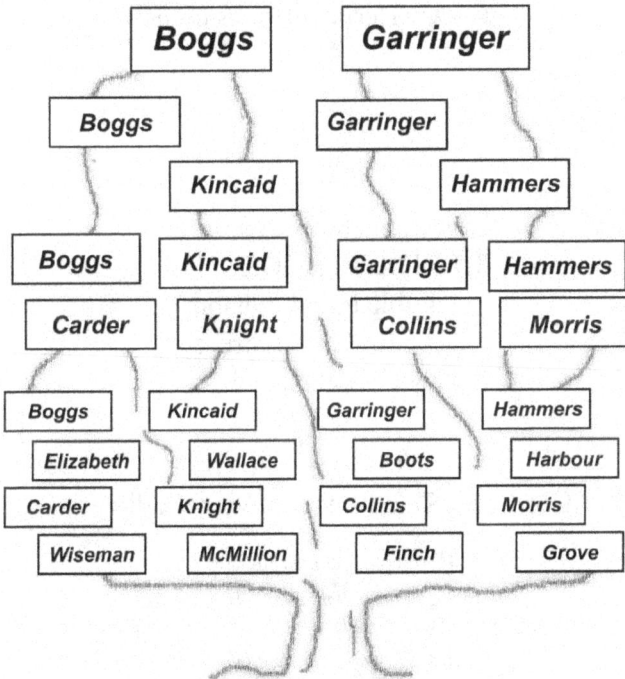

Boggs	Garringer

Boggs		Garringer	
	Kincaid		Hammers

Boggs	Kincaid	Garringer	Hammers
Carder	Knight	Collins	Morris

Boggs	Kincaid	Garringer	Hammers
Elizabeth	Wallace	Boots	Harbour
Carder	Knight	Collins	Morris
Wiseman	McMillion	Finch	Grove

David Vern Addington

HERITAGE BOOKS
2016

HERITAGE BOOKS

AN IMPRINT OF HERITAGE BOOKS, INC.

Books, CDs, and more—Worldwide

For our listing of thousands of titles see our website
at
www.HeritageBooks.com

Published 2016 by
HERITAGE BOOKS, INC.
Publishing Division
5810 Ruatan Street
Berwyn Heights, Md. 20740

Copyright © 2001 David Vern Addington

Heritage Books by the author:

*An Addington - Chalfant Family History: With a
History of the Addington Family in Randolph County, Indiana*

A Boggs/Garringer Family History

All rights reserved. No part of this book may be reproduced or
transmitted in any form or by any means, electronic or mechanical,
including photocopying, recording or by any information storage
and retrieval system without written permission from the author,
except for the inclusion of brief quotations in a review.

International Standard Book Numbers
Paperbound: 978-0-7884-1725-2
Clothbound: 978-0-7884-6315-0

Dedication

to

Ashley and Carmen

and

to their families to come

Table of Content

Acknowledgments

This book is about my maternal grandparents Plummer and Hilda (Garringer) Boggs. I first developed an interest in the genealogy of our family in the mid 1970s when I sat down and had some very interesting talks with my grandmother. She gave me information on her direct knowledge of the family and also gave me several family photos which I treasure to this day and have included some in this book.

I hope my family as well as others enjoy the information contained in this book. I have tried to base everything on documented data. Where I have used my best guess about relationships, I will so state or label with a question mark to indicate some doubt about the information or an assumption on my part.

Genealogy is tremendously interesting to those in its clutches. The remains of our ancestors are but graves, old yellowed records, perhaps an old photo and memories of our most recent ancestors whom we knew as children. This book would not be possible without the many published genealogies I have reviewed and referenced and the help of many people with whom I have worked and corresponded over the many years of this project.

I would like to thank my wife and daughters, Dixie, Ashley and Carmen for their support and patience during this project. My parents, Vern and Louise (Boggs) Addington, were most helpful and visited relatives and undertook some of the research work in Randolph County I was unable to do. My sister, Ann (Addington) Abel, was most helpful for her suggestions and editing of the final text. My thanks to my cousin Susan (Boggs) Latour (Springfield, Virginia) for her help on the research and editing of this book. My cousin Martha (Boggs) Howell supplied several photos and family stories and much encouragement in finishing this project.

For their help and information on the Boggs family, I would like to thank my uncles Keith, Edwin, Bob, and Phil Boggs, my great aunt the late Mrs. Virdie Gilmore (Farmland, Indiana), Mrs. Alice C. Grady (Stow, Massachusetts) and Marilyn Schuelzky (Fort Wayne, Indiana).

My great aunt, the late Mildred (Garringer) Gilpin, of Hollywood, Florida, was very supportive and supplied me with many stories, insights and some photos. Milton Masing of Lawrenceburg, Indiana, has done extensive work on the Garringer family and provided me with information from his sources. Rick Hambrock of Portland, Indiana, provided me with substantial information on the Garringer family in Indiana and I consider him the expert on this family.

I would like to thank Paula Kelly of San Francisco for her help and support on making some small progress on our branch of the Kincaid family. Gilmer W. Callison of Tucson, Arizona, provided me with information on the Knight family and several family stories. Helen Knight Williams of Annapolis, Maryland, graciously provided me with additional information on the Knight family. I thank Alwyn Carder of Redkey, Indiana, for his help and research on the Carder family and his memories of the Boggs and Carders.

Marilyn Peterson of Fort Lauderdale, Florida, was most helpful in deciphering much of the confusing data about the Collins family. Monisa Wisener, the Randolph County Historian, has been most helpful and provided assistance and encouragement.

Thank you to all the other researchers and close and distant family members with whom I have interacted in the last twenty plus years.

David Vern Addington, PhD
Houston, Texas
November 2000

The Samuel Plummer and
Hilda Irene (Garringer) Boggs Family

Samuel Plummer Boggs was born on 2 Apr 1893 in Greenbrier County, West Virginia near the small town of Falling Spring, also called Renick. He was the only surviving son of Noah Edward "Ed" and Clora Jane (Kincaid) Boggs. He had three sisters: Lottie, Virdie and Opal. Both the Boggs and Kincaid families were of Scottish descendency. The name Samuel was a very prevalent name from the Kincaid side of the family; however Plummer was the name he commonly used. Plummer Carder was a brother to Samuel Plummer Boggs' grandmother Phoebe (Carder) Boggs so that is probably the source of the name. Plummer spent his early days on their West Virginia farm until about 1904 when the family moved west to Decatur, Illinois, where Clora Jane (Kincaid) Boggs' brother was living. They stayed there for about a year and then returned to Greenbrier County. About a year later, they moved to Jay County, Indiana, and settled southeast of the town of Redkey. Ed's brother Thomas and sister Rebecca (Boggs) McMillion had previously settled near Redkey. The Boggs' farm was located on the southern Jay County border just east of current road Indiana 1.

Hilda Irene Garringer was born in Green Township of Randolph County, Indiana, on 28 Mar 1898 to Isaac Luther Garringer and Bertha Achsah Hammers. The Garringers and Hammers families are both of German origin, and both date back in the United States to before the American Revolution. Hilda was the second child of Isaac Luther and Bertha Achsah (Hammers) Garringer. She had an older sister Helen Marie, a younger sister Mildred Martha and a younger brother Lloyd Milton. Isaac Garringer farmed a section of land in Green Township, and that is where Hilda grew up.

According to a story Hilda told to one of her granddaughters, she met Plummer at church when they were playing a game which sounds like the children's game of Duck-Duck-Goose. Unfortunately, the year of their meeting is not known, but the following letter from Plummer to Hilda was written a year before their marriage. It was mailed to Miss Hilda Garringer, Farmland, Indiana, and postmarked Redkey Jan 15 1918 and cost 3 cents to send. It represents a different side of Plummer not known to his many grandchildren and is presented here for that enlightenment.

Redkey, Ind.
Jan. 14, 1918

Dear Hilda - Man that I have to write an apology for old <u>King Winter.</u> The sooner I do it the better it will be for me I suppose. Well doesn't this weather beat all. Can you beat it? I think that we could well say that we were snow bound as there were snow drifts as high as my head between the house and barn and the lane to the road to the house was drifted from one to three feet deep. We have got part of it shoveled out and trying run over the remainder but that isn't quite a success.

How did you enjoy the show last Sat. night? That is just our luck to miss seeing the Soldier Boys and who stole the pearls and what became of that old man's tooth. I was betting that it would blow up as it began to hurt him so suddenly.

I think that that storm was the worst that I ever saw or remember and you know how good my memory is and I had one of the most urgent calls along about 4:00 o'clock Sat. evening which was concerning life or death and it fell my lot to see which it was. Well this is the way of it. You know this old batchelor that lives in that quaint old house just north of us. Well his guardian called out here and wanted some one to go and see about him for he did not know how much food he had. I started up there horse back and after climbing over two to three snow drifts I arrived there and found him cutting wood in the front room. I asked if he had anything to eat and he said that he had enough to do until morning. I told him who had sent me. Then he asked if we had a phone? I said yes. Then he said you must call him and tell him to mind his business I am getting along alright.

Now could you just imagine how he was getting along without any wood only as he cut it. As I came back home I had to bad[?] the wind and I thought that it would blow me off the horse.

We got out to town about noon today and they were just getting the roads cleaned. The steam roads were just beginning to go a little there was one train, a passenger came in that was 48 hours late one evening was broke down and the other was almost dry. and I think everyone on it was pretty hungry so they almost eat out Redkey. It stopped for about a hour and you could see people running every where buying something to eat quite a few of them were soldier boys. And the old darkey porter was running back to the train and as he cut across the street he struck some ice with such force that he threw his bucket about ten feet in the air and his feet almost as high then he skidded about ten feet, it was quite a bit funnier that Mildred's mishaps maybe she could sympatize [sic] with him.

The first mail that has come to Redkey for two days came this morning. There has been not interurbans through Redkey since Fri. night but they thought that they would get through today.

I am beginning to think that I am the victim of ill luck for I first got beat four or five games of seven-up. Yes by the way I have learned a new game to play with the new cards. and oh yes I almost forgot to tell you about the acident I had last night a week ago. The horse run into the side of the bridge and broke the shaves out of the buggy, but I made out to get home with them and then found out that I had lost one of my overshoes and had to go back after it. Can you beat it?

I expect that you are getting tired of reading so I will close for this time hoping to see you by Sat. night if nothing prevents.

I am
Plummer

Samuel Plummer Boggs and Hilda Irene Garringer were married on 11 Jan 1919. They lived with Plummer's family for the first year of their marriage. They then rented and moved to a farm in Monroe Township in Section 1, about 1 mile north and 1 mile west of Farmland. About 1923, they moved to another farm about 1 mile east of Farmland, in section 8. Late in 1929, they moved to another farm in Monroe Township, section 34 about 3/4 of a mile north of the Rehoboth Church. In 1933 the family again picked up and moved to north of Muncie near the intersection of Wheeling Pike and Shaffer Road. Then in 1939 they moved to another farm north of Muncie on State Road 3, just south of Shideler Road. In 1941, Plummer was able to buy a farm in Liberty Township of Delaware County about 1 mile east of Selma and one mile south of that town. This is what I always remember as my grandfather's farm and I spent many happy days exploring the farm and watching my grandfather milk his cows. Plummer continually worked and upgraded this farm milking a herd of cows and growing grain to feed them and to sell.

Plummer and Hilda Boggs had five children, four sons and one daughter: Lloyd Keith Boggs, born 2 Apr 1920; Frances Louise Boggs, born 17 Jun 1922; James Edwin Boggs, born 16 Mar 1924; Robert Eugene Boggs, born 15 Apr 1926; and Philip Alan Boggs, born 4 Nov 1928.

Boggs family picnic, August 1928
Picture taken at McCullough Park, Muncie,
back row: Ray Kincaid, Plummer's cousin (name unknown)
middle row from left: Keith, Louise, Fancheon, Plummer's cousin
(name unknown), Edwin, front: Bob

Louise Boggs, 1937, 4H Contest Dress

The Plummer Boggs Family, 1942
Front (left to right): Plummer, Hilda, Edwin
Back: Louise, Bob, Philip, Keith, Marie (Creviston)

Plummer Boggs' Sons, 1942
Front: Edwin and Bob Boggs
Back: Keith and Philip Boggs

Remembrances of growing up in the Boggs family
by Keith Boggs:

Dad used to keep from fifty to fifty-five milk cows from 1930 on
and we milked them by hand and in 1938 we were able to buy
one Surge milking unit, so it would milk two cows while we were
milking another. Then in 1938 we were able to purchase another
unit, and then it would keep one person busy running the two
units. Talk about going modern; that was the easy life. In 1932
we had eight head of horses, two mules, an International 10-20
tractor that pulled two 14 inch plows and Dad farmed around
four hundred acres which was a lot of land in those days. We
had several sows and pigs, too. We expected to be in the barn by
four o'clock and have the horses, hogs and cattle fed and milked
by seven o'clock so I could catch the bus to school by seven thirty.
(I was caught asleep in study hall a few times, as long as I didn't
snore, they let me sleep.)

Dad and two hired hands would go to the corn field and shuck
corn by hand and bring the wagons in at dark and after the
milking was done and everything fed, we would eat supper

around seven-thirty or eight. After supper we would take our lanterns and go out and shovel off the two loads of corn, getting done by eleven o'clock if we were lucky. The hired hands made seventy-five cents a day if mother fed them, or if they brought their lunch, they got a dollar and a quarter.

When it rained and you couldn't do anything else, you got a spade, shovel, ax, mattock and spud (that's a long steel bar with a sharp edge on one end) and went out and dug out tree stumps. In those days there were several tree stumps in the fields that you were trying to farm.

In the summer time at least two times you would need to take the wagons down to the river to soak the wooden wheels so the iron rims would not come off. The flies were biting the horses and they were stomping their feet and switching their tails and you were trying to get the wheels soaked first but you were the one that really got soaked.

In 1933 as we did every year we dug a big hole and lined it with straw and then we dug our potatoes, put them on the straw, then covered them with straw and put chicken wire over this and covered it with dirt. We would do the same with our apples, (but never put apples and potatoes together for the gas from the apples would rot the potatoes). In January we ran out to dig the potatoes and they were rotten; the rats had dug farther out than our chicken wire and gotten into the potatoes. They were rotten as well as our apples. You talk about a tragedy! We lived the rest of the winter on milk toast and black apple butter that you could buy for fifteen cents a quart. Dad had to butcher another hog so we would have enough to eat. He could have sold the hog for four dollars.

In order to conserve electricity we had one light bulb in the barn to milk by and three bulbs in the entire house. Mother cooked on a wood stove and on an oil stove in the summer time when it was real hot. During this time most people were in the same situation as we were. Mother raised ducks to pay for my clarinet and she raised turkeys to buy the piano so Louise could take piano lessons. When I sold my clarinet I remembered this and gave Mother the money for I know how hard she had worked to do this for me.

7

***

Remembrances of Grandma Boggs by one of her granddaughters, Mary Ann (Boggs) Lowther:

After Grandpa Boggs died, I spent a lot of time at the farm. Grandma Boggs was frightened to be alone at the farm at night. One summer, I spent every single night at the farm. She helped me with my reading and taught me even more about the piano. She laughed and played games with me. She certainly could play a mean game of gin rummy. She loved to play games and cards. We would go out and gather chicken eggs together. I helped her sew. She made me beautiful doll clothes, all on an old treadle machine! I cooked with her. We made delicious lemonade. I helped her in the yard. We visited with the friends who came over. She made wonderful breakfasts each and every morning, and then I would help with the dishes. She would wash them in very hot water and heat the kettle up,. After it started to whistle, she would warn me to "STAND BACK" and scald all the dishes so everything would be sanitary. I helped with the laundry and was fascinated by the old crank machine in the shed. She ironed everything including the sheets. Her cookies were the best in the world and some times I have guilt that I don't make 1/100 times the wonderful things that she made for my boys to enjoy. She let me ice the cookies. I loved that terrific old tricycle in the milk house. Her greatest joy was when the other grandchildren were coming to visit. I remember being so happy that She was so happy they were coming over. Her glow lasted several days after they had been there. I think that her mother dying so young had such a tremendous impact (it would on anyone) that she really identified with all her grandchildren and the joys and sorrows that they experienced.

It was always such a treat when cousin Debbie and I both got to spend the night. Once, when we were four, or fiveish, we caught lightning bugs and put them between her sheets to scare her. Imagine our horror when we had to sleep in that bed instead. The next day we confessed to her what we had done and she laughed until she cried and couldn't catch her breath. She always made Debbie and I breakfast and served it on special ornate rose dishes. They were later stolen in the "Break-in at the Farm." I always search for those plates when I go to antique stores to this day trying to find something like them and I never have. Breakfast consisted of bacon, home grown eggs, toast, and wonderful home made hot chocolate. My husband is the only chef in the world who can come close to cooking like Grandma Boggs.

Remembrances of Edwin and Bob Boggs
as recorded by Susan (Boggs) Latour:

Plummer Boggs and his sisters attended Green Township High School in Randolph County. At 15 Plummer left school to work on a farm in Illinois. Then he went to live in West Virginia. At 17, he returned to Jay County. Living on the Jay/Randolph county line, he drove the hack (school bus) to Green Township High School because he lived the farthest from the school. Thus he was 21 when he graduated from Green Township High School in the same class as his younger sister Lottie.

Hilda Garringer graduated from Farmland High School and attended Indiana University for one year. When her mother, Bertha, died, she returned home to care for Mildred and Lloyd, her siblings.

Neither family wanted Plummer and Hilda to marry. Because Plummer farmed with his dad, his family probably did not want him to leave. Plummer's sisters also made Hilda feel uncomfortable. Since Hilda was raising her brother and one younger sister, her father was probably not eager for her to leave home.

After they were first married, Plummer and Hilda lived with his parents and sisters for a year. Eager to be on their own, Plummer and Hilda moved to a Garringer farm north of Farmland, Indiana. Next they rented the Bly Bayles farm located north and east of Farmland. Each of their moves was probably in February or March because tenant farmers always moved in early spring so that they would be able to put in the crops for the upcoming growing season. At harvest, the landowner split the crops with the farmer. Owners always looked favorably at the number of children a family had because that indicated how many hands could work the farm. From the Bayles farm, the family moved in 1928 to the Janney farm north of Parker and worked it for five years. In 1933 they became tenant farmers on the Marsh farm on Wheeling Pike in Muncie, Indiana. They stayed on that land until 1939 when the owner sold the farm, and Plummer moved his family to the Riggin farm on Highway 3 north of Muncie. In 1940, the government farm assistance program provided loans to farmers to help them buy 160 acres of land, but Plummer was not selected to participate that year. Farmers would have a 30-year mortgage that had to be paid in full at the death of the applicant. In 1941, Plummer applied for and received a government loan to help him purchase his 80-acre farm east of Selma, Indiana.

Often the size and condition of the farmhouse determined how the family lived. On the Marsh farm, all four boys slept in one bedroom of the small farmhouse, and Louise slept in the front room. On the Selma farm, the wash house was adjacent to the farmhouse. The family used this for laundry, bathing, and cleaning. Hilda, a meticulous housekeeper, would set out a fresh set of clothes in the wash house for Plummer to put on when he came into the house at the end of his workday. She did not want dirt from the farm to come into her house. They cut wood to heat their houses. Since the bedrooms were unheated, the boys remember sleeping back to back to stay warm. Using kerosene lanterns was commonplace until Plummer installed electricity in the Selma home in 1941. Their outhouse was located by the grape arbor, and the grandchildren remember making many trips to that structure. It was not until the early 1960s that Plummer and Hilda installed a bathroom in their home.

Everybody had work to do on the farm. Chores might include carrying water and feed to the animals, mowing the yard, or scrubbing clothes on a washboard. Saturdays were hard workdays. If it was harvest season, the boys would shuck an entire cornfield by hand. The boys remembered farming with draft horses; Plummer bought a tractor in the late 1930s. He planted crops as well as raised cows and pigs. The boys were not allowed to be in the house during the day. Louise helped Hilda in the house while the boys worked on the farm. Hilda sometimes helped Plummer milk the cows. While they lived on the Marsh farm on Wheeling Pike, Howard Epperson, a hired hand, stayed with them during the week.

The children also had time to play. Eddie remembers playing croquet on hot summer evenings. When they were not working, the boys played a lot of basketball in the barn. Christmas was usually celebrated by only the immediate family. Receiving an orange was a highlight of this holiday. Birthdays were special for each child. Hilda would bake each child's favorite cake: Robert's choice was angel food cake; Eddie's was spice cake. French chewing, a taffy-like candy, was another family treat. During the winter months, they would pull it on a Sunday afternoon.

Hilda cooked and baked on a wood stove for which Plummer had cut wood. She bought her first electric stove in 1933 because the Marsh farm had electricity. The family ate all three meals together. Each child had an assigned seat. If chicken was served, each child had his designated piece with the older children having first pick.

Monday was laundry day, and Hilda always served cabbage on those days. She also made her own soap. During the school year, each boy had one pair of pants and several shirts, which they washed on the weekends.

The three older children attended Parker School for their early elementary years, but for most of the children's school years, the family lived in Delaware County, Indiana. Keith and Louise graduated from Royerton High School. When Plummer bought the Selma farm, Eddie transferred to Selma High School for his senior year. Bob and Phil also graduated from Selma High School. In the 1960s, many Indiana schools consolidated. Royerton, DeSoto, and Eaton high schools united to become Delta High School. Center and Selma schools combined to become Wapahani High School.

Hilda had a strong sense of what was appropriate behavior. She was always concerned about what the neighbors might think. For example, she would not walk on a downtown street. Instead, Plummer had to drive her. She never did laundry on Sunday because people might see clothes drying on the clothesline. Socially, she was a member of a home economics club. Hilda always wore a dress and carried a handkerchief; in the summers, she added a sunbonnet to her ensemble. Hilda would wear a dress hat for special occasions, and her favorite color was blue. She gardened every summer. All the children had to work in the garden, and she canned meat, vegetables, and lots of jellies. Because she raised chickens, eggs were plentiful. She made noodles with the yolks, and angel food cakes with the whites. Butterscotch pies were another specialty of hers. Hilda gave birth to all her children at home, had high blood pressure, and had her gall bladder removed. Hilda did not drive. When she was learning to drive a car, she hit the garage. She never drove again.

Hilda and Plummer never went to church. Perhaps one reason was that Hilda did not have dress clothes. When they lived on Wheeling Pike, the children attended College Avenue Methodist Church; when they lived on the Riggin farm on Highway 3 North, they were members of Eden United Church of Christ. Plummer always rested on Sunday. He was a quiet man with rather large hands. Standing 5' 11", he had brown hair and blue eyes. A cigarette smoker, he never smoked in the house. At 60, he got false teeth but would not wear them (the dentures must have hurt). As a result, he ate lots of peanut butter and bread. Plummer cut the boys' hair. Infrequently, the boys would go to a barber in Farmland to get a 25-cent haircut and be treated to a big candy bar. When the boys misbehaved, he used a razor strop to discipline them. He rarely dressed up, but when he did, he always wore a dress hat. He visited many friends in Selma in the hardware and grocery stores. He disliked doctors and would not stay in the hospital when he had his heart attack in his early 60s.

Plummer never played ball with the boys; he did not have the time. He always had a farm dog, usually a German shepherd. Fred Roy, Jacks (a ferocious dog), and Sheik were three of his dogs. He listened to the Cincinnati Reds baseball games on the radio as he milked the cows. Plummer kept whiskey in the barn or garage and would often sweeten it with hard rock candy. Hilda never drank. Plummer managed the family's finances; Hilda had to ask him for money.

One memory of Edwin's is that Plummer and Granddad Garringer attended the World's Fair in Chicago (probably 1936). Hilda's sisters Helen and Mildred lived in Gary and Chicago at the time, so the men stayed with them. After Plummer returned home, the children remembered seeing all his clothes hanging on the clothesline outdoors. The children guessed that he had brought home bedbugs because Helen lived in such poor conditions and that Hilda was getting rid of the pests.

Plummer was distant with his children. When it was time for Edwin to get his driver's license, he had to drive himself to the license branch because Plummer had gone to the back woods. When the examiner asked who his adult sponsor was, Edwin knew he was in trouble because he had driven to the test without having a valid driver's license. The man behind him in line stepped up and volunteered to be his licensed driver during the test. Edwin surmised that this man recognized him as a basketball player and did him quite a favor. Edwin got his license and returned home. Plummer never asked what had happened.

Edwin remembers spending two summers in the 1930s living with his grandmother, Clora Boggs. She was widowed and needed him to do chores for her. There were no other children nearby to play with; because the house had no electricity, he went to bed in a very dark bedroom. On weekends, he would return home.

Granddad Ike Garringer had little to do with the family; he was aloof. After Bertha's death, Hilda's father, Ike Garringer, would travel to Florida in the winter, taking his son Lloyd, to build houses. He spent most of his money while there.

Plummer and Hilda raised their five children during the Depression without financial assistance from either of the Garringer or the Boggs families. Their children remember two parents who never fought, who provided a warm home, adequate clothing, and hearty meals, and who taught them strong values. During World War II, these parents watched and waited as their sons Keith, Bob, and future son-in-law (Louise's husband), Vern Addington, served in the U.S. Army and as Edwin served in the U.S. Navy. Each of these men survived the war and returned home to their families.

Plummer and Hilda's lives were not much different from every other tenant farm family struggling during hard financial times. Their work ethic, solid values, and sheer diligence enabled them to offer the next generation a better life. They moved often, they had five children, and they did what they had to do to survive. They experienced a century that changed from a horse and buggy world to one where man landed on the moon. They saw their children obtain advanced degrees, marry successfully, find fulfilling jobs, and have healthy, happy grandchildren. In their own quiet ways, they gave us all quite a legacy.

* * *

The four sons and one daughter of Plummer and Hilda Boggs married and started their own households. Each Thanksgiving and Christmas would be spent with ever expanding families and more and more grandchildren until a total of sixteen grandchildren arrived. Summer gatherings would include softball games in the large barnyard and hitting the ball over the fence into the cow pasture was a great thrill. Homemade ice cream was a specialty and always appreciated by the grandchildren.

Plummer suffered a heart attack in 1962 but recovered completely and continued farming. Three years later he died of heart failure on 9 Apr 1965. He was buried in Woodlawn Cemetery at Maxville where the parents and grandparents of Hilda are also buried.

The livestock and farming equipment were put up for auction that summer and Hilda moved into nearby Parker City in a house next to her son Philip and his family. The farm was later sold and two lots were sold on the western line and houses constructed on them.

Hilda "Grandma Boggs" lived on Main Street in Parker City from 1965 till 1976 when she moved to Fulton Street. Her first great grandchild arrived in 1969 and family gatherings saw many more follow. Hilda developed throat cancer in 1983 and died on 26 Dec 1983 in Parker City at her home. She had eighteen great grandchildren at the time of her death and eight more after that date. She is buried beside Plummer in the Woodlawn Cemetery at Maxville.

The following obituary was printed in the Tuesday, 27 Dec 1983 edition of the *Muncie Star*:

PARKER CITY, Ind. - Hilda I. Boggs, 85, wife of Plummer Boggs, died Monday in her home after an extended illness.

She was a Randolph County native but spent most of her life in Delaware County. She graduated from Farmland High School and attended Indiana University.

She was a member of Parker City United Methodist Church, the church's Dorcas Circle, and Parker City Garden Club, and she was a charter member of Modern Farm Wives Home Economics Club.

Survivors include a daughter, Louise (Mrs. Vern) Addington, Anderson; four sons, Keith and Robert, both of Selma, Edwin, Muncie, and Philip, Dunkirk; a sister, Mildred Gilpin, Hollywood, Fla.; 16 grandchildren, and 18 great-grandchildren.

Services will be at 10 a.m. Thursday in Meeks Mortuary with Rev. James Butler officiating. Burial will be in the Woodlawn Cemetery, Maxville. Calling hours at the mortuary are 3-5 and 7-9 p.m. Wednesday or before services Thursday.

Keith Boggs, son of Plummer and Hilda

Lloyd Keith Boggs, the first son of Plummer and Hilda was born on 2 Apr 1920 on a farm near Farmland, Indiana. He grew up in Randolph and Delaware Counties on several different farms. He married Marie Elizabeth Creviston on 26 Jun 1941 near Muncie. Keith entered the Army in Jan 1943 and served until Dec 1945. After the war he began working for Warner Gear in Muncie and Keith and Marie built a house southeast of Muncie. In 1956 they bought a farm north of Selma, Indiana, on what is now road 200N, just east of road 400W. Keith worked for Warner Gear for 40 years before retiring to their farm. Marie earned bachelor's and master's degrees in elementary education from Ball State Teachers College and taught in the West View Elementary School for over 30 years until her retirement in 1985. Keith and Marie Boggs had three daughters: Rachel Ellen, born 25 Jun 1949; Martha Elizabeth, born 14 Dec 1951; and Mary Ann, born 23 Nov 1956.

Rachel Ellen Boggs graduated from Earlham College in Richmond, Indiana, and married Allan Kaufman on 16 Jun 1969 in Wayne County, Indiana. They have two children, Lisa Beth Kaufman, born 27 Dec 1969 in Richmond, Indiana, and Joshua Allan Kaufman, born 18 Nov 1974 in Ann Arbor, Michigan. Rachel and Allan later divorced and Rachel returned to school earning a M. D. from the University of Toledo. Martha "Marty" Elizabeth Boggs graduated from Indiana University with a B. S. in Education and received a M. Ed. from the University of Arizona in 1978 and taught school in Arizona for four years. She later moved to the Dallas area where she taught for seven years and married George Howell on 28 Feb 1982 in Arlington, Texas. They have one son, Adam Christopher Howell, born 7 May 1985, in Arlington and continue to reside there. Mary Ann Boggs married John Lowther on 14 Feb 1980 in Indianapolis, Indiana, and they moved to Arizona two weeks later. They currently own and operate a construction company in the Phoenix area. They have two sons, John Keith Lowther, born 1 Oct 1983 in Phoenix and Max Conrad Lowther, born 23 Dec 1988, also born in Phoenix. Marie (Creviston) Boggs died on 29 Sep 1993 and is buried in the Mount Tabor Cemetery in Delaware County, Indiana.

Louise Boggs, daughter of Plummer and Hilda

Frances Louise Boggs was born on 17 Jun 1922 on a farm about one mile northwest of Farmland. Louise attended school at several different locations as the family moved and graduated in 1940 from Royerton High School which was located north of Muncie. She attended Ball State Teachers College starting in the fall of 1940 where she met Vern Addington in her junior year. Vern was drafted into the army in 1943 and they continued corresponding until he was released from active duty in late 1945. Louise graduated from Ball State in 1944 with a Bachelor's Degree in Home Economics. She then taught school in the Farmland and Parker Township school systems. Louise Boggs married Vern Addington on 24 May 1946 in Cowan before a minister with her brother Keith and his wife Marie as witnesses. Vern completed his degree at Ball State and the family moved to a house on Main Street in Farmland, Indiana. Vern taught school at Lincoln School in 1947 and 1948. In 1950 the Addington family moved to another house in Farmland on Mulberry Street. Vern and Louise

Addington had three children while living in Farmland: Ann Frances Addington, born 11 Jun 1947, David Vern Addington, born 4 Aug 1948 and Dale Lee Addington, born 5 Dec 1950.

Vern Addington taught school for three years and then accepted a job with the J. I. Case Company as a sales representative in farm implements. In 1952 the family moved to Twelve Mile, Indiana, and spent 5 years there. In 1957, they moved to Greenwood, Indiana, where they lived for two years. In 1959, they moved to the St. Louis, Missouri, area where they lived in the northern suburbs of Moline Acres. In 1962, they moved to Anderson, Indiana, and bought a home on Dogwood Drive in the South Edgewood addition. All three children graduated from Madison Heights High School in Anderson. After teaching for many years, Louise also returned to Ball State to earn a MS degree in 1965. She taught home economics at the high school and middle school level for over thirty-eight years, including the last twenty-five years in the Noblesville School System. Vern and Louise are retired and still reside in Anderson, Indiana. In their retirement, Vern and Louise have been very active volunteers with several community agencies in the Anderson area, particularly with the historic Paramount Theater.

Of the children of Vern and Louise, Ann Frances Addington graduated from Ball State University in 1969 with a BA degree in English. She also earned a MS degree in Library Science from Indiana University. She has taught English and been a school librarian in the Kokomo area schools for over fifteen years. Ann married Capt. Richard Abel on 24 Apr 1971 at Grissom Air Force Base. They have one daughter, Amy Louise Abel, born 6 Mar 1978 in Kokomo, Indiana. The Abels continue to reside in Kokomo, Indiana. The oldest son, David Vern Addington, graduated from Purdue University in 1970 with a BS degree in Chemical Engineering with Highest Distinction. He served in the U. S. Air Force from 1971 until 1974 in Germany and Alabama. He returned to graduate school and received MS and PhD degrees in Chemical Engineering from The University of Michigan. David moved to Texas and has worked in the production side of the oil industry since his graduation. David married Dixie Carol Behr, daughter of A. J. "Dick" and Evelyn (Brammer) Behr on 29 Dec 1979 in Richardson, Texas. They have two children: Ashley Lynn Addington, born 20 Nov 1982 in

Dallas, Texas, and Carmen Elizabeth Addington, born 1 Nov 1985 in Dallas. The youngest son of Vern and Louise, Dale Lee Addington, graduated from Purdue University in 1972 with a BS degree in Economics. He married Tammi Carson on 10 Jun 1972 in West Lafayette, Indiana. Dale first worked for many years for Sears, Roebuck and Company and later in other management positions. Dale and Tammi (Carson) Addington have two sons: Stephen Carson Addington, born 16 May 1982 in Findlay, Ohio, and James Michael Addington, born 28 Aug 1984 in Findlay. Dale and Tammi and their family still reside in Findlay, Ohio.

Edwin Boggs, son of Plummer and Hilda

James Edwin Boggs, born 16 Mar 1924, grew up in Randolph and Delaware Counties on several different farms and served in the Navy during World War II from Jul 1944 until Mar 1946. He married on 27 May 1944 in Muncie to June Berry. After the war, Edwin and June moved a farm northeast of Muncie (on now Riggin Road) where they have lived for over fifty years. Edwin and June had four children, all born in Muncie: Susan, born 22 Feb 1945, Stephen Edwin, born 3 May 1947, Dianna June, born 2 Jun 1950 and Charles Hamilton, born 21 Nov 1951.

Susan Boggs graduated from Ball State University with a B.S. in Education in May 1967 and has taught at the high school level for many years. She earned a MS degree in Education from Butler University in June 1972. Susan married Dennis Bruce Latour on 2 Jun 1968 near Muncie. Susan and Dennis have two children: Jennifer Susan, born 27 May 1972 in Indianapolis, Indiana, and Jeffrey Allen, born 15 Sep 1976 in Indianapolis. Jennifer graduated from Indiana University in 1994 and currently resides in Boston, Massachusetts. Jeffrey is attending George Mason University and plans to graduate in Dec 2000. He resides in Springfield, Virginia. Dennis and Susan live in Springfield, Virginia, where they have resided for many years. Stephen Edwin Boggs graduated from Ball State University in 1969 and married Letha Knerr on 18 Aug 1968 in Martinsville, Indiana. They have lived in Indianapolis, St. Louis, Chicago and Cincinnati where they continue to reside. Dianna Boggs attended Ball State University and married Jerry Richard Eiler on 7 Mar 1970 in Muncie, Indiana. They have two daughters: Lora Diane, born 8 Oct 1971 in Muncie and Christy Elizabeth, born 12 Feb

1974 in Muncie. Christy Eiler married Joseph Michael Knight on 3 Apr 1999 in Muncie and they currently reside there. Lora Dianne Eiler currently resides in Dallas, Texas. Charles Boggs married on 20 Oct 1972 in Muncie, Indiana, to Pam Caldwell Hammers. Charles and Pam have two children: Anna Stasha, born 17 Sep 1974 in Muncie and Charles Edwin, born 13 Jul 1976 in Muncie, plus Charlie adopted Pam's daughter Michlynn Hammer Boggs, born 16 Jun 1970. Charles and Pam later divorced. Anna Stasha Boggs married Eric Scott Baker in Muncie, Indiana on 20 May 2000. Charles Edwin Boggs married Stormie Ann Morgan on 27 Feb 1999 in Muncie, Indiana. They have two daughters, Courtlinn Kileigh Boggs, born 15 Oct 1966 in Muncie, and Carlie B. Boggs, born 13 Jul 2000.

Robert Boggs, son of Plummer and Hilda

Robert Eugene Boggs, "Uncle Bob," grew up on his father's farm and went into the Army in May 1945, returning in Nov 1946. He returned to Ball State University and earned his BS degree in 1950 and later an MA degree. Bob married Helen Roberta Wright on 4 Mar 1955 near Muncie, Indiana. Bob taught for 2 years in Butler Township, Miami County, Indiana, for 5 years in Harrison Township, Delaware County, Indiana, and for 32 years in the Selma (later Wapahani) schools and coached several sports. He later became an assistant principal there before retiring in 1989. Bob and Helen have three children: William Robert "Bill", born 6 Feb 1956, in Muncie, Debra Lea, born 17 Dec 1957 in Muncie, and Rodney Eugene, born 6 Dec 1961. Bob and Helen make their home north of Selma, Indiana.

William Robert Boggs graduated from Ball State University and currently lives in Muncie, Indiana. Debra Lea Boggs graduated from Indiana University and married Mark Charles Ladendorf on 20 Jun 1981, in Muncie, Indiana. Debra and Mark reside in Fishers, Indiana, and have two sons: Lance Robert, born 27 Apr 1986, in Indianapolis and Luke Mark Ladendorf, born 9 May 1989 in Indianapolis and one daughter Hannah Lea Ladendorf, born 27 Apr 1993. Rodney Eugene Boggs attended Ball State University and Indiana University and married Lisa Marie Burwell in Indianapolis on 5 Nov 1988. Rodney and Lisa live in Brookville, Indiana, and have two children, Bryant Eugene, born 24 Jan 1989, and Elizabeth Marie, born 26 Oct 1990, both in Indianapolis.

Philip Boggs, son of Plummer and Hilda

Philip Boggs married on 23 Nov 1947 in Muncie, Indiana, to Jean Ann Gowin. Philip and Jean Ann first lived in Parker City while Philip worked for Chevrolet in Muncie for about ten years before going into farming. Philip and Jean Ann bought a farm near Dunkirk, Indiana, where they raised their family. They have since retired and moved to Muncie where they keep extremely busy with volunteer work at a Muncie hospital.

Philip and Jean Ann had three children all born in Muncie, Catherine Ann, born 22 Sep 1948, Rebecca Jane, born 11 Nov 1952 and Philip Patrick, born 30 Jul 1955. Catherine graduated from Ball State University and then married on 26 Feb 1972 in Muncie, to David Hearld. They had two children, Angela Jane, born 29 Sep 1972 and Jason Ray, born 11 Nov 1982. Cathey and David later divorced. Rebecca "Becky" first married John Morris and married second Tom Mench. Rebecca and Tom have two children, Michael Thomas, born 29 Jun 1979, in Richmond, Indiana and Andrea Elizabeth, born 7 Dec 1984, in Cincinnati, Ohio. Becky and Tom currently reside in Cincinnati. Pat Boggs married Joyce Lowe on 26 Jan 1979 and they have one daughter, Michelle Leann, born 8 Dec 1980 plus Joyce's daughter Adrian Deann, born 27 Apr 1976.

Plummer Boggs, the farmer as his grandchildren knew him
early 1960s

Plummer and Hilda Boggs
1962

Plummer and Hilda (Garringer) Boggs' Grandchildren, 1958
front row from left: Charles, Pat,
Billy on tricycle, Dale, Becky, Martha,
back row from left, Dianna, Rachel, Cathy, David, Steve,
Ann holding Mary Ann, Susan holding Debbie

Philip, Louise Addington, Edwin, Keith and Bob Boggs
Hilda (Garringer) Boggs
1983

Randolph County History

A review of the history of Randolph County seems appropriate since the ancestral families of Hilda Irene Garringer were early settlers and Hilda spent her entire life in Randolph and nearby Delaware County. The land that is now Randolph County was part of the original Northwest Territory ceded to the struggling United States after the Revolutionary War. Before that the land had been wilderness for thousands of years with only the native American Indians sparsely occupying the land and leaving no permanent settlements.

Numerous relics of the prehistory of Randolph County have been found. Several Indian burial mounds of various sizes were found in the county by the first settlers. Unfortunately, most were destroyed in the process of developing and cultivating the land. Before the appearance of white settlers in Indiana, the region was occupied by the tribes belonging to the Miami confederacy. The main tribes inhabiting Indiana were the Miamis, the Pottawatomies, the Weas, the Delawares and the Kickapoos. The Indians were quite prevalent and Indian trouble came to a head in 1812 and 1813. The trouble had settled down by 1814 and in a treaty made at Fort Wayne in 1818, certain tracts were reserved for the Indians.

The first settlers in central Indiana were in Wayne County which is located just south of Randolph County. Wayne County settlers started moving in about 1800. Many of these settlers were from North Carolina, disliked slavery and were looking for a new free land to settle. The special 1807 census of the Northwest Territory shows only a few thousand people living in the state of what is now Indiana.

Randolph County lies in the eastern part of Indiana on the Ohio border. The county is about twenty-one and three quarters miles from east to west and twenty-one miles from south to north encompassing nearly 457 square miles. Randolph County is bounded on the north by Jay County, on the east by Mercer and

Darke Counties in Ohio, on the south by Wayne County, and on the west by Delaware and Henry Counties. Two Indian boundaries pass through the county, both in a southwesterly direction. The first resulted from a treaty made at Greenville, Ohio in 1795 by Gen. Anthony Wayne and several tribes. The second line was drawn up for a treaty made with the Indians in 1809 by Gen. Harrison, the Governor of the Indiana territory. It was called the twelve mile boundary because the Indians ceded a strip twelve miles wide, just west of the previous boundary. When Randolph County was first created by the Legislature in 1818, it embraced only the land east of the twelve mile border. In December 1819, the Legislature fixed the boundaries as they now stand.

There are no mountains nor even high hills in Randolph County. The land is mainly low and level and often needs drainage. Randolph County is drained by the start of two major rivers, the Mississinewa River in the northern part of the county and by the White River running through the center of the county. Many of the streams and the two rivers were used in the early days for water power for grist-mills, saw-mills and other machinery. When the first settlers arrived the county was thickly timbered with a tall, heavy forest, having a wonderful undergrowth of shrubs, wild grasses and weeds. The trees were beech, sugar tree, ash, oak, poplar, walnut, elm, hickory, buckeye, linn, wild maple, hackberry, coffeenut, honey locust and cottonwood. The main game were deer, squirrels, turkeys, pheasants and bears with some wolves, raccoons and various kinds of wild cats. Wild hogs became quite prevalent after the first settlers arrived and some of their domestic animals escaped to the wild.

The first white settlers in Randolph County starting moving into the southeastern townships in 1814, mainly moving up from Wayne County. The new county formed by the Legislature in 1818, was named Randolph from the old Randolph County in North Carolina, because many of the residents within its limits had come from that county in the "Old North State" and, because a member of the Legislature, living within its bounds, was also a native of the same. Winchester was located as the county seat of Randolph County at the same time. The first acknowledged settlement in Randolph County was made in April 1814 in Greensfork Township by Thomas Parker (a Quaker from North

Carolina) with his wife and three children. A considerable amount of land entries were made in 1814 and 1815, although often the owners did not occupy the land for several years. The land entries in the first two years were mostly in Greensfork, Washington and White River Townships in the southeastern portion of the county. There were even more land entries in 1816, 1817 and 1818 but then settlement slowed with almost no new growth from 1820 to 1828. Land entries were at a relative low level until 1831 when they increased and by 1837, almost all of the land had been "taken up." Land speculators had some of the land and many tracts laid unoccupied for many years. Whereas land entries for about 32,000 acres were entered on between 1815 and 1817, the years of 1832 through 1837 saw 172,000 acres claimed.

The ancestral families of Hilda Irene Garringer settled mainly in Monroe and Green Townships in the northwestern part of Randolph County and were some of the very earliest settlers. Monroe and Green Townships were the last areas of Randolph County to be settled. The Garringer and Boots families came to this area in 1832. The 1882 History of Randolph County states that Alexander Garringer and Martin Boots were the first settlers in Green Township living near the location of the town of Fairview. Elijah Harbour moved into this area by 1834. The Hammers family was in Monroe Township by about 1836. The Morris and Grove families were later settlers moving in about 1854. The other ancestral families of Collins and Finch lived a little further north, just over the county border in Jay County.

The early settlers were strongly religious people and churches were soon organized and built. Often a church would be convened at someone's house until a crude but suitable building could be built. It appears that the Friends and Methodists were probably the first to organize and build churches in Randolph County.

Winchester was the first town established in the county. Gov. Jennings appointed David Wright Sheriff and asked him to organize the county. Five individuals donated 158 acres of land to help establish the site of Winchester, which was accepted by a set of commissioners appointed by David Wright. For several years after 1818, until the northern counties were organized, Winchester was the seat of justice for all the white people north, including those at Fort Wayne. Lots were laid out in the fall and winter of 1818 and sold the following spring. Contracts to build the first courthouse ($254.50) and the first jail ($125) were let in December 1818 and were accepted by the commissioners in October 1820. The first house was built in the spring of 1819 on lot no. 9 and was a round log-cabin, owned and occupied for many years by Martin Comer. Winchester grew slowly and by 1830, there were still but only a dozen houses or so. It was still mainly just the seat of justice and little else. Most people lived a rural agricultural life and had no need of visiting the town.

The cabins that the early settlers built were crude and built from round logs of eight to ten inches in diameter. Sizes were from small cabins of twelve by fourteen feet to maybe eighteen by twenty-five feet. Small cabins usually had one door and maybe one window while large cabins had two doors and several windows. Cabins were one story of about eight feet with a loft above in the roof. A fireplace and chimney occupied one wall and opened into the house. At the "raising," neighbors from miles around would come and lend their aid. The use of glass windows in houses was not prevalent until about 1850. Eventually as saw mills were built, the quality and size of the cabins improved.

Early education in Randolph County was usually done at home since schools were few. The few schools that were available were usually associated with local churches. Before 1850 nearly all schools were supported by subscriptions and often times poorly supported. More public funds were allocated after this, but the school systems did not seem well organized until into the 1870s. The level of the education depended greatly on the family's commitment to educate their children. The Union Literary Institute was founded in Ridgeville in the 1846 and educated blacks along with some white settlers' children. Ridgeville College was founded in 1867 by the Free Will Baptists and survived until 1902.

The population of Randolph County by the 1840 census was 10,684. The county continued to grow to 14,785 by 1850, 18,997 by 1860 and to 26,768 by 1880. The population was evenly distributed but with a few towns of size. By 1880, only Union

City (2,478), Winchester (1,965), Ridgeville (775) and Farmland (669) had substantial populations.

When the Civil War started in 1861, Randolph County showed its loyalty and devotion to that noble cause. Although exact numbers are not known, over 2,000 men from Randolph County served in the volunteer forces, this from a total population of about 19,000 in 1860. At least 250 of these brave volunteers lost their lives due to combat or disease in helping to insure the survival of the Union.

A majority of the above history is taken from *History of Randolph County, Indiana with Illustrations and Biographical Sketches* which was published by the Rev. Ebenezer Tucker in 1882. Rev. Tucker spent over three years traveling around the county and interviewing numerous early settlers and gathering the early history of Randolph County. This oversize 512 page book is a monumental achievement and should be consulted to truly understand the hardships and environment of the early pioneers who settled Randolph County.

In more recent history, Randolph County has remained an agricultural based economy. The population of Randolph County has grown only slowly being about 28,900 in 1980. The population has shifted more to the cities as modern mechanization has resulted in larger farms.

Randolph County has taken pride in its history, its people and its accomplishments. The Historical and Genealogical Society of Randolph County has undertaken the task of organizing and recording this rich history. The Society published in 1990 an updated history of *Randolph County, Indiana 1818-1990* which covers the last one hundred years of the county's history.

Woodlawn Cemetery

Woodlawn Cemetery is located at Maxville, north of the old Maxville Road and it is sometimes referred to as the Maxville Cemetery. Maxville is located about two miles southeast of

Farmland and six miles west of Winchester. The old section of the cemetery is located on the south side of Maxville Road with the oldest burial stone being dated 1832. The first section of the cemetery on the north side of the road was laid out in 1875 and new sections have been added several times since then. The latest section was the Rhody section, laid out in 1970 south of Maxville Road and east of the church.

Samuel Plummer and Hilda (Garringer) Boggs are buried in section 7H in the northeast portion of the cemetery. Hilda (Garringer) Boggs has a significant number of ancestors and relatives buried in Woodlawn Cemetery, this probably being the reason that she chose this cemetery when Plummer died in 1965. Hilda's parents, Isaac Luther and Bertha (Hammers) Garringer are buried not far away to the south of Plummer and Hilda's grave. Hilda's maternal grandparents, Elijah Oliver and Elizabeth (Morris) Hammers, are also buried nearby. Elijah's parents and Hilda's great-grandparents, Abraham and Nancy (Harbour) Hammers are buried on the far west side of the cemetery in section 2. Hilda has two sets of Garringer uncles and aunts and one set of Hammers uncles and aunts buried in the cemetery. There are also numerous great aunts and uncles buried in Woodlawn Cemetery from the Garringer, Hammers, Grove, and Morris families. Plummer's sister, Virdie, and her husband, Revillo Gilmore, are buried in the newer Rhody section of the cemetery.

Greenbrier County History

Greenbrier County, West Virginia, plays an important part in all of the ancestral families of Samuel Plummer Boggs. The Boggs family was in Greenbrier County by 1771 and the Kincaid family settled there about the same time. Other families associated with these like the McMillion, Cavendish and McClung families were also very early settlers in Greenbrier County. The most recent and thorough history of Greenbrier was written in 1986 by Otis K. Rice and published by the Greenbrier Historical Society, entitled *A History of Greenbrier County*.

Greenbrier County is the second largest county in West Virginia with 1022.8 square miles and is located in the far southeastern part of the state. The name Greenbrier was first applied to the river bearing that name about 1740 while the county was not formally organized until 1778. When the county was first organized it consisted of the present Greenbrier County plus everything running north of the Kanawha River to a line about 40 degrees north of west from the far most northeastern corner of the current county and west all the way to the Ohio River. Later the western part of the original Greenbrier County was organized into the counties of Fayette, Nicholas, Kanawha, Clay, Roane and the southern counties of Summers and Monroe plus parts of several other counties.

The eastern portion of Greenbrier County lies in a valley and ridge geographic region while the western portion of the county lies in a part of the Appalachian Plateau. The highest point in Greenbrier County is at Grassy Knob at 4,372 feet above sea level while the lowest point on the Greenbrier River is at 1,520 feet. The eastern part of the county contains a substantial area of relative broad flood plains. The Greenbrier River dominates the eastern half of the county. It begins south of the county in the Allegheny Mountains and enters Greenbrier County along the border with Monroe County, then meanders in a northeastern direction passing east of Lewisburg and Falling Spring. A major tributary Anthony Creek enters the river south of Falling Spring.

Greenbrier County contains numerous caves in which artifacts and bones from prehistoric man have been found indicating the county has been occupied many thousands of years ago. Two major Indian trails, the Seneca Trail and the Kanawha Trail, pass through the county, indicating that even though the county was not heavily settled by Indians, they often passed through.

The most notable features of the county when the first European settlers moved in were the great forests and savannahs. White pine forest stood east of the Greenbrier River while the western forests contained many different trees, most of significant commercial value. The forest provided a great variety of animals for hunting so the early settlers were rarely without meat. Greenbrier County has several mineral springs where the minerals precipitate out on the surface forming various colors which have been named for the larger springs, such as White Sulphur, Black Sulphur and Blue Sulphur Springs.

The first expedition to explore the Greenbrier area was sent out in 1671 by the owner of a trading post at Petersburg. Other fur traders may have been in the region earlier but this was the first group to bring back definitive information on the region. The Blue Ridge Valley of Virginia was not opened to settlement until about 1730 when land was made available under easy terms to attract settlers. By 1750 the valley was well populated and further west was looked upon as the next frontier. Two large land grants for the Greenbrier Valley were made on 25 Apr 1745 to groups of various influential people. They were required to settle one family for each 1000 acres within four years. Initially the groups were not able to attract settlers due to the uncertainty between England and France of claims to this area so extensions were allowed in the settling of the land.

Land surveys were first made in 1750/52 so at least a few land speculators were busy gathering up the land and a few settlers were braving the frontier to have access to the land. In 1755, an expedition against the Indians by British General Edward Braddock met disaster at the Forks of the Ohio and led to more uncertainty and insecurity in the Greenbrier area. Indian attacks also increased with the Shawnees going on some raids in the Greenbrier River area and most of the settlers fled eastwards for safety. By 1758, the British had gained the upper hand over the

French and most of the Indian tribes made peace with the British. By 1761, the British gave more priority to this region of Virginia and settlers starting returning but Indian troubles again increased.

The Greenbrier settlements felt the impact of the Indian uprisings when in 1763 the war chief Cornstalk appeared in the Muddy Creek settlements. Using the guise of being friends, they often intermingled with the settlers and then on a pre-arranged signal would attack their hosts and often killed entire families and settlements. In 1764 the Indians were brought under control by an expedition led by Col. Henry Bouquet and many captured settlers were released from Indian control. Over the next 5 years, treaties were negotiated with the Indian tribes that opened up the land that is now known as Greenbrier County. The year 1769 saw more land surveys made in Greenbrier County as land speculators again started acquiring and trading properties.

Settlers again started moving into the Greenbrier area but Indian troubles remained. In 1774, that trouble came to a head at a point called Point Pleasant, the confluence of the Kanawha and Ohio Rivers. There Virginia forces and settlers under Andrew Lewis met a large Indian force and defeated them at a high cost to both sides. Many men from Greenbrier were fighting in those forces and several died including a Thomas McClung. Many members of the ancestral families of Samuel Plummer Boggs were present at the battle. Many were also wounded including a John McMillion who is probably related to our McMillion family. Others who fought in this battle were James, William and Charles Boggs and a William Kincaid.

One record of the early settlers of Greenbrier County comes from the records of a trading post that Sampson and George Mathews operated in Greenbrier in the 1770s. Their store was located near the mouth of Howard Creek on the Greenbrier River. Surviving records from ledgers dated 1771 to 1773 list customers and their purchases. The records showed that the store served a wide area around Greenbrier and provided many necessities and bartered for many goods since currency was scare on the frontier. Among the customers of ancestral families of Samuel Plummer Boggs were Francis, James, Sr., James, Jr. and William Boggs and Samuel and George Kincaid.

When the Revolutionary War started, the British tried to enlist the aid of the Indians on the western frontiers to attack the settlers. They were only partially successful but it greatly added to the insecurity felt by the residents of the Greenbrier area who were so remote from the rest of Virginia. A few forts were built in the area to supplement several private forts already constructed. An important battle occurred in Greenbrier in 1778 at Fort Donnally which was located about 10 miles northwest of Lewisburg in what is now known as Rader's Valley. Twenty-five men held off an aggressive Indian attack for half a day until a relief force under Matthew Arbuckle arrived, surprising the Indians and scattering them. There were a few minor battles in Greenbrier after Fort Donnally but it was a uneasy peace with settlers needing to always be on guard against small groups of Indians.

The County of Greenbrier was formed out of Botetourt County by the General Assembly in 1777 to take effect on 1 Mar 1778. The county extended westward beyond its current western border with the population of the county being between three and four thousand at this time. The Indian troubles abated somewhat but were still present in Greenbrier County until 1794 when General Anthony Wayne defeated the Indians at the battle of Fallen Timbers. The Treaty of Greenville in the next year finally gave Greenbrier settlers the security for which they longed.

The early settlers had many difficulties with land titles in western Virginia because of the way that land was granted to select companies and individuals who then resold the land to individual tenants. There were many non-resident land speculators who held large holdings and probably never had entered the county. Many of the early settlers also bought large areas of land on speculation and accumulated thousands of acres. Among those listed in 1783 as large land holders were Thomas Kincaid with 1590 acres. Eventually, the land title problems were resolved with the establishment of government land offices but it was well into the 1820s before order was well established.

Additional counties were formed out of the original Greenbrier County as was expected when the vacant lands to the west were occupied. Kanawha County was formed in 1789 as the first new county with little fanfare. However, the formation of Monroe

County to the south in 1799 created public uproar at the loss of the tax base for supported Greenbrier projects. Many prominent individuals fought the creation of that new county but no change occurred and Monroe County was formed. Some of the prominent names mentioned in the political process in this period were William and Andrew McClung, William H. Cavendish and Samuel Kincaid.

The town of Lewisburg was officially established in 1782 and it soon grew to be the dominant seat of government and commerce. The first courthouse was build in 1785 and the need for additional space resulted in a second larger courthouse being built about 1800. By 1819 a federal district court had begun to meet in Lewisburg. In 1831, the Virginia Supreme Court started holding an annual session in Lewisburg. In 1837, the county built a new courthouse.

The majority of the settlers in Greenbrier County were Scotch-Irish, English and German in ancestry with probably the largest group being Scotch-Irish. There were also some Welsh, Irish and Dutch settlers. The large Scotch-Irish population brought with them Presbyterianism whose churches were prevalent very early. Baptist and Methodists also created many churches in Greenbrier County. The Old Stone Presbyterian Church in Lewisburg was built in 1796 and is said to be the oldest church building west of the Allegheny Mountains in continuous use.

The economic growth and diversification of Greenbrier County were steady. In 1785 the legislature authorized the construction of a wagon road at least thirty feet wide from Lewisburg west to the falls of the Kanawha which became known as the old state road. Later additional toll roads were opened and Lewisburg became a stopping point along the way to western trade. By the 1820s Greenbrier County was beginning to be known for the fine horses it bred. Cattle breeding was also growing strong and sheep and hogs were also being raised in quantity.

The medicinal qualities of the water at White Sulphur Springs were identified as early as 1772. After the Revolutionary War the springs were developed by Michael Bowyer. By 1810 there were 10 log buildings and the number of visitors increased considerably. Further building and development occurred and by the 1830s, White Sulphur Springs was one of the nation's most fashionable resorts. In 1854 the White Sulphur Springs Hotel was built and became known as "Old White." The resort provided a good market for supplies and produce from the surrounding area and farmers sold a number of horses to the hotel patrons.

In politics Greenbrier County was very early a staunch supporter of Federalism. The county supported very strongly the War of 1812 and sent many volunteers. After the war Greenbrier County supported nationalism and often felt neglected by the state government. The citizens of Greenbrier County supported the writing of a new state constitution in 1828 by a large majority but then were disappointed with the results of the new constitution that was written. Greenbrier was a strong supporter of the Whig party in the 1830s and 1840s. As the sectionalism of the 1850s approached, Greenbrier found itself in a dilemma. It had always looked towards the national government for support and direction yet it realized how affected it was by southern culture. In the 1860 presidential election, Greenbrier supported the Constitutional Union Party of Bell and Everett as a way to preserve the union. When the southern states started withdrawing from the Union, various factions showed strong sympathies for the both the union and southern causes. Once Virginia seceded from the Union, Greenbrier generally gave its loyalty to Virginia and the Confederacy. Greenbrier did not send any representatives to the Wheeling conventions that were the start of the organization of the state of West Virginia.

In mid 1861, federal successes caused an alarm in Greenbrier and southern troops maneuvered through the county but no battles were fought there. In May 1862 a small battle occurred around Lewisburg in which the Union was victorious. Later in the year, southern forces regained control of the area. In 1863 two battles occurred in the area. On August 26-27, the union was successful at the Battle of White Sulphur Springs and also successful at the Battle of Droop Mountain on November 6. The people of Greenbrier suffered during the war years with shortages of food, clothing and other necessities. Although a majority of the population was in sympathy with the south, the people accepted the defeat and turned their focus towards reconciliation of the country. Greenbrier County very slowly began to participate in the politics of their new state of West Virginia. For the next five years, politics in Greenbrier were heated as the supporters of the confederacy were brought back into the political process.

Agriculture had been significantly hurt by the war as crops were damaged or not planted and most of the stock had been sold or used by both armies. It took a decade or two for agriculture to return to its previous levels. In 1898 it was estimated that eighty percent of the population of Greenbrier County still worked in agriculture and related areas. In 1870 the first railroad reached into Greenbrier County and a new industrial age began for the county. Lumber became a big business in the county and sawmills were built along the Greenbrier River which was used to transport logs to the mills. There had been a minor amount of coal mining in the late 1800s but it was not until after 1900 that major coal mining took place in Greenbrier County.

There are several place names and geographical features in Greenbrier County that are associated with and named for ancestral families of Samuel Plummer Boggs. Data taken from the United States Geological Survey GNIS database lists three named summits in Greenbrier County named after Boggs. The highest is Boggs Knob near Rainelle on the west side of the county with an altitude of 3600 feet (lat 37 55 10, long 80 46 49). There is another Boggs Knob (lat 38 00 29, long 80 22 43) of altitude 2628 feet in the Trout Mountains just west of Renick or Falling Spring. This feature is very near the land owned by John A. Boggs, Plummer's grandfather so we can assume it was named for some branch of our Boggs family. There is also a Boggs Hilltop near Ronceverte in the southern part of the county.

Boggs Run is a small creek running southeast off of the Greenbrier River about one half mile east of the town of Falling Spring. There is a Boggs Creek just south of Rainelle in the western part of the county. Take Boggs Creek Road off of Road 24 south of Rainelle to get to Boggs Creek. There is also a Boggs Run to the northeast of the town of Loveridge in the northern part of the county. Kincaid Run is a small creek off the Greenbrier River just to the east of Droop Mountain. McMillion Creek is located north of the town of Lile in the northwest part of the county.

The John A. Boggs family farm was just west of the town of Falling Spring in Greenbrier County. Falling Spring is a small town about 16 miles north of Lewisburg, the county seat. The post office address for Falling Spring is Renick and the town is also known by that name. Renick is named for the family of Renick who were very early settlers in this area of Greenbrier County.

Boggs Knob, Greenbrier County, West Virginia
near the town of Renick

The Ancestry of Samuel Plummer Boggs

Samuel Plummer Boggs' ancestry is mainly Scottish or Scottish-Irish and English. Certainly the Boggs and Kincaid families were of Scottish descent. The following is a listing of the direct line ancestors of Samuel Plummer Boggs that are known at this time. In this identification scheme, double the number of the individual to identify the father and double the number plus one to identify the mother.

6. Samuel Plummer Boggs
   b. 2 Apr 1893, Greenbrier Co., WV
   m. 11 Jan 1919, Randolph Co., IN
   d. 9 Apr 1965, near Selma, Delaware Co., IN
   bur. Woodlawn Cem., Maxville, Randolph Co., IN

12. Noah Edward "Ed" Boggs
   b. 10 Nov 1864, Greenbrier Co., WV
   m. 11 Mar 1891, Greenbrier Co., WV
   d. Nov 1932, IN, bur. Hillcrest Cem., Redkey, IN
 24. John A. Boggs
   b. 12 May 1828, Greenbrier Co., VA
   m. 9 Sep 1851, Taylor Co., VA ·
   d. 26 Nov 1893, Greenbrier Co., WV
   bur. Boggs Homestead, west of Falling Spring, WV
 48. Alexander Boggs
   b. Apr 1792, Greenbrier Co., VA
   m. 1812/15, prob. Greenbrier Co., VA
   d. 5 Mar 1876, Greenbrier Co., WV
   96. Francis Boggs, Jr.
   b. c1722, Ireland
   m. 1760, Philadelphia, PA
   d. c1795, Greenbrier Co., VA
   192. James Boggs, Sr.
   b. c1702, Londonderry, Ireland
   m. c1720, Ireland
   d. 1763, Chester Co., PA
   384. James Boggs
   b. c1667, Londonderry, Ireland

d. 1736/7 New Castle Co., DE

786. possibly John Livingston

193. Agnes ?

97. Martha Elliott

d. c1818, Gallia Co., OH

194. Andrew Elliott

d. c1765, Chester Co., PA

49. Elizabeth ?

b. c1794, MD or VA

d. 1876/80, Greenbrier Co., WV

25. Phoebe E. Carder

b. 7 Aug 1828, Taylor Co., VA

d. 9 Jan 1899, Greenbrier Co., WV

50. Joseph Carder

b. 1791, Culpeper Co., VA

m. 18 Feb 1817, Harrison Co., VA

d. aft. 1860

100. John Carder

b. c1767, Culpeper Co., VA

m. c1789, prob Culpeper Co., VA

d. 1850/4, Taylor Co., VA

200. probably John Carder of Culpeper Co., VA

201. probably Frances ?

101. Mary ?(Day)

d. 6 Mar 1836, Taylor Co., VA

51. Rebecca Wiseman

b. 1797, Woodstock, VA

d. 1850/3, Taylor Co., VA

102. Thomas Wiseman

b. c1767, Philadelphia Co., PA

m. 1788, Harrison Co., VA

d. c1840, MO

204. George Wiseman

b. c1731 Philadelphia Co., PA

d. will dated 11 May 1816, Grafton, VA

408. Thomas Wiseman

b. England

m. 1707, Germantown, PA

409. Elizabeth Renberg

205. Hannah Spader

103. Elizabeth Anderson

b. 1766, Waterford, Ireland

206. James Anderson, Jr.

    m. 27 Dec 1764, Kill St. Nicholas, Ireland

    412. James Anderson, Sr.

        m. 15 Mar 1736, Dublin, Ireland

    413. Eliza Kane

207. Susannah Paul

13. Clora Jane Kincaid

    b. 2 Nov 1870, Greenbrier Co., WV

    d. 18 Jun 1955, Farmland, Randolph Co., IN

    bur. Hillcrest Cem., Redkey, IN

    26. William Samuel Kincaid

        b. 10 Dec 1844, Greenbrier Co., VA

        m. 21 Oct 1869, Greenbrier Co., WV

        d. 27 Feb 1882, Greenbrier Co., WV

        52. James Kincaid

            b. c1816, Greenbrier Co., VA

            m. 29 Jun 1843, Greenbrier Co., VA

            d. aft 1880, Greenbrier Co., WV

            104. Samuel Kincaid

                b. 1788, prob. Greenbrier Co., VA

                m. 20 Jun 1812, Greenbrier Co., VA

                d. 28 Dec 1866, Greenbrier Co., WV

                208. prob Andrew Kincaid

                    416. prob. Andrew Kincaid

                        b. c1740

                        d. 1810, Greenbrier Co., VA

                        832. prob. Thomas Kincaid

                            d. 1750, Augusta Co., VA

                    417. Mary ?

                209. Rebecca ?

            105. Katherine McClung

                b. 1788, VA

                d. 5 Jun 1874, Greenbrier Co., WV

                210. James McClung

                    d. 1789/90

                    420. John McClung, Jr.

                        b. Ireland

                        d. 1788, Rockbridge Co., VA

                        840. John McClung, Sr.

                            b. c1670, Scotland

                    421. Rebecca Stuart

212. Nancy Dickenson
    424. adp. dau of Col. Dickenson
53. Mary Jane Wallace
  b. 24 Apr 1824, Greenbrier Co., VA
  d. bef 1880, Greenbrier Co., WV
  106. Robert Boyd Wallace
    b. c1788, Rockridge Co, VA
    m. 16 Nov 1808, Monroe Co., VA
    d. 19 Jun 1838, Greenbrier Co., VA
    212. Robert Wallace
      b. c1750, prob. Augusta Co., VA
      m. c1773, prob. Augusta Co., VA
      d. bef. 9 Sep 1812, Augusta Co., VA
      424. Samuel Wallace
        d. c1765 Augusta Co., VA
    213. Esther Boyd
      b. c1750, prob. Augusta Co., VA
      426. Robert Boyd
      427. Eleanor Porterfield
  107. Mary Alexander
    b. c1794, VA
    d. 5 Apr 1855, Greenbrier Co., VA
    214. Mathew Alexander
    215. Jane Black
27. Rachel Ellen Knight
  b. 15 Sep 1847, Greenbrier Co., VA
  d. 17 Nov 1930, Greenbrier Co., WV
  54. Andrew Knight
    b. 10 Oct 1804, Greenbrier Co., VA
    m. 6 Mar 1834, Greenbrier Co., VA
    d. 14 Feb 1889, Greenbrier Co., WV
    108. James Knight, Jr.
      b. 10 Dec 1780
      m. 25 Nov 1802
      d. 1855, Greenbrier Co., VA
      216. James Knight, Sr.
        b. c1741, possibly Bath Co., VA
        d. 16 Dec 1794, Greenbrier Co., VA
      217. Mary ?
        b. c1746
        d. 29 Oct 1808 (62 yrs.)
    109. Margaret Cavendish

b. 1790

d. 1858, Hunter, Greenbrier Co., VA

218. William Hunter Cavendish

   b. c1740, Ireland

   m. (3rd) 13 Jun 1780

   d. c1818, Bath Co., VA

219. Jane Murphy

   d. 1800/1804

55. Rebecca McMillion

  b. 1807, Greenbrier Co., VA

  d. 10 Nov 1884, Greenbrier Co., WV

110. John McMillion

   b. Dec 1771, Fauquier Co., VA

   d. bef. 1850, Greenbrier Co., VA

220. John McMillion

    b. 1 Jan 1735/36, prob. Fauquier Co., VA

    d. will written 25 Aug 1800

      440. John McMillion

       b. 9 Mar 1703/04

      441. Anne Frances Harrison

       b. c1711

       882. Thomas Harrison

       883. Anne Sothia Short

221. Martha Palmer

    b. 25 Feb 1742/43

    d. aft. 1800

    442. Parmenas Palmer

    443. Mary Ann Draper

111. Rachael Hutchinson

   b. 1776

The Boggs Family

Our Boggs family was originally of Scottish descendency but spent some time in Ireland before migrating to America. History of the early Boggs families in America is fragmentary and there appears to have been several immigrants who came at different times. All of these Boggs families appear to be of Scottish-Irish ancestry and most may have been related in Scotland and Ireland but there are too few records to prove their relationships. The Boggs family was originally Scottish but many of the family moved to Ireland because of political problems before they later immigrated to America. A "Boggs Newsletter" was published and edited by Mrs. Alice Grady of Stowe, Massachusetts, from 1977 to 1987 and served as an early source of exchange for genealogists studying the various Boggs families. Published research on the Boggs family continued with the Boggs Family History Quarterly published by Robert J. Boggs of Florida. Much information on the Boggs families was published but there are numerous branches of the family and there remains uncertainty on how many of the families are related.

Our branch of the Boggs family is sometimes known as the "Greenbrier" Boggses because of their concentration at one time in Greenbrier County, Virginia, now West Virginia. It appears that a James Boggs, a widower with two daughters and seven sons emigrated from Londonderry, Ireland, to Philadelphia in 1724. Two years later, he moved and purchased 100 acres in White Clay Creek Hundred, New Castle County, Delaware, from James Chambers, recorded on 17 Nov 1726. New Castle County was one of three Delaware counties originally known as the three lower counties of Pennsylvania.

Other Boggs Ancestral Lines

There appear to be several different Boggs families who immigrated to America. Most all are Scotch-Irish in ancestry and most came from Northern Ireland although some may have come directly from Scotland. They came at different times but most came before the Revolutionary War. They predominately settled in Pennsylvania or Virginia although some settled in New York, Maine and the Carolinas. It has not been possible to connect all these Boggs families together and there are at least ten or more different Boggs lines in the United States. Some of these and possibly many could be related back in Northern Ireland or Scotland but time and the lack of records mean that we will probably never know the connection.

Our Boggs family that started with the James Boggs who came to New Castle County, Delaware, in 1724 is probably by far the largest line of Boggses in America. Some of the other Boggs lines in America are:

Captain John Boggs, served in the Revolutionary War and at the close of the war moved to Wheeling, Virginia, on the Ohio River. In 1798, he sold this land and moved to the Scioto Valley. Son John Boggs, Jr. served as a Major in the War of 1812 and lived in Zanesville, Ohio.

A John Boggs, who was born about 1665 in Scotland, moved to Ireland and then to America about 1715 where he settled in Chester County, Pennsylvania. John and his wife, name unknown, had at least five children, William, Joseph, Margaret, John and Alexander. Son Joseph Boggs later migrated to South Carolina.

Andrew Boggs and wife Ann Patton came from Ireland about 1730 and settled in Lancaster County, Pennsylvania. One of their sons was a James Boggs who lived in Allegheny County and died in the Pittsburgh area in 1784.

A John Boggs who was born in 1720 in Ireland married Mary Keys. He immigrated to America and had one son, James L. Boggs, who lived in Virginia, the Carolinas, Ohio and finally settled in Lawrence County, Kentucky. James L. Boggs is the ancestor of a large family of Boggses from Kentucky.

A Hugh Boggs was born in Londonderry, Northern Ireland, and immigrated to Berkley County, Virginia, where he had at least two sons, William and Ezekial. Ezekial lived in Ohio County, Virginia.

A Samuel Boggs who was born in Ireland immigrated to Maine where he prospered and later died in Warren, Maine, in 1769.

A Charles Boggs who was born in Ireland immigrated to Bath County, Virginia where he had a large family including eight sons. Lilburn Boggs, who was governor of Missouri from 1836-1840, descends from this line.

Brothers John, Aaron and Thomas Boggs settled in South Carolina and they have not been connected to any other Boggs line.

John Boggs and his wife, Margaret Kee, settled in Pendleton County, Virginia.

James Boggs, a physician, is found in New Jersey.

A Francis Boggs who married Jane Morrison Campbell settled in Allegheny County, Pennsylvania, where he died in 1826.

James Boggs of Londonderry

The surname Boggs originated in England and Scotland and is derived from the birthplace or dwelling-place of the family. It simply means at or by the bog with addition of the suffix -s meaning "Bogg's son." The name Bogg and Bogges are seen as early as 1327 in England.

The earliest ancestor that we have definite information about is the James Boggs who immigrated to America in 1724. James Boggs was born in Londonderry about 1667 and family tradition says he was the son of John Livingston who was a Covenanter in Scotland. The Covenanters were a religious group who allied themselves against Charles II of England in the mid 1600s. After the monarchy was restored to England in 1660, the Covenanters were exiled from Scotland and John Livingston was among them. He settled in the bogs near Londonderry in the northern part of Ireland with his presumed brother Hugh. It has been said that they were originally known as Livingstons of the bogs and this was later shortened to just Boggs. It is unlikely that the surname

Boggs arose independently in Gaelic Ireland because the word bog is of English origin. Boggess is another spelling which often times is the same family but not necessarily always so.

Another Boggs history has the father of James Boggs, the Immigrant, as being a William Boggs who was born in Lononderry, Ireland about 1625. He married about 1650 and is listed on the tax roles is 1663 as living within the liberties of Londonderry. The reported father of William Boggs was James Boggs who was born in Scotland about 1600. This James Boggs immigrated to the North of Ireland sometime between 1603 and 1625. His name is found on various documents in Londonderry in 1630, 1641 and 1643.

The origin from the Livingston family has been in our family tradition for many years. Further research may clarify the family origin or we many never know the exact origin. Both of the above versions of the origin of the James Boggs who immigrated to America in 1724 are still just family traditions and neither has been proven in this author's view.

After moving to Delaware by 1726, James Boggs built his farm with several outbuildings and later owned some land at neighboring Mill Creek Hundred, New Castle County, purchased from James Chambers and recorded on 17 Nov 1726. James died about 1736/7 since his will was dated 9 Feb 1736 or 1737. To the best of our knowledge based on research by several Boggs genealogists, James Boggs had the following nine children, all born in Ireland:

(1) John Boggs, b. 1700, Ireland, d. 1751, lived in Nottingham
    Township of New Castle County, DE
    m. Margaret Ogelbay
(2) Francis Boggs*, b. 1702, Ireland, d. 1763, Chester Co., PA
    m. c1720, Ireland, Agnes ?
(3) James Boggs, Jr., b. 1704, Ireland, d. c1779, Augusta Co., VA
    m. 1726, New Castle Co., DE, Elizabeth Bryan
(4) Mary Boggs, b. c1710, Ireland, d. aft 1763, Chester County,
    PA
    m. Francis Morris
(5) Robert Boggs, b. 1712, Ireland, d. 2 Apr 1804,
    New Castle Co., DE

m. 3 Mar 1741, New Castle Co., DE, Margaret Robinson
(6) Rebecca Boggs, b. 1714, Ireland, d. after 1763 Chester Co., PA, dnm
(7) William Boggs, b. 1716, Ireland, d. 1790 Chester Co., PA
    m. 1733, New Castle Co., DE, Jane Stein
(8) Alexander Boggs, b. 1718, Ireland
    m. 1759, Philadelphia, PA, Elizabeth Lloyd
(9) Ezekial Boggs, b. c1719, d. 1756, New Castle Co., DE
    m. c1742, Strabane Co., Tyrone, Ulster, Ireland, Elizabeth Baird

The "*" symbol in a descendants list is used to identify a direct line ancestor of Samuel Plummer Boggs or Hilda Irene Garringer.

James and Elizabeth (Bryan) Boggs were in Fallowfield Township of Chester County, Pennsylvania, by 1736 and then moved to Augusta County, Virginia, about 1747. Children listed by them are: Robert, b. 1723, James, b. 1725, Henry, b. 1727, Thomas, b. 1729, Jennat, b. 1729, Alexander, b. 1733 and John, b. 1735. There were several Boggs families in Augusta County in the early 1800s and they are probably descendants of James and Elizabeth Boggs.

No records of any offspring of John and Margaret (Ogelbay) Boggs are currently known.

More is known about the descendants of Robert and Margaret (Robinson) Boggs. Their children are thought to be:
(1) James Boggs, b. 1742, d. young
(2) Robert Boggs, Jr., b. 9 Sep 1746, d. 25 Aug 1827, Boonesborough, KY
    m. 5 Apr 1782, Greenbrier Co., VA, Sarah McCreary Huston
(3) William Boggs, b. 9 Sep 1746, dnm, d. in Revolutionary War
(4) James Boggs, b. 10 Sep 1747, d. Madison Co., KY
(5) Agnes Boggs, b. 4 Feb 1749, d. bef. age 21
(6) Elizabeth Boggs, b. 11 Feb 1751, dnm
(7) Benjamin Boggs, b. 12 Mar 1753, dnm, d. in Revolutionary War
(8) Moses Boggs, b. 12 Nov 1756, d. 22 Feb 1833, Muskingham Co., OH
(9) John Boggs, b. Jan 1759, d. 5 Apr 1847, Madison Co., KY
    m. Elizabeth Pearson
(10) Joseph Boggs, b. 2 Jan 1761, d. 13 Jul 1843, Madison Co., KY

Robert Boggs, son of Robert and Margaret Boggs, moved first to Fort Harrod, Kentucky, and then later to Boonesborough, Kentucky. Sons James, Jr., John and Joseph Boggs all moved to Madison County, Kentucky.

William Boggs, son of James, Sr. married Jane Stein and they had the following children:
(1) James Boggs, b. 21 Jul 1735, d. 1 Nov 1805,
    Washington Co., PA
    m. 1765, Hannah Rice, m. 2nd Sarah Brown
(2) John Boggs, b. 23 Feb 1737, d. bef. 1780, served in the
    Revolutionary War
(3) Margaret Boggs, b. 23 Feb 1738/9, m. James Johnson
(4) Robert Boggs, b. 6 Apr 1741, m. Elizabeth Brown
(5) William Boggs, Jr., b. 14 Mar 1743, d. 4 Mar 1833, dnm
(6) Jane Boggs, b. 10 Apr 1745, d. 3 Sep 1830, dnm
(7) Elizabeth Boggs, b. 31 Jul 1747, d. 3 Mar 1835, dnm
(8) Rebeca Boggs, b. 31 Jan 1749/50, d. 19 Jan 1835
(9) Mary Boggs, b. 24 Mar 1751, dnm
(10) Agnes Boggs, b. 17 Feb 1752, m. William McWilliams
(11) Joseph Boggs, b. 1 Oct 1754
(12) Moses Boggs, b. 6 May 1757, d. Jul 1845

James Boggs, the son of William and Jane Stein, was a Captain in the Pennsylvania Line during the Revolutionary War. James married twice and died in Washington County, Pennsylvania, in 1805.

Francis Boggs, Son of James, the Immigrant

Our Boggs line descends through Francis Boggs who was born 1702 in Ireland. Francis and his wife Agnes, maiden name unknown, migrated with his father to New Castle County in 1724. After the death of his father, he moved about 1737 to East Fallowfield Township in Chester County. He was a miller by trade and settled on the Brandywine River. He and his family were members of the Doe Run Presbyterian Church on Strasburg Road. He died there in 1763.

To the best of our knowledge, Francis and Agnes Boggs had at least seven children:

(1) William Boggs, b. 1721, Londonderry, nfi
(2) Robert Boggs, b. c1723, Londonderry, nfi
(3) James Boggs, b. c1725, New Castle Co., DE, d. Feb 1806,
    Greenbrier Co., VA
    m. 25 Jan 1751, Wilmington, DE, Margaret Jane Sharp
(4) Francis Boggs, Jr.*, b. 1726/32, New Castle Co., DE, d. c1795,
    Greenbrier Co., VA
    m. 1760, Philadelphia, PA, Martha Elliott
(5) Ezekial Boggs, b c1734, d. 7 Jun 1815, St. Clairsville, OH
    m. 1756, Jane Johnson
(6) Agnes Boggs
    m. 15 Aug 1762, Philadelphia, PA, Davidson Filson
(7) Samuel Boggs, d. c1815, Mason Co., KY

Son James Boggs married 25 Jan 1751 to Margaret Jane Sharp at
Old Swede's Church in Wilmington, Delaware. Some researchers
have said his name was James Charles Boggs but most of the time
he is just referred to simply as James. James and Margaret
(Sharp) Boggs were the parents of nine children, many of whom
settled in Greenbrier County, Virginia. James and Margaret
Boggs first lived in Chester County, Pennsylvania, and about
1763, they moved to Augusta County, Virginia. They moved to
Greenbrier County, Virginia, (now West Virginia) about 1771. In
Greenbrier County, James Boggs built a sawmill and a gristmill
along the Greenbrier River and Spring Lick Creek.

James and Margaret (Sharp) Boggs had nine children:
(1) William Boggs, b. c1751, d. c1835, KY, removed to Clark Co.,
    KY
    m. Ann Clendenin
(2) Francis Boggs, b. c1754, Chester Co., PA, d. 1837, Braxton
    Co., VA
    m. 1777, Mary Clendenin
(3) James Boggs, Jr., b. c1756, PA, d. 10 Apr 1809, Gallia Co., OH
    m. Jane Watts (or Grant)
(4) Elizabeth Boggs, b. c1758
    m. William Glackin, removed to TN
(5) Ezekial Boggs, b. 1760, d. after 1830, Greenbrier Co., VA
    m. 10 Dec 1788, Margaret Boggs, d/o Francis and Martha
    (Elliott) Boggs
(6) John Boggs, b. 14 Feb 1763, d. 15 Nov 1861, Roane Co., VA
(7) Samuel Boggs, b. 1765, d. after 1832, Gallia Co., OH

m. Ellen Watts
(8) Andrew Elliott Boggs, b. 1767, d. 27 Jan 1854,
Kosciusko Co., IN
m. 1st 5 Mar 1791, Susannah Bowen
m. 2nd 21 Apr 1836, Delaware Co., IN, Elizabeth (Peragin)
Friend
(9) Alexander Boggs, b. 1770, d. after 1816, Gallia Co., OH
m. 6 Apr 1795, Agnes "Nancy" Boggs, d/o Francis and
Martha (Elliott) Boggs

James Boggs wrote his will dated 10 Jul 1803 and died sometime in late 1805 or early 1806 since the will was probated in February 1806. Margaret (Sharp) Boggs survived him and died some time after 20 Apr 1816 when she is mentioned in some court documents. Of the children of James and Margaret (Sharp) Boggs, Ezekial stayed in Greenbrier County but the others moved west.

It is reported that three of the sons of James and Margaret (Sharp) Boggs fought at the Battle of Point Pleasant in 1774: William, Francis and James, Jr. This battle was a major confrontation in 1774 with the Indians on the Ohio River at influx of the Great Kanawha River. This was also known as "Lord Dunmore's War" and some consider it as the First Battle of The American Revolution but it really is not. About 1100 Indian warriors under the Shawnee chief Cornstalk attacked an army of about an equal number of western Virginia militiamen under Colonel Andrew Lewis.

Beside fighting at the Battle of Point Pleasant, William Boggs, b. 1751, also served with William Clendenin's Regiment in Kanawha County. By 1784, William owned 580 acres in Greenbrier County but later sold that and moved to Clark County, Kentucky. He later moved to Knox County, Ohio, where he married a second time to Elizabeth Lawson on 7 Mar 1801 and where he later died about 1835.

The movement of the Boggs family into Greenbrier County, Virginia began early. James Boggs, born c1725, and his wife Margaret Jane Sharp moved to Greenbrier County by 1771. His brother Francis Boggs, born c1730, is thought to have moved to Greenbrier County about 1786. The 1771-1779 Ledger of the

Mathews Trading Post lists several Boggs customers. This trading post was located on the Greenbrier River just south of where Howard's Creek enters the Greenbrier. Francis Boggs is listed in entries in 1771-1774, 1776 and 1779. James Boggs Senior is listed on dates in 1771, 1773, 1774 and 1777. William Boggs (James' son) is listed in 1771-1777. James Boggs, Jr. is listed in 1773, 1774 and 1777.

These two branches of the Francis Boggs family, born c1702, form the basis for what is often called the "Greenbrier" Boggs. Of the two Boggs brothers who moved their families to Greenbrier County, Francis died first in about 1795 and James died in Greenbrier County in February 1806. The family was centered in Greenbrier County for several decades but then started to move further west for access to better land.

At least three sons of James Boggs, James, Jr., Samuel and Alexander, moved to Gallia County, Ohio. Son William Boggs, born 1751/2, moved his family to Clark County, Kentucky. Son John Boggs and most of his family moved to Roane County, Virginia (now West Virginia). Son Francis Boggs who married Mary Clendenin moved to Nicholas County and later many of his descendants were in Braxton County, Virginia (now West Virginia).

Son John Boggs married Susan Drennin on 25 Apr 1786 in Greenbrier County. He moved his family to Roane County, Virginia (now West Virginia) about 1830 where he had large land holdings of over 1500 acres. Most of his children married in Roane County, and John died there at a ripe old age in 1861.

Another son, Andrew Elliott Boggs, evidently was quite a wanderer since he seemed to be at the forefront of the movement to the frontier. In about 1803 he moved his family to Gallia County, Ohio and then in 1816 moved on to Jackson, County, Ohio. About 1825 he moved to Henry County, Indiana and later moved to Delaware County, Indiana. Here is an excerpt from article in the Centennial Edition (1827-1927) of "The Muncie Sunday Star" Sunday, September 25, 1927:

"Andrew Boggs First Settler"
Hamilton Township Lands Did Not Attract Many Persons Until 1829

Andrew Elliott Boggs, formerly a citizen of Ohio, was the first white settler of Hamilton Township according to data gathered by county historians several years ago. The township which is situated in the north part of the county was slow to attract settlers and it was not until 1834 or 1835 that even a small number of land entries were made.

At what date Mr. Boggs settled in Hamilton Township is not known, but in the spring of 1829, he was living with his wife and child and a stepson, Nicholas Friend, in a log hut erected by himself and stepson on the land owned by Owen Russell in that year. He had cleared a small piece of ground and was trying to earn subsistence for his family from the products of his "clearing." Mr. Russell gave him a yoke of oxen for his labors on the land. Several years later he moved to Blackford County.

Andrew Elliott Boggs first married Susannah Bowen on 5 Mar 1791 in Greenbrier County, Virginia. Andrew and Susannah had fourteen children, the first five born in Greenbrier County, the next five in Gallia County, Ohio and the last four born in Jackson County, Ohio:

(1) Anthony Bowen Boggs, b. 12 Aug 1793, Greenbrier Co., VA, d. 1873, CA
m. 17 Sep 1816, Jackson, Co., OH, Mary Friend
(2) Sarah Boggs, b. 1794, d. 1829, Jackson Co., OH
m. 18 Jul 1816, Gallia Co., OH, William McCarley
(3) Jane Sharp Boggs, b. 10 May 1798, d. 26 Sep 1830, Kosciusko Co., IN
m. 18 Feb 1817, Jackson Co., OH, Joel L. Long
(4) Alice Boggs, b. 7 Oct 1799, Greenbrier Co., VA, d. 11 Apr 1870, Jamestown, OH
m. 10 Nov 1820, Jackson Co., OH, James F. Long
(5) Mary Boggs, b. 12 Apr 1802, Greenbrier Co., VA, d. 1849, OH
m. 3 Feb 1825, Henry Co., IN, Matthew Williams
(6) Cynthia Boggs, b. 26 Oct 1803, d. 22 May 1857, Leesburg, IN

m. 25 Oct 1824, Jackson Co., OH, James Hale

(7) James Boggs, b. 19 Feb 1807, d. 7 Nov 1842, Kosciusko Co., IN
    m. 1 Jul 1827, Henry Co., IN, Martha H. Stinson

(8) Hannah Boggs, b. 25 Feb 1809, d. 7 Mar 1888, Xenia, OH
    m. 6 Nov 1826, Greene Co., OH, Joseph Dean

(9) William Bowen Boggs, b. 25 Dec 1812, d. 22 Mar 1906,
    Kosciusko Co., IN
    m. 6 Jul 1837, Lydia Groves
    m. 2nd 5 Oct 1851, Kosciusko Co., IN, Sarah Yisley Mingle

(10) Mahala Boggs, b. 5 Mar 1814, d. 10 Jun 1901, Marshall Co., IN
    m. 12 Nov 1829, Obed Swain, m. 2nd 24 Oct 1841 Thomas
    Sumner

(11) Lewis Boggs, b. 16 Jun 1816, Gallia Co., OH, d. 16 May
    1888, Marshall Co., IN
    m. 20 Feb 1840, Kosciusko Co., IN, Sarah Devault

(12) Julia Ann Boggs, b. 12 Nov 1818, Jackson Co., OH, d. 20
    Feb 1910, Marshall Co., IN
    m. 3 Mar 1836, Wayne Co., IN, Benoni Jordan

(13) Andrew Hamilton Boggs, b. 7 Mar 1821, Jackson Co.,
    OH, d. 7 Mar 1917, Kosciusko Co., IN
    m. 14 Dec 1843, Kosciusko Co., IN, Martha Ann Thomas
    m. 2nd 18 Sep 1889, Kosciusko Co., IN, Abbie (Silver) Shoup

Susannah Boggs died on 4 May 1834, in Henry County, Indiana, at the home of her son, Anthony Bowen Boggs. Andrew evidently had left his family earlier since in 1829, he was living in Center Township of Delaware County, with a woman twenty years younger than he and her children. This was probably Elizabeth (Peragin) Friend whom he married in Delaware County on 23 Apr 1836. On 24 Apr 1834, Andrew Boggs was commissioned a justice of the peace for Delaware County. However, by 20 Sep 1836, he had entered on land in Licking Township of Blackford County, Indiana. He was also commissioned Associate Judge of Blackford County and held the first term of the circuit court at his home on 23 Sep 1839. A year later in 1840, he sold that land and moved to Huntington County, Indiana. His second wife, Elizabeth, died some time before 1850, and Andrew later lived with his step-daughter Electra and her husband, Joseph Blount. Andrew died 27 Jan 1854, at the home of his youngest son, Andrew Hamilton Boggs, and is buried in Leesburg Cemetery, Kosciusko County, Indiana, where his tombstone reads: "In memory of Andrew Boggs, d. 27 Jan 1854, in his 87th year."

Francis Boggs, son of James and Margaret (Sharp) Boggs, was born in 1754 in Chester County, Pennsylvania, and moved with his family to Augusta County, Virginia, in 1762 and then in 1771, moved to Greenbrier County. He is reported to have fought with his five brothers at the Battle of Point Pleasant with British regulars against the Indian Cornstalk. Francis Boggs married Mary Clendenin in 1777 probably in Greenbrier County. Francis and Mary (Clendenin) Boggs moved to Nicholas County, Virginia (now West Virginia) about 1798 where they lived on Big Elk River. Francis Boggs applied for a pension from the government based on his military service but it was rejected, probably because most of his service was against the Indians rather than the British. Francis Boggs died in Braxton County, Virginia, in 1837 and Mary Clendenin Boggs died in 1853 in Roane County, Virginia.

Francis and Margaret (Clendenin) Boggs had the following children:
(1) James Clendenin Boggs, b. 20 Feb 1778, Greenbrier Co., VA, d. 1846, Braxton Co., VA
    m. 11 Jun 1799, Kanawha Co., VA, Polly Lemasters
(2) John Clendenin Boggs, b. 16 Feb 1780, Greenbrier Co., VA, d. 17 Jul 1842, Braxton Co., VA
    m. 19 Feb 1801, Anna "Nancy" Lemasters
(3) Rebecca Boggs, b. 1781, Greenbrier Co., VA, d. 1821, Braxton Co., VA
    m. 1801, James Frame
(4) Mary Boggs, b. 1784, Greenbrier Co., VA, d. bef. 1837
    m. 19 Mar 1804, Kanawha Co., VA, James Sparks
(5) Charles Boggs, b. 27 May 1787, Greenbrier Co., VA, d. 27 Sep 1873, Roane Co., VA
    m. 12 Feb 1809, Kanawha Co., VA, Jane Lemasters
(6) Jane Boggs, b. 1791, Greenbrier Co., VA, d. 1836 Braxton Co., VA
    m. 7 Aug 1818, Nicholas Co., VA, John Stewart
(7) William Boggs, b. 1792, Greenbrier Co., VA, d. 7 May 1868, Gilmer Co., WV
    m. 20 Dec 1812, Harrison Co., VA, Sarah Stump
    m. 2nd 12 May 1865, Gilmer Co., WV, Louisa Griffith

(8) Andrew Boggs, b. 1795, Greenbrier Co., VA, d. 12 Nov 1859, Braxton Co., VA
m. 1813, Christina Shock

(9) Elizabeth Boggs, b. 1797, Greenbrier Co., VA, d. Sep 1873, Braxton Co., VA

(10) Margaret Boggs, b. 1799, Nicholas Co., VA, d. 1831, Braxton Co., VA
m. John L. Davis

(11) Miriam Boggs, b. 1809, Nicholas Co., VA, d. aft. 1880 Kanawha Co., VA
m. Hugh Griffith

Francis Boggs, Jr., Son of Francis Boggs, Sr.

Our Boggs lineage is through Francis Boggs, Jr., born about 1730 who married Martha Elliott sometime before 1773 in Philadelphia. There are some records that suggest Francis had an earlier marriage. It appears from various resources that Francis and Martha Boggs had the following children although only Elizabeth and Alexander are proven by records:

(1) Margaret Boggs, d. after 1830 Greenbrier Co., VA
m. 10 Dec 1788, Ezekial Boggs (first cousin, son of James and Margaret (Sharp) Boggs)

(2) Andrew Elliott Boggs, b. c1765, PA, d. 20 Aug 1840, Gallia Co., OH
m. 6 Jan 1794, Greenbrier Co., VA, Hannah Bowen

(3) James Boggs, b. c1772, d. prob. Gallia Co., OH
m. 16 Aug 1797, Isabelle Waddell

(4) Agnes "Nancy" Boggs, b. c1775
m. 6 Apr 1795, Greenbrier Co., VA, Alexander Boggs (son of James and Margaret (Sharp) Boggs)

(5) Elizabeth Boggs, b. c1785, PA, d. Sep 1855, Greenbrier Co., VA, dnm

(6) Francis Boggs, III, b. 27 May 1786, prob. PA, d. 20 Jan 1853, Warren Co., IN
m. 23 Jul 1809, Greenbrier Co., VA, Jane Blair
m. 2nd 19 Sep 1844, Warren Co., IN, Nancy Clark
m. 3rd 2 Oct 1850, Warren Co., IN, Violette Tolliver

(7) Alexander Boggs*, b. 1793, Greenbrier Co., VA, d. 5 Mar 1876, Greenbrier Co., WV
m. Elizabeth ?, d. 1876/80

Francis Boggs moved his family to Greenbrier County about 1786. Originally he was called Francis, Jr. but his nephew Francis Boggs, son of his brother James also moved to Greenbrier County around 1785-1790. After his nephew moved in, our Francis was referred to in county records as Francis, Sr. while his nephew was referred to as Francis, Jr. Senior and Junior during this time period did not always mean father and son but were often used to mean older and younger. Our Francis died in Greenbrier County about 1795. Of the children of Francis and Martha (Elliott) Boggs, several of them moved their families west to Gallia County, Ohio, presumably because of the ready availability of better farm land. Sons Andrew and James moved to Gallia County between 1810 and 1820. Daughter "Nancy" who married her cousin Alexander Boggs also moved to Ohio. Margaret who married her cousin Ezekial stayed in Greenbrier County where she died sometime after 1830. Martha (Elliott) Boggs lived with her children after the death of husband Francis and moved to Gallia County, Ohio. Her will was presented to court on 24 Feb 1818 so she must have died sometime shortly before that.

The 1790 Virginia census lists seven Boggs households in Greenbrier County: Ezekial, Francis, Sr., Francis, Jr., James, Sr., James, Jr., Samuel and William. Francis, Sr. and James, Sr. are the sons of Francis and Agnes Boggs. William, Francis, Jr., James, Jr. Ezekial and Samuel are the sons of James, Sr. The titles of Sr. and Jr. here mean older and younger. Francis, Jr. (b. 1754, son of James) was a nephew to Francis, Sr. The 1800 Virginia census was destroyed and the 1810 census for Greenbrier County is missing, so no information is available from the census for this time period.

Francis Boggs, III, the son of Francis and Martha (Elliott) Boggs, married first Jane Blair on 23 Jul 1809 in Greenbrier County and later moved west to Indiana between 1820 and 1830 although he may have spent some time also in Illinois. He finally settled in Warren County, Indiana, where he married twice more and died there in 1853.

Andrew Elliott Boggs, the son of Francis and Martha (Elliott) Boggs, married Hannah Bowen on 6 Jan 1794 in Greenbrier

County. Andrew Boggs moved his family to Perry Township in Gallia County, Ohio about 1810.

Our direct line ancestor, Alexander Boggs, stayed in Greenbrier County as did his sister Elizabeth who never married. Elizabeth lived most of her life in Alexander's household, dying in March 1855.

Alexander Boggs, Son of Francis and Martha (Elliott) Boggs

Alexander Boggs' wife was named Elizabeth as listed in the later census records but we do not know her maiden name and no marriage record has been found. A search of the Greenbrier marriage records in the period 1810-1820 show that some marriage records may have been lost in this period. From 1812 to 1816, in 1818 and in 1820 there are no marriage records starting with "B"s as if these pages were lost. This is the time that Alexander would have married based on his family profile shown in the 1820 and 1830 censuses. We will probably never know Elizabeth's maiden name.

One researcher in the Boggs Newsletter (Vol. 10, 1987, pg 2) claimed that Alexander had an earlier first marriage to Martha LeForge on 24 Oct 1813 in Fleming County, Kentucky. That Fleming County record actually reads as Alling Bogs marrying Marth LeForge. There are no other Boggs marriages in Fleming County and no Boggs were found in land deeds in the county. The 1800 Kentucky tax list shows an Alexander Boggs, Sr. and Jr. in Logan County and the 1820 census shows an Alexander Boggs in Franklin County, Kentucky of age 26-45, living alone. No Allen Boggs has been found in any of the early Kentucky census records. There were several Boggs families in Kentucky, one of which was probably connected to this marriage record. I have found no records or evidence that our Alexander Boggs of Greenbrier County was ever listed as Allen or was ever tied to Kentucky. Tying our Alexander Boggs to this marriage record is incorrect. The same listing includes a Joseph E. and Vincent Boggs as possible sons of Alexander or his father and these are also incorrect. Unfortunately, these 1987 errors have been propagated into several Boggs' lists since then. There are several other errors and assumptions in this reference that need to be noted and corrected.

Our Alexander Boggs is in the 1820 Virginia census in Greenbrier County age 26-45 with wife and children 1M<10 and 2F<10. Elizabeth is apparently Alexander's first and only wife. Unfortunately, no death record for Elizabeth has been found and we do not know her maiden name. In the 1850, 1860 and 1870 census her birth state is listed as Virginia; however, the 1880 census for two sons John A. and Benjamin F. lists Maryland as her birth state. Also it appears that Alexander's older sister Elizabeth is living with the family as she is in the 1840 and 1850 census. Also listed in 1820 in Greenbrier County are Ezekial, John, James and Laurence Boggs. Ezekial and John are Alexander's cousins and James and Laurence are John's sons. By 1820 all of the other Boggs families have moved on to other counties north and west of Greenbrier or to the states of Ohio and Kentucky.

The 1830 census shows Alexander's family as 2 M5-10, 1 M30-40, 2 F<5, 1 F5-10, 2 F10-15, 1 F30-40 and 1 F40-50. The young sons are Benjamin Franklin and John A. The youngest daughters are Sarah (b. c1822), Ruhanna Ann (b. c1823) and Elizabeth (b. c1828). The oldest female is Alexander's sister Elizabeth who was born in 1785. There appears to be two other daughters, ages 10-15, but we do not know their names. Also listed in Greenbrier County are households headed by Ezekial, Hamilton, Stephen and William Boggs. Also listed are Thomas and John Bogges with a different spelling of the last name.

The 1840 census shows Alexander and Elizabeth with their large family of 2 M15-20, 1 M40-50, 1 F5-10, 2 F10-15, 1 F15-20, 2 F20-30, 1 F40-50 and 1 F50-60 (Alexander's sister). Again there are apparently two daughters born before 1820 listed. Other Boggs families in Greenbrier County are William, Fielding, Ezekial, Stephen and Jane Boggs and they are all cousins of Alexander. Thomas Bogass listed in the census is also a cousin. There is a Enoch Boggess listed in Greenbrier County but he has not been identified as a family member but may be.

The 1850 census lists Alexander and Elizabeth Boggs with children Benjamin Franklin, Sarah, John A., Elizabeth, and Almira still living at home. The earlier census data indicate there were probably two daughters born before Benjamin Franklin Boggs who are not found in the 1850 census. A search of the marriage records of Greenbrier County for the period 1840-1850 did not find any Boggs marriages that would correspond to Alexander's daughters. Neither of these two daughters is listed in Alexander's will so they may have died before 1850. The Jane Boggs who married Mathew V. Peers on 30 Sep 1852 and is listed in Alexander's will is probably daughter Almira "Jane." In one later census, her name is spelled as Alcinda. Another is Ruhanna Ann who married Jacob McCarty on 1 Sep 1842. By the 1850 census they had four children: Samuel A., born c1844; Elizabeth J., born c1846; Mahala M., born c1848; and Melissa R., age one month.

Alexander and Elizabeth Boggs' children were:
(1) Benjamin Franklin Boggs, b. c1820, VA, d. 15 Jul 1882
     m. 27 Nov 1857, Greenbrier Co., VA, Sarah F. Cochran
(2) Sarah Boggs, b. c1822, VA, d. ? aft. 1860, listed in 1876 will
(3) Ruhanna Ann Boggs, b. c1823
     m. 1 Sep 1842, Jacob McCarty
(4) John A. Boggs*, b. 12 May 1824, VA, d. 26 Nov 1893
     m. 9 Sep 1851, Taylor Co., VA, Phoebe E. Carder
(5) Elizabeth Boggs, b. c1828, d. Mar 1854, dnm
(6) Almira Jane Boggs, b. c1833
     m. 30 Sep 1852, Greenbrier Co., VA, Mathew V. Peers
(7) probable daughter, name unknown, b. 1815/20, d. aft. 1840
(8) probable daughter, name unknown, b. 1815/20, d. aft. 1840

The 1850 Virginia census lists Alexander's sister Elizabeth as age 70, born in Virginia, thus giving her a birthdate of 1779/80. Greenbrier County death records show Elizabeth died in September 1855 but list her age at that time as 70 and says she was born in Pennsylvania. Parents were listed as Francis and Martha Boggs and the death was reported by Alex Boggs, brother. Alexander's daughter Elizabeth died of bilious colic in March 1854 at the age of 26 according to county records, and she was buried at the Old Stone Church Cemetery in Lewisburg, West Virginia.

The 1860 Virginia census lists the households of:
Alex Boggs*, age 66, Farmer, b. VA

Elizabeth*, 70, VA
Sarah, 38, VA

John A. Boggs*, age 40, b. VA
Phoebe E., age 30, VA
Joseph A., 8, VA
Cornelius C., 5, VA
Rebecca, 3, VA
Thomas G., 1, VA
Francis A. Carder, also in household

Benjamin F. Boggs, age 40, b. VA
Sarah, 23, VA
Robert S., 1, VA

Other Boggs households in 1860 Greenbrier County, Virginia, census are headed by: William (age 62), Stephen (age 55), Gehiel (age 44), another Stephen (age 54) and Jane (age 55). All were listed as having a Lewisburg P. O. address.

The 1870 census lists
John Boggs*, age 46, b. VA
Phoebe, age 42, VA
Cornelius, 17, VA
Rebecca, 14, VA
Thomas G., 11, VA
Edward*, 7, VA
Mary, 2, VA
Alexander*, 79, VA
Elizabeth*, 76, VA

Alexander Boggs died on 5 Mar 1876 at the age of 83. His name was listed simply as Alex and his parents were listed on the death record as F. M. Boggs and Greenbrier County is listed as the birthplace. In his will, he lists his wife Elizabeth and son Benjamin as executors. Also listed are Anna McCarty, Jane Peers and Sarah Boggs. It is not clear why John is not listed; presumably he already received his share. Elizabeth must have died after 1876 but before 1880 because she is not found in the 1880 census. No death record for Elizabeth was found. If Alexander had two daughters born before 1820, neither one was listed in his will so they must have been deceased before Alexander's death.

Benjamin Franklin Boggs was married to Sarah F. Cochran on 27 Nov 1857 in Greenbrier County. They had the following children:
(1) Samuel R. Boggs, b. 25 Sep 1858
(2) Martin L. Boggs, b. 28 Feb 1860
(3) Emily J. Boggs, b. 1862
     m. 10 Nov 1886, George W. Winden
(4) John G. Boggs, b. 1865
     m. 13 May 1891, Sarah C. Gabbert
(5) Elizabeth N. Boggs, b. 1867
(6) Washington L. Boggs, b. 1869
     m. 22 Jun 1898, Luella McLaughlin
(7) Medora M. Boggs, b. 1870
(8) William L. Boggs, b. 28 May 1872
(9) Mary F. Boggs, b. 10 Jun 1875, d. young
(10) Charles Boggs, b. 26 Mar 1877

Benjamin Franklin Boggs died on 15 Jul 1882. The death records say his father was A. Boggs, mother was J. Boggs, the cause of death was diarrhea and the report was made by J. A. Boggs, brother.

Daughter Ruhanna Ann Boggs married Jacob McCarty on 1 Sep 1842 in Greenbrier County. In the 1850 census they are still in Greenbrier County with four children. They later moved to Pocahontas County, West Virginia, where they are shown in the 1870 and 1880 census. In both of those censuses, her name is simply listed as Hannah. Jacob and Ruhanna Ann (Boggs) McCarty had the following children:
(1) Samuel A. McCarty, b. 1844, Greenbrier County, VA
(2) Elizabeth McCarty, b. 1846, Greenbrier County, VA
(3) Mahala McCarty, b. 1848, Greenbrier County, VA
(4) Rachel M. McCarty, b. 1850, Greenbrier County, VA
(5) Julia A. McCarty, b. 1854
(6) Nancy E. McCarty, b. 1858
(7) George McCarty, b. 1861

Daughter Almira Jane Boggs married Mathew V. Peers on 30 Sep 1852 in Greenbrier County, Virginia. The marriage license actually reads Alcinda Jane Boggs. M. V. and Alcinda J. Peers are found in the 1860 census in Greenbrier County with children Martha Elizabeth, born 25 Oct 1855, and Thomas S., born 1858. They also had a son William who was born 23 Sep 1853 but died young and is buried in the Old Stone Church Cemetery in Lewisburg. Jane Peers is listed in 1876 in her father Alexander's will. However, the 1880 Ohio County, West Virginia census lists a Math Peer of the appropriate age with a younger wife named Elizabeth. Jane may have died sometime before 1880.

John A. Boggs, son of Alexander and Elizabeth Boggs

Marriage records in Taylor County, Virginia, show that John A. Boggs and Phebe E. Carder applied for a marriage license on 8 Sep 1851 with consent papers signed by Joseph Carder. They were married on 9 Sep 1851 by the Rev. James Gawthrop, Minister of the Commonwealth of Virginia. Phoebe Carder was the daughter of Joseph and Rebecca (Wiseman) Carder. The Carders lived in Taylor County, now West Virginia as shown in the 1850 and earlier censuses. Taylor County is several counties north of Greenbrier County so it is not clear how John and Phoebe met. One family story says that the two counties were connected by a heavily traveled river route and they met when John was trading along the river. A look at the map does not show a direct river route so this is doubtful.

Our John Boggs is often listed in census data with the middle initial A. I have never seen his middle name spelled out but I assume that it was probably Alexander after his father.

The children of John A. and Phoebe E. (Carder) Boggs were:
(1) Joseph A. Boggs, b. 26 Jun 1852, d. 6 Jan 1863
(2) Cornelius C. Boggs, b. 19 Mar 1854, d. 1909, Greenbrier Co., WV
    m. 13 Jan 1881, Greenbrier Co., WV, Luella E. Alderson
(3) Elizabeth Rebecca Boggs, b. 29 Oct 1856, d. aft. 1920, IN
    m. 1877, Greenbrier Co., WV, Marion D. McMillion
(4) Thomas G. Boggs, b. 8 May 1859, d. aft 1920, CA
    m. 28 Aug 1884, Greenbrier Co., WV, Mary E. Peers
(5) George H. B. Boggs, b. 9 Oct 1862, d. 23 Jan 1863
(6) Noah Edward "Ed" Boggs*, b. 10 Nov 1864, d. Nov 1932, Jay Co., IN

m. 11 Mar 1891, Greenbrier Co., WV, Clora Jane Kincaid
(7) Mary F. J. Boggs, b. 25 Jun 1868, d. 3 Feb 1871

The 1880 West Virginia census shows in Greenbrier County:
John A. Boggs, age 56, b. WV, father b. VA, mother, b. MD
Phoebe E., 50, WV,VA,WV
Cornelius, 25, VA
Thomas G., 21, WV
Noah E.*, 16, WV

Of the sons and daughters of John and Phoebe Boggs, Elizabeth Rebecca married Marion D. McMillion on 12 Sep 1877 in Greenbrier County. Marion and Becky McMillion moved to Jay County, Indiana, sometime around 1890. They had two surviving children, Albert R., born Jun 1878 in West Virginia and Dennis C., born Apr 1888 also in West Virginia. The McMillions are found in the 1900 census in Richland Township in Jay County, Indiana, but later moved into Muncie where they are found in the 1920 Indiana census.

Cornelius Carder Boggs married Luella Alderman on 12 Jan 1881. In the 1880 West Virginia census Luellin Alderman was listed as age 21 and living in the John Boggs household as a servant. Cornelius and Luellin (Alderman) Boggs had the following children:
(1) Maggie Boggs, b. c1882, d. 18 Dec 1884
(2) James R. Boggs, b. Feb 1884
(3) Lydie J. Boggs, b. Mar 1889, d. 31 Mar 1891
(4) Joseph Boggs, b. Feb 1895
There may have been other children who died in childhood. Cornelius died in 1909 and Luella is listed as a widow in the 1910 Greenbrier County, West Virginia, census with her two surviving sons.

Thomas G. Boggs married Mary Etta Peers on 28 Aug 1884. Mary Etta Peers was probably related to the Peers family of Mathew Peers who married Thomas' Aunt Jane Boggs. Noah Edward Boggs married Clora Jane Kincaid in Greenbrier County on 11 Mar 1891 with Rev. L. S. Huffman performing the ceremony.

John A. Boggs died of heart disease on 26 Nov 1893 in Greenbrier County. His death record lists his parents as Alex and Eliz

Boggs. Phoebe E. (Carder) Boggs survived her husband by over 5 years and died on 9 Jan 1899. They are buried on the old Boggs farm just west of Falling Spring (Renick), West Virginia.

John A. and Phoebe (Carder) Boggs, about 1890

Of the four children of John A. and Phoebe (Carder) Boggs who survived to adulthood, three moved west to Indiana before 1910. The one who did not was Cornelius who had married Luella Alderman. He remained in Greenbrier County and died there in 1909.

Thomas Boggs and his wife Mary Etta Peers migrated to Jay County, Indiana, about 1896. The 1900 Jay County census shows them living in the city of Redkey on North Spencer Street. Thomas and Mary Etta (Peers) Boggs had the following children:
(1) Herman J. Boggs, b. May 1885, WV
(2) Nila Marguerite Boggs, b. Jun 1896, IN
(3) Lizzie V. Boggs, b. Jan 1898, IN
(4) Florence Irene Boggs, b. Mar 1900, IN
There may have been more children who died young based on the separation of birth dates. Perhaps he moved his family west to Indiana for health reasons.

Marion D. McMillion with his wife Rebecca Boggs also moved to Indiana settling in Jay County. They are shown in the 1900 census in Richland Township of Jay County, Indiana, with sons Albert R., born Jun 1878, West Virginia, and Denny C., born Apr 1888, West Virginia.

Noah Edward "Ed" Boggs, son of John A. Boggs

Noah Edward "Ed" Boggs was the last of John A. Boggs' children to marry when he wed Clora Jane Kincaid on 11 Mar 1891 in Greenbrier County. Clora Jane Kincaid was born 2 Nov 1870, the daughter of William Samuel and Rachel Ellen (Knight) Kincaid. Ed and Clora Jane Boggs were the parents of Samuel Plummer Boggs.

Ed Boggs moved his family west about 1904 to Decatur, Illinois, where Clora Jane (Kincaid) Boggs' brother was living. They stayed there for about a year and then returned to Greenbrier County. About a year later they moved to Jay County, Indiana, and settled southeast of the town of Redkey. Ed's brother Thomas and sister Rebecca (Boggs) McMillion had previously settled near Redkey. Clora also had two cousins, Phoebe (Carder) Ritter and Mont Carder who had settled in Jay County. Thomas later moved his family to California and died there. Rebecca (Boggs) McMillion later lived in Muncie where she probably died.

Ed and Clora Jane Boggs had six children, four of whom survived, the first five born in Greenbrier County:
(1) daughter, b. 6 Mar 1892, d. 6 Mar 1892
(2) Samuel Plummer Boggs*, b. 2 Apr 1893, d. 9 Apr 1965
(3) Lottie Ellen Boggs, b. Sep 1895, d. 5 Mar 1989
(4) Virdie Ora Boggs, b. 3 Apr 1897, d. 17 Feb 1991
(5) Mattie Opal Boggs, b. 9 Oct 1900, d. 28 Aug 1974
(6) James Boggs, b. 22 Apr 1909, d. 22 Apr 1909

Lottie Ellen Boggs, who was born in Sep 1895 in Greenbrier County, moved with her family to Indiana and became a home economics teacher and first taught in Milwaukee. She returned to Indiana and married Roscoe Sumner. Roscoe and Lottie had no children, and he died in 1939. Lottie was then on the Purdue extension staff until she retired in 1962. Lottie lived her remaining years in Alexandria, Indiana. Lottie survived to the age of 93 and died on 5 Mar 1989 in Farmland, Indiana.

Virdie Ora Boggs, who was born on 3 Apr 1897 in Greenbrier County, married Revillo W. Gilmore on 30 May 1918 in Indiana. They had one daughter Jacquelyn Sue Gilmore who was born 13 May 1928. Jacquie Sue married Edwin Hodgin and they had one son Kurt Gilmore Hodgin who was born 27 May 1966. Revillo died in 1972. Virdie died on 17 Feb 1991 and is buried in the Woodlawn Cemetery at Maxville beside her husband.

Mattie Opal Boggs, who was born on 9 Oct 1900 in Greenbrier County, married Harold Worden in Jan 1918 in Indiana. They had one daughter Fancheon Madonna Worden who was born 3 Aug 1918. Mattie Opal (Boggs) Worden died on 28 Aug 1974. Fancheon married Harold E. Hodson on 1 Aug 1941 and they had one daughter, Pamela Hodson. Pamela Hodson married Thomas Vincent and they currently live in Yukon, Oklahoma.

Clora Jane (Kincaid) and Noah Edward "Ed" Boggs
date unknown

Clora Jane (Kincaid) Boggs, Plummer Boggs' mother

Plummer, Virdie and Lottie Boggs
childhood photo about 1899

Green Township High School Basketball Team
Plummer Boggs in center

Green Township High School
Senior Class of 1915
Plummer Boggs clowning at second from right

Green Township High School, Senior Class of 1915
Samuel Plummer Boggs 7th from right in back row
Lottie Boggs 4th from right in front row
Clifford French 3rd from right in back row
Other graduates in the class were Ralph French, Lloyd Stilwell, Jacob
Woodard, Arthur Zimmerman, Charley Wood, Hazel Life Schnitzer, Ethel
Life Ralston, Oma Pursley Summers and Esther Pearson Stromberg

Front: Virdie, Opal and Lottie Boggs taken in April 1919
Rear: Noah Edward "Ed", Clora Jane (Kincaid), Plummer Boggs

Hilda Irene (Garringer) and Samuel Plummer Boggs
about 1919

Front: Opal (Boggs) Worden and Hilda (Garringer) Boggs,
Rear: Harold Worden and Plummer Boggs
about 1919

Samuel Plummer and Hilda Irene (Garringer) Boggs, 1918 or 1919

Virdie (Boggs) and Revillo Gilmore
Golden Wedding Anniversary, May 30, 1968

Remembrances of the Boggs and Carders
by Alwyn Carder

Note: Alwyn Ardath Carder is a son of Fremont and Elizabeth (Flesher) Carder, grandson of John Anderson and Mary (Rinker) Carder, and great grandson of Joseph and Rebecca (Wiseman) Carder. He currently lives on his grandfather's home place south of Redkey, Indiana. Alwyn was a high school teacher and college professor and has done extensive genealogy on the Carder family.

My Aunt Phoebe Carder Boggs on my father's side was one of the sisters to grandfather John Anderson Carder. Everyone said that Ed Boggs (Noah Edward) looked more like his uncle John Carder than any of John's sons did. He acted like grandfather John, talked like him, stood with arms akimbo and crossed on chest with legs far apart, and stood for no nonsense.

Your great great grandmother Phoebe Carder who married John Boggs was my great Aunt Phoebe. From the photo you sent me, I can see she must have looked like the Wisemans, with I suspect blue eyes. The Carders were more severe, with mostly dark or black eyes, and they were pretty "Cardery," rather high tempered and serious, with a tendency to be a little overbearing and important. Yes, Ed had some of that too.

Now my father said that Aunt Phoebe Boggs visited out here at her brother John's sometime in the Nineties. Her sister, Rebecca Rinker, had come in from Illinois (Gales County) to visit here too.

After Aunt Phoebe left by train, my grandfather John and his sister Rebecca Rinker went by train to Grafton (Taylor Co., WV) to visit with their brother Cornelius Carder (Uncle Neece) who lived on the old home place on Carder Hill above Fetterman (Fetterman old town before Grafton and became a western suburb of Grafton).

Now Rebecca, Phoebe (pronounced Phebe) and Cornelius are Wiseman names which appear in old Wiseman records and some of the Wiseman family are down in Fayette County (just west of Greenbrier County).

Now Aunt Phoebe Boggs was one of nine children. She had three sisters, Elizabeth Rinker, Josina (Aunt Sweeney) Williams, and Rebecca Rinker. She had several brothers, but I think Aunt Phoebe was the oldest of the children born 1828, then Uncle Isaac. My grandfather John not born until 1833. There was also Uncle Jesse of Illinois, Uncle Cornelius of home place, and Uncle Joseph Plummer. He was named after a Colonel Plummer back there and there is a Plummer Knob near Pruntytown in old Harrison County but may be in Taylor County. Taylor County was created out of other counties in 1844.

Uncle Plummer (my great uncle) fought on the Yankee side from Indiana and his relatives back in Virginia never quite understood this. Plummer had come out here and entered land around Selma and would have been drafted.

When the war was over, he survived but was rather at outs with his family. He went west with the army. He was killed in 1880's near Walla Walla, Washington. A watch fob, a picture of an unknown girl, and some other personal trinkets came back by army to Virginia to Uncle Cornelius. A picture came here to my grandfather John. We never learned who the girl was, whether daughter or young girl he married, or just sweetheart. Rumor says he was married shotgun fashion while in camp there. He had a liaison with the commanding officer's daughter, had child by her, and so couldn't get out of it. He had a good job in quartermasters corps but if his commanding officer even suspected that he might try to edge out of his predicament, he might have put him in the front lines of infantry.

Uncle Plummer, so the army letter said, was caught in an ambush in a mountain pass. They tried to put revolvers up beside rifles when ammunition ran out but the Indians were not to be so easily fooled. Now I don't know whether this was before or after the terrible massacre at Little Big Horn.

Uncle Plummer's name is listed with the famous 19th Indiana, the Iron Brigade and his name is on the list on the wall of the historic and huge Indiana Soldiers and Sailors Monument on monument circle, Indianapolis and I saw that name years and years ago.

Uncle Isaac was a sutler or commissary and PX agent with a wagon in the Southern Army. Uncle Jesse so they said was a bugler and drummer with the confederate army. He survived and went west to southern Illinois.

Uncle Cornelius was impressed by the southern Porterfield army at the very first battle which was at Phillipi then Rich Mountain. He had to furnish a team of horses and wagon to haul, but he managed to be free when the army retreated and withdrew south to Staunton over the mountains when Federals got the upper hand at that battle. This was a month or so before Manasses on the Bull Run in Fairfax County.

I don't know what all grandfather John did, but I have his Confederate Enfield musket rifle, made in Birmingham Small Arms in England and it is a John Tower model. He commanded his offspring "Don't Ask."

I was last in Greenbrier County in 1951 in July or August. It was hot and I climbed back an old creek bed to come to Aunt Phoebe's old homestead the back way since it was only a half mile or so. Had I gone the other way, I would have had to take a car over a rocky almost abandoned country road up that rocky hill and come into the Boggs homeplace from the front. When I was there people by the name of Fields owned the land and farmed it. The old large double story log house, rather of a large lodge type, was still standing but roof about gone. The garden was kept up and the grapevines and berry vines. They all knew about Ed Boggs, some of the older folks remembered him and showed where the land was.

At the back of the land up on a knoll with trees was the cemetery and there is where Aunt Phoebe and John Boggs are buried along with some younger children (presumably who died in infancy). Now there were other brothers they told me about such as Cornelius Quillan and another one. But your great gran was not one to know or talk about genealogy, so Virdie said and Clora too.

Ed died suddenly in November of 1932 and I was early in high school. The funeral was at home on the old home place. (We called it the old John Current Homestead since the Currents came from Virginia and entered the land there in the 1840's. The back of grandfather's south land (he had 400 together with my grandmother Marye Virginia) nearly touched the Current Boggs land and by the road it is only about two miles from me if I go around.

Clora died sometime, in 1955. She was a great lady, soft spoken of few words. I knew and liked her. Your Aunt Charlotte (Lottie) was very gracious, a teacher and Purdue professor, cultivated and taciturn with those Wiseman or Boggs blue eyes. Either she or your Samuel Plummer was the oldest. They moved out here, I think in the teens at the time of World War, maybe as early as 1912 or 1911, Lottie and Plummer were in the same grade. They graduated from high school from Green Township High School in Randolph County, Indiana, which was 1 1/2 miles south of them and both of them graduated in 1915. Now I barely remember your grandfather Plummer Boggs, and don't remember of seeing him at all in later life.

For some reason Lottie, Virdie never spoke of him, and didn't seem to know about him when we would ask. He moved south and was never around this area much. The same for your Aunt Opal. We never knew her very well for she lived at Alexandria her married and divorced life. Some of the relatives, my father and my own Uncle Cornelius Carder said that they thought the reason there were hard feelings there was because Ed favored his only son Plummer. He financed him, mortgaging his own land to get Plummer started in farming his own land. Well, then came the hard times of the late twenties, the depression and Ed was left with a huge mortgage. When Clora had Charlotte to sell the land (after she Clora got down sick after a stroke) there was little left after the mortgage. Now we don't know that for a fact, but that is the family rumor.

Other Indiana Boggs Families

Our Boggs family was rather late moving to Indiana with two related families moving to Jay County about 1895/6 and Ed and Clora moving their family here in 1906.

The 1850 Indiana census, the first census to give state of birth, shows 40 Boggs families and 8 Boggess families in Indiana. The largest number of these families seem to come from Pennsylvania with Boggs families in Wayne, Shelby, Jay, Whitley, Warren, Carroll and Jennings Counties. Several Boggs families are from Virginia in Kosciusko, Clark, Greene, Union and Clinton Counties. The Ripley County Boggses are from Kentucky, the Jackson County Boggses are from North Carolina and the Bartholomew County Boggses are from New York.

We do know that one line related to our Boggs family moved to Indiana rather early. Andrew Elliott Boggs, a son of James and Margaret (Sharp) Boggs as related above had moved into Henry County by 1825 and then moved to Hamilton Township of Delaware County by 1829. Andrew stayed there only a few years before he sold his land and moved to Kosciusko County where many of his children also settled. Andrew Boggs died in 1854 in Huntington County while living with his daughter's family.

There were other Boggs from Virginia who settled in Indiana. A James Boggs, who was born in Virginia around 1764 moved to Clark County, Indiana, sometime before 1820. An Eliam Boggs, who was born about 1800 in Virginia, first moved to Butler County, Ohio, and then moved about 1837 to Clinton County, Indiana. Joel Boggs, who was born in 1808 in Virginia, moved to Green County, Indiana, sometime before 1837. A Norval Boggs, who was born in Virginia about 1816, moved to Union County, Indiana, sometime before 1838.

Another Boggs family settled in Randolph County when a Volney Boggs who was born in Ohio in 1855 moved to the Union City area about 1880. This Boggs family was in Covington, Ohio, before moving to Indiana and before that the family had moved from Virginia. Volney Boggs had three sons John, Charles and Everett and descendants of this Boggs family still live in the Union City area. It has not been possible to determine the origins of this Boggs family in a limited amount of research done.

John H. and Laramie Boggs family moved from West Virginia to Wayne Township of Randolph County between 1912 and 1915. This family came from Braxton County, West Virginia, and is distantly related to our Boggs family. John H. Boggs is a fourth cousin, once removed, from Plummer Boggs. The name of his son Burke Boggs was seen and heard in the early 1900s but our Boggs family did not know that he was distantly related. This John H. Boggs was the son of William Newlon and Delilah (Mollohan) Boggs, who was a son of Benjamin Lemasters and Jane (Cutlip) Boggs, who was a son of James Clendenin and Mary (Lemasters) Boggs, who was a son of Francis and Mary (Clendenin) Boggs. This Francis Boggs was born in Chester County, Pennsylvania, moved with his family to Greenbrier County and later moved to Braxton County, Virginia, (now West Virginia) and is the patriarch of the Boggs in Braxton County.

The Kincaid Family

Samuel Plummer Boggs' mother was Clora Jane Kincaid. The Kincaid family is of Scottish descendency and our branch of the Kincaids apparently arrived in America as early as 1715. The family first settled in Pennsylvania, then to Augusta County, Virginia and then later moved to Greenbrier County, now part of West Virginia. Clora Jane Kincaid, who was born on 2 Nov 1870 in Greenbrier County, was married to Noah Edward Boggs on 11 Mar 1891. They had one surviving son, Samuel Plummer and three surviving daughters Lottie, Virdie and Opal. About 1906 the family moved from Greenbrier County, West Virginia, to Indiana settling near Redkey in Jay County. Clora was a member of the Christian Church and was active in church work for many years until her illness near the end of her life. Ed Boggs died in 1932. Clora Boggs moved to Alexandria and made her home with her daughter, Opal Worden, until her death on 18 Jan 1955.

The Kincaid surname is a place name taken from the lands of Kincaid in the Parish of Capmsie, Stirling County, Scotland. It is taken from Gaelic and at least four meanings have been suggested: "at the head of the quagmire," "at the head of the pass," "head of the sacred place" and "head of the battle."

A family history of our Kincaid family has evolved over time. The earliest documentation for this family tradition appears to be the chapter on the Kincaid family is the 1951 book *the Renicks of Greenbrier*. The author of this chapter was Dr. Herbert Clarke Kincaid who was born at Summersville, West Virginia, on 16 Oct 1883 to Robert Alexander and Mary Thomas (Patton) Kincaid. His Kincaid line descends from the Kincaids that arrived in Greenbrier County, West Virginia, by 1777.

The earliest recorded Kincaid to immigrate to America was a Daniel Kincaid who first appeared in New Hampshire in 1689. Several other immigrants then appeared and many moved to Pennsylvania. One early immigrant related to our Kincaid line is a David Kincaid who immigrated in 1715. The tradition according to Dr. Herbert Clarke Kincaid is that the Kincaid clan was loyal by blood ties to the Stuarts in Scotland and that David Kincaid, brother of the then Laird, took part in the unsuccessful Stuart Rebellion in 1715. He was forced to leave Scotland after the rebellion was put down. David Kincaid first came to Spotsylvania County, Virginia, and later moved to Albemarle County, then to Augusta County, and finally to Bath County where he died. Another early Kincaid immigrant is a Thomas Kincaid who came first to Lancaster, Pennsylvania, about the same time in 1715. Thomas Kincaid later moved to Augusta County, Virginia where he bought land in 1747 on the Calfpaster River. Thomas Kincaid is believed to be a brother of the above David Kincaid.

In Scotland in December 1745, Charles Stuart made another attempt to retake the throne but was defeated at a battle in Stirlingshire. Four sons of Alexander Kincaid, Samuel, George, James and Robert Kincaid, fought with the Stuarts but were captured in a rear-guard action. Alexander Kincaid is believed to be a brother of the David Kincaid who immigrated in 1715 making the four sons David's nephews. The story is told that the wives of the two married brothers, Samuel and George, plus the four brothers were spirited out of the English camp and put on board a ship to America. On the advice of their Uncle David they settled in Augusta County, Virginia.

David Kincaid does appear in Spotsylvania and Orange County, Virginia, land records in the 1730's. There is a reported marriage record of a David Kincaid to Winifred Hobson (Tillary) (widow of Samuel Tillary) in 1729 in Spotsylvania County. From 1752, David Kincaid's name appears in land records with other Kincaids with first names Joseph, John, Mathew, Thomas and Borrough Kincaid. David Kincaid left a will in Washington County, Virginia, which lists wife Winifred and sons, John, Hobson, Burrough and Joseph. There may have been a daughter Jean who married into the Isabella family.

In 1747, Thomas Kincaid moved from Pennsylvania and purchased 263 acres of land in Augusta County, Virginia, on the Calfpaster River. This land adjoins the 520 acres that David Kincaid and his son John purchased later in 1764. This Thomas Kincaid died intestate in 1750 leaving a widow Margaret (possibly last name Lockhart) and at least one son named William.

Dr. Herbert Clarke Kincaid states that there appeared to be four branches of Kincaids in Augusta County in the 1700s. He states that William, Matthew, James, John, Thomas, and Andrew are names that appear to be common to all of these families. Samuel, George, and Robert appear to be found only in his family line.

The father of the four brothers, Samuel, Robert, George, and James, who came to America in 1746 was Alexander Kincaid. Alexander was a pharmacist in Edinburgh and is believed to be a brother to the David and Thomas Kincaid of Augusta County, Virginia. Alexander Kincaid had another son, also named Alexander, who did not migrate to America and was a printer in Edinburgh.

Of the four brothers who immigrated, George Kincaid settled in what is now Allegheny County, Virginia, where he was killed in an Indian raid in 1756 and his wife and three children were captured. They were not returned until 1764. His son Samuel was a lieutenant in the Virginia militia and was wounded in Indian fighting near Wheeling. Samuel later moved to Pennsylvania.

George's brother, James Kincaid, went south and little is known about him. One record says he was buried at St. Helena, Lees County, Kentucky.

The two other brothers who immigrated to Augusta County, Virginia, were Robert and Samuel. Robert Kincaid bought land in 1763 in Beverly Manor in Augusta County, Virginia. About 1770 they moved to the Falling Spring area in Augusta County. Robert Kincaid and his wife Anna Helena had sons Andrew, Joseph, Thomas, Matthew, James and John. Son Andrew married Ann Kincaid, daughter of his uncle Samuel. Son John Kincaid married Alice Dean in 1787. Son James Kincaid married Elizabeth Dean in 1786.

Samuel Kincaid, the fourth immigrant, first bought land in Beverly Manor in 1754, purchased from Adam Thompson. He held this land for many years and later he sold it to his son,

Samuel, Jr. About 1765 Samuel, Sr. moved to the Falling Spring area in Botetourt County, now Allegheny County where he purchased 283 acres from William Hamilton. Later Samuel sold this land to his son-in-law Andrew Kincaid.

Family tradition says that when the Revolutionary War began, Samuel Sr. went to Pittsburgh in 1775 with his old friend and neighbor, Capt. John Wilson and was wounded in the thigh while on that service. He evidently never recovered fully from that wound and died in 1780. According to papers in the Virginia State Library, Capt. John Wilson's Company listed Samuel Kincaid, wounded, received 19 days pay, 3 pounds, 7 shillings, advances on pay-wound, balance 3 pounds, 7 shillings.

Samuel Kincaid, Sr. and his wife (name unknown) had the following children:
(1) Alexander, died young
(2) Samuel Kincaid, Jr., b. 1734, Scotland, d. 23 Jan 1819,
    Greenbrier Co., VA
    m. c1775, Margaret Clarke
(3) George Kincaid, m. c1770, Margaret "Peggy" Renick
(4) James Kincaid, moved to KY about 1800
(5) Ann Kincaid, m. 11 Feb 1782, first cousin Andrew Kincaid
(6) Robert Kincaid
(7) Hugh Kincaid
(8) William Kincaid

Most of the Kincaids that settled in the Greenbrier County area were descendants of this Samuel Kincaid, Sr. or descendants of the Thomas Kincaid who died in 1750 in Augusta County. The Mathews Trading Post on the Greenbrier River in Greenbrier County lists among its customers a Samuel Kincaid in 1771 and a George Kinkead in 1774.

Of the children of Samuel Sr., we know the most about Samuel, Jr. He was a Captain in the Botetourt Militia and his company was at Pittsburgh in 1775. About 1775, he married Margaret Clarke, daughter of his neighbor James Clarke. Samuel Kincaid, Jr. became a large land holder in Greenbrier County and at one time held over 10,000 acres of land. Samuel Jr. was also prominent in politics and served as sheriff of the county in 1807-1809. His will was dated in 1816 and proved in 1819. Listed in his will were children: Samuel, who married Sallie Kester; Harriet Frances, George, James, Sally, Betty and Ann.

George Kincaid, son of Samuel Sr., served with his brother James in Capt. Robert McClanachen's Company of Greenbrier Valley Volunteers and in the Botetourt Regiment, at the Battle of Point Pleasant. George married about 1770 Margaret "Peggy" Renick. George is not mentioned in many of the county records of Greenbrier County but he raised a large family of eleven sons and two daughters. The book *the Renicks of Greenbrier* lists his children as Samuel (m. Mary Allison), Thomas (m. Jemima Allison and later migrated to Illinois), Margaret (m. Daniel Allison and moved to Gallia County, Ohio), Andrew, John, Renick, William, Hugh, and Phebe (twin with Hugh who were the youngest, born 15 Apr 1795). George inherited nothing from his father who had died intestate; however, he did receive 200 acres in 1787 for his military service.

Hugh Kincaid, son of Samuel Sr., raised his family in Greenbrier county and in 1782 had 95 acres of land "joining Renick." William Kincaid, another son of Samuel Sr., also entered on land in Greenbrier County to the amount of 400 acres in 1782.

The other ancestor of many of the Kincaids of Greenbrier County was Thomas Kincaid who died in 1750 in Augusta County. Thomas Kincaid and his wife, Margaret (maiden name unknown) had the following children:
(1) William Kincaid, b. c1735/6, d. 1823 Augusta Co., VA
    m. 30 Nov 1756, Eleanor Gay
(2) John Kincaid, b. c1740, d. aft. 1807
    m. c1765, Anne Graham
(3) Andrew Kincaid*, b. c1740, d. 1810, Greenbrier Co., VA
    m. Mary

Thomas Kincaid who was born c1737/8 and later married Hannah Tincher is also listed as a son of Thomas and Margaret Kincaid in one published genealogy. However, other researchers think this Thomas is a son of John Kincaid. This is but one of several Kincaid connections that are uncertain and still debated by Kincaid researchers.

Our Kincaid line descends from Andrew and Mary Kincaid who moved to Greenbrier County by at least 1793 when they bought 170 acres of land on Anthony Creek. Andrew Kincaid died in 1810 and the children listed in his will were:

(1) Andrew Kincaid*, m. Rebecca ?
(2) John Kincaid
(3) Robert Kincaid
(4) James Kincaid
(5) Thomas Kincaid
(6) Sarah Kincaid, m. Kincaid Caldwell
(7) Elizabeth Kincaid, m. Miller
(8) Ann Kincaid, m. Richard Gratner
(9) Mary Kincaid, m. Wyatt
(10) Margaret Kincaid, m. William Slone

The ancestry of Plummer Boggs' mother Clora Jane Kincaid has been traced directly back to William Samuel Kincaid, born 1844; whose father was James Kincaid, born 1816; whose father was Samuel Kincaid, born 1788, who married Katharine McClung on 20 Jun 1812 in Greenbrier County. Land records in Greenbrier County show Andrew and Rebecca Kincaid selling land for the sum of $1 to Samuel Kincaid on 23 Sep 1812 with witnesses Robert Kincaid and Lanty Kincaid. This is land that Andrew bought in 1807 from Chesley Rodgers. Robert Kincaid is probably Andrew's brother and Lanty Kincaid is a cousin. It is assumed that Andrew and Rebecca Kincaid are Samuel's parents and they were selling him land for an very nominal sum of $1 shortly after his marriage to Katharine McClung.

There are some research notes of a Robert D. McMillion, a great grandson of Samuel Kincaid who in 1934 "thought" that Samuel's father was a Hugh Kincaid. These records have been examined and no records other than family stories support this thesis. With today's more available records, the land deed in 1812 seems to be the strongest link to assume that Andrew and Rebecca Kincaid are the parents of our Samuel Kincaid.

The 1790 Greenbrier County census lists eleven Kincaids: Andrew, George, James, John (3), Samuel (2) and Thomas (2). Samuel, George, James, and Hugh are sons of Samuel, Sr. with one John being a grandson of Samuel, Sr. Thomas, Andrew and another John are sons of the Thomas Kincaid who died in 1750 in

Augusta County. The other John, Thomas and Samuel are grandsons of the Thomas Kincaid of Augusta County.

The 1800 and 1810 censuses for Greenbrier County were lost or destroyed so the movement of the Kincaids in and out of Greenbrier County is difficult to determine during this time period. Samuel was a common male name in the Kincaid family and it is often difficult to identify a specific Samuel. The 1820 Greenbrier census lists nineteen Kincaid households with five Samuels listed on two concurrent pages. They are listed as Capt. Samuel, Samuel, Sr., Samuel, Jr., and two listed without any title. Samuel, Sr. is listed as age 45+ while the other four are shown as being 26-45 years old. The 1830 Greenbrier census lists twenty-one Kincaid households with four Samuels shown. In the 1840 census there were eleven Kincaid households in Greenbrier County with two Samuel Kincaids, age 50-60.

There is strong evidence that James Kincaid was the son of a Samuel Kincaid, born 1788. In both the 1850 and 1860 Greenbrier County census, William and Samuel are listed living next to each other. Data from the 1880 census supports this fact since James had a brother Hugh who is listed earlier in the household of the older Samuel Kincaid.

Samuel Kincaid was born in 1788 in Virginia, probably Greenbrier County. His wife Katherine was born in 1789 also in Virginia. A marriage record in Greenbrier County shows a marriage of Samuel Kincaid to Katharine McClung on 20 Jun 1812. One transcription of Greenbrier County marriage records shows the date as 20 Jun 1818 but a review of the original marriage records confirmed the correct year as 1812.

Based on the census records, Samuel and Katherine (McClung) Kincaid had the following children:
(1) Joseph Kincaid, b. c1813, d. aft 1860
(2) James Kincaid*, b. c1816, d. aft 1880
    m. 29 Jun 1843, Mary Jane Wallace, d. before 1880
(3) Samuel Kincaid, b. c1819
    m. 26 Nov 1840, Catharine Hawver
(4) Hugh Kincaid, b. c1827, d. aft. 1880
    m. 17 Mar 1870, Jemima McMillion
(5) Robert Kincaid, b. c1829, d. 1853/60

m. c1848, Margaret ?

Samuel and Katherine Kincaid probably also had one daughter who was listed as age 5-10 in the 1830 census but was not listed in 1840 or later censuses. She may have died by 1840 or married young and was not listed with the family in that census.

Samuel Kincaid died on 28 Dec 1866 according to Greenbrier County death records with the cause listed as old age. Katherine (McClung) Kincaid died on 5 Jun 1874 at the age of 85. No will has been found but their son James evidently inherited the family farm.

Son Hugh married Jemima McMillion, and was a farmer in Greenbrier County. They had children Robert, born c1870 and Catharine A., born c1873.

Son Robert Kincaid probably died between 1853 and 1860 since his daughter Virginia, born c1849, and sons, Samuel, born c1851, and Robert, born c1852, are shown living in their grandfather's household in the 1860 census.

Our direct line ancestor is James Kincaid who was born in 1816 in Greenbrier County. A marriage license which was dated 29 Jun 1843 was issued to James Kincaid and Mary Jane Wallace so they were probably married shortly after that. Later census records show she was born in 1829 in now West Virginia. James and Mary Jane Kincaid had the following children:
(1) William Samuel Kincaid*, b. 10 Dec 1844, d. 27 Feb 1882 (pneumonia)
    m. 21 Oct 1869, Rachel Ellen Knight
(2) George Robert Kincaid, b. c1846, d. 4 Dec 1869 (consumption)
(3) Mary C. Kincaid, b. 1 Mar 1855, d. 6 Dec 1927
    m. Calvin Huston Hanna
(4) Margaret Susan Kincaid, b. 11 Dec 1859, d. 24 May 1933
    m. Francis Clark Hanna
(5) Elizabeth Nancy Kincaid, b. c1867
    m. John Knapp
There may have been others who did not survive childhood since the birthdates are spread out irregularly.

Mary Jane (Wallace) Kincaid is not found in the 1880 census so she must have died some time before then. James Kincaid is found in the 1880 census with daughter Mary C. keeping house and daughters Margaret and Elizabeth still at home. Living next to him is his brother Hugh.

William Samuel Kincaid married Rachel Ellen Knight on 21 Oct 1869 in Greenbrier County. Rachel Ellen Knight was born 16 Sep 1847 also in Greenbrier County, the daughter of Andrew and Rebecca (McMillion) Knight. Plummer Boggs' mother, Clora Jane Kincaid, was the first born child of Samuel and Rachel.

Samuel and Rachel (Knight) Kincaid had the following children:
(1) Clora Jane Kincaid*, b. 2 Nov 1870, d. 18 Jun 1955, Randolph Co., IN, bur. Redkey, IN
    m. 11 Mar 1891, Greenbrier Co., WV, Noah Edward Boggs
(2) Della Rebecca Kincaid, b. 28 Sep 1872, d. 26 Feb 1958
    m. 13 Mar 1895, Edgar Huff
(3) Mary Uginia "Eugie" Kincaid, b. 27 May 1874, d. 22 May 1908
    m. 5 Sep 1894, Marion Burr
(4) James Andrew Kincaid, b. 6 Oct 1875, d. 7 May 1944
    m. 25 Jun 1903, Annie C. Sward
(5) Mattie Ora Kincaid, b. 22 Sep 1877, d. 9 Mar 1957
    m. 2 Oct 1901, Mason Knapp
(6) William Robert Kincaid, b. 10 Sep 1879, d. bef. 1955
    m. Lillian (surname unknown)
(7) Samuel Alexander Kincaid, b. 13 Mar 1882, d. bef. 1955
    m. 20 Jul 1905, Emma C. Sward

William Samuel Kincaid died of pneumonia at the age of 37 on 27 Feb 1882, some 15 days before the birth of his seventh child. This left Rachel Ellen (Knight) Kincaid with seven young children to raise. After her children were raised, Rachel married a widower, James C. McCoy, on 26 Nov 1902.

In Clora Jane Boggs' obituary, survivors were listed as sister Mrs. Della Huff of White Sulphur Springs, West Virginia, and Mrs. Mattie Knapp of Alexandria, Virginia. Her brother, Samuel Alexander Kincaid, moved his family west and settled in McLean County, Illinois, as shown by the 1920 census.

The McClung Family

Katherine McClung is a great great grandmother of Samuel Plummer Boggs through marriage into the Kincaid family. Katherine married Samuel Kincaid on 20 Jun 1812 in Greenbrier County, Virginia. Katherine was born in 1788 in Virginia, probably in Greenbrier County.

The McClung family is of Scotch-Irish descent and the earliest known records of the family were in Galloway, Scotland. Tradition says that three McClung brothers named James, John, and Robert left Scotland about 1690 and settled in Ulster, Ireland. They were Presbyterians and left Scotland on account of religious persecution. They appear to have first settled in Larne, County Antrim. This was a time of a large migration of Scots to the area around Ulster. Many of the descendants of these Scots later migrated to North America in the mid 1700s. They were called Scotch-Irish but there was little intermingling with the true Irish in this section of Ireland. Many of these Scotch-Irish who immigrated settled in the Shenandoah Valley of Virginia and some later moved further west into Greenbrier County. The Scotch-Irish are known as a liberty-loving race.

The family name McClung probably evolved from the word Lang (meaning long in Scot) with the Celtic prefix Mac (later shortened to Mc) added later.

The first McClung to immigrate to North America was a Thomas McClung who first settled near Christiana, Pennsylvania, in 1729. About 1731, John McClung migrated to Boston and later to Lancaster County, Pennsylvania, by 1734. He was later joined by his father, James, and the rest of that family. About 1742, James with his sons William and Hugh migrated to Augusta (now Rockbridge) County, Virginia. Later the families migrated in many directions in search of new land.

Another immigrant to North America and our ancestor was a John McClung who is said to be a cousin to William and Hugh.

John McClung was born in Scotland and immigrated to Ireland in 1690 and then later to America.

John McClung, Sr. was the father of John McClung, Jr. who was probably born in Ireland, and migrated with his father first to Pennsylvania, and then to Rockbridge County, Virginia. John, Jr. was a farmer and owned 278 acres of land in Rockbridge County in what was known as the "Forks." John, Jr. married Rebecca Stuart, the Stuarts being an influential family in Virginia. Rebecca died before her husband and John Jr. lived with his daughter Nancy Moore in his later years. John Jr. died about 1788 in Rockbridge County. County records show that an inventory of his estate was made 7 Jun 1791 with the estate being valued at 3 pounds 16 shillings. Seven of John McClung's sons settled in Greenbrier County, Virginia, so this branch of the family is often known as the Greenbrier "McClungs." During the Civil War, it is said that two companies of cavalry, the "Greenbrier Swifts" and the "Nicholas Grays" contained thirty-two McClungs.

John and Rebecca (Stuart) McClung had the following children:
(1) Thomas McClung, d. 10 Oct 1774, killed at Battle of Point Pleasant
    m. Nancy Black
(2) Joseph McClung, m. Miss Bell
(3) William McClung, b. c1738, d. 18 Jan 1833, aged 95
    m. Abigail Dickson
(4) James McClung*, d. c1790, will written 10 Aug 1789, probated 28 Sep 1791
    m. Nancy Dickenson
(5) John McClung, b. c1733, d. 1830 aged 97 years
    m. Sarah McCutcheon
(6) "Capt." Samuel McClung, b. c1744, d. Apr 1806
    m. Rebecca Bourland
(7) Edward McClung, d. c1792
    m. Letitia Weymer Black
(8) Charles McClung
(9) Nancy McClung
    m. Capt. William Moore
(10) Janett McClung
    m. David Moore

We know few details about James McClung, except that his will was made out on 10 Aug 1789 and probated on 28 Sep 1790. James married late in life to Nancy Dickenson who was of unknown parentage. Nancy was captured by the Indians as a child and later found and adopted by a Col. Dickenson.

James and Nancy (Dickenson) McClung had six children:
(1) Jane McClung
    m. Robert Steel
(2) Nancy McClung
    m. Joseph Dixon
(3) Elizabeth McClung
    m. 8 Mar 1802, George Matthews
(4) William McClung, b. 1 Apr 1787, d. 10 Aug 1866
    m. Margaret Bollar
(5) Mary McClung
    m. Adrian Anglin
(6) Katherine McClung*, b. c1788, VA, d. 5 Jun 1874, Greenbrier Co., WV
    m. 20 Jun 1812, Greenbrier Co., VA, Samuel Kincaid

Katherine McClung married Samuel Kincaid in 1812 and they had at least seven children. They both appear in the 1850 and 1860 census. Samuel died in 1866 and Katherine died in 1874.

In Greenbrier County, there were several marriages of McClungs to Kincaids, Knights and McMillions so these Scotch-Irish families must have known each other and been in close contact for several generations.

Most of this information about the McClung family comes from a 1904 McClung genealogy published by Rev. William McClung.

The Knight Family

Rachel Ellen Knight was the mother of Clora Jane Kincaid and the maternal grandmother of Samuel Plummer Boggs. She was born 16 Sep 1847 in Maysville, Greenbrier County, Virginia, (now West Virginia) to Andrew and Rebecca (McMillion) Knight. She grew up in the central part of Greenbrier County and at the age of 22 married William Samuel Kincaid on 21 Oct 1869. William and Rachel Ellen Kincaid had seven children from 1870 to 1882. William Kincaid died at Falling Spring on 27 Feb 1882 while Rachel was expecting their seventh child. Fifteen days after his death their last child, Samuel Alexander, was born.

Rachel Ellen (Knight) Kincaid raised her family with help from relatives until most of the children were married. On 26 Nov 1902, she re-married to James C. McCoy, age 65. His previous wife had been Eliza Brown. They lived near Renick and Brownstown until his death on 6 Jan 1917. Rachel Ellen lived to the ripe old age of 83 dying on 17 Nov 1930.

Rachel Ellen (Knight) Kincaid McCoy

Below is a typed copy of a diary written by Jennie Eldora (Knight) Ball, not dated, but evidently written in late 1927 when she visited relatives in Greenbrier County. She talks about many Knight relatives and the wonderful beauty of the countryside. The author has included the diary because it contains a wonderful description of the people and beauty of this countryside.

* * *

Had a fine trip from Cincinnati to Ronceverte. Had a long ride along the Ohio from Cincinnati. Watched it in the moonlight till it became foggy, then went to sleep. When I wakened in the morning, we were in the mountains and traveling along the Greenbrier River. Got in Ronceverte about 8 o'clock. Telephoned right away to Mason Knapps, then went to the hotel to wait for them to come for me. Had my breakfast of a real jelly omelet, then wrote letters.

Mason Knapp's sister came for me in a Ford and the ride was beautiful - over a paved road all the way. Turned up the lane at a real up-to-date consolidated school to the once fine old mansion of the Knapps, built before the war. Great big high rooms with fireplaces in all the rooms. The whole place takes one back to the old times. Aunt Ellen, the only one of father's family left, lives here with her daughter. She is tall like father, but does not resemble him in looks. She is 80 years old but seems so much younger. The Knapp family consists of Mr. and Mrs., two married daughters, one lives here in the yard, one in Lewisburg. Katharine is in Washington training to be a nurse, Amanda and Della drive their Ford into Lewisburg to school and Mary in school here.

It is warm today although they have fires in the grates. Mary and I carry water from the spring over a hill. Mountains are in every direction and fine farming land in this valley. It would be beautiful here in summer, but we couldn't have the fires in the grates then, so I'm glad I'm here now for it is beautiful now, too.

Amanda and Della milk a dozen cows or more before they go to school, then they fix themselves up and are as pretty as any city girls you ever see. They have 500 chickens with a dandy chicken-house and sell lots of eggs.

Saturday I went to Lewisburg with Della to take the cream. Stopped to see Emma Knight who is Uncle Alex's daughter who is housekeeper for a lady in Lewisburg. Then we went on to Ronceverte for chicken feed. Beautiful road clear down at the foot of a mountain.

Then in the pm or rather at noon, went to a land sale. It was lots of fun but I've taken a terrible cold to pay for it.

Saturday night Cora and George came, drove through from Iowa. Sunday Cousin Emma came out for the day. Had such a delicious dinner, a real Southern one. George took us for a ride over a fine paved road on the White Sulphur Springs road. Never anywhere have I seen such beautiful scenery.

Monday I stayed in bed until eleven expecting to get up just in time for dinner but Aunt Ellen came in with the nicest breakfast and so I had two meals pretty close together. Cora and I took a walk down, away down, a rocky road to an old mill and a covered bridge. A beautiful mountain stream - I would never grow tired of this place, so quiet and peaceful.

Tuesday, Nov. 15, Cousin Tom Knight came for us shortly after noon and we drove to his home at Williamsburg. He got a distant cousin Sam McMillion to come with him for he had a bigger car, a Chandler. The road was paved all the way except for a short distance from Williamsburg. He wound among the mountains, up and down, over Brushy Ridge Mountain, on the Midland Trail, turning off over a single track pavement called Shoestring Trail.

Tom had just butchered so we had fresh sausage and visited all evening.

Wednesday, Kittie Sammons came over about four miles on horseback and we have visited all day. It's been dark and gloomy, rained some. Fog has hung over the mountains all day. Quite a sight. Have been eating persimmons. My mouth is all puckery.

Thursday, Nov. 17 - Cousin Tommy borrowed a car and we were to sight-see and visit some more cousins. We got as far as Williamsburg and went in to cousin Emma's home which is now rented and found her pictures and saw so many interesting things. Among the pictures I found one of a baby, written in father's handwriting - Cora Knight, Oct 26, 1868. Another of Cora and Jim when Cora was perhaps five. She remembers father taking them to town to Des Moines for the picture. Mother had put an apron over Cora's Sunday dress and father forgot to take the apron off and had forgotten to smooth her hair and it's standing up all over her head, but she has new shoes, but Jim is bare foot. Another beautiful picture of mother and Aunt Sallie. Needless to say, we stole all of them.

Saw the most beautiful bedspreads or coverlids. Opened Emma's mother's trunk and found beautiful handmade linen, a beautiful shawl, her sun bonnet, etc. All this time rain was pouring so we had to return home. Late in the afternoon Tom and I took the little Ford and went for the mail but didn't get any!

The mud was awful. The water was running down from the mountains and things looked full. Went on to the cemetery where Cousin Minnie, who only died three years ago, is buried. Saw so many graves of family names. Many of them were relatives. Drove a little further to see an old log schoolhouse used for the negro children at that time, built by Uncle Alex when he was a young man. Saw a fine negro man there who told us much about it but he said, "Land sakes, Mars Knight, that schoolhouse was built "fore yous and I was born!"

After supper we went to spend the evening with the Humes. Mrs. Hume is a sister of Cousin Tommie's wife - also third cousins of ours. They are such interesting people. They have six children. The two oldest boys, university graduates, both teaching. Two daughters and one other son teaching. The girls had such beautiful handwork of all kinds, also the mother. They have a nice house with electric lights, etc. Mr. Hume knew father and, my, I felt like I was relation to all West Virginia when they began to tell of our relatives. It was getting cold when we walked home.

Friday morning - Cold as blixen. Went to the kitchen and such a sight from the window - a snow storm on the mountains. Cold Knob, the highest peak, is covered with snow. Also Meadow Mountain, not a bit of sunshine all the time at Tommies so didn't get any pictures, but we started out about 9:30 with all the wraps we could carry. Tom drove - but over Friers Hill was bad, but I've been more scared. However, was glad it was frozen.

Tom and Mr. McClintic stayed for dinner. Then Kittie let us hunt among old books for father's. Some were his old school books. The oldest book was on Joseph McMillian and the date was Dec 31, 1818. Other names in the book were John McMillian (or McMillion) and John W. Knight 1810, 1811. These must have been uncles or father's since the book was kept in the family. We saw grandmother's old spinning wheel. We hunted around and talked so much that I felt so spooky when I went to bed I couldn't sleep.

Saturday - Still cold, awfully cold down to 26 above zero. We climbed to the top of Geo Mountain where we could see far in every direction. Snow topped mountains and some of the valley still green, but no sunshine for pictures. The top of this mountain was warm and Kitty says that the sheep often go to the top of this when it is very cold on account of it being warmer.

We sent to the spring from which the water is piped to the side of the house where it is a running stream all the time. An old trough hollowed from a tree is still there although not used, where they watered the stock. The old barn that father help build still stands but is quite feeble. The great evergreen as high as any tree around was planted by father as a boy. The cabin where he was born was very near - only a pile of rock and a hollow place in the ground mark the place. The house not standing was built, begun before the war and finished after. He helped in the building until he went to war. One of the most interesting things we have seen today was an old chestnut tree. Kitty took us away down the valley until we came to Miery Branch - a beautiful little mountain stream. We followed it for some distance through thick woods. Aunt Ellen had told me of how Father and Uncle Alex had left home and were going to enlist in the Union Army. As they were walking along father said to Uncle Alex, "I just can't go on. I must turn back." So they parted. Father came back home and told his folks, anyway his mother, that he was joining the Confederates. He could not stay at the home for he might be taken by the Union Army at any time. So he took some comforts that grandmother gave him and agreed that he would sleep under this same chestnut tree that we have seen today. Then in the morning he would slip off through the woods. When, grandmother and Aunt Martha, Kittie's mother, went to the tree in the morning, he was gone and we saw the limb today where they found the covers. They never saw father again until the war was over, father married and settled in Iowa. He came back about the year 1878. Uncle Alex was not in any battles but was in the train service while father was in the commissary department so they were never forced to fight against each other. We picked some chestnuts from under the tree then gathered some mountain laurel which was beautiful.

We carried some bread and milk and jam, etc. in by the living room fire and had our suppers all cozy. Now we are ready for bed.

Sunday, Nov. 20. Still cold but the sun is shining bright. Waited until nine o'clock, then went out and took pictures. Took the old pine tree father planted so many years ago, the pile of stones left from the house where father was born, several pictures of the house as it now stands, then went to the old chestnut tree by Miery Branch in spite of the vicious ram. Had to go across the cornfield to escape him and Cora lost her rubbers, but we got there and took two pictures. Hope they are good. About eleven Denny Callison came for us. The ground was frozen when he came so we hurried dinner hoping to have the trip before the roads got soft. Kittie had a dandy dinner and I was hungry after so much walking. Kittie got some chickens and ducks, and about two o'clock we started out bags and baggage. We were not on pavement, the roads were rocky, but not slick. Went past the McMillion church about two miles from Kittie's. The church was organized in 1850 and the first members were six McMillions and their wives. Grandfather and grandmother Knight - she was a McMillion - gave the land. They have a nice building now. We wandered around the cemetery a bit. Saw grandfather's and grandmother's graves but found no stones for which I felt so badly. So many names on the grave stones that were familiar, a great many that were relatives. A short distance on we came to the old home where Grandmother Knight was born. The buildings were all changed but a beautiful spot. After going some distances and winding some more for it was mostly up and down or winding, we came to the most forsaken spot in all creation. Away off in sort of a gully between mountains was where Grandfather Knight's father settled. How they lived and what on one could not imagine. The next thing was fording Spring Creek. I supposed we had come to the end of things but if we didn't go straight through, car and all. Then came the thrill that excelled all so far and there have been many. We climbed Spring Creek Mountain. It was rock road, narrow. What would have happened if we had met a car or had something go wrong with the car. We'll never know, nothing went wrong. When we got on top we just stopped and looked and coming down, it was not so steep, so we were more comfortable. And to think that the mail carrier went over that road every day.

We came to a nice little town, Renick on the R. R. Only a couple of hundred or so people, but a fine consolidated school and good churches. Everywhere we go we find the people cultured, well-educated and real.

On through Renick through the valley to White Oak Grove where Aunt Ellen (father's youngest sister) lived and raised her family. (Clora Boggs, Della Huff, Eugie Burr who died, Mattie Knapp, Jim, Will and Sam Kincaid). After the family were all gone she married Jim McCoy and we passed their house just a few miles further on at Brownstown. We again crossed the upper end of Spring Creek Mountain, then through Renicks Valley to Droop Mountain. The climb up was rocky but not scary. Away down in the valley we could see the beautiful Greenbrier River and father's description of that beautiful stream made it all seem so real. We soon ran into the Senica Trail, a splendid highway crossing the state from north to south. We now had some six miles right on top of the mountain. Almost level, good homes and farms for there were so many clearings. Lots of pine trees are mixed with oak and maple and beautiful mountain laurel. Then we began the decline of Droop Mountain. The road was much like the Harney Peak road in the Black Hills.

We saw just where a battle had been fought. History gives that as the Battle of Droop Mt. The Confederates were coming up the Mt. and the Union soldiers were going down. The Union won, of course. Down a little farther Cousin Denny stopped the car and we got out to look. We could see far below the most beautiful valley we had seen yet called the Little Levels. In one direction the town of Hillsboro and far up the valley where mother was born.

It didn't look so far across, but in order to get there we had to go clear down the mountain in the opposite direction, then five miles after leaving Hillsboro. We could see the Greenbrier River at many places on the way out but far above it all the time. When we were nearly home, we picked up Denny's and Rexford's children coming from their church service.

We passed Mother's old home and a short distance farther came to Rex and Denny's home. A nice fire was burning so we warmed up. I went into the kitchen for a drink and there found a big fireplace with two big logs that they said were about 3 1/2 ft. long, each burning. This fireplace burns all the time and I never got very far for it is so cheerful. Rex's family consists of Virginia, 12 yrs. old who is very interested in her 4-H club. This club is very strong through here. Virginia took as her project sheep raising and had her own sheep and raised it and has it all written up in such an interesting way. Henry is nine, Hubert about seven and Gilmer five.

Monday we just visited mostly and looked around this very interesting place. Denny went into town and found a history of Pocohantas County. This gives us an interesting history from the beginning in this county. An old gentleman, Mr. Cutlip, while younger than mother, knew so much of the family and told us so many interesting stories. He told one good joke on Israel Callison, my grandfather. He and his brother, Josiah, and a lot of other men were on a fox hunt and decided to have a chicken roast while they were out. They were to steal the chicken from a widow woman who had a very bad temper, so part were to do the stealing while the others hunted up the other things for the feed. After they started, the one set of men thought they would steal the chicken from Israel Callison, my grandfather, just for a joke. They brought it back and Israel said "My, that looks like our old spotted hen." but the men never let on.

The next day Israel saw the widow coming to their house across lots and he imagined she looked pretty mad. He made his escape and stayed away all day. He never did know the joke but everybody else did and it has been handed down to the great grandchildren.

Tuesday - In the morning we washed and in the afternoon Dennie's brother Elba took us to see their aunt and our second cousin once removed. She lives in Hillsboro and is now 87 years old and was a school mate of mother until mother moved away to Illinois in 1855 when she was 13 years old. Her name is Mattie Bright. She came tripping into the room as spry as a sixteen year old girl. Just a little woman, so straight and prim. She got her open fire fixed to suit her, then we visited. Her home was the home of Dennie and Rex now. The claim or homestead was taken from the government by one James Callison from Ireland but of English descent. He settled right on this place and had several thousand acres of land. Later he moved to Tennessee and the land has been handed down. The sons James and Anthony were the ones who were on the place here. The son James prospered but Anthony did not so James gave him 160 acres of the farm. Josiah, son of James, fell heir to this place and Israel (my grandfather) fell heir to the other place. The buildings are all changed over there but this place has remained very much the same.

After their visit with Mattie Bright, we drove on farther over the highway to get some wool to Stamping Creek, then came home a much lower road by Denmar.

Wednesday - In the morning we called on Dennie's mother, who with her son lives on this place but in a fine new house. In the afternoon we went to see an old church where mother went to church, Droop Church. The pews are handmade and it has a gallery where the negros sat. The cemetery there has many Callisons and Brights. After this we visited the school here for they had a Thanksgiving program. After school we sent to Beard with Dennie for he was taking Elba to the train. He was going to spend Thanksgiving with his girl at Roanoke. Just for a joke we slipped a letter of congratulation in his traveling bag for him to find when he opened his bag. Coming home we stopped and got mountain laurel to send home. Came home and had oysters for supper. Then Cora and I dressed a turkey for the Thanksgiving dinner tomorrow. I've never been away from home folks for Thanksgiving but know that you are having a good time.

Thursday and Thanksgiving. First thing for breakfast we had some of those great big oysters fried. Say - good. We helped with the work what we could, then by that time it was raining. Denny went over for his mother and Aunty just the same and we had a most delicious dinner together. The rest of the day was spent doing nothing.

Friday morning Denny took Kitty, Cora and I to Beard for an 8:40 train and so ends one of the best times of the whole trip although there have been so many. Kitty got off at a little station and would go back to her home with the mailman. We came on down the line along the Greenbrier River to Ronceverte, changed trains there on to the main line for Alderson. Cleo, Kitti's and Rex's sister was to meet us. She was so fine looking and young to have a daughter in college. The road was paved all the way to her home so we had a nice ride out. Fine old southern home she has. Her husband is quite old, more like her father. She has seven children, five boys and two girls. Two are quite small and are live wires. Cora has such a cold. Went with Cleo to feed her turkeys. She has some fifty and has already sold that many. She expects to clear $500 from them.

Saturday - Cora still feels bad so she is not enjoying her visit so much. Went to a 2:30 train to go back to Mason Knapps for over Sunday. We thought we were going to miss the train for now one seemed to have the time but when we got started we didn't know just what we might miss for Charles drove like Jehu the 2nd. We just seemed to go over fences, mountains and rivers and never even took the corners. We must have gotten there before we started for we were a half hour early. They have a new federal prison there, the only one of its kind in the U.S. so they decided to show us that in the half hour. So off we went again with Cleo all the time calmly telling Charles to please not drive so fast but evidently Charles did not hear. At the gate we met about 75 convicts, men working on the grounds, had been brought up from North Carolina. They were going to a movie in town. We waited for them to get out, then the gatekeeper told us we could not drive in, so we only saw the gate to the wonderful woman's prison. We turned around and after Charles had taken the corner off of several of those prisoners, the other learned to get out of the way. I wasn't afraid of them for I knew they could never catch Charles. We went to the depot then and waited the rest of the time there. We expected Della to meet us at Ronceverte but she was not there so I phoned out and it's some job to get anyone on those country lines. I had to yell so loud I wasn't sure but some of them would hear me without the phone. Della came after us. It was nice to think we were to have our last visit there where Aunt Ellen was. I'll never forget Aunt Ellen. So calm, so much of dignity. The modern grandmother can in no way compare with her.

After her husband died, which was before Sam was born, she cared for and earned the living for them all and now at eighty she is strong and well. We just visited that evening and watched them fix some hams to put away for they had been butchering. Cora did not rest well that night.

Sunday - We helped some with the work and about ten Cousin Tom and Dess came, then Della, another of Aunt Ellen daughters, with her son and daughter-in-law. Tom went for Emma in Lewisburg and altogether we had 22 for dinner. And there were some of the things we had: roasted pork loin, cabbage salad, potatoes, macaroni and cheese, salt rising bread, sweet potatoes and pineapple ice cream with applesauce cake and white cake. I got some pictures for the day was sunshiny, just like spring. We all had a good time. Della looks like Mattie, both are rather witty. Just full of fun.

Monday - Up long before daybreak. We had expected to go to Washington, then down to Norfolk, but Cora's cold was so bad and she had slept very little for several nights so we decided to go straight to Norfolk. Della hurried her milking so she could take us to Ronceverte before school.

Rachel Knight's father was Andrew Knight, born 10 Oct 1804 in Greenbrier County, Virginia. On 6 Mar 1834 he married Rebecca McMillion, daughter of John and Rachael (Hutchinson) McMillion.

Andrew and Rebecca had seven children with Rachel Ellen being the youngest.
(1) John Wesley Knight, b. 2 Jan 1835, d. 28 Dec 1918
    m. 25 Dec 1866, Margaret A. Callison
(2) Betty Ann "Betsy" Knight, b. 4 Mar 1836, d. 4 May 1843
(3) James Knight, b. 6 Oct 1837, d. 22 Mar 1908
    m. 1883, Kate Kincaid
(4) Caroline Jane Knight, b. 15 Nov 1839, d. 24 Jul 1858
(5) Alexander Knight, b. 10 Jul 1842, d. 12 Jul 1912
    m. 11 Jan 1871, Susan Whiting
(6) Martha Mirienda Knight, b. 27 Aug 1845, d. 23 Jan 1919
    m. 2 Nov 1881, Samuel P. Sammons
(7) Rachel Ellen Knight*, b. 16 Sep 1847, d. 17 Nov 1930
    m. 21 Oct 1869, William Samuel Kincaid
    m. 2nd 26 Nov 1902, James McCoy

John Wesley Knight was born in Greenbrier County but migrated west while the rest of the family stayed in Greenbrier County. He married Margaret Abigail Callison on 25 Dec 1866 in Abington, Illinois. Shortly after that he moved his family to Warren County, Iowa, where all seven of their children were born. Jennie (Knight) Ball who wrote the above diary is a daughter of John Wesley Knight.

James Knight who was born in 1837 fought in the Civil War on the Confederate side with the 14th Virginia Cavalry. He married later in life to Kate Kincaid, daughter of Richard Kincaid. They had two girls, Pearl and Maybell, and one son who died in infancy. On the following pages is a letter written by James Knight during the Civil War. It tells of the hardships suffered by all and the hope that the war will soon end and their families can be reunited.

Union March 1st 1864

Andrew Knight
Hazeville Va
　　　　Dear Father

As this day is too
wet to travel I will write you a few lines I have
written frequently but have no assurance that you have
Received any of my letters but I will Continue to
write occasionaly Some of my letters perhaps may Chance
to come to hand I am in fine health

I came to this county a short time ago expect to
Remain here for some weeks Wesley is at Dublin he
has been there for some time and will Remain for an
indefinite time Ludington is at Dublin he expects
to finish packing beef in a few weeks he will then move
back to this place Perhaps I can then get time to Come home
a few days We have four hundred Cattle
in this County and have but very little to feed on if this
month should be hard we will be very apt to lose Some
Cattle we will have to depend pretty much on the blue grass
sods to bring them through. my horse in good
condition he would make a splended plough horse this Spring

I was sorry to hear of you loosing your horse such a
horse is hard to Replace I saw R F Dennis at Chris-
tainsburg he told me he had seen your horse in Roanoke and
had written to you I was then in two hours Ride on the
cars of where he seen the horse and intended giving imediately
in pursuit but just then Wesley wrote to me that
uncle Abe had gone I have lately understood that he dos not
come up with horse I think from what Dennis told me that it was not your horse

100

The Currency bill lately adopted by Congress has put Confederate money at a very low ebb. The bill requires that all money above the denomination of five dollars shall be bonded by the first of April, at which time there will be a new issue put in circulation. The present five dollar notes will be good until the first July, at which time they are required to be bonded.

The late military bill requires all between the age of seventeen & eighteen and forty five and fifty to be organized into a Reserve Corps.

The tax bill is very sweeping in its character. It is very oppressive on speculators. I hope it will have a tendency to stop speculating.

Congress will assemble again on the first monday in May. I look for a very active campaign as soon as the spring opens. I believe that the coming season will decide and terminate this war.

I would advise you not to go to the mountain to make sugar. I think you are too far advanced in life to stand the exposure. besides those of the family left at home would have more to do, and more exposure during your absence.

Try to put out a crop and endeavor to raise your subsistence during this war and I after the war is over. I hope the little family that is now scattered to and fro may yet be reunited around the domestic circle.

Ever Your affectionate Son James

101

Rachel's brother, Alexander Knight, was an influential farmer in the Williamsburg district of Greenbrier County. He was a deputy sheriff and later sheriff in years 1871-76. In the Civil War he served three years under General Crook as trainmaster. Alexander Knight married Susan Whiting, the daughter of Ebenezer and Sally (McMillion) Whiting, and they had one son, Andrew Thomas, born 4 Mar 1874, and two daughters, Minnie Lake, born 6 Jul 1878, and Emmie Frances, born 20 May 1881.

Rebecca (McMillion) Knight died 10 Nov 1884 and Andrew Knight died 14 Feb 1889. Both are buried in what is known as the McMillion Knight Cemetery on Friars Hill about 4 miles northwest of the town of Renick.

Andrew Knight, born 1804, was the son of James Knight, Jr. and Margaret Cavendish. James Knight, Jr. was born 10 Dec 1780 in Virginia. On 25 Nov 1802 in Greenbrier County, he married Margaret Cavendish, the daughter of William Hunter and Jane (Murphy) Cavendish.

The Cavendish Connection

William Hunter Cavendish was born in Ireland about 1740 and later immigrated to North America. It was said that William Hunter Cavendish was connected to the aristocratic House of Cavendish in England and this was freely discussed among the people in early Greenbrier County. One story says he came to this country with his widowed mother and two sisters, and there is a record of a Margaret Cavendish coming to North America on the convict ship *Litchfield* in 1752. This timing is about right and this Margaret may be his mother. That she came on a ship with felons does not indicate that she was bad because many victims of politics also came on these ships. The story is that they settled in Virginia on the James River not far from Lexington. The place where they settled in still known as Cavendish Farm.

The young William Hunter Cavendish appears to have reflected the education and breeding of his royal background at an early age. One biography in a Greenbrier County history says: He came to this county in 1765 (another says 1769) and settled one mile north of Fort Donnally, lived here during the Indian troubles and after the treaty of peace with them, went to their encampment and brought away David and Nancy Williams, white children the Indians had captured. Greenbrier County records show William made numerous land transactions in the county between 1782 and 1804 and owned an extensive amount of land.

William Hunter Cavendish was a lawyer and had many political offices and dealings. He was a quarter-master general during the Revolutionary War 1778-82 and provided much needed supplies from the Greenbrier area. He was the first County Clerk of Greenbrier County and served often in the Virginia Assembly during 1790-1804. He was appointed on the first board of visitors of Washington College, Lexington, Virginia, in 1796. The duties of the board of visitors were to appoint the president and professors, make inspections, and to have control of all property belonging to the college. William Hunter Cavendish also served for two years as sheriff of Greenbrier County during which time he lived in Lewisburg.

Records are somewhat unclear but it appears William Hunter Cavendish married four times. His first wife was a Lewis and his second wife was Mary (McCoy) Williams, widow of John Williams. He married his third wife, Jane Murphy on 13 Jun 1780. Jane Cavendish died sometime before 1804. His fourth wife was Alice (Mann) McClintic whom he married on 10 May 1804. William Hunter Cavendish died between 14 August and November 1818 in Bath County, Virginia.

William Hunter Cavendish had the following known children:
(1) William Cavendish, Jr.
    m. 6 Feb 1794, Jane McCoy
(2) Margaret Cavendish*, b. Apr 1784, d. 3 Jul 1853
    m. 25 Nov 1802, James Knight, Jr.
(3) Joseph Cavendish
    m. McCoy
(4) William Cavendish
    m. Rachael Hull
(5) Mary "Polly" Cavendish
    m. 27 Aug 1798, Isaac Callison
(6) Jane Cavendish

m. May 1804, Joseph McClung
(7) Rebecca Cavendish
m. 25 Jan 1816, Alexander McClung
(8) Andrew Cavendish, b. 24 Mar 1787,
d. c1870, Fayette Co., WV
m. 27 Apr 1809, Janet McClung

Returning to the Knight family, James and Margaret (Cavendish) Knight had many children. Some are confirmed by county and family records, but some are only listed as children in his will. To our best knowledge, their children were:
(1) Elizabeth (Jane) Knight, b. 10 Aug 1803, d. 2 Apr 1858
m. Feb 1827, John Williams
(2) Andrew Knight*, b. 10 Oct 1804, d. 24 Feb 1889
m. 6 Mar 1834, Rebecca McMillion
(3) Mary "Polly" Knight
m. 31 Mar 1831, Samuel Hinkle
(4) George W. Knight, 16 Aug 1807, d. bef. 1870
m. Susan Wallace
(5) Thomas B. (Tom) Knight, b. c1815
m. 18 Dec 1867, Jane Wolfenbarger
(6) Abigale (Abby) Knight, b. 4 Nov 1817, d. 20 Mar 1879
m. Beverly McMillion
(7) Alexander Knight, b. c1819
(8) Nancy Knight
m. 25 Dec 1839, George Lewis
(9) Cavendish Knight
(10) James Knight
(11) William Knight
(12) Kenny Knight
(13) Caroline Knight
m. Joe McMillion
(14) Rebecca Knight
m. F. H. Luddington

James Knight, Jr. died in Greenbrier County in 1855. His wife, Margaret (Cavendish) Knight, died on 3 Jul 1853 at Hunter in Greenbrier County.

James Knight, Jr. was the son of James Knight, Sr. who was born about 1741 and died on 16 Dec 1794, probably in Greenbrier

County. James Knight, Sr.'s wife was named Mary, family name unknown and she died on 29 Oct 1808 at the age of 62 years. James Knight, Sr. moved his family from Warm Springs, Bath County, Virginia, to Greenbrier County in 1790. James and Mary Knight had the following children:
(1) George Knight, b. 11 Nov 1777
(2) James Knight, Jr.*, b. 10 Dec 1780, d. 1855
(3) Rebecca Knight, b. 23 Mar 1784
      m. 9 Nov 1809, Greenbrier Co., VA, David Williams
+ possibly others unknown

James Knight, Sr. evidently fought in the Revolutionary War since his name is listed in a book entitled *West Virginians in the Revolution* by Ross Johnson. Before a Greenbrier County court, James Knight, Jr. and Rebecca Williams, formerly Rebecca Knight, certified to the Department of War that they were the children and sole heirs of James Knight, Sr. who was a regularly enlisted soldier of the Revolutionary War.

There is evidence that James Knight, Sr. came from Bath County, Virginia. Several researchers have searched for his ancestors but no further connections have been found. There are numerous Knight families in North America and it is doubtful if his ancestry can be further determined.

The McMillion Family

Rebecca McMillion was a great great grandmother of Samuel Plummer Boggs. She was born about 1807 and married Andrew Knight on 6 Mar 1834 in Greenbrier County, Virginia (now West Virginia).

The McMillion family appears to have been in Greenbrier County in its early development stages. The 1783-86 *Heads of Families for Greenbrier County* lists Jno. McMillian, Danl McMullen and Jno. McMullen as head of households. Rebecca's father John was born December 1771 to a John McMillion and his wife Martha Palmer so it is probably her grandfather John who is listed in the head of households

Our McMillion family starts with a John McMillion who was born 9 Mar 1703/04 and married an Anne Frances Harrison. Anne Frances Harrison was born about 1711 and is the daughter of Thomas and Anne Sithia (Short) Harrison.

John and Anne McMillion had 6 children:
(1) Elizabeth Harrison McMillion, b. 1730
    m. Doc John Briscoe
(2) John McMillion*, b. 1 Jan 1735/36
    m. Martha Palmer
(3) Ruth Harrison McMillion, b. 1745
    m. Gerrard W. Briscoe
(4) Cathbert McMillion, b. 1746
(5) Ann Frances McMillion, b. c1748
(6) Samuel L. McMillion

Our line descends through son John McMillion who married Martha Palmer on 4 Sep 1761. Martha Palmer was born 25 Feb 1742/43 and is the daughter of Parmenas and Mary Ann (Draper) Palmer. John McMillion is listed in 1765 and 1767 on the tithables list for Loudoun County, Virginia. From 1768 to 1774, both John McMillion and his brother Joseph are listed on the Loudoun County tithables lists. John and Martha McMillion also lived in Fauquier County, Virginia, before moving to Greenbrier County.

Land records in Fauquier County show John McMillion purchased land on the Fauquier-Loudoun border on 27 May 1776 and sold the same land on 23 Aug 1783. The names of John McMillion, Sr. and his wife Martha appear in land records in Greenbrier County when they bought land in 1791, 1796, and 1798. John McMillion wrote his will on 25 Aug 1800 and his wife Martha was still alive at that time. His will was probated in June 1804 so he probably died shortly before that date.

John and Martha McMillion had 12 children:
(1) Nancy McMillion, b. 4 Nov 1762
    m. 1779, Benjamin Hamrick
(2) Joseph McMillion, b. 15 Oct 1764, d. 9 Jul 1855
    m. 22 Jul 1791, Greenbrier Co., VA, Jane Hannah
(3) Mary McMillion, b. 18 Dec 1766
    m. Jonathan Kidd, m. 2nd Patrick Constantine
(4) Elizabeth Margaret McMillion, b. 18 Nov 1768
    m. James "David" Williams
(5) John "Jack" McMillion, Jr.*, b. Dec 1771
    m. Rachel Hutchinson
(6) Martha "Patsie" McMillion, b. 18 Mar 1773,
    will probated Feb 1846
    m. 7 Jan 1791, John Williams
(7) Hannah McMillion, b. 23 May 1775, d. 1854
    m. Jacob Hutcheson
(8) Daniel McMillion, b. 10 Jun 1777
    m. 19 Sep 1805, Nancy Lewis
    m. 2nd 15 Jul 1826, Margaret Carrell
(9) William McMillion, b. 18 Dec 1779, d. 7 Jul 1826
    m. 14 May 1801, Margaret Blair
    m. 2nd 2 May 1804, Elizabeth Betsey Perkins
(10) Jane "Jennie" McMillion, b. 25 Feb 1782
    m. 24 May 1805, James Hume
(11) Catharine "Katy" McMillion, b. 15 Jan 1784, d. aft 1850 dnm
(12) Sarah "Sally" McMillion, b. 25 Jan 1786
    m. 1811, Nicholas Kire

Son Joseph McMillion was a soldier in the Revolutionary War. In a pension file for Virginia No. 23820, it says that Joseph McMillion was born in Fauquier County in 1763, the son of John and Martha McMillion. Joseph was drafted in Fauquier County about 24 Feb 1781 serving under Captain T. Morehead in the

Virginia militia and under Colonel Armstead Churchill in Gen. Meadow's Brigade. The record further says that Joseph married on 22 Jul 1791 to Jane and moved from Fauquier County to Greenbrier County in 1785. Joseph received a pension for his service at the rate of $20 a year beginning 4 Mar 1831. His widow, Jane Hannah, was allowed bounty land in 1856 under warrant No. 47435 on account of his service.

Joseph McMillion married Jane Hannah, daughter of James W. and Eliza Hannah. Joseph and Jane had 10 children:

(1) John McMillion, b. 7 Nov 1794
    m. Jane Virginia McMillion
(2) James McMillion, b. 30 Sep 1796
    m. Eliza Jane Rader
(3) Nathaniel M. McMillion, b. 20 Jan 1801
    m. Isabella "Peggy" Burr
(4) Daniel McMillion, b. 1807
    m. 22 Sep 1831, Alice Aisley McCoy
(5) Nancy McMillion, b. 1808
    m. James Ewing
(6) Joseph Jr. McMillion, b. 1810
    m. Alice "Alley" Knight
(7) Elizabeth "Betsy" McMillion, b. 1811
    m. William McCoy
(8) Margaret "Peggy" McMillion, b. 8 Jul 1820
    m. Aaron Burr, Jr.
(9) Lydia McMillion
    m. Alex Groves
(10) Julia A. McMillion, b. 1821
    m. James McMillion (a cousin)

Our direct line ancestor John McMillion married Rachael Hutchinson in Greenbrier County on 10 Apr 1793. The Hutchinson family had been in Greenbrier County since its founding and a John Hutchinson was an early sheriff of the county in 1785. The 1790 Greenbrier census lists 4 Hutchinson families: John, Sr., John, Jr., George and William. One of these must be Rachael's family, but it has not been determined which one.

John and Rachael (Hutchinson) McMillion had the following children:

(1) Martha McMillion, b. c1793
    m. William McClung
(2) Hannah McMillion, b. c1795
    m. 19 Nov 1829, Greenbrier Co., VA, John McClung
(3) Jane McMillion, b. c1797, d. 14 Jun 1858
    m. 15 Jun 1815, John McMillion
(4) Elizabeth McMillion, b. c1801, d. 3 Mar 1853
    m. 23 Aug 1821, Greenbrier Co., VA, William Neal
(5) Rebecca McMillion*, b. c1807, d. 10 Nov 1858
    m. 5 Mar 1834, Andrew Knight
(6) Andrew McMillion, b. c1809, d. aft 1860
    m. 3 Sep 1835, Greenbrier Co., VA, Jane McClung
(7) Beverly Waugh McMillion (son), b. 20 Sep 1811,
    Greenbrier Co., VA, d. 6 Jun 1880
    m. 24 Dec 1835, Abigail Knight
(8) Caroline McMillion, b. c1811, Greenbrier Co., VA
    m. 19 Nov 1857, Greenbrier Co., VA, Alex Knight
(9) John McMillion
    m. 27 Feb 1836, Eliza McClung
(10)Ann Vance McMillion, b. Jan 1817, Greenbrier Co., VA, d.
    31 May 1888
    m. 24 Sep 1868, William McClung

John McMillion died in 1848. His will reads:

I give to my son, Andrew, that part of land on which I live,
also, 50 acres on Spring Creek. Also give my son Beverly, 60
acres on Spring Creek. Give to son, Andrew, 49 1/2 acres. I
give to my son, Beverly, and my three daughters Martha
McClung, Caroline and Ann McMillion 514 acres on Spring
Creek. The sum to be equally divided between them.

Devisees
wife Rachel
sons Beverly, Andrew, John
daughters Ann, Caroline, Jane, Hannah McClung, Elizabeth
Neal, Martha McClung

Will Book No. 2, Dated 30 Apr 1848

Rebecca McMillion is not listed in John's will so perhaps she had already received her inheritance. She is listed as his daughter in a biography of her husband, Andrew Knight.

Andrew McMillion, son of John and Rachael (Hutchinson) McMillion, married Jane McClung and had a family of seven children: Matthew, John W., William R., Mary, Anderson, Andrew and Marion D. Marion D. McMillion later married into the Boggs family when he married Elizabeth Rebecca Boggs (an aunt of Plummer Boggs) and they later migrated west to Jay County, Indiana. This may have been some of the ties that later brought the Ed Boggs family to this area of Indiana.

The 1820 Virginia census lists John and Joseph (age 45+) in Greenbrier County plus Daniel, John Jr., William and James (age 26-45) and a James (age 16-26) as household heads.

The 1830 census lists households of Joseph (age 60-70), John (age 50-60), Daniel (age 50-60), Martha (age 80-90), John (age 40-50), James (age 40-50), Ralph, and Elizabeth (age 40-50).

The 1840 census lists households of Joseph (age 70-80), John (age 60-70), Daniel (age 60-70), Ralph (age 40-50), Eli (age 30-40), Allen (age 20-30) Andrew (age 30-40), Daniel (age 30-40), Elizabeth (age 50-60), George (age 20-30), Joseph Jr. (age 20-30).

The 1850 and all the later censuses show that many descendants of the McMillion family remained in Greenbrier County. There is a McMillion cemetery located at the McMillion Methodist Church in Friars Hill, Greenbrier County, West Virginia. There are a number of McMillions buried there.

Most of the early information on the McMillions comes from a report done by Mrs. Clyde Garner which was obtained from the Greenbrier Historical Society. My thanks to Adrienne Pappas of Fairfax, Virginia, and Thomas Wade McMillion of Waynesboro, Virginia, for information on the McMillion family.

The Carder Family

The Carder family is connected to the ancestry of Samuel Plummer Boggs through Phoebe E. Carder who was married to John A. Boggs on 9 Sep 1851 in Greenbrier County. Phoebe Carder was the daughter of Joseph and Rebecca (Wiseman) Carder. The Carders lived in Taylor County, Virginia, (now West Virginia) as shown in the 1850 and earlier censuses. Taylor County is several counties north of Greenbrier County, so it is not clear how John and Phoebe met. The only explanation may be that Greenbrier County residents often moved their farm produce down the river and perhaps this is the way that John and Phoebe met. Other members of the Carder family did not appear to move into Greenbrier County.

Phoebe's father John Carder was born in 1791 in Culpeper County, Virginia, the son of John and Mary (Day) Carder. John Carder moved his family west in 1802 to Harrison County, Virginia (now West Virginia.) Joseph Carder married on 18 Feb 1816 in Harrison County to Rebecca Wiseman, the daughter of John Wiseman. Joseph and Rebeca (Wiseman) Carder had the following children, all born in Taylor County:
(1) Isaac Carder, b. 17 Oct 1819, d. 9 Oct 1855
    m. Nancy Brooks
(2) Plummer Carder, d. 1880s in the West
(3) Elizabeth Carder
    m. John Rinker
(4) Phoebe E. Carder*, b. 1828, Monongalia Co., VA, d. 9 Jan 1899, Greenbrier Co., WV
    m. 9 Sep 1851, Taylor Co., VA, John A. Boggs
(5) Jesse "Jose" Carder, b. 23 Apr 1830
    m. Laura Martin
(6) Josina Carder, b. 1832
    m. Thomas Williams
(7) John Anderson Carder, b. 19 Nov 1833, d. 27 May 1908
    m. May Jane Rinker
(8) Rebecca Carder, b. 1835
    m. Samuel Rinker
(9) Joseph Carder, b. 1837, d. young

(10) Cornelius Carder, b. 13 Mar 1842, d. 10 Jan 1814
    m. Mary Ellen Peacock
(11) Clarinda Carder, b. 1845, d. prob. young
(12) Frances Augusta Carder, d. young

Rebecca (Wiseman) Carder apparently died between 1850 and 1860 because Joseph Carder married a second time to Mary "Polly" Rogers who was born 20 Sep 1815. His second wife was called Aunt Polly by his children. Joseph Carder died some time between 1861 and 1863.

Most of Joseph's children remained in Taylor County but some emigrated away. Jesse Carder and his family immigrated to Illinois where Jesse died and he is buried at Denver, Richland County, Illinois. John Anderson Carder married in Taylor County, Virginia, to Mary Jane Rinker in December 1858 but later moved to Jay County, Indiana. They lived at Eaton, Delaware County, Indiana, and are buried at Hillcrest Cemetery in Jay County, Indiana. The youngest daughter Frances Augusta Carder went to live with the John Boggs family but died before reaching maturity.

Plummer Carder moved to Indiana some time before or at the beginning of the Civil War. He was about to drafted so he enlisted in the 19th Indiana Regiment which became famous as part of the "Iron Brigade." After the war he moved west and was back in the army when he died in an Indian attack in the 1880s in Washington state. This Plummer Carder is the source of the name "Plummer" for Samuel Plummer Boggs.

Joseph Carder's father was a John Carder who was born about 1767 in Culpeper County, Virginia. *The Charles Brinkman Papers 1869-1938* state the following about this John Carder:

John Carder fought in the Revolutionary War at age 16, serving with the "Culpeper Freedom Riders." He also rode with the Culpeper Minute Men to offer his services to Governor Patrick Henry in Williamsburg at the time of the Virginia Colony's uprising and the flight of the English Governor, Lord Dunmore. These records also state that as a Revolutionary War veteran, John Carder attended the inaugural ceremonies of George Washington at New York City in 1789.

John Carder went to Harrison County, Virginia, (now West Virginia), where his first land purchase, 700 acres from John Prunty, was recorded in 1802 in the area north of Pruntytown (then Williamsport) and northeast of Grafton. By 1844, this part of Harrison County had been split off to form Taylor County.

According to Emeline Breakiron and Anna Carder Reed, John Carder traded with the Indians, bought furs from them and sold the furs down river, using the profits to buy land. The Indians respected him and never harassed him. On one occasion, two Indian fur traders came up Lost Run from Tygart River into Carder Run and old John Carder invited them up onto the hill and had breakfast with them.

The 1810 census of Harrison County, Virginia, lists John Carder in the "45 and over" bracket, indicating a slightly earlier birth date than that shown by the 1850 census. The 1850 census of Taylor County, Virginia, shows John Carder, age 83, living in the household of his oldest son, Isaac.

John Carder is said to have married Mary Day, but there is some question about her maiden name. John and Mary (Day?) Carder had the following children:
(1) Isaac Carder, b. 18 Dec 1790, Culpeper Co., VA, d. 9 Dec 1865, Taylor Co., WV
   m. 8 Mar 1814, Harrison Co., VA, Tabitha Bennett
(2) Joseph Carder*, b. 1791, Culpeper Co., VA, d. 1861/3
   m. 18 Feb 1817, Rebecca Wiseman
   m. 2nd Mary "Polly" Rogers
(3) Thomas Carder, b. c1793, Culpeper Co., VA, d. bef. 1850
   m. 14 Jan 1813, Harrison Co., VA, Jemima Riley
(4) John Carder, Jr., b. 1795/8, Culpeper Co., VA, d. c1826
   m. 20 Dec 1819, Fanny Hawkins
(4) Mahalia Carder, b. c1797, d. bef. 1850
   m. 1814, Harrison Co., VA, Robert Johnston
(5) Ealon Carder, b. 1806, d. 18 Aug 1882
   m. 15 Jul 1824, Harrison Co., VA, George Wiseman
(6) Lucinda Carder
   m. 31 May 1820, Harrison Co., VA, John Cross

Mary (Day) Carder died sometime before 1850 while John Carder died sometime after the 1850 census.

Of the children of John Carder, son Isaac Carder and his wife Tabitha Bennett had fourteen children all born in Taylor County, Virginia. Isaac died on 9 Dec 1865 in Taylor County and court records show his estate appraised at $5,317. Thomas Carder married Jemima Riley in 1813, and they had at least four known children but probably more (8 children shown in the 1830 census). Thomas died sometime between 1830 and 1850 since his widow Jemima is shown living with her son George in Richie County, Virginia, in the later year. John Carder, Jr. married Fanny Hawkins in 1819 and they had four children before John died about 1826.

There are records of some earlier Carders in Virginia before John Carder's birth about 1767. Some later migrated to Culpeper County but to date they have not been tied to our John Carder. John is probably a descendant of these Carders, but it has not be yet confirmed.

Most of the above information has been taken from genealogical research done by Alwyn A. Carder of Redkey, Indiana and also from the book *Carder, An American Family* by W. Ashley Carder of Columbia, South Carolina.

The Ancestry of Hilda Irene Garringer

Hilda Irene Garringer was born 28 Mar 1898 to Bertha Achsah Hammers and Isaac Luther Garringer. The Garringer and Hammers families are both of German origin and both date back in the United States to before the American Revolution. Both the Garringer and Hammers families were very early settlers in Randolph County, Indiana. The Garringer family arrived between 1832 and 1833. The Hammers family arrived in 1836.

The two families form the basis for this ancestral search, but many other families are associated with them through marriage. Families associated with the Garringer line are the Collins family of Virginia, the Boots/Stieffel family of Pennsylvania, the Finch family of Ohio and Virginia, the Smith family of Virginia, and the Peterson/Bidert family of Pennsylvania. Families associated with the Hammers family are the Morris family of Virginia and Ohio, the Harbour family of Virginia, the Grove family of Virginia, the Fry family of Pennsylvania, the Capps family of North Carolina, and the Cooper family of Virginia.

Hilda Irene Garringer's ancestry is mainly German and also has several English family ties. Certainly the Garringer, Hammers and Boots families were of German ancestry. The following is a listing of the direct line ancestors of Hilda Irene Garringer that are known at this time. In this identification scheme, double the number of the individual to identify the father and double the number plus one to identify the mother.

    7. Hilda Irene Garringer
      b. 28 Mar 1898, Randolph Co., IN
      m. 11 Jan 1919, Randolph Co., IN, Samuel Plummer Boggs
      d. 26 Dec 1983, Parker City, IN, bur. Woodlawn Cem.,
      Randolph Co., IN

14. Isaac Luther Garringer
  b. 15 Jun 1874, Randolph Co., IN
  m. 10 Aug 1895, Randolph Co., IN
  d. 2 Jun 1940, Randolph Co., IN
  bur. Woodlawn Cem., Randolph Co., IN
  28. David C. Garringer
    b. 4 Aug 1838, Randolph Co., IN
    m. 6 Mar 1871, Randolph Co., IN
    d. 10 Dec 1895, Randolph Co., IN,
    bur. Hopewell Cem., Randolph Co., IN
    56. Isaac Jacob Garringer
      b. 7 Mar 1812, Fairfield Co., OH
      m. 16 Mar 1834, Delaware Co., IN
      d. 16 Jan 1870, Randolph Co., IN
      bur. Garringer Homestead Cem., Monroe Twp.,
      Randolph Co., IN
      112. David Garringer
        b. 12 Oct 1772, Frederick Co., VA
        m. 27 Oct 1795, Berkeley Co., VA
        d. 11 Nov 1865, Fayette Co., OH
        bur. Cochran Cem., Perry Twp., Fayette Co., OH
        224. David Gerringer
          b. c1735, Edenkoben, Pfalz, Germany
          m. c1765, prob. Frederick Co., MD
          d. will probated, 10 Aug 1812, Berkeley Co., VA
          448. Emig Geringer
            b. c1682, Edenkoben, Pfalz, Germany
            m. 15 Apr 1728, Edenkoben
            d. 16 Feb 1737, Edenkoben
            896. Gorg Diether Geringer
              b. c1651, Germany
              m. c1673, Germany
            897. Maria Clara
              b. c1653, Germany
          449. Anna Maria Neu
          225. Barbara
            d. 15 Mar 1814, Berkeley Co., VA
      113. Elizabeth Smith
        b. 1775, (?) Frederick Co., VA
        d. Sep 1848, Randolph Co., IN,
        bur. Garringer Homestead Cem., Monroe Twp.,
        Randolph Co., IN

226. Alexander Smith

227. Mary Wright

57. Sally "Sarah" Boots

  b. 23 Mar 1814, Ross Co., OH

  d. 8 Aug 1882, Randolph Co., IN

  bur. Garringer Homestead, Monroe Twp., Randolph Co., IN

  114. Garrett Boots (b. Stieffel)

    b. c1765, PA

    d. 1819, Fayette Co., OH

    228. Adam Boots (b. Stieffel)

      b. 1733, Mangabohrnn, Germany

      d. 18 Aug 1803, Hardy Co., VA (now Grant Co., WV)

    229. Barbara

      d. after 1808

  115. Elizabeth Peterson (b. Bidert)

    b. c1770, Hardy Co., VA

    d. c1825, Fayette Co., OH

    230. John Martin Peterson (b. Hans Martin Bidert)

      b. 20 May 1730, Near Barenmyle, Switzerland

      m. 19 Jan 1768

      d. May 1820, Hardy Co., VA (now Grant Co., WV)

      460. Hans Jacob Bidert

        bap. 7 Nov 1706, near Barenmyle, Switzerland

        m. 13 Feb 1728

        d. 1785, Hardy Co., VA (WV)

        920. Hans Jacob Bidert

          b. 17 Sep 1676

          1840. Niclaus Biderb

          b. 8 Aug 1622, nr. Langenbruck or Rheinfelden, Switzerland

            3680. Niclaus Biderb

              b. 23 May 1595, Switzerland

              7360. Wolfgang Biderb

                b. 1550/60 Switzerland

                m. 2nd 19 Sep 1586

              7361. Bropstin vonHeldarband

            1841. Barbara Flattner

          921. Elizabeth Camperin

        461. Sarah Mohlerin

        b. Switzerland

        d. 1787, Hardy Co., VA (WV)

    231. Rosina Teter (b. Dieter)

        b. c1728

        d. 1804, Hardy Co., VA (WV)

        462. George Teter (b. Dieter)

            b. Wurtenburg, Germany

            d. 1744, Orange Co., VA

        463. Margaret Ludman

29. Amelia Alisa Collins

  b. 30 Jun 1844, Jay Co., IN

  d. 9 Jun 1908, bur. Hopewell Cem., Randolph Co., IN

  58. Joseph Collins

    b. c1809, VA

    m. (2nd) 7 Nov 1839, Jay Co., IN

    d. 25 Feb 1873, Jay Co., IN

    bur. Bost Cem., Jay Co., IN

    116. John Collins, III

      b. 5 Jan 1782, VA

      d. 13 Sep 1838, Jay Co., IN

      bur. Bost Cem., Jay Co., IN

      232. John Collins, Jr.

        b. c1750, Frederick Co., VA

        m. c1771

        d. 1835, Warren Co., OH

        464. John Collins

          b. c1715, Ireland

          d. 1790/95

      233. Hannah Cozad

        466. Rev. Jacob Cozad

        467. Elizabeth Sutton

    117. Elizabeth Liggett

      d. 30 Aug 1838, Jay Co., IN

      bur. Bost Cem., Jay Co., IN

  59. Harriet Finch

    b. 16 Mar 1821, Columbiana Co., OH

    d. 2 Aug 1884, Collett, Jay Co., IN

    bur. Bost Cem., Jay Co., IN

    118. William Finch

      b. 1785, MD

      d. 16 Oct 1863, Jay Co., IN

      236. Thomas Finch

237. Alice Stevens
119. Amelia Jackson
    b. 1791, VA
    238. James Jackson
    239. Martha Thomas

15. Bertha Achsah Hammers
    b. 30 Jan 1877, Randolph Co., IN
    d. 29 Oct 1918, Randolph Co., IN,
    bur. Woodlawn Cem., Randolph Co., IN
    30. Elijah Oliver Hammers
        b. 10 Jun 1845, Randolph Co., IN
        m. 1 Oct 1864, Randolph Co., IN
        d. 10 May 1920, Randolph Co., IN
        bur. Woodlawn Cem., Randolph Co., IN
        60. Abraham Hammers
            b. 14 Nov 1817, Greene Co., PA
            m. 19 Nov 1839, Randolph Co., IN
            d. 7 Aug 1894
            bur. Woodlawn Cem., Randolph Co., IN
            120. Peter Hammers, Jr.
                b. c1786, PA
                m. c1808, Greene Co., PA
                d. 1838, Licking Co., OH
                240. Peter Hammer
                    b. 19 Aug 1757, Burks Co., PA
                    m. c1779
                    d. 18 Apr 1838, Monongalia Co., VA.
                241. Elizabeth White Bonser
                    d. 1797, PA
            121. Mary Fry
        61. Nancy Harbour
            b. 9 Sep 1821, Fayette Co., OH
            d. 24 Apr 1892, Randolph Co., IN
            bur. Woodlawn Cem., Randolph Co., IN
            122. Elijah Harbour
                b. 1 Apr 1788, Montgomery Co., VA
                m. c1809, OH
                d. 13 Sep 1872, Randolph Co., IN
                bur. Fairview Cemetery, Randolph Co., IN
                244. David Harbour
                    b. 1765, Pittsylvania Co., VA

m. 17 Aug 1787, Montgomery Co., VA
d. 1854, Cabell Co., VA
488. Elijah Harbour
  b. c1735/40, VA
  m. c1758, VA
  d. 1769, Pittsylvania Co., VA
  976. Thomas Harbour
    b. 1675/95, Wales
    m. 1705/25, Charles City Co., VA
    d. After 1777, VA, prob. Henry Co.
  977. Sarah Witt
    1954. John Witt, Jr.
489 Prudence Pusey
  b. c1741/3, VA
  d. 1816, Sullivan Co., IN
  978 Robert Pusey
  979 Magdalena Van Meter
245. Mary Spurlock
  d. bet. 1796 and 1802, prob. KY
  490. John Spurlock Sr.
123. Rhoda Capps
 b. 22 Apr 1788, SC
 d. 15 Jul 1870, OH
 bur. Fairview Cemetery, Randolph Co., IN
246. Dempsey Capps
  b. c1760, NC
  m. c1783
  d. 1839, IL
  492. John Capps
    b. c1735, VA
    d. 1806/7
    884. John Capps
      b. c1705, VA
      d. 1752/3, VA
      1768. Richard Capps
        b. 1654, VA
        m. bef. 1693
        d. 1720
        3536. William Capps
          b. 1612 or 1618
          d. 1666
          7072. William Capps

b. c1575, Ireland

d. 1629/1653, VA

7073. Catharine ?

d. bef. 16 Feb 1623

3537. Margaret ?Moonhouse

d. 1696/1701

1769. Jane ?

d. bef. 1715

885. Dinah Whitehurst

493. Martha ?

247. Sallie Pool (Overman)

b. 8 Nov 1756

d. 18 May 1840

31. Elizabeth Morris

b. 25 Sep 1845, Fayette Co., OH

d. 7 Jun 1922, Randolph Co., IN

bur. Woodlawn Cem., Randolph Co., IN

62. George Morris

b. 17 Mar 1824, Fayette Co., OH

m. 20 Jan 1845, Clinton Co., OH

d. 11 Jul 1901, Guthrie Co., IA

124. David Morris

b. 10 Jan 1796, NC

d. 17 Sep 1879, Fayette Co., OH

248. Isaac Morris

b. Wayne Co., NC

m. 14 Sep 1788

d. c1825

496. Zachariah Morris

b. 23 Sep 1722

m. 1 Nov 1752

d. 2 Mar 1809

992. John Morris

b. 3 Mar 1680

m. 4 Sep 1703

d. 20 Sep 1739, Perpulmans Co., NC

993. Mary Symons

b. 4 Dec 1687

d. 14 Aug 1745, NC

1986. Thomas Symons

b. c1648

1987. Rebecca White

3974. Henry White
d. 1669/70
3975. Rebecca Arnold
497. Anne Williams
b. 12 Dec 1727
d. 28 Apr 1795
249. Millicent Bundy
b. 1769
125. Nancy Cooper
b. 27 Jan 1801
d. 3 Dec 1835, Fayette Co., OH
63. Anceline Grove
b. 28 Jun 1828, VA
d. 2 Mar 1864, Randolph Co., IN
126. Abraham Groves
b. c1804, VA
m. 1827, Frederick Co., VA
d. 29 Sep 1876, Randolph Co., IN
bur. Rehobeth Cem., Randolph Co., IN
252. Jacob Grove
b. c1774, VA
m. 1795, Frederick Co., VA
d. aft 1850, Clinton Co., OH
504. John Grove
253. Catharine Lonas
b. c1775, VA
d. aft 1850, Clinton Co., OH
127. Elizabeth Reed
b. c1810, Frederick Co., VA

The Garringer Family

The first known ancestor of our Garringer family in America is a David Gerringer who first shows up in records of Frederick County, Maryland, as early as 1769. The family name has been spelled many ways throughout the years but in early records it is often spelled with an "e" and either one or two "r's." Spellings beside Garringer are Garinger, Geringer, Gerringer, Gearinger and Gehringer. There appears to be no special meaning as to how the family name is spelled, but the name was recorded however the writer felt it sounded. Our David Gerringer moved to Berkeley County, Virginia (now West Virginia) some time before 1795 and lived there until he died in 1812. His wife's name was Barbara, but her maiden name is not known.

Descendants of David Gerringer in Ohio have held an Ohio Garringer Reunion every year for over fifty years. In the early 1980s a committee of this reunion was set up to research the available records to try to determine the ancestry of that David Gerringer. The committee, headed by Caroline (Garringer) Shaper, met from 1982 to 1984. After the committee disbanded, Caroline Shaper continued the research on her own and published a book *Unpuzzling One David Geringer/Gerringer/ Garinger/Garringer* in 1992 which gives the findings. She was able to trace this family back to Germany.

Our David Gerringer is first shown to be in Frederick County, Maryland in 1769 when he recorded a deed to land he bought from Richard Butler for 15 pounds. In this deed his name is spelled as David Carrenger. The name of David Gearinger later shows up in records in 1789 when a request is made to resurvey the same land. David Carringer's name appears in the 1770-1773 debt book for Frederick County for this land called Stoney Meadow. David Gearinger's name appears in the 1793 Frederick County tax assessment records for the same land. This land is located south of current town of Foxville, Maryland, south of the intersection of Catoctin Hollow Road and Mink Farm Road. In other records in Frederick County, David Geringer appears on the rolls of military recruits in 1775, and in 1776 the name of David Kerringer is listed in a report on warrants which levied sums against persons for misbehavior. David Garringer's name appears in the will of a Samuel Shertz which was presented in court on 3 Apr 1783 and had to be translated from German.

There are some land records in 1792 which show David Garinger in a deed with the heirs of a Henry Garinger, late of Frederick County who died intestate. This suggests that David and Henry might have been brothers. Henry Garinger and his wife Rosina have been traced back to the First Reformed Church of Lancaster, Pennsylvania, where a son and three daughters were baptized in the period 1760-1769. A Henry Garringer of age 25 enlisted in 1757 in an Augusta regiment and on his enlistment, he stated that he was born in Germany and was a weaver by occupation.

In the same Lancaster County church records, a David and Anna Marie Geringer had two children baptized, a John Jacob in February 1760 and a John David in December 1760.

A search of German records shows that the family name Geringer and its variations are most prevalent in the Rheinland Palatinate area of Germany. A search of the church records there showed the family of an Emig Geringer to be in the town of Edenkoben. Edenkoben is on the west bank of the Rhine River about 30 kilometers southeast of the town of Kaiserslautern. Emig was listed as a master weaver. Emig Geringer was christened on 11 Nov 1682, married Anna Maria Neu on 15 Apr 1728 and died on 16 Feb 1737. Emig and Anna Maria Geringer had three children christened in the local church. They were: Johann Nikolaus, christened on 20 Feb 1730; Johann Hendrich, christened on 17 Aug 1732; and David christened on 5 Nov 1735. The later two appear to correspond to the Henry and David Geringer who show up in Pennsylvania and later Maryland. Further research showed that the parents of Emig Geringer were a Gorg Diether and Maria Clara Geringer. Searches of passenger lists did not show these Geringer brothers but they are most likely our Geringer ancestors.

Our David Gerringer is listed in the 1790 census in Frederick County, Maryland, with 2 males over 16, 2 males under 16 and 3 females in the household.

The children of David and Barbara Gerringer that are known were:

(1) Mary Garringer, b. 8 Feb 1766
    m. 1784, John Culp
(2) Elizabeth Garringer
    m. c1792, Matthis Zinner
(3) Madalenah Garringer, m. ? Miller
(4) David Garringer, Jr.*, b. 12 Oct 1772, Frederick Co., MD, d. 11 Nov 1865, Fayette Co., OH
    m. 27 Oct 1795, Elizabeth Smith
(5) John Garringer, b. 13 Aug 1777, d. 9 May 1861
    m. Elizabeth ?
(6) Sevil Garringer, b. c1782, d. 1869
    m. Thomas Canby
(7) Jacob Garringer, b. c1784, Frederick Co., MD, d. Pontiac, IL
    m. 19 Nov 1806, Martha Ann "Patsy" Moore

David and Barbara Garinger purchased a piece of land in Frederick County called "Green Brier" on 22 Aug 1792 and then immediately sold that land to their son-in-law John Culp. In 1793 they sold the rest of their land before moving to Virginia. They located a few miles northwest of the town of Martinsburg, Virginia (now West Virginia). David Gerringer's name appears on the tax list in Berkeley County from 1803-1808. He is listed in the 1810 Berkeley County census as David Girenger.

David Garringer's will was written 13 Jul 1805 and was admitted for probate on 10 Aug 1812 and is listed below:

In the name of God, Amen, I David Garringer of the County of Berkeley and the State of Virginia though weak in body yet through the Mercy of God being of sound mind and memory do make and publish this my last will and testament

Item first I give to my well beloved wife Barbara all my land where I now live and also all my moveable property during her life My personal property I give to wife Barbara to will to whoen she thinks proper at her death After the death of my wife I give the land where I now live to my son David and my daughter Sevil to be equally divided between them in quantity and quality.

Item I give to my son David twenty-five pounds Pennsylvania currency I give my daughter Sevil twenty-five pounds the above currency to be made out of my personal property I give to my daughter Mary Culp five shillings I give to my daughter Elizabeth Zener five shillings I give to my daughter Madelenah Miller five shillings I give to my son John five shillings which is their full portions beside what I formerly gave them. I give to my son Jacob a tract of land I purchased of Henry Huffman near Sleepy Creek.

I do constitute and appoint my wife Barbary and Monnos Plotner my Executors of this my last will and testament revoking all others made by me. In witness whereof I have here unto set my hand and seal the 13 day of July 1805.

> his
> David   Garringer
> mark

Signed and sealed in presence of Charles Orrick, Isaac Kroeson, Johnson Moore at a Court held for Berkeley County the 10th day of August 1812.

The last will and testament of David Garringer was produced in Court and proved by oaths of Charles Orrick and Isaac Kroeson two of the witnesses thereto and ordered to be recorded.
> D. Hunter C. B. Court

It is assumed that David Garringer died sometime shortly before 10 Aug 1812 when his will was admitted into court. His wife Barbara died two years later. Her will puts her death sometime between 15 Mar and 11 Apr 1814.

Of the children of David and Barbara Garringer, daughter Mary was born on 8 Feb 1766 according to a church confirmation record. She married John Culp (name also written as Johan Kolb) in 1784. They lived in Frederick County, Maryland, until about 1810 or 1811 when they moved to Berkeley County, Virginia (West Virginia). John Culp's will was filed in Morgan County in 1829, and Mary was believed to have died about 1836, also in Morgan County. They had one known son, Frederick Culp, and possibly others unknown. One deed, signed John Culp, Sr. and Mary Culp, Sr., gave land to grandchildren John Culp, Jr. and Mary Culp, Jr.

David and Barbara's daughter Elizabeth is only mentioned in the will but some indirect evidence indicates she may have married Matthis Zinner. Daughter Madalenah is also only mentioned in the will and evidently she married a Miller. Daughter Sevil may have been younger since she married later to Thomas Canby on 31 Oct 1809. Thomas and Sevil had five or six children, some of the names which are known: John, David, Beulah and Nancy. Thomas Canby died in March 1850, and Sevil died in Sep 1869.

David and Barbara Gerringer's son John was born 13 Aug 1777 in Frederick County, Maryland. He married about 1803 to Elizabeth, family name unknown although some have claimed it to be Bowersmith. They moved to Berkeley County, Virginia, and later moved to Ohio by 1810. They are found in Wayne County, Ohio, in the 1820 census, Holmes County in the 1830 census, Lucas County in the 1840 census, and Fulton County in the 1850 and 1860 census. Cemetery records in Dover Township of Fulton County list John Geringer, died 9 May 1861, aged 83 years, 8 months and 26 days, and Elizabeth Geringer, died 9 Oct 1854, age 71 years. John and Elizabeth Geringer had at least five children:
(1) Benjamin Geringer, b. c1804
    m. 4 May 1824, Wayne Co., OH, Mary Ann Rouse
(2) Nancy Geringer, b. c1806
    m. 19 Aug 1833, Holmes Co., OH, John McConkey
(3) Sarah Geringer, b. c1808
    m. 20 Oct 1836, Holmes Co., OH, Isaac Darnell
(4) Elizabeth Geringer, b. 4 Aug 1819, Holmes Co., OH
    m. 20 Jun 1841, Lucas Co., OH, John Warner
(5) John Jacob Geringer, b. 23 Jan 1828, Holmes Co., OH, d. 13 Jul 1916, Ringgold Co., IA
    m. Dorothy Ayers

Jacob was the youngest son of David and Barbara Geringer and was born about 1784 in Frederick County. Jacob married Martha Ann "Patsy" Moore, daughter of Johnstone and Martha (Kitzmuller) Moore, on 19 Nov 1805 in Berkeley County. Jacob and Martha moved to Fairfield County, Ohio, about 1816 and were there in the 1820 census. Jacob and Martha owned some land in Delaware County, Ohio, and may have lived there before they moved further west. They may have moved to Jay County, Indiana, before they moved on to Livingston County, Illinois, where it is said that Jacob died sometime before 1850. Martha was living with a son in Livingston County when the 1850 census was taken.

Confirmed evidence has not been found on the names of the children of Jacob and Martha "Patsy" (Moore) Garringer. Census data say they had 7 or 8 children. The following are most likely the children of Jacob and Martha:
(1) David Garringer, b. c1807, VA, d. 1863, Jay Co., IN
    m. Tamara Adams
(2) John Garringer, b. 1809, VA, d. 1833, Delaware Co., OH
    m. Anne ?, m. 2nd Esther Adams
(3) Jacob Garringer, b. 1812, VA, d. after 1852, Jay Co., IN
    m. Margaret Felkey, m. 2nd Harriet Lewis
(4) Mary Ann Garringer, b. c1815, VA, d. 1859, Jay Co., IN
    m. Reuben Lewis
(5) Benjamin Garringer, b. c1820, OH, d. 1884, Jay Co., IN
    m. Sarah McCartney, m. 2nd Mary Harford
(6) Isaac Garringer, b. c1822, OH, d. c1865, IA
    m. Rachel Biggerstaff
(7) Alexander Garringer, b. 23 Jan 1824, Delaware Co., OH, d. 27 Aug 1901, Jay Co., IN
    m. 24 Nov 1850, Jay Co., IN, Elizabeth "Betsey" Bonnell
(8) Martha Garringer, b. c1828, OH, d. 1863, Randolph Co., IN
    m. William Sutton

David Garringer, son of David and Barbara Garringer

Our direct line ancestor is David Garringer Jr., son of David and Barbara Garringer. Often times this David Garringer's name is seen as spelled with an "e" rather than an "a" and he was nicknamed "Cripple Davy." He married Elizabeth Smith (or Smyth) on 27 Oct 1785 in Berkeley County, Virginia. Elizabeth Smith was born in 1775 in Frederick County, Virginia, and was the daughter of Alexander Smith (or Smyth) and Mary Wright. Alexander Smith is listed as a patriot in the book *West Virginia Revolutionary Ancestors* by Ann Walker Reddy.

David and Elizabeth Garringer had six children:
(1) John Garringer, b. 14 Aug 1796, Berkeley Co., VA, d. 14 Jul 1852, Howard Co., IN
m. 23 May 1823, Elizabeth Johnson
(2) Alexander Garringer, b. 5 Feb 1800, Berkeley Co., VA, d. 1851, Howard Co., IN
m. 3 Aug 1818, Mary Ellen Boots
(3) David Garringer, b. 25 Oct 1803, Berkeley Co., VA, d. 16 Sep 1869, Fayette Co., OH
m. 20 Sep 1825, Cyrene Yeoman
(4) Elizabeth Garringer, b. 17 Feb 1806, Berkeley Co., VA, d. 20 Mar 1848, Fayette Co., OH
m. 14 Aug 1831, Acquilla Jones
(5) Mary Garringer, b. 27 Jan 1810, OH, d. 27 Jan 1886, Fayette Co., OH
m. 1 Jul 1830, Elias Brakefield
(6) Isaac Jacob Garringer*, b. 7 Mar 1812, OH, d. 16 Jan 1870, Randolph Co., IN
m. 16 Mar 1834, Delaware Co., IN, Sarah Boots

In 1805 David and Elizabeth Garringer sold all of their land in Berkeley County, Virginia, and moved their family to Ohio in the following year. They first settled in Fairfield County, Ohio, but about 1816 or 1817 moved to Perry Township, Fayette County, Ohio. David Garringer bought 215 acres on the north bank of Paint Creek where he built a log house. This was to be their house for the next eight years. David Garringer was a carpenter by trade.

Of the children of David and Elizabeth Garringer, daughters Mary and Elizabeth, and son David, all married and remained in Fayette Co., Ohio.

David Garringer married Cyrene Yeoman by whom he had nine children:
(1) Sarah Garringer, b. 19 Oct 1826, d. 4 Jun 1914
m. 10 Aug 1845, Henton Hoppes
(2) Angeline Garringer, b. 19 Nov 1828, d. 2 Jan 1915
m. 27 Feb 1848, Abraham Booco
(3) Amanda Garringer, b. 3 Sep 1831, d. 13 Feb 1904
m. 24 Jan 1847, James Stokesbury
(4) Albert Garringer, b. 21 Mar 1834, d. 6 Sep 1923

m. 31 Oct 1858, Angeline Little

(5) Samantha Garringer, b. 7 Aug 1836, d. 15 Sep 1916
    m. 22 Oct 1857, Atthemas Hendrickson

(6) Osa D. Garringer, b. 7 Jun 1839, d. 7 Dec 1916
    m. 15 May 1859, John Weller

(7) Thomas Benton Garringer, b. 14 Oct 1841, d. 14 Sep 1923
    m. 22 Oct 1872, Melissa Ann Catherine Parrett

(8) Stephen Garringer, b. 17 Apr 1844, d. 8 Feb 1923
    m. 22 Mar 1865, Rebecca Ann Borton

(9) Ira James Garringer, b. 1 Jan 1848, d. 25 Oct 1925
    m. 18 Dec 1871, Lucy Ellen Smith, m. 2nd Mary Slager

Evidently this David Garringer was quite a successful farmer and stock raiser because at one time he owned 1400 acres of land in Fayette County and he left substantial amounts of land and money to each of his children in his will. David Garringer died on 17 Sep 1869 in Fayette County. Cyrene (Yeoman) Garringer died 21 Oct 1888 in Fayette County. The children of David and Cyrene remained in Ohio and form the ancestors of the large concentration of Garringers in this area of Ohio. Details of their descendants are given in the book by Caroline Shaper which was previously cited.

Of the other children of David and Elizabeth (Smith) Gerringer, John and Alexander both married in Fayette County, Ohio, but later moved to Randolph County, Indiana. Alexander Garringer made the first land entry in Green Township, Randolph County, Indiana in 1832. He and Martin Boots were the first settlers in Green Township. John Garringer's first land entry in Green Township was in early 1833. Isaac Garringer evidently followed his brothers because in late 1833, his name was also entered on some land in Green Township. Alexander Garringer's property was across the river south of the town of Fairview. The town of Fairview was first laid out in 1838. Alexander originally had a little store at his cabin south of the river, but he moved his general goods store over to the site of the town and "set up" in 1839. He also had an accompanying smith shop. Isaac also bought land in Monroe Township and was located on the now state road, both north and south. John and Alexander Garringer later sold their lands in Randolph County sometime after 1840 and moved to Howard County, Indiana.

John Garringer, son of David and Elizabeth (Smith) Garringer, moved with his parents to Fayette County, Ohio, where on 1 May 1823 he married Elizabeth Johnson. Land records in Fayette County show John owned land in Wayne Township. John Garringer first entered on land in Green Township, Randolph County, Indiana, on 30 Mar 1833 and probably moved there about that same time. His name is listed on several land transactions in Randolph and the nearby Jay County, where they were living in 1837. Sometime after 1840, John and Elizabeth moved to Howard County, Indiana, where they are found in the 1850 census in Howard Township. John died on 14 Jul 1852, aged 52 years, according to his tombstone in Salem Cemetery in Howard County. Elizabeth is found in the 1860 census in Niles Township, Delaware County, Indiana, along with two of her children. She died sometime before 1870, probably in Delaware County.

John and Elizabeth (Johnson) Garringer had ten children:
(1) Eliza Garringer, b. 23 May 1824, Fayette Co., OH, d. 10 Mar 1874, Delaware Co., IN
    m. 17 Oct 1843, Jay Co., IN, Joshua F. Maitlen
(2) Margaret Garringer, b. c1826, Fayette Co., OH, d. c1862
    m. 20 Apr 1848, Howard Co., IN, Oliver Tyre
(3) Elizabeth Garringer, b. c1829
    m. 14 Apr 1849, Howard Co., IN, Edmond Mannen
    m. 2nd 1866, John G. Hochstedler
(4) Drucilla Garringer, b. c1831, Fayette Co., OH, d. c1875, Putnam Co., MO
    m. 13 Jul 1848 Howard Co., IN, David Garringer
(5) Nancy Garringer, b. c1832, Fayette Co., OH, d. aft. 1853
    m. May 1850, Howard Co., IN, Elijah Tyre
(6) Jacob Garringer, b. c1834, Randolph Co., IN, d. c1865
    m. 10 Mar 1858, Howard Co., IN, Margaret Rich
(7) Rhoda Ann Garringer, b. 25 Dec 1835, Randolph Co., IN, d. 22 Feb 1914, Cloud Co., KS
    m. 11 Dec 1853, Delaware Co., IN, Wm. B. Maitlen
    m. 2nd Jesse McDowell
(8) John Garringer, b. 18 Oct 1836, Randolph Co., IN, d. 28 Jul 1902, White Co., IN
    m. 6 Mar 1864, Howard Co., IN, Jane Travis
(9) Amanda Garringer, b. c1838, Jay Co., IN
    m. 15 Oct 1856, Howard Co., IN, Richard Bodle

(10) James E. Garringer, b. 8 Oct 1842, Howard Co., IN, d. 28 Sep
1865, Delaware Co., IN

Most of the children of John and Elizabeth (Johnson) Garringer
remained in Delaware or Howard County, Indiana. Daughter
Drucilla later moved to Missouri where her younger children
were born and she later died. Daughter Rhoda Ann and her
family later moved to Kansas.

The second son of David and Elizabeth (Smith) Garringer,
Alexander Garringer, was born 25 Feb 1800 in Berkeley County,
Virginia. On 6 Aug 1818 in Fayette County, Ohio, he married
Elizabeth Boots, a daughter of Garrett and Elizabeth (Peterson)
Boots. Alexander operated a farm in Wayne Township and later
may have moved to Green Township. Alexander also owned
land in Delaware County, Ohio and may have lived there during
late 1830. Alexander's first land entry was in Green Township of
Randolph County, Indiana on 5 Oct 1832. He probably moved
there in 1833. He purchased land in Albany, Delaware County,
Indiana, in 1839 but probably never lived on it. Sometime around
1845, Alexander moved his family to Howard County, Indiana,
where he died intestate some time before 16 Jun 1849 when court
records show an administrator was appointed for his estate.
Alexander is believed to be buried in the Salem Cemetery, but no
tombstone has been found.

Alexander and Elizabeth (Boots) Garringer had the following
children:
(1) Mary Garringer, b. c1819, Fayette Co., OH
    m. 14 Nov 1842, Randolph Co., IN, Thomas Love
(2) David Garringer, b. c1821, Fayette, OH
    m. 13 Jul 1848, Howard Co., IN, Drucilla Garringer
(3) Isaac Garringer, b. 12 Jan 1824, Fayette Co., OH
    m. 2 Sep 1849, Howard Co., IN, Mary Louisa Martin
(4) Sarah Jane Garringer, b. Aug 1825, Fayette Co., OH
    m. William H. Good
(5) Alexander Garringer, b. Oct 1827, Fayette Co., OH
    m. 10 Oct 1849, Phebe Betson, m. 2nd Rebecca Simons
(6) Absolum Garringer, b. 12 Jan 1829, Fayette Co., OH
    m. 15 Apr 1850, Howard Co., IN, Delila Ann Martin
(7) Samuel Garringer, b. 26 Mar 1831, Fayette Co., OH

(8) Elizabeth Rebecca Garringer, b. c1833, Randolph Co., IN, d.
Feb 1864, Putnum Co., MO
m. 14 May 1853, Howard Co., IN, Joseph U. Martin
(9) Solomon Garringer, b. 10 Apr 1835, Randolph Co., IN
(10) William Garringer, b. 16 Aug 1840, IN

About 1854, Elizabeth (Boots) Garringer along with some of her children moved to Missouri. Elizabeth died in Lovinia, Putnam County, Missouri about 1877. Sons Solomon and Alexander were in Iowa County, Iowa, in the 1870 census.

Returning to the previous generation, both David "Cripple Davy" and Elizabeth "Betsey" Garringer lived long lives. Elizabeth died in her 73rd year and is buried in the Garringer family plot in Monroe Township, Randolph County, Indiana. David Garringer died 11 Nov 1865, age 93 years, 29 days and is buried in Cochran's Cemetery, near New Martinsburg, Ohio. There are family stories of some kind of a disagreement between David and Elizabeth because David stayed in Ohio while Elizabeth moved to Indiana and lived with her three sons who were living there.

Isaac Jacob Garringer, son of David and Elizabeth Garringer

Our direct line ancestor is Isaac Jacob Garringer, the youngest son of David and Elizabeth (Smith) Garringer. Isaac followed his brother John and Alexander to Indiana and first entered on land in Green Township on 24 Aug 1833. Isaac married Sarah "Sally" Boots, daughter of Garrett and Elizabeth (Peterson) Boots, on 16 Mar 1834 in Delaware County, Indiana. Sarah Boots was a younger sister of Mary Ellen (or Elizabeth) Boots who married Alexander Garringer, Isaac's brother.

Isaac and Sally Garringer lived their entire married lives in Randolph County, Indiana, and had a family of 12 children, all of whom were born in Randolph County. Their children were:
(1) Simon Garringer, b. 7 Sep 1835, IN, d. 9 May 1863, dnm
(2) Delilah Garringer, b. 13 Jan 1837, d. 7 Jun 1872
m. 24 May 1860, Henry Dull, m. 2nd 25 Aug 1866, Christian Ziegler
(3) David C. Garringer*, b. 4 Aug 1838, d. 10 Dec 1895
m. 6 Mar 1871, Amelia Alisa Collins
(4) Samuel Garringer, b. 31 Aug 1840, d. 13 May 1912

m. 19 Dec 1861, Susannah Troyer

(5) Phoebe Garringer, b. 23 Nov 1842, d. 20 Nov 1923
    m. 16 Aug 1861, William Bales

(6) Isaac B. Garringer, b. 25 Nov 1844, d. 8 Nov 1924
    m. 3 Oct 1868, Sarah C. Godwin

(7) Lewis Garringer, b. 19 Jan 1847, d. 3 Oct 1916, Pulaski Co.,
    AR
    m. 31 Dec 1871, Ann Bartlette
    m. 2nd 20 Feb 1876, Randolph Co., IN, Hannah E. Garringer

(8) John Garringer, b. 7 Feb 1848, d. 4 Nov 1914
    m. 8 Aug 1874, Louisa Garringer

(9) George W. Garringer, b. 21 Apr 1851, d. 15 May 1931
    m. 13 Feb 1886, Martha A. Cox

(10) Uriah Garringer, b. 14 Mar 1853, d. 18 Jul 1920
    m. 1 Nov 1877, Mary Elizabeth Godwin

(11) Sarah Ellen Garringer, b. 29 Jan 1855, d. 31 Jan 1936
    m. 12 Dec 1872, William Harrison Collins

(12) Henry Garringer, b. 23 Jan 1857, d. 25 Feb 1950
    m. 19 Aug 1879, Ida A. Moore, m. 2nd Martha Moore

(13) Sarah Garringer, b. c1858, d. 1870/80

The following is a interesting letter written by Isaac Garringer to his sister Mary Brakefield. It was written in 1869 given his reference to his son Isaac's being married last fall. Son Isaac married Sarah Goodwin on 3 Oct 1868.

Dear Sister:

I take the present opportunity to let you know that I and my wife aint very well at present. But I have hope that these few lines find you all well. I have neuralgy in my head, I have if oft times, that I can hardly live. -- My Delilah has not been well, since her last child was born, she took cold in her breasts, and they gathered several times, and now she has sarasipleus.

The rest of the children are well, Isaac was married last fall. David is not married yet. Delilah has three children. Phoebe has four children. Samuel has one child.

There aint any of brother John's family here, but two of them, two live in Iowa; and the rest are at the reserve. His wife, and Margaret, and Jacob, and James are all dead.

Alexander, wife and children live in Missouri, - the rebels killed Absalom and Samuel Boots in Missouri.

I have had some bad luck. I have loaned out four hundred fifty dollares, and the man has broke up and lost it. They have passed a law in the state, where they want to build a turn pike road, for to tax the land one mile and a half on each side of it, and they are going to make one through my land, and if they do, I will have to pay about fifteen hundred dollars, or they will sell my land.

You wrote about getting tombstones for mother's grave; I think that David got all of her money; and father told me that he had given Silas Brakefield five or six hundred dollars, for to loan out, and I think it looks a shame that they wont honor her enough to get tombstones, with their money; for I think they have anymore right to any more than their share, anyhow.

My health is not very good, at the best, and I do not know if I will ever get to come there or not. If you ever get to come out here, you must write, what day of the week or month, you will start; and we will meet you there. Come from Dayton, Ohio to Union City, then to Farmland. You didn't write what had become of your youngest girl. Write soon.

signed-- Isaac Garringer

Isaac Jacob Garringer was a very successful farmer and began with 80 acres in Monroe Township but at one time owned 940 acres of land, of which he gave to each of his children eighty acres. Isaac Garringer died on 16 Jan 1870, probably less than six months after the above letter was written. He was buried in the Garringer family plot on the original farm in sections 35 of Monroe Township. His wife, Sarah (Boots) Garringer survived him by twelve years and died in 1882. A 12 foot spire marks the spot of their entombment.

Garringer Homestead Family Cemetery, 1978
Green Township, Randolph County, Indiana

Of the children of Isaac and Sarah, most stayed close to the soil
and made their living at farming. Sons David, Samuel, Isaac, and
Henry were farmers in Green Township. Sons John, George, and
Uriah were farmers in Monroe Township. Simon was an
exception and was a grocer at Antioch. Lewis was a farmer in
Pike Township of Jay County. Phoebe Garringer who married
William Bales lived near Redkey. Ten of the thirteen children of
Isaac and Sarah (Boots) Garringer married and many had large
families so Isaac and Sarah had at least eighty-one known
grandchildren. Most of these remained in Randolph County
where there are still many descendants particularly in Green and
Monroe Townships.

David Carson Garringer, son of Isaac and Sarah (Boots) Garringer

Son David Carson Garringer is the direct line ancestor. In the
second year of the Civil War in response to the call for more
troops, David C. Garringer enlisted in the volunteer army on 11
Aug 1862 in Randolph County for a 3 year term. In the
enlistment records he is recorded as 23 years old and being 5 feet,
11 inches tall with a dark complexion, black eyes and black hair.
He enrolled in Capt. William Burris' company which was
recruited mostly from Farmland and later this company became
Company A of the 84th Indiana Infantry. The 84th Indiana
Infantry was mustered into federal service on 3 Sep 1862 at
Richmond, Indiana with Nelson Trusler as Colonel. Its first

service was in the defense of Cincinnati during the invasion of Kirby Smith. In February 1863 the regiment moved to Louisville and then moved on to Nashville in March 1863. David C. Garringer was reported as absent, sick at Ashland, Kentucky in January 1863, and also absent sick in August 1863 at Nashville. David C. Garringer participated with the 84th Infantry in the battles of Chickamauga, Chattanooga and the Atlanta campaign. David Garringer was wounded on 3 Jun 1864 in a battle at Dallas, Georgia. He was shot in the left arm, a blow that fractured that arm. He was recovering at the Army hospital in Nashville in July 1863 and then was later transferred to the Army Hospital at Madison, Indiana. He was furloughed from that hospital on October 1, 1864 for further recovery at home. Evidently he recovered and rejoined the regiment in January 1865 and served for the duration of the war until he was mustered out with the regiment on 14 Jun 1865 at Nashville.

A distant cousin of David Carson Garringer, David V. Garringer (son of John Garringer) also fought in the Civil War. He enlisted in the 19th Indiana Infantry, a unit that became famous as part of the "Iron Brigade" of the Army of the Potomac. The 19th Indiana Infantry participated in many battles including the Battle of 2nd Bull Run, Antietam, Fredericksburg, Gettysburg, and the Wilderness to Petersburg. David V. Garringer was wounded at Laurel Hill, near Spottsylvania Court House, Virginia, on 8 May 1864. He was promoted to corporal and later transferred to the 20th Indiana Infantry. He was mustered out along with that regiment on 19 Jun 1865.

A few years after the war, David C. Garringer married Amelia Alisa Collins on 6 May 1871 in Jay County, Indiana. Amelia A. Collins was born 30 Jun 1844 in Jay County, Indiana, to Joseph Coltmus Collins and Harriet Finch. David and Amelia Garringer had 5 children:
(1) James Milton Garringer, b. 17 Nov 1872, d. 4 Aug 1931
    m. 18 Feb 1897, Addie Heath, b. 1876, d. 1945
(2) Isaac Luther Garringer*, b. 15 Jun 1874, d. 2 Jun 1940
    m. 10 Aug 1895, Bertha Achsah Hammers
    m. 2nd 1 Sep 1923, Charity (Marquis) Clements
(3) Sarah Melissa Garringer, b. 10 Oct 1875, d. 1 Apr 1958
    m. 24 Dec 1890, William B. Life
(4) David Arthur Garringer, b. 25 Apr 1881, d. 1 Jun 1940

m. 27 Jun 1903, Iva Perle Pittenger
(5) Elizabeth Catherine Garringer, b. 20 Jan 1887, d. 1 Mar 1888

Of the five children of David and Amelia Garringer, Elizabeth Catherine was the youngest by several years. At her birth the other children were ages 6, 11, 12 and 14 and "Katey" as she was nicknamed was the baby of the family. Evidently she was dearly loved by the whole family because when she died at the age of 14 months in 1888, her loss was deeply felt by all. A lock of her hair was taken and kept with the family Bible which is currently in possession of the author. Katey was buried at Hopewell Cemetery next to where her parents were later buried.

The oldest son of David and Amelia, James Milton Garringer, married on 18 Feb 1897 to Addie Pearl Heath, the daughter of John T. and Delilah (Pitser) Heath, and they lived in Farmland for most of their lives. Milton died on 4 Aug 1931 and Addie died in 1945 and they are buried in Tomlinson Cemetery in Delaware County, Indiana.

Daughter Sarah Garringer married to William Life on 24 Dec 1890. They had nine children: David, Carl, Homer, Herschal, Bessie, Ethel, Beulah, Geraldine and Clara. Sarah (Garringer) Life died on 1 Apr 1958. Son David Arthur Garringer married on 27 Jun 1903 to Pearl Pittenger and they had children: Clarence, Thelma, Margaret, Harriet, Sarah Milton, Rozella, Iva Jean, and Betty Louise. David Arthur Garringer died on 1 Jun 1940.

David Carson Garringer wrote his will and it was recorded on 14 Feb 1895 (Randolph Co., Indiana Will Book 4, pg. 306/7):

I David Garringer of Green Township in the County of Randolph and state of Indiana, do make and publish this my last will and testament in manner and form following, that is to say.

1st It is my will that my funeral shall be conducted without pomp, unnecessary parade or ostentation, and that the expense thereof together with all my just debts be fully paid.

2nd I give devise and bequeth to my beloved wife Amelia Garringer the farm on which I now reside containing one hundred and sixty acres, it being situated in Green Township

Randolph County Indiana, to have and to hold, and to derive all benefits to be derived therefrom, during her widowhood and in case my said wife should remarry, then it is my will that me Real Estate should be divided as follows. After my said wife shall have received her one third, the remaining two-thirds of said Real Estate to be divided in equal shares between my three sons, James M. Garringer, Isaac L. Garringer, David A. Garringer, and my daughter Sarah M. Life or their heirs.

3rd I give and devise to my beloved wife all my live stock, horses, cattle and swine, by me now owned and kept on said farm, and all house hold furniture and other items not particularly named and otherwise disposed of and also all money I may have on hands at the time of my decease together will all notes that my be outstanding at the time of my decease with full power to collect the same, and for my said wifes own use, after all my just debts and funeral expenses shall have been paid.

4th I do hereby nominate and appoint my said wife Amelia Garringer my executor of this my last will and testament hereby authorizing and impowering her to compromise, adjust, release and discharge in such a manner as she may deem proper the debts and claims due me.

In testimony hereof, I have hereunto set my hand and seal this 14th day of February 1895.
/s/ David Garringer
Signed and acknowledged by said David Garringer as his last will and testament, in our presence, and signed by us in his presence.
/s/ William M. Fowler
/s/ Uriah Garringer
/s/ Isaac Garringer

David C. Garringer died on 10 Dec 1895 and was buried in Hopewell Cemetery in Green Township, Randolph County. Amelia (Collins) Garringer died on 9 Jun 1908 and is buried beside her husband.

The David C. Garringer Family
Front: Sarah (Life), Arthur, David C. Garringer, Amelia (Collins)
Rear: Isaac Luther, James Milton

The following obituary was written by Jacob Life and published in an unknown newspaper:

David Garringer was born August 4, 1848, and, after two years of indescribable suffering, fell asleep December 10, 1895, aged 51 years, 4 months and 6 days.

He was joined in marriage with Amelia A. Collins on March 6, 1871. This union was blessed with five children - three boys and two girls. One girl, little Katy, when about 13 months old, folded her loving arms in death and sailed to glory.

He enlisted in Co. A 84th Indiana Regiment, August 11, 1862 and was honorably discharged June 14, 1865.

He joined the United Bretheren Church and enlisted in the Army of the Lord in the month of February, 1886. As a soldier in this great army he was doubtless, and exception. When able he was at his post ready for service, which was a pleasure to him. Unlike so many professors he enjoyed giving to the support of the gospel. Knowing the life he lived and the triumphant death he died, doubt vanished.

Unquestionable assurance takes the throne and declares, "Asleep in Jesus, blessed sleep." He loved the gospel and requested of his loving and faithful wife, in the dead hours of night, to read to him from its sacred pages. It was good for his soul.

When asked if afraid to die, he replied "Oh, no, I'll soon be in Heaven." Sometime before he died he was noticed gazing upward and was heard to say: "Oh what do I see? A band of Angels after me." He requested all present to wish him good-bye and to meet him in heaven. Could we behold him as he enters the gate of gold! Could we watch him as he gazes on the enraptured scenes that fall on his immortal vision! Ah! could we see him as he, clothed in raiment white, outshining the noonday sun, waving palms of victory in his snow-white hands, while wave after wave of joy and suspeakable bliss bursts forth from his loving hearth, and the blessed Christ and the redeemed hosts join in a welcome that makes blessed Christ and the redeemed hosts join in a welcome that makes heaven's arches ring. Yes, we could see him as he is, we could doubtless ery with a voice that would leave earth and climb the sleepy steps of the skies, enter the home of the righteous and say "Stay, father, stay! our loss is your gain."

Sister Garringer loses a noble husband, the children, a king and loving father, the community a good neighbor, the country a good citizen.

Funeral was conducted by Revs. A. Rust and C. B. Small on Thursday, December 12.

Isaac Luther Garringer, son of David C. and Amelia Garringer

Isaac Luther Garringer married Bertha Achsah Hammers on 10 Aug 1895 and started farming in Green Township. Isaac and Bertha had four children:
(1) Helen Marie Garringer, b. 8 Jun 1896
(2) Hilda Irene Garringer*, b. 28 Mar 1898
(3) Mildred Martha Garringer, b. 14 Dec 1903
(4) Lloyd Milton Garringer, b. 12 Sep 1910

Isaac and Bertha later moved to a farm just on the north side of Farmland. Bertha was very intent on her children's getting an education and all the children graduated from high school and attended or graduated from college. Bertha had some medical problems and it was suggested that the girls be taken out of school to help out more on the farm but she would have none of that. Bertha died on 29 Oct 1918 and was buried in the Woodlawn Cemetery 2 miles southeast of Farmland. Shortly after Bertha died, Isaac moved his family into Farmland and lived in a house on West Main Street. Isaac also worked as a carpenter and even went to Florida for a couple of years to work. Isaac married a second time on 1 Sep 1923 to Charity Marquis Clements who was born in 1878. Isaac Luther Garringer died on 2 Jun 1940 and was buried in Woodlawn Cemetery next to his first wife, Bertha. Charity Garringer died in January 1973 and is also buried in Woodlawn Cemetery a couple of rows from Isaac and Bertha.

The oldest daughter, Helen Marie Garringer, graduated from college and became a teacher. She married Paul Williams and they had one daughter named Mildred Jane and one daughter who died at birth. Helen and Paul Williams later separated. Helen died on 29 Oct 1969 and is buried in Williamsburg Cemetery.

The only son of Isaac and Bertha Garringer, Lloyd Milton Garringer, was born on 12 Sep 1910. After graduating from high school, he became a carpenter and contractor, and later married June Ellen Hawk on 17 Nov 1942 in Indianapolis, Indiana. Lloyd served in the 101st Airborne Division during World War II and went into Normandy Beach on D-Day in a glider. He also participated in the Battle of the Bulge and won medals for bravery. Lloyd and June Ellen Garringer had one daughter, Kay Ellen. They later moved to Florida where Lloyd died on 18 Jan 1979 and was buried in Nokomis, Florida.

Daughter, Mildred Martha Garringer, graduated from college and became a teacher. She married on 1 Jan 1927 to Ralph Raymond Gilpin. Mildred and Ralph moved to northern Indiana where she eventually became an elementary and high school principal in the Gary, Indiana school district. Mildred and Ralph did not have any children. Upon retirement in 1965, Mildred and

Ralph moved to Hollywood, Florida. Ralph died on 16 Nov 1977 and is buried at the Hollywood Memorial Gardens. Mildred continued an active schedule up until her last year. She was a member of the Hollywood Hills United Methodist Church, Hollywood Womens Club, Emeritus Club of Indiana University and the Emeritus Club of the University of Chicago. Mildred died in Florida on 9 Apr 1999 and is buried beside her husband.

* * *

Remembrances of Mildred Garringer Gilpin

In 1893, a World's Colombian Exposition, also known as the Chicago World's Fair, was held in Chicago. Isaac (my father) and Uncle Jim went to the fair. As the two young farm boys were enjoying the exhibits a pick pocket relieved them of their money. They had to walk miles to their rooming house, someone kindly loaned them enough money for the return home trip. One building from the Exposition was standing when I attended the University of Chicago.

Hilda was born when Helen was 22 months old and my mother was ill for several months. Grandma Hammers kept the baby almost a year and the entire family - especially the twins doted on the baby. Hilda remained their favorite.

All of us took piano lessons at 50 cents a lesson. I suspect that money, or part of it, came from Mama's egg money. The money spent on me was wasted! I even took harmony. I played so badly at one church service when I was pushed into playing. Irene Ritter, my music teacher, spent two lessons getting me ready for the next ordeal. The summer before Mama died, my lessons ended.

Helen was a warm outgoing person who liked people and was an excellent teacher - home economics and art. After Mama died Helen came (at reduced salary) to teach at Farmland and look after Lloyd and me. To avoid being accused of favoritism she had me do clean up and scrub sinks etc. She was my Home Ec teacher.

In sewing we made layettes for World War babies. I unfortunately made one good button hole and was then assigned all button holes. I haven't made one since I left that class.

Helen was an inspired cook and improved every recipe she used. She was creative. The most attractive dress I had was a blue jersey with a panel embroidery yarn. She was no house keeper and her marriage was a disaster but she was a very special person. While dying she quoted "Crossing the Bar."

Farm Woman's Life

As you do your research, do you wonder what your ancestors were like, how they lived and how they would cope with change?

My life has been most interesting because I've lived from the horse and buggy to the moon age. Grandpa Hammers would not have died with a burst appendix nor grandma not been able to thread a needle if they had the medical help available today. My two implants (cataracts) have enabled me to read as much as I like and thread a needle. (I don't do this if I can avoid it.)

My mother lived 38 of her 41 years on a farm without electricity and inside plumbing. Like other women -

She bore her children at home with a relative (as Aunt Addie helped Hilda) and a country doctor.

She raised chickens, collected eggs and sold eggs for spending money.

She cooked and/or helped the hired girl prepare 3 meals a day - hearty meals. Breakfast wasn't cereal and juice - it was meat and potatoes etc. The stove was a wood burner and she tested oven heat by putting her hand in it.

She heated water in a wash boiler for laundry. A wash board and a push-pull washer were used. Clothes were hung outside - even freezing - later to be draped in the kitchen.

She heated water on the stove for our weekly baths in round tubs and each of us had clean water.

She heated irons on the stove for ironing - everything - sheets, pillow-cases and our dresses.

Daily, lamp globes were washed and filled bases. Slop jars were emptied, washed and aired.

She had the cellar stocked for winter with jam and jelly, canned fruit and vegetables, sauerkraut, lard, pickles, sausage covered with lard, sorghum, maple syrup, apples, celery in tubs. This meant a lot of work.

On Saturday she prepared for Sunday's company. She baked pies, two cakes (light & dark), made noodles, killed and dressed chickens. She never complained but we girls who had to wash dishes for Sunday's guests did.

She grew flowers! She did some work in the garden!

How did she do all she did? She seldom left home - sometimes to church - to county fair - to a family reunion. And she had us children help.

Hilda made bread for the family from the time she was 2 years old. We carried in wood, collected eggs, fed chickens, washed dishes, milked cows, washed the milk separator, ironed the easy things, etc. And we feel sorry for women who work!

My father, unlike some neighboring farms, did not have his daughters do field work. And we were kept away from the barn and "sex life" of the animals.

Bertha Achsah Hammers Garringer

My mother was named "after" her Aunt Achsah Taylor (Grandma Hammers' sister). My mother hated the name, Dad teased her by calling her "Achsay." (It is a biblical name.)

Bertha resembled her aunt - was slender. Aunt Achsah Taylor's daughter Ida Taylor Gantz was short and plump like Grandma.

My mother and father were "readaholics." Dad would read all night and then go to the fields to work. We had magazines and books - always books at Christmas and at birthdays. Helen and I early became avid readers.

Dad taught Bertha to shoot (shotgun) and encouraged her to ride "Lady" her own riding horse.

Bertha must have been a pretty girl - attractive to boys. My name Martha was from Mrs. Davis (Dr. Davis' wife). She had dated their only son before he died. We also had a fancy pen (pearl handle) given to her by another suitor Lee Driver. Lee became county superintendent and interviewed me before my first teaching assignment. I knew who he was but he didn't know who I was (I think). From picture I'd guess my father was the handsomest of the lot.

Isaac Luther Garringer

Dad was a victim of the times. Since his father had been injured in the Civil War the sons were taken out of school after 6th grade yet Dad could help me with high school math. The appeal of farming was animals. He liked horses and was proud of his teams of horses. Mama had her riding horse named Lady. Lady loved mama but nipped any of us girls. Dad accused us of teasing her but we didn't. She was just a one woman horse. We children had a very small pony for Lloyd, an average sized pony for me and a pinto for Helen and Hilda. Dad would have been an excellent veterinarian. After my mother died Dad left the farm and "took up" carpentry.

Memorial

A large stained glass window in the sanctuary of the Hollywood Hills United Methodist Church is a memorial to Mr. and Mrs. Isaac L. Garringer. It has symbols of King David and Sermons of the Great Hebrew leaders.

Mildred Martha (Garringer) Gilpin

On my birth certificate my mother's name was Hammer.

My life has been busy and interesting. I went to school when I was five years old. Fortunately I could read because I was the only first grader. Mr. Uphaus had eight grades in this one room school house so he didn't spend much time with me. I did accumulate a lot of information! When I was in 3rd grade we were taken to Parker consolidated school by bus drawn by horses. Since we were at the end of the line we left home while it was dark. Helen and Hilda had to watch me or I would eat my lunch enroute! In 1921 I was graduated from Farmland H. S. - valedictorian in class of 21! Some honor - I wish I had a copy of my speech.

At the time I received a diamond ring from Mrs. Martha Davis. Later after she died her lawyer told my father she intended to change her will and leave me the farm which is the Purdue Experimental Farm but she died before the change was made.

I attended Ball Normal School 2 years and 2 summers; with three years training I began teaching at Jefferson School near Winchester. While I was at Ball Normal, Hilda was thrilled when my picture appeared in the Muncie Star. I was 3rd of 5 in a beauty contest. She saw the picture before I learned of this dubious honor. Voting was done secretly in chapel. Since I worked at 25 cents per hour in the library, students knew me.

After I saved enough money I transferred to U. of Chicago and received a Ph.D. in Philosophy. Later I received a MS in Education from Indiana U. As a graduate student I had my own ideas. When called upon I once said, " The book says . . . . but I think . . . . " The professor said, "We have a rare bird. She knows what the books says and she knows what she thinks." Again, I blushed.

Most of my life I was in school as a student or teacher. First, I taught Latin and English; I was a guidance counselor and wrote a guidance manual used by other schools. Then I went into administration.

Like Dad I like animals and have had 4 pet cats. My present cat is a 13 1/2 lb Tomkinese. Friends give me cat mementos so they think of me as the "cat lady" although I have more than 30 Hummels. The one I like best is a large "Three School Girls."

I remember being told that I was a "quarter horse." English and Dutch on mother's side. Weren't the Hammer ancestors Dutch? I've a 100 year old picture (about 7 X 9 inches) of my great grandfather and his family in front of his house. The house itself resembles some I saw in Amsterdam. The picture is very fragile. I hesitate to leave it to be reproduced.

Dad's father's people were German but I thought there were some French ancestors - Finch? Bidert? Switzerland had three sections - German, French and Italian - as I learned when I was there.

Grandpa and Grandma Hammers were a child's answer to perfect grandparents. In the winter when I visited them after "supper" we sat by the base burner. Grandpa peeled apples and "scraped" them for me. Grandma sometimes popped corn. They told stories while we ate the apples Grandpa had taken from the outdoor fruit pit (hole with straw, covered over). The apples had a different flavor. Grandma told how some of her family had come to Indiana in a covered wagon. She told us how disgusted she was because her mother had so many babies so fast, she died when 30 or 31. She (Grandma) and Great Aunt Achsah starched their father's underwear. Of course, he made them wash out the starch.

Grandma was an excellent seamstress and a willing "patcher." She kept our clothes patched, buttons sewed on, etc. My mother was not a seamstress. A few weeks before school would begin

Miss Nettie Wood came for a week and made dresses and underwear for us three girls.

My mother had a heart problem from an early childhood bout with rheumatic fever. We often had a "hired girl"; Bessie Life, a cousin was my favorite. Since Dad had only girls, early on, we had a "hired hand" who stayed with us. My favorite was Omar Betts who, at Christmas, gave me a set of doll dishes.

We had a Kimball piano and all three of us took piano lessons. After Sunday dinner, friends and relatives (guests) gather in the parlor and my parents wanted us to perform. Helen and Hilda willingly played, singly or as a duet, but they were as unhappy as I when we had to play a trio. I was much younger and not gifted! Finally I learned to go to the barn and hide.

Since Helen and Hilda were older and Lloyd younger I turned to pet animals, excursions to the woods for flowers and nuts, and have always been able to be involved in many things - alone if necessary.

Isaac Luther and Bertha Achsah (Hammers) Garringer
Wedding Photo, 10 Aug 1895

Hilda and Helen Garringer
Childhood photo about 1901

Hilda, Mildred and Helen Garringer, about 1913

Bertha Garringer with son Lloyd

Farmland High School Senior Class of 1916
Front (left to right): Lorilla Thornburg, Hilda Garringer,
Lucille Mullen, Ruby Armstrong, Cadis Kem
Back: Theodore Oswald, Don Graham, Collins Black, Frank Burris,
Frank Reynold + unidentified

Ralph and Mildred (Garringer) Gilpin

By the 1920 census, the Garringer family had 41 families listed in the Indiana census in the counties of Randolph, Jay, Marion and Delaware.

Other Garringer Families in Indiana

Most of the Garringers that have lived or currently live in Indiana are part of our Garringer family. However, there were some other families of the same name that were not related to our family or are of an unknown distance from our family. A David Garringer and his family first show up in the 1850 Indiana census in Whitley County. David was listed as age 51, born in Ohio with wife Margaret, age 37, born in Germany and eight children born in Ohio and Indiana. Members of this family and descendants later moved to Elkhart County, Indiana, where some descendants continue to live to this day. No connection between this David Garringer family and our line is known at this time.

A John Garinger, born in Pennsylvania in 1834, and his family including his father Daniel moved to Jay County, Indiana, between 1863 and 1867 where they show up in Madison Township in the 1870 census. This Garinger family appears to come from Lehigh County, Pennsylvania. One son George is found with his family in the 1900 Randolph County census so some of their descendants did stay in the area. This Garinger family has been traced back to a Johann Adam Geringer who was born about 1721 in Germany and came to Northampton County, Pennsylvania by 1751. This family is apparently not closely related to our Garringer family.

A Fred Garringer, born 1840 in Germany, and his family show up in the 1880 Franklin County, Indiana, census and are more recent immigrants and are probably unrelated to our Garringer family.

The Hammer(s) Family

Bertha Achsah Hammers who married Isaac Luther Garringer was the mother of Hilda Irene Garringer. The Hammer or Hammers family emigrated from Germany in the early 1750s and first settled near Harrisburg, Pennsylvania, according to one old family letter. Unfortunately, we do not know the early names in this family or from what part of Germany they emigrated. However in 1757 in Bucks County, Pennsylvania, Peter Hammer was born into this family. Peter Hammer (once signed his name as John Peter Hammer on a deed and is listed in one census as John P. Hammer) is the earliest Hammer ancestor of which we have knowledge. The earliest records of this family show the family name to often be spelled Hammer without the "s." Later when the family moved to Indiana, the family name was most often spelled with the "s" but not always. There appears to be no great significance whether the family name is spelled in the singular or plural.

Peter Hammer lived a long and interesting life. He served in the American Revolution in several different military units. Peter Hammer married twice having eight children by his first wife and four children by his second wife. He died in Virginia at the age of 81.

Peter Hammer was born 19 Aug 1757 in Bucks County, Pennsylvania. At the age of eight, his family moved to New Jersey and after living there for three years, moved to York County, Pennsylvania. Peter lived here until he was twenty-seven. In 1775, Peter Hammer enlisted in the Pennsylvania troops at Little York, Pennsylvania, according to his pension claim first filed in 1832. On the following page is a copy of a letter from the Veterans Administration which lists the pertinent information found in the pension claim of Peter Hammer. This letter is taken from the book *The Hammers Genealogy, Descendants of Peter Hammer, 1757-1838* by Wayne Parker which was published in 1972.

C O P Y

VETERANS ADMINISTRATION

WASHINGTON, D.C.
BA-J/MCS
Peter Hammer W.5699

September 25, 1939

Mr. Wayne V. Parker
144 N. Sedwick
Wichita, Kansas

Dear Sir:

The data which follows were taken from papers on file in the pension claim, W.5699, based on the military service of Peter Hammer, the only soldier of that name that is found in the Revolutionary War records of this office.

Peter Hammer was born August 19, 1757, in Bucks County, Penn. The names of his parents are not shown. When six years of age, Peter Hammer moved to New Jersey and after living there three years he moved to York County, Penn., where he lived until he was twenty-seven years of age.

He enlisted at Little York, Penn., in 1775 and served as private with the Penn., troops as follows: in 1775, about three months in Captain Michael Doudel's company in a rifle corps regiment; from about the middle of June, 1776, until sometime in September 1776, in Captain William Bailey's or Bayley's company in Colonel Donelson's regiment; from September, 1776, until sometime in October, 1776, in Captain Christian Stake's company in Colonel Swope's regiment; from March 1780, a little over ten months in Captain James Mackey's company and during a part of this time in Colonel Thompson's regiment; in the fall of 1782, two months in Captain John Blennis' company.

From York County, Penn., Peter Hammer moved to Frederick County, Maryland, where he lived four years when he moved to Fayette County, Penn. After living there eight years he moved to Allegheny County (state not given) and after living there for five years he returned to Fayette County where he lived until 1810 when he moved to Monongalia County, Virginia.

Peter Hammer was allowed pension on his application executed August 28, 1832, at which time he was living in Monongalia Co., Va.

Peter Hammer married September 17, 1812, in Monongalia Co. Virginia, Sarah Pearce. Peter Hammer died April 18, 1838.

His widow, Sarah, married April 14, 1849, Isaac Rice of Marion County, Virginia, and he died August 19, 1851.

On account of the Revolutionary War service of Peter Hammer, Sarah Rice was allowed pension on her application executed August 2, 1852, at which time she was sixty years of age and was living in Marion County, Virginia.

In 1853 said Sarah was living and she was referred to as the widow of Peter or John P. Hammer but the soldier signed in person in 1832 as Peter Hammer.

In 1829 it was stated that Peter Hammer had twelve children by his first wife and four by his second wife but the names of the children were not given.

The name of the soldier's first wife and the date of this marriage were not given and the papers in this claim contain no further discernible family data.

Very truly your,

/s/ A. D. HILLER
Executive Assistant
to the Administrator

Peter Hammer was a blacksmith by trade. He was the youngest child in his family, and his father put him with a man to learn the blacksmith trade. He was a good workman and later was the foreman of a large establishment. In 1779, Peter Hammer married Elizabeth White Bonser (born Elizabeth White) in York County, Pennsylvania. She was a young widow with two small children, Nathaniel (b. 16 Dec 1774) and Sarah. In 1784, Peter Hammer moved his family to Frederick County, Maryland, where he stayed for four years before moving to Fayette County, Pennsylvania. In the 1790 Pennsylvania census Peter Hammer is listed in Frederick County with two males < 16, two males >16 and 4 females in the household. After living in Frederick County for seven years, he moved about forty miles above Pittsburgh on the Allegheny River. Elizabeth (White Bonser) Hammer died in 1797 or 1798 north of Pittsburgh in Allegheny County. After living five years in Allegheny County, Peter Hammer and his family returned to Fayette County.

Peter and Elizabeth (White Bonser) Hammer had 8 children:
(1) Joseph Hammers, b. 6 Apr 1780, near Little York, PA, d. 27 Feb 1863, Woodford Co., IL, bur. Hammers Cem., Panther Creek, near Panola, IL
    m. May 1803, Fayette Co., PA, Elizabeth Hanna, b. 22 Sep 1781, d. 15 May 1851
(2) Agnes Hammers, b. 15 Jun 1782, York Co., PA, d. 16 Jul 1829
    m. James Woodmansey
(3) Elizabeth Hammers, b. c1784, York Co., PA, d. IN
    m. Joseph Hanna
(4) Peter Hammers, Jr.*, b. c1786, York Co., PA, d. 1838, Licking Co., OH
    m. prob. c1808, Greene Co., PA, Mary Fry, d. 1838, Licking Co., OH
(5) Anna Hammers, b. c1788, PA
    m. 1st Samuel Hanna, d. 1814
    m. 2nd Joseph McDonald
(6) Mary Hammers, b. c1791, d. IN
    m. ?William Carothers
(7) John Hammers, b. c1792, went south and probably died there according to one story
(8) Phebe Hammers, b. c1794, d. ?
    m. ? Stevens ? m. 2nd Okey McCabe

Of the children of Peter and Elizabeth Hammer, the first born son Joseph was trained as a blacksmith as his father. When Elizabeth died, she left several young children, Joseph took care of Elizabeth and Agnes until they married. It was probably at the time of Elizabeth's death that son Peter, Jr. was put to an apprenticeship at the tanner's trade. After the two older daughters married, Elizabeth took care of Mary, and Agnes took care of Phebe. John stayed with his father, and Anna lived with her father part of the time but later stayed with Agnes and Elizabeth.

In 1810, Peter Hammer moved to Monongalia County, Virginia (now West Virginia). Two years later at the age of 55 on 12 Sep 1812 he married Sarah Pierce. Sarah was born in 1792 in Virginia. Peter and Sarah (Pierce) Hammer had 4 children:
(1) Delilah Hammers, b. Oct 1813, Monongalia Co., VA, d. 27 Sep 1874
   m. c1836, John Martin Fleming
(2) Augustus Hammers, b. c1818, VA
(3) Rebecca Hammers, b. c1820, VA
(4) Permela Hammers, b. c1821, VA

In the 1820 Monongalia County census, a John P. Hammer of the correct age is listed in the eastern part of the county. This listing is another indication that his full name may have been John Peter Hammer. In 1832, Peter Hammer was living in Monongalia County and was awarded a pension (executed 12 Aug 1832) for his military service. He claimed to have marched through Pennsylvania, New Jersey, Delaware and New York during his service. The pension application of 1832 was granted in 1833 but was suspended in 1835, reason unknown. Peter Hammer died 18 Apr 1838 in Monongalia County, Virginia, but his place of burial is unknown.

Peter Hammer's widow, Sarah, remarried on 14 Apr 1849 to Isaac Rice of Marion County, Virginia. Sarah's second husband died shortly after on 19 Aug 1851. In 1852, Sarah Rice, living in Marion County was allowed a pension based on the Revolutionary War service of Peter Hammer. The DAR recognized Peter Hammer as an American patriot, and several descendants have become members based upon his service.

Joseph Hammer, the first born son of Peter Hammer, married Elizabeth Hanna in May 1803 in Fayette County, Pennsylvania. Elizabeth was born in Fayette County, Pennsylvania, the daughter of Robert and Mary Hanna. The Hanna family had emigrated from Ireland to America some years earlier. In 1807, Joseph Hammer moved his family to Greene County, Pennsylvania where the family continued to expand. Most of his children married in Greene County and then in 1849, Joseph Hammer moved further west to Woodford County, Illinois. His wife Elizabeth died there in 1851 and Joseph died there in 1863. They are buried in the Hammer Cemetery, Panther Creek, near Panola, Illinois.

Three of the daughters of Peter Hammer married and evidently their families moved to Indiana. Daughter Agnes married James Woodmansey, and a James Woodmansee is listed in Jackson County, Indiana, in the 1820 Indiana census. Daughter Elizabeth married Joseph Hanna, and a Joseph Hanna of the appropriate age is shown on the same page of the 1820 Jackson County, Indiana census. Daughter Mary Hammer is listed in one Hammers' genealogy as marrying William Carothers and moving to Indiana where she died some time before 1857.

Little is known about son John Hammer who is only listed as going south and no further information in one Hammer genealogy. There is a John Hammer in the 1810 Greene County, Pennsylvania census and a John Hames in the 1820 Greene County census. John Hammer seems to disappear after the 1820 census, so he may have died or moved on to elsewhere.

Peter Hammers, Jr., son of Peter and Elizabeth (White) Hammer

Limited information is known about Peter Hammer's namesake, his second son also named Peter. The younger Peter Hammers was born about 1786 either in York County or Fayette County, Pennsylvania. At a young age he was trained in the tanner's trade. Peter Hammers married Mary Fry, probably in Greene County, Pennsylvania about 1808, but the exact date is not known.

The 1810 Pennsylvania census lists a Peter Hammer as living in Greene County. His family is listed as 1M16-26, 1F<10, and

1F16-26. Joseph Hammer, his older brother, is listed as living in Green Township while a John Hammers is listed as living in Marion Township of Greene County.

According to the 1820 census, Peter Hammers was living in Whitely Township of Greene County, Pennsylvania. At that time his family consisted of 2M<10, 1M26-44, 2F<10, 1F10-15 and 1F26-44. Peter and Mary (Fry) Hammers apparently had nine children but their identities have been difficult to determine.

In 1828, Peter Hammers moved to Licking County, Ohio, where he bought for $200, 100 acres of land in Range 13, Township 2, Section 2, Granville Township from David Gospel. A Peter Hammer or Creamer (hard to decipher) has been found in the 1830 Licking County, Ohio, census so he may be our relative. In 1833, Peter Hammers bought two additional parcels of land in nearby McKean Township, 116 acres from Jesse Gosnell and 125 acres from George and Betsey Roe. On 28 Dec 1835, Peter Hammers sold 60 acres of his original land purchase for $60 to a James Hammer, presumably a son. Assuming that James Hammers was at least 20 years old, that would make his birthyear 1815 or earlier, consistent with the 1820 Pennsylvania census of 2 males less than 10 years old.

There are few references to Hammer vital records in Licking County, Ohio, and the marriage records from 1829 to 1839 were lost in a courthouse fire. One record shows a Katherine Hammery marrying Samuel Messery on 2 Oct 1828 with written consent of Peter Hammery, and this is one of Peter's daughters.

There are several references in Licking County, Ohio, records to a. Fry family who moved there early in the county history. A John Fry who was born in 1802 in Greene County, Pennsylvania, is listed in one county history as moving to Licking County in 1810 and is most likely a brother or cousin to Mary Fry who married Peter Hammer. Another Fry family appears to be from Virginia and may not be related. Land records show several references to the Fry family, so several of Mary Fry's relatives must have also moved to Licking County. The 1830 Ohio census shows a Peter Fry (age 60-70) who could be Mary Fry's father.

To the best of our knowledge, the children of Peter and Mary (Fry) Hammers are:

(1) Samuel Hammers, b. c1810, PA, d. after 1850, m. Elizabeth ?
(2) James Hammers, b. c1811, PA
(3) Catherine Hammers, b. c1812, PA, d. after 1850
    m. 2 Oct 1828, Licking Co., OH, Samuel Mesarvey
(4) Anna "Amy" Hammers, b. 4 Aug 1816, Greene Co., PA, d. 7 Sep 1899, Randolph Co., IN
    m. Licking Co., OH, Alfred McCamy, b. 1 May 1813, OH, d. 13 Apr 1895
(5) Abraham Hammers*, b. 14 Nov 1817, PA, d. 7 Aug 1894
    m. 19 Nov 1839, Randolph County, IN, Nancy Harbour
(6) Mary Hammer, b. c1820
    m. 16 Jan 1840, Randolph Co., IN, William Sinclair Page
(7) Sarah Hammers, b. c1821, Greene Co., PA, d. 1899, IN
    m. 4 Feb 1840, Randolph Co., IN, Henry G. Hulderman, d. 3 Jun 1863
(8) Joseph Hammers, b. Sep 1829, OH, d. Aug 1903
    m. 22 Mar 1853, Randolph Co., IN, Achsah Jane Howery, b. 1835, IN, d. 16 Jan 1917

The 1840 Ohio census index shows only one Hammer(s) in Licking County, a Samuel Hammer (age 30-40). Samuel Hammer is also listed in the 1850 Licking County census in the town of Brownsville, age 40, occupation cooper. His place of birth was given as Pennsylvania so that is consistent with being a son of Peter Hammers, Jr. The census shows his wife as Elizabeth, age 41 and children Jappard, Mary, Angeline, Robert, Martha and Jarrel, all born in Ohio. There is also a James Hammet listed in the 1840 Licking County census, age 20-30 with wife and two sons less than 5 years old. This is probably Peter's son James to whom he sold land in 1835.

There are few other references to Hammers in Licking County records. One county record mentions a Daniel Hammers, 1843-1943, buried in the County Home Cemetery in Union Township, so this may be a grandson of Peter Hammers, Jr.

Some of the information we have about the Peter Hammers, Jr. family comes from a known descendant of Sarah Hammers Hulderman and consists of an old picture of some of his family and a piece of cardboard, with one end torn off, but had the following written on it:

The Hammers Family all born in (rest torn off)

Sarah Hammers
Anna Hammers
Katy Hammers   (3) girls
Joseph Hammers
Abram Hammers
Saul Hammers
Jim Hammers (4) boys
Father and Mother, Peter and Zeld (rest torn off)

According to a Randolph County, Indiana biography on Peter's son Abraham Hammers, Peter Hammers in 1836 traded his farm in Licking County, Ohio, and came to Randolph County, Indiana, and bought 160 acres of land in Monroe Township. He resided there for one summer and then returned to Ohio, where he died in 1838 according to the same biography. Mary (Fry) Hammer also died in 1838 on the family farm in Ohio. The place of their burial is unknown.

Son James is probably the James Hammet who is listed in the 1840 Licking County, Ohio, census. James has not been found in the 1850 Licking County, Ohio, census but there is a James Hamer in the 1860 Licking County, Ohio, Etna Township census. James is 49, born in OH (this may be an error) with wife Nancy and fourteen children ranging in ages from 1 month to 26 years. There is a record of a James Hammer marrying a Sarah Walker on 27 Oct 1842 in Randolph County, Indiana, but it is not clear who this James is and whether he is a member of our Hammers family.

Daughter Catherine who married Samuel Mesarvey in Licking County is later found in the 1850 Randolph County, Indiana census with husband Samuel (b. c1798, Maine) and children:

(1) George Mesarvey, b. c1830, OH
(2) Samuel Mesarvey, b. c1834, OH
(3) Jenett (Janet) Mesarvey, b. c1835, OH
(4) Abram Mesarvey, b. c1840, IN
(5) Nancy E. Mesarvey, b. c1846, IN

Janet later married John Q. Adams and they had children Abraham, William Loring, Millicent, Nancy Jane, Cora Belle, Charles, and Lula.

Peter's daughter Mary was born in 1820 in Pennsylvania and married 16 Jan 1840 in Randolph County, Indiana, to Sinclair Page. Sinclair and Mary Page had at least two children
(1) Nancy Page, m. Arney
(2) Sinclair John Page
John Page and his wife also had a daughter Mollie who was raised by Joseph and Achsah Hammers but never officially adopted by them. Mary "Mollie" Page married John Life and after his death, she married Carey Ross.

Peter's daughter Sarah was born in 1821 in Pennsylvania and married Henry G. Hulderman on 4 Feb 1840 in Randolph County, Indiana. They lived in Jay County, Indiana, and had the following children:
(1) Mary Etta Hulderman, b. 1841
(2) Nancy E. Hulderman, b. 1843
(3) James W. Hulderman, b. 1844
(4) Lewis E. Hulderman, b. 1848
(5) Catharine M. Hulderman, b. c1851
(6) Abram R. Hulderman, b. c1854
(7) Joseph J. Hulderman, b. c1857
(8) Silas J. Hulderman, b. c1859
Henry died in 1863, and Sarah died in 1899 and both are buried in Rehobeth Cemetery, Randolph County, Indiana.

The Randolph County biography of son Abraham said he bought out the other eight heirs to rights for the land in Monroe Township so we can assume he probably had eight brothers and sisters alive in 1839.

Peter's son Joseph Hammers was born in 1830 in Ohio and in the 1850 census is in Monroe Township of Randolph County living in the household of brother-in-law and sister Alfred and Amy McCama. Joseph Hammers married Achsah Jane Howery on 22 Mar 1853 in Randolph County with minister Elijah Harbour performing the ceremony. Elijah Harbour is the father of Nancy (Harbour) Hammers and father-in-law to Abraham. Joseph and Achsah Hammers lived only about a mile north of Abraham

Hammers' farm in Monroe Township. Joseph and Achsah had several daughters who died young, Laura, died 1862, Mary, died 1862, and Sarah Ann, died 1856, all buried together in Rehobeth Cemetery. Joseph Hammers died in August 1903 and Achsah Hammers died in January 1917 and they are buried in Woodlawn Cemetery. This Achsah Hammers would be a great aunt to Bertha Achsah Hammers, so this might be how this biblical name entered the family.

There was another Hammer family in Randolph County before Abraham moved there, but they do not appear to be related to our Hammer family. David Hammer was born about 1767, married in 1789 to Charlotte Jay in Newberry County, South Carolina. This Hammer family was Quaker and migrated north to Clinton County, Ohio, in about 1805 with other Quakers in their protest over slavery. David's name appears on a 1810 Clinton County tax roll. David Hammer moved his family to Randolph County by 1820 since his family is listed in that census. David and his wife Charlotte had the following known children: Margaret, born 1792; Rachael, born 1797; David, born 1801; Ann, born 1804; William, born 1807; and Mary, born 1809. Ann married Edward Thornburg on 24 Jul 1822 in Randolph County. Son David married Mary Lewellen in Randolph County on 1 Jan 1826. In 1839, David Hammer and most of his family migrated to Lee County, Iowa, where he died on 26 Dec 1845 according to records of the New Garden Quaker Meeting. Some of his descendants appear to have stayed behind in nearby Henry County.

There was a John Abraham Hammer who was born in Bedford County, Pennsylvania, in 1825 who moved to Randolph County between 1862 and 1866 and lived in Stoney Creek Township near Windsor. He married Elizabeth Andrews or Anders, and they had five children. John Abraham Hammer died in 1913, and his wife Elizabeth died in 1921 in Randolph County. This John Abraham Hammer was a son of John Michael and Anna (Slick) Hammer, Jr. who was a son John Michael and Margaret Hammer, who was a son of Johann Frantz and Rebecca (Eisen) Hammer who was born in Palatinate, Germany between 1720 and 1730. This Hammer family is not believed to be related to our Hammers family.

Abraham Hammers, son of Peter and Mary (Fry) Hammers

Abraham Hammers was born on 14 Nov 1817 in Greene County, Pennsylvania, and moved with his family to Licking County, Ohio, in 1828. At the age of 19, he moved to Monroe Township, Randolph County, Indiana, where his father had owned 160 acres in Section 26. After his father had returned to Ohio and then died in 1838, Abraham bought out the interest of the other eight heirs and built a log cabin on the land. In Randolph County on 19 Nov 1839, he married Nancy Harbour, one of eight children of Rev. Elijah and Rhoda (Capps) Harbour. The Tucker 1882 *History of Randolph County, Indiana* said Abraham was a member of the United Brethren Church and a Republican in politics.

Abraham and Nancy (Harbour) Hammers had five offspring:
(1) Elijah Oliver Hammers* (twin), b. 10 Jun 1845, d. 10 May 1920
    m. 1 Oct 1864, Randolph Co., IN, Elizabeth Morris
(2) Mary Elizabeth Hammers (twin), b. 10 Jun 1845, d. before 1894
    m. 2 Aug 1866, Randolph Co., IN, James Richwine
(3) Abraham Preston Hammers, b. 1852, d. aft. 1920
    m. Laura A. Sommerville
    m. 2nd 6 Feb 1875, Ann E. Odle
(4) William Blane Hammers, b. 8 Aug 1858, d. 3 Sep 1891
    m. Irene Groves
(5) Nancy J. Hammers, b. 1860, d. 6 Oct 1911
    m. c1879, Hamilton Pursley
Elijah and Mary were fraternal twins.

Abraham Hammers was a highly respected citizen, and he helped build many of the pikes in Monroe Township and the surrounding county. He served several terms as township supervisor. He was a local preacher in the Methodist Episcopal Church for thirty years. Abraham Hammers began with 160 acres from his father and at one time owned 440 acres of land. He gave 80 acres apiece to each of his sons and 40 acres to his daughter Nancy.

Nancy (Harbour) Hammers died 24 Apr 1892 and was laid to rest in Woodlawn Cemetery. Abraham Hammers died two years later in 1894 and was buried next to his wife. A large marble spire marks their graves on the far west side of Woodlawn

Cemetery at Maxville. In Abraham's will, recorded 14 Aug 1894, he named his sons Elijah and Abraham as executors. He gave to granddaughter Maud Hammers, daughter of son William B. Hammers, dec'd, real estate. To children of dec'd daughter Mary E. Richwine, viz Samuel Wesley Richwine, Viola Richwine, Abraham B. Richwine and Egbert Richwine - Samuel Wesley $100; the other 3 children to have $800 each. To daughter Nancy J. Pursley $1000; already had received $1500. Residue of property to children Elijah O. Hammers, Abraham Preston Hammers and to Nancy J. Pursley.

Nancy (Harbour) Hammers

Abraham Hammers

Abraham Hammers House
and Family Gathering, about 1888

Elijah Oliver Hammers, son of Abraham and Nancy Hammers

Elijah Oliver Hammers married Elizabeth Morris on 1 Oct 1864 in
Randolph County. Elizabeth Morris was the daughter of George
and Anceline (Grove) Morris and was born in Ohio. Elijah grew
up in Monroe Township helping his father on the farm and came
of age during the start of the Civil War, but evidently he did not
serve in the war. Elijah was a farmer and initially helped farm his
father's land, eventually farming 120 acres of his own land.

Elijah Oliver and Elizabeth (Morris) Hammers had four children:
(1) Arthur Leroy Hammers, b. 7 Feb 1865, d. 3 Apr 1879
     bur. Rehobeth Cemetery, Randolph Co., IN

(2) Bertha Achsah Hammers*, b. 30 Jan 1877, d. 29 Oct 1918
     m. 10 Aug 1895, Isaac Luther Garringer
(3) William Blane Hammers, b. 4 Aug 1885, d. 1950
     m. 22 Jun 1911, Opal McGuire
(4) Lucy Irene Hammers, b. 4 Aug 1885, d. 29 Jan 1961
     m. 19 Feb 1910, William Hervet Huston

The name Achsah for the first born daughter is a biblical name
and is a family name passed down. Elizabeth (Morris) Hammers
had a sister named Achsah who married Hiram Taylor. Elijah O.
Hammers also had an aunt Achsah who married his father's
brother Joseph.

Elizabeth (Morris) and Elijah Oliver Hammers
Taken 1916 or 1917 with their dog "Bravo"

Elijah Hammers owned a farm in Green Township and was quite
successful accumulating over 400 acres. Elijah and Elizabeth
were strong believers in getting their children an education.
Daughter Bertha Achsah graduated from high school in Farmland
even though the family farm was many miles away in Green
Township. It was said that every Sunday evening, her father
would hitch up the buggy and drive Bertha the seven miles to
Farmland where she would stay with relatives and then pick her
up on Friday afternoon after school was out for the week. This
thirst for education Bertha would instill in her children. Elijah O.

Hammers died on 10 May 1920 and is buried in Woodlawn Cemetery. Elizabeth (Morris) Hammers died on 7 Jun 1922 and is buried beside her husband.

Of the children of Elijah and Elizabeth (Morris) Hammers, the oldest son Arthur Leroy Hammers died in 1879 at the age of 13. William Blane Hammers married Opal McGuire and they had two children, John Oliver Hammers who did not marry and Margaret Helen Hammers, who married Maurice Jordan. Lucy Irene Hammers married William Hervet Huston and they had one son, William Hervet, Jr.

The Boots/Stieffel Family

The Boots (originally Stieffel in German) family is associated with the Garringer family by the marriage of Sarah Boots to Isaac Garringer in 1834. Sarah Boots is a maternal great grandmother of Hilda Irene Garringer.

Members of the Stieffel family immigrated to America in 1752. This family starts with Adam Stieffel who was born in 1733 in Mangabohrnn, Germany. In the book *Pennsylvania German Pioneers*, Vol. 12, p. 601, Hans Melchior Stieffel and Hans Adam Stieffel were listed as passengers on the ship *Phoenix* landing on 2 Nov 1752. It is unclear where the Stieffel brothers settled, but some evidence suggests that it was in Berks County, Pennsylvania, north of Philadelphia. The story of this German family is well documented in numerous records accumulated by Clyde S. Boots of Isabel, Kansas, whence a majority of the following is taken.

From church records it is known that Adam Stieffel's wife was named Barbara, but her maiden name is not known. Based on the birthdate of their first child, they were probably married about 1763/4. Adam Stieffel and his family next surface in the church records of the North Mill Creek Lutheran Church near Dorcus, Hardy County, (now Grant County, West Virginia) Virginia. It is uncertain when they moved to Hardy County but it was before 1777.

Adam and Barbara Stieffel are believed to have the following children:
(1) Garrett Stieffel*, b. c1765, d. bef. 4 Dec 1819, Fayette Co., OH
    m. c1786, prob. Hardy Co., VA, Elizabeth Peterson
(2) Adam Stieffel, II, b. 19 Jul 1767, prob. Hardy Co., VA, d. 17 Mar 1830 or 3 Jul 1830, Greene Co., OH
    m. Mary Elizabeth Ketterman
(3) Barbara Stieffel, b. 4 Mar 1770, prob. Hardy Co., VA, d. 31 Jul 1800, Hardy Co., VA, dnm

(4) John Stieffel, b. 1773, prob. Hardy, Co., VA, d. 17 Jan 1792, Hardy Co., VA

(5) Martin Stieffel, b. 1777, Hardy Co., VA, d. 13 Sep 1842, Marion, IN
    m. 18 Jun 1804, Ross Co., OH, Eva Arrahood
    m. 2nd 1 Sep 1805, Ross Co., OH, Mary Odle

(6) Mary Stieffel, d. bef. 1830
    m. Hardy Co., VA, Michael Ault

(7) George Stieffel, "children of son George" mentioned in will of Adam in 1803, nfi

(8) Eve Stieffel, only reference to Eve is one family history where she is listed as a sister of Martin (Stieffel) Boots

Records of the North Mill Creek Lutheran Church in Petersburg, Virginia (now West Virginia), show that on 21 Mar 1799 Adam Stieffel, Sr., Adam Stieffel, Jr., Barb Stieffel "frau," Elizabeth Stieffel "frau" and Marte (prob. Martin) Stieffel attended communion service. Sometime about 1801 all the members of the Stieffel family changed their name to Boots. There may have been a trend about this time to Americanize family names, but the reason for the choice of Boots is unknown. Evidence that pinpoints the data of the change in the family name comes from Hardy County, Virginia, records. On 10 Dec 1800 Adam and Garrett Stieffel witnessed the will of Valentine Post. Then a few months later, Adam Boots witnessed the will of Sebastian Hagler. After 1801 the family name Boots is used exclusively except in one or two instances.

Adam Boots wrote his will in 1803 and it follows:

In the name of God Amen I Adam Boots of the County of Hardy and being weak and sick but of Perfect Mind and Memory, thanks be given unto God, calling to mind the mortality of my body and knowing that it is appointed for all men once to die, do make and ordain this my last Will and Testament that is to say Principally and first of all I give and recommend my soul unto the hands of Almighty God that gave it and my body I recommend to the Earth to buried in a Christian decent manner at the discretion of my Executors noting but at the general resurection I shall receive the same again by the mighty power of God and as touching such worldly estate wherewith it hath pleased God to bless me in this life I give devise and dispose of in the following manner and form.

First. I give and bequeath unto my beloved son Garret Boots the lower part of the plantation whereon I now live including up Mill Creek to Coopers Mill road in a square line across which I freely give unto his heirs forever.

Secondly. I give and bequeath unto my beloved son Adam Boots the upper part of my plantation above mentioned including down Mill Creek to the said Coopers Mill road aforesaid which I freely give unto him and his heirs forever and I desire that my two sons namely Garret and Adam Boots pay unto my son Martin Boots the sum of fifty pounds as part out of the land to be paid after my death and further I desire that the said Garret and Adam Boots pay unto my daughter Mary Ault's children, namely Elizabeth Ault, Mary Ault, Susannah Ault, Michael Ault, Jacob Ault and Barbary Ault the sum of three pounds each after my death and as they become of age and I further desire that the said Garret and Adam pay unto my son George Boots children the sum of five pounds each after my death as they become of age and do nominate and appoint my beloved wife Barbary and my son, Adam Boots Executor and Executrix of this my last will and testament and I do utterly disallow revoke and disannul all and every other former Testament will legacies bequeaths by me in any wise before willed and bequeathed ratifying and confirming this and no other to be my last Will and Testament in witness whereof I have hereunto set my hand and Seal this 19th day of April 1802.

Sealed signed & acknowledged   s/Adam Boots (Seal)
in the presents of us
s/ Conrad Carr
s/ Leonard Hagler

Adam Boots died on 18 Aug 1803 in Hardy County, Virginia, and is probably buried in the North Mill Creek Lutheran Church graveyard. Adam's wife Barbara died after 1808, but we do not know the exact date.

In the early 1800s the sons of Adam Boots moved their families from Virginia (now West Virginia) to Ohio. Martin Boots was in Ross County, Ohio, by 1804. He first married Eva Arrahood in Ross County on 18 Jun 1804. Evidently she died quite soon after their marriage since on 1 Sep 1805, Martin Boots married Mary Odle in Ross County.

In 1806 Garrett Boots and his wife Elizabeth sold their land in Hardy County, Virginia, and moved to Ross County, Ohio. The 1810 tax records of Ross County list a Garrett Boots. Martin and Garrett Boots remained in Ross County until about 1816. At which time, Garrett Boots moved to Fayette County, Ohio. Martin Boots was in Franklin County, Ohio, in 1821.

Garrett Boots married Elizabeth Peterson (born Bidert) probably in Hardy County, Virginia, about 1786 based on the birthdate of their first child. Elizabeth Peterson was the daughter of John Martin Peterson (born Hans Martin Bidert) and Rosina Teter (born Rosina Dieter).

The Peterson/Bidert Family

The Peterson/Bidert family are of German extraction and their name change evidently indicates a mass adoption of American names by many German families in this region of the country. This family has been researched by Clyde S. Boots of Isabel, Kansas. The Bidert family can be traced back to a Wolfgang Biderb (the family name appears to be spelled Biderb in Switzerland and Bidert after moving to America) who was born about 1550 near Langenbruck or Rheinfelden, Switzerland. Wolfgang married on 13 Jun 1581 to Katerina Heurin Von Hagendorf and married second on 19 Sep 1586 to Maria Bropstin Von Holderband. Wolfgang and Maria had a son Niclaus Biderb who was born 23 May 1595. Niclaus married Margreth Hockendorn and had a son Niclaus who was born 8 Aug 1622. This Niclaus married Barbara Plattner and they had a son Hans Jacob Biderb who was born 17 Sep 1676 near Langenbruck, Switzerland. Hans Jacob Biderb married Elspeth Tschamper Von Brittnau and they had a son Hans Jacob Biderb, Jr. who was born 17 Sep 1706.

Hans Jacob Biderb, Jr. married Sarah Mohlerin on 13 Feb 1728 in Switzerland. They had four known children born in Switzerland before they migrated to America in 1736 and settled in Grant County, Virginia, now Hardy County, West Virginia. Their second son was Hans Martin Biderb who was born 20 May 1730 in Barenwyle, Switzerland. About 1764, Hans Martin Bidert married Rosina Teter (born Dieter) probably in Hardy County, Virginia. Their daughter Elizabeth was born about 1770 in Hardy County and she married Garrett (Stieffel) Boots in about 1786. It appears that the Bidert family changed their family name to Peterson about the same time that the Stieffel family made the change to Boots.

Returning to the Boots family, Garrett Boots was born about 1765, probably in what is now Hardy County, West Virginia.

Garrett and Elizabeth (Peterson) Boots had twelve children:
(1) Martin S. Boots, b. 1 Mar 1787, Hardy Co., VA, d. 8 Mar 1865, Guthrie Co., IA
   m. Susannah Shoemaker
(2) John Boots, b. 25 Feb 1788, Hardy Co., VA, d. 7 Mar 1855, Blackhawk Co., IA
   m. 28 Jul 1816, Fayette Co., OH, Rhoda Ann Mann
(3) Barbara Boots, b. c1792, Hardy Co., VA
   m. 15 Aug 1816, Fayette Co., OH, William Archer
(4) Jamima Boots, b. c1794, Hardy Co., VA
   m. 1818, Fayette Co., OH, Daniel Culver
(5) Rosannah Boots, b. c1796, Hardy Co., VA
   m. 1816, Fayette Co., OH, Johnson Thurman
(6) Elizabeth Boots, b. 1 Sep 1798, Hardy Co., VA
   m. 1818, Fayette Co., OH, Alexander Garringer
(7) Solomon Boots, b. 3 May 1801, Hardy Co., VA, d. 30 Sep 1840, nr. Albany, IN
   m. 16 Jan 1825, Fayette Co., OH, Mary Barger
(8) Phoebe Boots, b. 16 Apr 1804, Hardy Co., VA
   m. 1 Jul 1827, Fayette Co., OH, Henry McDonald
(9) Absolom Boots, b c1808, OH, d. ? aft. 1860, Platt Co., MO
   m. 19 Feb 1828, Fayette Co., OH, Elizabeth Parks, m. 2nd Mary Hill
(10) Mary Boots, b. 18 Aug 1811, Ross Co., OH, d. 24 Mar 1893, Delaware Co., IN
   m. 5 Feb 1833, Fayette Co., OH, Uriah Pace
(11) Sarah Boots*, b. 28 Mar 1814, OH, probably Ross Co., d. 8 Aug 1882, Randolph Co., IN, bur. Garringer Homestead Cem., Monroe Twp., Randolph Co., IN
   m. 16 Mar 1834, Delaware Co., IN, Isaac Jacob Garringer
(12) Samuel Boots, b. c 1817, OH, d. 1861, near Osceola, MO

m. Lydia Ann ?

Garrett Boots died sometime in 1819 in Fayette County, Ohio, but the exact date is not recorded. His will was proved in that county on 4 Dec 1819. In his will his widow Elizabeth and son-in-law Daniel Culver were appointed administrators. In 1823, his widow Elizabeth Boots was living in Fayette County, Ohio, at which time she signed a deed with her brothers and sisters as the heirs of Martin Peterson. In 1830, it appears that Elizabeth Boots is living with her son Absolom's family. She probably died sometime between 1830 and 1840 since she is not with her son's family in the latter census.

Of the children of Garrett and Elizabeth Boots, the following is known. Solomon and Mary (Barger) Boots had seven children: Martin, Elizabeth, Jemima, Mary, John, Absalom, and Samuel. Solomon died in Delaware County, Indiana, and Mary remarried to Ezra Bantz.

Son Samuel Boots married Lydia Ann, last name unknown, and moved to Pike County, Illinois, by 1846. Sometime after 1854, they moved to St. Clair County, Missouri. Samuel and his brother Absolom got caught up in the civil unrest in Missouri at the start of the Civil War. In 1861, raiders led by John Morton caught the brothers in a boat on the Osage River and shot both. Samuel was killed and Absolom seriously wounded. One record says only that Absolom was wounded while another source says he was also killed.

The first born of Garrett and Elizabeth Boots, Martin Boots (once signed his name Martin S. Boots) served in the War of 1812 from Ohio. Before 1819, he married Susannah Shoemaker near Chillicothe, Ohio. Martin moved to Randolph County, Indiana, in 1832, moved in 1855 to St. Clair County, Missouri, and in 1862 moved to Guthrie County, Iowa. Martin and Susannah Boots had the following known children:
(1) Elizabeth Boots, b. 17 Feb 1819, Franklin Co., OH, d. 11 Jun 1893, IN
    m. 31 Jul 1838, Randolph Co., IN, Samuel Caylor
(2) Eli Boots, b. 6 Mar 1821, Franklin Co., OH, d. 3 May 1914, Guthrie Co., IA
    m. 19 Sep 1844, Selma, Delaware Co., IN, Eunice Jones

(3) John Boots, b. 26 Feb 1823, Franklin Co., OH, d. 9 Nov 1892, Albany, IN

m. 6 Aug 1846, Jay Co., IN, Harriet Jane Current

(4) Susannah Boots, b. c1828, OH

m. 7 Sep 1848, Randolph Co., IN, John B. Lewellen

(5) Rachel Boots, b. c1830, OH

m. 10 Dec 1850, Randolph Co., IN, Daniel Dillman

(6) Solomon Boots, b. c1834, Randolph Co., IN

m. Sarah O. Anderson

(7) Mahala Boots, b. c1837, Randolph Co., IN

m. ? Peterson

(8) Martin Boots, Jr., b. 31 Jan 1841, Randolph Co., IN

m. 1861, Sarah Ann Lewellen

(9) Elijah Boots, d. young

In 1832, Martin Boots and Alexander Garringer moved their families to Green Township, Randolph County, Indiana, and were the first settlers in that township. Alexander Garringer had previously married Elizabeth Boots, Martin's sister.

The 1840 Indiana census lists a Marton Boots living in Green Township of Randolph County. Also listed as living in Delaware County, Indiana, were Addin (Adam) Boots, John Boots and Lvir (Levi?) Boots. This John Boots is the second son of Garrett Boots. Addin Boots is Adam Boots III, a son of Adam Boots II. Another son of Adam Boots, II, Martin Boots born 1803 in Virginia, married Rhoda Strong Dillon on 21 Dec 1826 in Greene County, Ohio. This Martin Boots moved sometime after 1850 to Randolph County, Indiana, where three of his children married.

In the late 1840s Alexander and Elizabeth (Boots) Garringer moved to Howard County, Indiana, where they later both died. In about 1855 Martin Boots moved his family to St. Clair County, Missouri. Several of his brothers including John also moved their families at the same time. In this era Missouri became a very troubled state and a battleground between pro-slavery Southerners and abolitionist Northerners. In 1861 Samuel Boots, a son of Garrett Boots, was shot and killed by bushwhackers while in a boat on the Osage River, near Osceola, Missouri. His brother, Absolom, was wounded at the same time Samuel was killed.

John Boots, the second son of Garrett and Elizabeth (Peterson) Boots married Rhoda Ann Mann in Fayette County, Ohio, on 28 Jul 1816. They had ten children:

(1) Martin Boots, b. 25 Sep 1817, Fayette Co., OH, d. 9 Jul 1907, Hampton, IA
    m. 23 May 1844, Delaware Co., IN, Rebecca Jones
    m. 2nd Mrs. Elma Manifold
(2) Aaron Boots, b. 13 Apr 1819, Fayette Co., OH, d. 4 Sep 1865, Randolph Co., IN
    m. 15 Feb 1844, Randolph Co., IN, Nancy Wirt
(3) Marietta (or May Etta) Boots, b. 17 Aug 1821, Fayette Co., OH
    m. 25 Aug 1842, Delaware Co., IN, John Simmons
(4) Isaac Garrett Boots, b. 13 Apr 1823, Fayette Co., OH, d. 14 Jan 1898, Delaware Co., IN
    m. 12 Nov 1846, Julia Ann Jones
(5) Elizabeth Boots, b. 13 May 1826, Fayette Co., OH
(6) Rhoda Ann Boots, b. 13 Jan 1828, Fayette Co., OH
    m. 15 Mar 1855, Delaware Co., IN, William Hanna
(7) Warner Boots, b. 16 Jun 1830, Fayette Co., OH
(8) Harriett Boots, b. 13 Oct 1832, Fayette Co., OH
    m. 19 Aug 1852, Delaware Co., IN, Elmore W. Ridout
(9) Joseph Mann Boots, b. 1 Apr 1836, Randolph Co., IN, d. 1920, IA
    m. Sarah Ann Ridout
(10) Benjamin Boots, b. 28 Mar 1839, Randolph Co., IN, d. 1860 MO

This John Boots moved his family to Delaware County, Indiana, about 1835. Several of their children married in Delaware County. Rhoda Ann (Mann) Boots died on 4 Mar 1845 in Delaware County and is buried in Albany, Indiana. John Boots moved his family to Iowa sometime after 1855 where he developed a farm in Blackhawk County, dying there shortly after he moved.

Aaron Boots, a son of John and Rhoda (Mann) Boots, married Nancy Wirt in Randolph County and had children Israel, Sarah, Solomon, Lewis, George, Noah, James and Mary. Aaron died in 1865 and is buried in the old abandoned Steubenville Cemetery south of Redkey, Indiana. Most of their children married in Randolph County but later moved west.

Sarah Boots, daughter of Garrett and Elizabeth Boots

Sarah Boots was the 2nd youngest of the twelve children of Garrett and Elizabeth (Peterson) Boots. She was born on 28 Mar 1814 in Ross County, Ohio. She was only 5 when her father Garrett died and but 11 when her mother Elizabeth died. She was probably raised in the family of her older brother Martin or John Boots and came to Indiana with those families in about 1828.

On 16 Mar 1834, Sarah Boots married Isaac Jacob Garringer in Delaware County, Indiana. Although Sarah was her given name, she was commonly called Sally. Isaac and Sarah had 12 children which they raised on a farm in Randolph County, Indiana. Sarah outlived her husband by 12 years and died on 8 Aug 1882. Isaac and Sarah are buried in the Garringer family plot in Monroe Township, Randolph County.

The Harbour Family

Nancy Harbour was a maternal great grandmother of Hilda Irene Garringer and married into the Hammers family. She was born on 19 Sep 1821 in Fayette County, Ohio. Her parents were the Rev. Elijah and Rhoda (Capps) Harbour. The Harbour family was one of the early settlers in Green Township of Randolph County, Indiana, moving there in 1833 or 1834. On 19 Nov 1839, Nancy Harbour married Abraham Hammers in Randolph County. Nancy and Abraham Hammers had five children and lived the rest of their lives in Randolph County. Nancy (Harbour) Hammers died on 24 Apr 1892 and is buried in Woodlawn Cemetery at Maxville, Randolph County, Indiana.

The Harbour family history was researched by Hazel Mildred Harbour Williams and published in a book by her husband Louis J. Williams in 1982 after her death. A Harbour-Harbor-Harber Family Association has been formed and holds annual reunions and issues a family newsletter. Much of the early history of the Harbour family that follows is taken from that book and the family newsletters. Hazel Mildred Harbour (1889-1970) was a great granddaughter of the Rev. Elijah and Rhoda (Capps) Harbour.

Nancy Harbour's father, the Rev. Elijah Harbour, was born 1 Apr 1788 in Montgomery County, Virginia. He grew up in Virginia and moved to Ohio in 1809 or before. He stopped for a while in Highland County and then later moved on to adjoining Fayette County. He is first listed in the census records in the 1820 Ohio census as living in Green Township of Fayette County. He appears on the tax rolls in Fayette County from 1816 until 1836. In 1833 or 1834 he moved his family to Green Township of Randolph County, Indiana, but did not apparently sell his land in Ohio until a few years after he moved to Indiana.

Nancy Harbour's mother was Rhoda Capps who was born 22 Apr 1788 in South Carolina, according to census records. She was the daughter of Dempsey and Sallie Pool (Overman) Capps.

Dempsey Capps was living in Madison Township of Highland County, Ohio, by 1811 and probably before. Highland County is adjacent to Fayette County. Although no marriage record has been found, it is assumed that Elijah Harbour and Rhoda Capps were married in Fayette or Highland County, Ohio, in 1809 based on the birthdate of their first child.

Elijah and Rhoda (Capps) Harbour had eight children:
(1) Sarah Harbour, b. 9 Jul 1810
      m. 27 Sep 1826, William Simmons
(2) Thomas E. Harbour, b. 8 Jan 1813, d. aft. 1880, prob. IA
      m. c1833, Mariah Zimmerman
(3) Mary "Polly" Harbour, b. 19 Dec 1815, d. 27 Mar 1910
      m. 3 Aug 1833, John Draper
(4) Dempsey Capps Harbour, b. 23 Aug 1818, d. 27 Aug 1897
      m. 20 Apr 1839, Sarah Godwin
(5) Nancy Harbour*, b. 9 Sep 1821, Fayette County, OH, d. 24 Apr 1892, Randolph Co., IN
      m. 19 Nov 1839, Randolph Co., IN, Abraham Hammers
(6) Rhoda Harbour, b. 8 Oct 1823, d. 1 Apr 1910
      m. 5 May 1848, Wesley Draper
(7) Elizabeth Harbour, b. 21 Oct 1826, d. 21 May 1889
      m. Samuel Life
      m. 2nd Andrew Davids
(8) Elijah E. Harbour, b. 16 Oct 1831, Fayette Co., OH, d. 18 Mar 1865, Randolph Co., IN
      m. 30 Mar 1851, Susannah Davis

Rev. Elijah Harbour was a self-educated man and served as a justice of the peace in Randolph County. He was a minister of the Methodist Episcopal Church and served as pastor of the Fairview Church for many years and was known as "Father" Harbour to all. Elijah Harbour was a skillful hunter and often shared game with his neighbors and parishioners. He was also an excellent carpenter and often when he conducted funerals, the deceased would be buried in a coffin made by him.

The following biographical sketch about the Rev. Elijah Harbour is taken from the Tucker's 1882 *History of Randolph County, Indiana*. "Rev. Elijah Harbour came to Green Township, Randolph, in about 1833 or 1834. He raised a large family and spent a long life upon the homestead of his choice, dying at length in 1872, after tarrying upon these mundane shores more than his full fourscore years - eighty-four years, five months and twelve days. His wife Rhoda, had preceded him to the Scared Land more than two years. She died 30 May 1870, aged 82 years, two months and twenty-three days. Mr. Harbour was a Methodist and a local preacher, and was active and successful in helping to spread the knowledge and the practice of godliness through these frontier regions. The religious exercises in connection with the interment of his earthly remains were largely attended, and they were followed to the grave by a large throng of sympathizing neighbors and friends." Elijah and Rhoda (Capps) Harbour are buried in Fairview Cemetery, Randolph County, Indiana.

Of the children of the Rev. Elijah and Rhoda (Capps) Harbour, we know the following: Son Thomas E. Harbour married Mariah Zimmerman, had seven children and moved to Guthrie County, Iowa, where he is found in the 1880 census and presumably he later died in Iowa. Dempsey Capps Harbour married Sarah Godwin, the daughter of Nathan and Elizabeth (Wirt) Godwin, had 8 children and remained in Randolph County where he died in 1897. Elijah E. Harbour married Susannah Davis, had five children and remained in Randolph County where he died on 18 Mar 1865. According to the Randolph County Coroner, Elijah E. Harbour died by his own hand, reason not given.

David Harbour, father of the Rev. Elijah Harbour

The Rev. Elijah Harbour was the son of David and Mary (Spurlock) Harbour. David Harbour was born in 1765 in Pittsylvania County, Virginia. He married Mary Spurlock on 17 Aug 1787 in Montgomery County, Virginia. She was the daughter of John Spurlock, Sr. David and Mary (Spurlock) Harbour had four children:
(1) (Rev.) Elijah Harbour*, b. 31 Mar 1788, Montgomery Co., VA, d. 31 Mar 1872, Randolph Co., IN
   m. c1809, Fayette or Highland Co., OH, Rhoda Capps
(2) Nancy Harbour, b. c1790, Montgomery Co., VA
   m. c1807, Isaac Overman
   m. 2nd Highland Co., OH, George Rains
(3) Mary "Polly" Harbour, nfi
(4) Rhoda Harbour, b. c1796, Bourbon Co., KY, bur. Pope Cem., Highland Co., OH

m. c1832, Highland Co., OH, Jared Harbour

Mary (Spurlock) Harbour died sometime between 1796 and 1802 when David Harbour married 2nd 26 Feb 1803 in Bourbon County, Kentucky, Elizabeth "Betsey" Berry Bell, daughter of Basil Berry, Sr. and widow of John Bell. David and Betsey Harbour had four children:

(5) Jesse Harbour, b. c1804, d. 1880, Cabell Co., WV
   m. 10 Jan 1828, Jane Newman
   m. 2nd 21 Mar 1837, Jane Malcolm
(6) David Harbour, b. c1806, d. 1849, Putnam Co., VA
   m. c1827, Elizabeth McCallister
(7) Sarah Harbour, b. c1808
   m. 25 Dec 1827, Russell Newman
(8) Mary Bell Harbour
   m. 25 Jan 1820, Cabell Co., VA, John Smallridge

David Harbour evidently moved his family to Kentucky around 1796 and stayed there for 10 or 15 years before returning to Cabell County, VA. David was a Baptist preacher and performed the marriage ceremonies for his own children as well as his step-daughter and countless other marriages in Cabell County, Virginia. In the 1840 census he was found living with his son David, Jr. in Cabell County and in 1850, he was living with his son Jesse. David Harbour died in 1854 in Cabell County, Virginia.

Elijah Harbour, father of the David Harbour

David Harbour was the son of Elijah and Prudence (Pusey) Harbour. Elijah Harbour was born about 1735/40. He married about 1758 to Prudence Pusey, daughter of Robert and Magdalene (Van Meter) Pusey. Prudence was born about 1741/3 and after Elijah Harbour died in 1769 she remarried to Thomas Flowers. Prudence died about 1816 in Sullivan Co., IN. David and Prudence (Pusey) Harbour had four children:

(1) Thomas Harbour, b. c1759, d. 1796, Patrick Co., VA
   m. c1780, Keziah Townsend
(2) Sarah Harbour, b. c1762, d. 1814, IN
   m. c1780, Benjamin Turman, Jr.
(3) David Harbour*, b. 1765, Pittsylvania Co., VA, d. 1854, Cabell Co., VA
   m. 21 Aug 1787, Montgomery Co., VA, Mary Spurlock

m. 2nd 26 Feb 1803, Bourbon Co., KY, Elizabeth "Betsey" Berry Bell

(4) Mary Harbour, b. c1767, d. aft. 1834, Cabell Co., VA
    m. c1785, Jesse Spurlock

After Elijah's premature death while only in his 30s, his widow, Prudence, married Thomas Flowers and they had at least ten children. Son Thomas died in middle age. He was planning to move with the Turmans, Flowers and Spurlocks to Kentucky when he died.

Thomas Harbour, the emigrant and father of the Elijah Harbour

Elijah Harbour was the son of the original emigrant of the Harbour family, Thomas Harbour. Thomas Harbour was reputedly born in Wales in the period 1675/95. We know little about him until he shows up on 28 Sep 1728, on which date he received a land grant in Hanover County, Virginia, from the British Crown. Thomas appears to be a man of great wealth with large land holding and one active in community affairs where he lived. Thomas married in the period 1705/25 to Sarah Witt, daughter of John Witt, Jr. one of two Huguenot brothers, refugees from France.

Thomas and Sarah (Witt) Harbour had the following known children (order of birth uncertain):
(1) David Harbour, b. c1708-1726
(2) Talmon Harbour, b. c1718-1728
    m. c1745, Mary (Wright)
(3) Lavinia Harbour, b. c1720
    m. Charles Witt
(4) Mary Harbour
    m. Palatiah Shelton
(5) Abner Harbour, b. c1730, d. 1778, Henry Co., VA
    m. Joyce Thornhill
(6) Elisha Harbour, b. c1733
    m. Margaret ?
(7) Elijah Harbour*, b. c1735/40, d. 1769, Pittsylvania Co., VA
    m. c1758, Prudence Pusey
(8) Jane Harbour
    m. Elijah Witt
(9) Sarah Harbour

      m. David Witt
(10) Adonijah Harbour
      m. 25 Aug 1769, Pittsylvania Co., VA, Ann "Nancy" Dalton
      m. 2nd 3 Apr 1791, Surry Co., NC, Charlotte Gallihue
      (Dalton)

The date of Thomas Harbour's marriage and birthdates of his children have some uncertainty. It is known that in 1728, Thomas Harbour filed on 400 acres of land on the lower fork of Deep Creek in the area that is now Louisa County, Virginia. Later Thomas Harbour filed for land on three separate dates in Albemarle County, now Fluvanna County, Virginia. In 1734, he had a land patent for 400 acres, in 1737, a land patent for 1463 acres and in 1745 for another 400 acres. Thomas' father-in-law, John Witt, is also mentioned in several land patents in this area about the same time.

Thomas Harbour later moved to Patrick and Henry Counties in Virginia where he obtained 8 tracts of land totaling 1555 acres all entered on 28 Sep 1753. The tracts were in different areas so he may have been picking tracts for family members since they all had to be occupied under the provisions of the grants. From 1753 to 1777 there are a series of land transactions between Thomas Harbour and his sons, son-in-laws and other family members. On 31 Oct 1777, Thomas Harbour took the Oath of Allegiance in Henry County, Virginia. We do not know when Thomas Harbour died but it was sometime after 1777 nor do we know where he is buried.

The Capps Family

Rhoda Capps is a great great grandmother of Hilda Irene Garringer on her maternal side through marriage into the Harbour family and then into the Hammers family. Rhoda Capps was born on 22 Apr 1788 probably in North Carolina although one later census record lists her birth state as South Carolina. Rhoda Capps' parents were Dempsey and Sarah Pool (Overman) Capps.

The Capps family is of English descent and arrived in Virginia within a few years of the founding of Jamestown. The early records of the Capps family are related by Colonel William Couper in his Couper Family Genealogy which was published in the *Virginia Magazine of History and Biography* in 1951 (Vol. 59).

The earliest known ancestor is a John William Capps who married Mary Ann Moss. John William and Mary Ann (Moss) Capps had a son, William Moss Capps, who was born in 1575 in England. John William Capps died in 1599 in England. Son William Capps is recorded as coming to Virginia with the Sir Thomas Gates and Sir George Somers Expedition in 1609/10. His mother Mary Ann may have accompanied him since one record states she died in 1616 in Kickoughton, Virginia.

William Capps took up some land near Jamestown on Southampton Creek at a place known as "Little England." His name is found in several early records and he was a member of the first general assembly from (now) Hampton County in 1623. William Capps married Catharine Jernigan, but she died sometime before 16 Feb 1623. William died some time between 1629 and 1653 when the estate of William is listed in some court records. William and Catharine Capps had only one known son, William, who was born 1612/18.

This William Capps, the son, is found is Virginia records in 1645 with his occupation listed as carpenter. His name is found in land records in 1637 where the records refer to "Hampton River, commonly called Capps." It appears that what is now called Lafayette River in Norfolk City was originally called Capps Creek. William Capps married Margaret Sykes. William Capps' will was dated 6 May 1666 so he died around this time while his wife survived him by several years and remarried to Dennis Dawley. Her will was written in 1696 and probated in 1701 so she died some time in between. William and Margaret Capps had the following known children:

(1) William Capps, b. c1650, d. c1706
    m. Frances Cox
(2) Henry Capps, b. c1652, d. Jan 1689
(3) Richard Capps*, b. aft. 1654, will dated 6 Apr 1720, Princess Ann Co., VA
    m. Jane Langly, m. 2nd Margaret ?
(4) Jeane Capps

Richard Capps is found in (now) Princess Anne County land records patenting 390 acres in 1691. He married Jane Langly who died sometime before 1715 and Richard married second to Margaret, last name unknown. Richard had the following offspring, most by his first wife Jane:

(1) William Capps, b. c1680, d. 1744
    m. Elizabeth Marsh
(2) Phyllis Capps, mentioned in will
(3) Anne Capps, mentioned in will
(4) Elizabeth Capps, m. William Brimson
(5) John Capps*, b. c1705, d. 1753, Princess Ann Co., VA
    m. Dinah Whitehurst
(6) James Capps, minor in 1720
(7) Lewis Capps, minor in 1720
(8) Thorowgood Capps, b. c1699, d. aft. 1753
    m. Anne Langley
(9) Richard Capps, b. bef. 1685, d. c1729
    m. Anne (Land) Fountain

Richard's will was prepared on 16 Apr 1720 so he probably died shortly after this date.

Son John Capps lived in Princess Ann County, Virginia, and married Dinah Whitehurst. Dinah Whitehurst was the daughter of James and Mary (Godfrey) Whitehurst, Jr. James Whitehurst, Jr., was the son of James Whitehurst, Sr., and his wife Sarah Goldsmith. James Whitehurst, Sr., was the son of a Richard Whitehurst who owned land in Upper Norfolk County in 1639. Sarah Goldsmith was the daughter of a William Goldsmith who died in Norfolk County, Virginia in 1691/2. Mary Godfrey was the daughter of John Godfrey and his wife Mary. John Godfrey died in Norfolk County, Virginia, in 1708/10. This John Godfrey's father was also named John Godfrey and had arrived in Virginia in 1735 aboard the ship *Transport*.

John Capps' will was probated in 1753 so he died in that year or before. John and Dinah (Whitehurst) Capps had the following children:
(1) James Capps
(2) Amy Capps
(3) Hillary Capps, d. 1798
(4) Mary Capps
(5) Margaret Capps
(6) Charles Capps
(7) John Capps*, b. c1735, d. 1806/7
     m. Martha ?, m. 2nd Mary Rainey
(8) Solomon Capps, b. c1750, d. 1783

John Capps had the following children, mostly with his first wife Martha:
(1) John Capps, d. 1832
     m. 1815, Mrs. Mary Moses
(2) Solomon Capps, b. c1780, d. bef 1830
     m. Sarah Walker (Braithwait)
(3) Polly Capps, m. 1813, Henry Robinson
(4) James Capps, d. 1833
     m. 1814, Sally Iromer
(5) Charles Capps, m. Julia Whitehurst
(6) Dempsey Capps*, b. 7 Sep 1760, VA or NC, d. ? 1839, IL
     m. c1783, Sallie Pool (Overman), b. 8 Nov 1756, d. 18 May 1840
(7) Anne Capps
(8) Sally Capps, m. Anthony Lovett
(9) Amy Capps, m. 1830, Andrew Bonnett
(10) Andrew Capps
     m. 1820, Jacomine Moore, m. 2nd Mary Smith

(11) Caleb Capps, m. Elizabeth Whitehurst

Dempsey Capps was living in Highland County, Ohio, by 1811 along with a William Caps and James Capps (younger and assumed to be his sons).

The Bible of Nathan Overman has been published. Nathan was the son of Isaac and Sarah Pool Overman, born 8 Feb 1777. Along with numerous Overman entries, there were several births recorded for the surname Capps. Research of the Quaker records in North Carolina have helped figure out the connection. Isaac died young and his widow Sarah remarried Demsey (or Dempsey) Capps. The Bible lists the birth dates for Demsey, Sarah, and 6 children (including Nathan's full sister Sarah Overman):

"Demsey Capps was born September the 7th 1760.
Sarah (sic) Capps was born November 8th 1756.
Sarah Overman was born February 25th 1782.
Mary Capps was born July 18th, 1785.
Rhoda Capps was born April 22 1788.
William Capps was born June 17th 1791.
James Capps was born September 13th 1794.
Elijah Capps was born January 10th 1797."

Dempsey Capps was born in 1760, location unsure, probably Virginia but it could have been North Carolina. There are few records of Capps in North or South Carolina before this date. However, there was a large emigration of people out of Virginia down to North Carolina about this time.

On 15 Oct 1777 Dempsey Capps enlisted for 3 years in the North Carolina regiment of Colonel Gideon Lamb and served in the corps until 1782 when he was discharged from service in James Town, Virginia. He later served for an additional year in another North Carolina regiment and was stationed at Charlestown, South Carolina.

Records show Dempsey Capps to have lived in Highland County, Ohio, from 1811 until at least 1830. The 1810 South Carolina census does not list him so he may have been in Ohio before 1810.

Dempsey and Sarah (Pool) Capps had the following known children:

(1) Mary Capps, b. 18 Jul 1785
    m. ? Garrett
(2) Rhoda Capps*, b. 22 Apr 1788, d. 30 May 1870
    m. c1809, Fayette Co., OH, Elijah Harbour
(3) William Capps, b. 17 Jun 1791
(4) James B. Capps, b. 13 Sep 1794
(5) Elijah Capps, b. 10 Jan 1797

In the 1820 census his family is listed as Dempsey Capps 1M16-25, 1M45+, 1F16-18 and 1F 45+. The 1820 census also lists a James Capps, age 26-45, with wife and 2 children and a William Capps, age 26-44, with wife and four children. These are both sons of Dempsey. The 1830 Ohio census shows households of a Dempsey Capps and a James Capps in Fairfield Township of Highland County. DAR records list Dempsey Capps as a revolutionary soldier and list him as dying in Illinois in 1839.

Highland County, Ohio records in Order Book E, 1824-1829, pg. 101, April 25, 1825 give the following information on a petition by Dempsey Capps for a pension based on his military service:

On this twenty first day of April 1825 personally appeared in open Court (it being a Court of record for the Seventh Judicial Circuit in the State of Ohio) Dempsy Capps aged sixty five years resident in the state of Ohio who being first duly sworn according to law doth on his oath make the following declaration in order to obtain the provision made by the Acts of Congress of the 18th March 1818 and the first May 1820 that he the said Dempsy Capps enlisted for the term of three years on or about 15th October 1777 the precise date he does not now recollect, in the Company Commanded by Captain _____ in the Regiment Commanded by Colonel Gideon Lamb in the line of the State of North Carolina on the Contenental establishment; that he continued to serve in the corps until September 1782 when he was discharged from the said service in James Town in The State of Virginia. That immediately after his enlistment he marched with the Company to South Carolina having rendevouze a short time at Baron's Bridge was marched to Panersburg and was under the command of General Lincoln, he was attached to this place to the fourth North Carolina Regement under the command of Col. ___

Mebane and to the Command Commanded by Captain Reding Blount, from this place he marched to Charleston S. Carolina and remained there under General Lincoln for more than a year and until he and the city of Charleston were taken by the enemy by General Cornwallis, he then remained at Hadleys Point about 15 months a prisoner and was finally exchanged for by the United States and sent around on board of the British fleet to James Town in the State of Virginia and was sent to the Governor at Richmond and obtained his discharge and that he has no other evidence now in his power of his said services except the Testimony of Zebalon Overman an aged and respected citizen of the County of Highland & State of Ohio whose affidavit is hereto annexed. And in pursuance of the act of first May 1820 I do solmenly swear that I was a resident citizen of the United States on the 18th day of March 1818 and that I have not since that time by gift, sale or in any manner disposed of my property or any part thererof with intent thereby to diminish it as to bringing myself in the provisions of an Act of Congress entitled an 'Act to provide for certain persons engaged in the land and naval service of the United States in the Revolutionary War' passed on the 18th day of March 1818 and that I have not nor has any person in trust for me any property or securities contracts or debts due to me nor have I any income other than what is contained in the Schedule hereto annexed and by me subscribed, That my occupation is that of a farmer that I have no family except an old and infirm wife aged sixty nine years and that she is unable to contribute any thing to my support that my circumstances were such from to the first day of April 1824 as renderd it unnecessary to apply for the aforesaid provisions having lived with a son at that time from whom I received support but since that time I have removed myself and have not the aforesaid support. Schedule of my property Five head of cattle - apprised to $18.00 Twelve head of sheep 12.00 Five head of Hogs 6.50 four hundred cwt pork 8.00 Sixty five bushels corn 6.00 fifteen bushels wheat 3.75 two ten gallon Kettles 2.50 two ovens & pot 3.00 fire dog shovel & tong 2.00 two pot forks 1.50 Burea, cupboard & furniture 18.00 chair 2.00 table 2.00 Barrel 2.00 flax 2.00 Tea Kettle 1.50 tubs & buckes 2.00 table 2.00 I Certify the above schedule to be correct and true Witness my hand this 25th day of April 1825. Demy Capps Highland Com. Pleas April Tern 1825 Highland County Michael Lowman being in open court and duly sworn according to law deposeth and saith the schedule of property annexed to the declaration of Dempsy Capps was by him and William Parker examened and appraised and that each article of property therein contained is of the value of the amount to them annexed Michael Lowman Sworn to & subscribed in open court April 25th 1825 S Bell Clk Zabelon Overman aged 69 years being duly affirmed according to Law deposeth and saith he believes Dempsy Capps the applicant in the foregoing petition did regularly serve for the Term of three years in the revolutionary War on the continental establishment from the circumstance of his having seen his discharge purporting to that fact and from the circumstance of his having received a land warrant for his said services Zabulon Overman Sworn to and subscribed in open Court April 25, 1825 Saml Bell Clk"

The Collins Family

Amelia Alisa Collins is the paternal grandmother of Hilda Irene Garringer through marriage to David Carson Garringer. Amelia was born 30 Jun 1844 and she married David on 6 Mar 1871. The Collins family was of Irish ancestry and came to America before the Revolutionary War and settled in Virginia, then spent some time in New Jersey before moving to Ohio and then later to Jay County, Indiana, where Amelia was born.

The immigrant patriarch for our Collins family was John Collins who was born in Ireland about 1715. The first record of John in America, dated 22 Sep 1745, is found in Philadelphia where "John Collins, of Philadelphia, laborer, in consideration of 10.4 by him due and owing to Daniel Boyle of Philadelphia County yeoman, indents himself to Daniel Boyle for one year and a half from this date." John Collins is next found with a fellow immigrant Thomas McGuire on the tax roles of Frederick County, Virginia, where John Collins was assessed for 620 pounds of tobacco. Evidently, the holders of large land grants in Frederick County, Joist Hite and John van Meter, must have lent John Collins money to buy out his servitude and he agreed to tenant farming in Frederick County. Many large land grants were only given and held by the requirement that settlers be present on the land within some period of time.

He is next found when John Collins of Frederick County is granted by the right honorable Thomas Lord Fairfax a parcel of land in Hampshire County, Virginia, in 1749. Many years later he purchased a second tract of land of 400 acres in Hampshire County from Mary Wolfe on 12 Aug 1766. Apparently John Collins moved back to Frederick County sometime around 1765. By 1769 he had moved again and was living on 300 acres of land on Morgan Run, a branch of the Cheat River. A survey shows that John Collins' tract of land was adjacent to land of Rev. Jacob Cozad. A daughter of Jacob Cozad married one of the sons of

John Collins. The name of John Collins' wife is not known and she may have died before 1765 based on a 1765 land deed.

Sometime prior to 1785, John Collins moved back to Harrison County where he is listed in the 1785 census as living in the West Fork settlement. John Collins died sometime before 1795 while living on Stoney Run, Hackers Creek in Harrison County. A land deed dated 1795 for the sale of 400 acres of land in Hampshire County by John Jr. and his wife Hannah Cozad indicates that they obtained the land from John Collins, his father deceased. John Collins, Sr. died without a will and his sons apparently distributed his property without probate. Apparently each of three known sons, Thomas, John, Jr. and George, received a farm.

Thomas Collins received the land that John Collins, Sr. had received from Lard Fairfax in 1749. John Collins, Jr. received the land that his father had bought from Mary Wolfe in 1766. George Collins received the home place on Stoney Creek in Lewis County. George Collins' Revolutionary War pension record says that he settled on the land in 1791.

John Collins, Sr. and his wife, name unknown, had three known sons and probably other sons and daughters unknown:
(1) Thomas Collins, b. ?, d. 1820, Hampshire Co., VA
    m. 1774, Elizabeth Cresap, daughter of Col. Daniel and Ruth (Swearingen) Cresap
(2) John Collins*, Jr., b. c1750, Frederick Co., VA, d. c1835, Warren Co., OH
    m. c1771, Hannah Cozad, daughter of Rev. Jacob and Elizabeth (Sutton) Cozad
(3) George Collins, b. c1755, Hampshire Co., VA, d. 4 Sep 1833
    m. 1791, Mary Richard, m. 2nd 1798, Abigail Smith

John Collins, Jr. son of the Emigrant John Collins

John Collins, Jr. moved with his family to Monongalia County, Virginia, in 1769 and settled on Morgan Run, a fork of the Cheat River. There about 1771 he wed Hannah Cozad, the daughter of their neighbor Rev. Jacob Cozad. Shortly after their marriage they moved to New Jersey and were there until about 1785. In 1786, they were living in Fayette County, Pennsylvania, since their daughter Elizabeth was born there. Later they are living at the mouth of Big Buffalo on West Fork River in Harrison County, Virginia, on land John bought in 1785. In the winter of 1797-98 John Collins, Jr. moved his family to the Collins Settlement in Harrison County (now Walkersville, Lewis County, West Virginia). They lived there until 1817 when most of the Collins family moved to Salem Township, Warren County, Ohio. John Collins, Jr. died about 1835 in Warren County and it is said that he was buried in the old cemetery where the Rossburg Methodist Episcopal Church once stood. Hannah (Cozad) Collins probably died some time between 1828 and 1835.

John Collins, Jr. and his wife Hannah Cozad had the following children:
(1) Cornelius Collins, b. c1768, NJ, d. after 1850, IN
    m. 1 Oct 1798, Harrison Co., VA, Eleanor Richards
(2) Jacob Collins, b. 11 Sep 1773, NJ, d. 7 Mar 1837, Warren Co., OH
    m. 25 Mar 1795, Harrison Co., VA, Mary Elsworth, b. c1776, d. 1821 Warren Co., OH
    m. 2nd Nancy Sleeth
(3) George Collins, b. c1775, NJ, d. 7 Mar 1830, Warren Co., OH
    m. 1 Oct 1798, Harrison Co., VA, Abigail Smith
    m. ? 2nd 23 Sep 1819, Harrison Co., VA, Elizabeth Crossan
(4) Mary Collins, b. c1777
    m. 21 Jan 1793, Harrison Co., VA, Abraham Bennett
(5) John Collins*, III, b. 5 Jan 1782, VA, d. 13 Sep 1838, Jay Co., IN, bur. Bost Cem., Jefferson Twp., Jay Co., IN
    m. c1805, Harrison Co., VA, Elizabeth Liggett, d. 30 Aug 1838, Jay Co., IN
(6) Abigail Collins, b. 1785, NJ
    m. 1802, Joseph Bennett
(7) Elizabeth Collins, b. c1786, Fayette Co., PA
    m. 15 Apr 1801, Harrison Co., VA, John B. Burnsides
(8) Benjamin Collins, b. 3 Mar 1787, Harrison Co., VA, d. 16 Feb 1871, Union Co., IN
    m. Hannah Emory, b. 5 Jun 1787
(9) Isaac S. Collins, b. 1792, Harrison Co., VA, d. 11 Dec 1871, Calhoun Co., WV
    m. 6 Oct 1812, Harrison Co., VA, Rachel Cunningham
(10) Hannah Collins, b. Sep 1795, d. 4 May 1874, Liberty, IN
    m. 22 Dec 1814, Warren Co., OH, Joseph Liggett

John Collins, son of John Collins, Jr.

Our Collins line descends through son John Collins, sometimes referred to as John Collins, III. John Collins was born 5 Jan 1782 in Virginia, probably Harrison County. John married Elizabeth Liggett about 1805, probably in Harrison County although no marriage record has been found. This family moved with the other Collins families to Warren County, Ohio, about 1817. The 1820 Ohio census shows 10 Collins households in Salem Township of that county.

In this period in Warren County, Ohio, there was another unrelated Collins family which had been in New Hampshire. There were several intermarriages between these two families so the records can be confusing. Later, some of these New Hampshire Collins families also moved west to Jay County, Indiana.

The 1830 Ohio census lists John Collins in Warren County along with 10 other Collins families. John Collins and a few of his children moved to Jay County, Indiana, about 1836. Elizabeth (Liggett) Collins died on 30 Aug 1838 and John Collins, III died on 13 Sep 1838 and both are buried in Bost Cemetery. A biography of Samuel Blazer who married their daughter Prudence said that both of Prudence's parents died of fever soon after coming to Jay County.

Records from the Bost (also called Flesher) Cemetery in Jefferson Township, Jay County, Indiana show the following:
Collins, John, d. 13 Sep 1838, aged 56y, 8m, 8d
Elizabeth, wife of John Collins, d. 30 Aug 1838, ae 53y, 11m, 22d
Collins, Joseph, d. 25 Feb 1873, ae 62y, 2m, 24d
Susan, wife of Joseph Collins, d. 19 May 1838, ae 27y, 2m, 1d
Harriet Ann, wife of Joseph H. Collins, d. 2 Aug 1884, ae 63y, 4m, 17d

John and Elizabeth (Liggett) Collins had the following children:
(1) Mary Collins
    m. 2 Jan 1823, Warren Co., OH, Harrison Watkins
(2) John Collins, b. 1802/1810, d. bef. 1849
(3) George Collins, b. 1802/1810, d. bef. 1849

(4) Joseph Collins*, b. 1 Dec 1810, VA, d. 25 Feb 1873, Jay Co., IN, bur. Bost Cem., Jefferson Twp., Jay Co., IN
m. c1834, OH, Susan ?, d. 19 May 1838, Jay Co., IN, bur. Bost Cem.
m. 2nd 7 Nov 1839, Jay Co., IN, Harriet Finch*, b. 16 Mar 1821, OH, d. 2 Aug 1888
(5) Jesse C. Collins, b. c1811, OH
m. Eliza Cook, d/o John and Mary Cook
(6) Prudence Collins, b. 4 Aug 1820, Warren Co., OH
m. 9 Apr 1840, Jay Co., IN, Samuel Blazer
(7) Elliott Collins
(8) Elizabeth Collins, b. 25 Jul 1829, Warren Co., OH, d. aft. 1883
m. c1845, Joseph Kidder
(9) Hannah Collins, d. bef. 1849
m. 18 Dec 1828, Warren Co., OH, Elias Jackson
(10) Susan Collins, d. bef. 1849
m. 18 Dec 1828, Warren Co., OH, Henry L. Williams
(11) Harrison Collins, d. bef. 1849 (reported in Feb 1849 legal document)

Harrison Collins, a minor and probably the youngest of the children of John and Elizabeth Collins, died some time shortly before 1849. An 1849 legal document from Jay County, Indiana, requests that his share of his father's real estate be assigned to his brothers and sisters and lists them confirming the above family. In 1849 son Joseph Collins and daughters Prudence (Collins) Blazer and Elizabeth (Collins) Kidder live in Jay County. Sons George and John Collins and daughters Susan (Collins) Williams and Hannah (Collins) Jackson are deceased. The remaining siblings are all said to be residents of the State of Ohio.

The 1840 Indiana census lists the following Collins in Jay County: Cornelius Collins, 1M20-30, 1M60-70, 1F 20-30, (Cornelius, uncle to Joseph Collins below)
Joseph Collins*, 1M<5, 1M10-15, 1M30-40, 1F<5, 1F10-15
Amos Collins, 1M<5, 1M10-15, 1M15-20, 1M40-50, 1F5-10, 1F10-15, 1F30-40
Jesse Collins, 1M15-20, 1M20-30, 1F<5, 1F15-20 (Jesse, brother to Joseph)

The 1850 Indiana census lists six Collins families in Jay County, Indiana:

Pike Township
Joseph Collins*, 41, VA
Harriet*, 29, OH
Mary, 15, OH
Martin, 13, OH
Susan, 9, IN
Elizabeth, 8, IN
Amelia*, 6, IN
Catherine, 4, IN
Joseph, 2, IN
William H., 1, IN

Joseph B. Collins, 27, OH (s/o Amos, d. 21 Feb 1896, age 71, Jay
Co., IN)
Mildred, 21, OH
William T., 2, IN
Elisha, 9/12, IN

Amos Collins, 51, Maine (s/o Benjamin of the NH Collins family)
Abigail, 47, VA
Mary, 18, OH
Elizabeth, 15, OH
Cornelius, 10, OH
George, 3, IN

Robert Collins, 24, OH (s/o Amos)
Sarah, 24, OH
Oceanna, 5, IN
John G., 3, IN
Abigail, 1, IN

Noble Township
James Collins, 35, OH (prob. brother to David below)
Nancy, 40, PA
William, 7, IN
Sally A., 6, IN
Rachel, 5, IN
Melissa, 4, IN
John, 2, IN
David, 1/2, IN

Knox Township

David Collins, 37, OH
Sarah E., 23, PA
Elizabeth J., 2, IN
Cornelius Collins, age 82, b. NJ (uncle to Joseph)

Joseph Collins and his first wife Mary Ann had 2 children:
(1) Mary Collins, b. c1835, OH
(2) Martin Collins, b. c1837, OH

Joseph Collins and his second wife Harriet Finch had the following children:
(3) Susan Collins, b. c1841, IN
(4) Elizabeth Collins, b. c1842, IN
(5) Amelia Alisa Collins*, b. 30 Jun 1844, IN, d. 1908, Randolph Co., IN, bur. Hopewell Cem., Randolph Co., IN
    m. 6 Mar 1871, Jay Co., IN, David C. Garringer
(6) Catherine Collins, b. c1846, IN
(7) Joseph Collins, b. c1848, IN
(8) William Harrison Collins, b. c1849, IN, d. 2 Apr 1930
    m. 12 Dec 1872, Randolph Co., IN, Sarah Ellen Garringer
(9) Melissa Collins, b. c1852, IN
(10) John Collins, b. c1854, IN

Joseph Collins died on 25 Feb 1873 and his second wife Harriet died on 2 Aug 1881 and both are buried in Bost (also called Flesher) Cemetery in Jefferson Township of Jay County. There are several descendants of this Collins family who still reside in Jay and Randolph Counties.

Their daughter, Amelia Alisa Collins, was born on 30 Jun 1844 in Jay County. Amelia married David Carson Garringer on 6 Mar 1871 in Jay County. Their son, Isaac Luther Garringer, was born on 15 Jun 1874 and was the father of Hilda Irene Garringer. David C. Garringer died on 10 Dec 1895 at the age of 57. David had been severely wounded in the Civil War and his death may have been related to problems relating to that wound. Amelia (Collins) Garringer died on 9 Jun 1908 and both are buried in Hopewell Cemetery in Green Township of Randolph County.

Amelia (Collins) Garringer, date unknown

Amelia (Collins) Garringer, widow of David C. Garringer
This house was built by David Garringer in 1894 or 1895.
The girl with Amelia is Ethel Finch, a niece who lived with Amelia.

The Finch Family

Harriet Finch is a paternal great grandmother of Hilda Irene Garringer through marriage to Joseph Collins. Harriet Finch was born 16 Mar 1821 in Ohio to William and Amelia (Jackson) Finch. The family moved to Indiana about 1837 and Harriet married Joseph Collins on 3 Nov 1839 in Jay County, Indiana, after his first wife died in 1838.

This Finch family goes back to Maryland where William Finch, the father of Harriet, was born in 1785. William's parents were Thomas and Alice (Stevens) Finch. Thomas Finch appears in the 1790 head of households list of Maryland in Frederick County as does a John Finch who is apparently his brother.

From the records of Frederick County, Maryland, there is a John Finch mentioned in a will in 1750 and a John Finch listed as a debtor in 1756. A Johann Finch was christened in St. Peters Lutheran Church at Woodshore in Frederick County on 4 May 1769. Parents were Matthis and Anna Marie Finch.

Finch is a more common surname than many so it makes research into this family line more difficult. There is an excellent book, *Finch Families of Dixie*, which lists many Finch families but the author has not been able to tie our Finch family into any of these lines. There were some Finch families in Maryland quite early. Several records show a Francis Finch in Kent County, Maryland as early as 1659. There are several references to a Finch family in Prince George's County, Maryland, from 1681 to 1776 with the first name Thomas and William being frequently mentioned. No link has been found to this Prince George's County Finch family and our Thomas Finch of Frederick County in the work done to date but there may be some link. Much of this early research was obtained from Vianna Finch of Sheridan, Missouri.

Thomas Finch married Alice Stevens on 13 Dec 1783 in Baltimore, Maryland. Thomas and Alice Finch of Frederick County, Maryland, had known and probable children:

(1) William Finch*, b. 1784, MD, d. 16 Oct 1863, Jay Co., IN
    m. 1809, VA, Amelia Jackson, d. 9 Apr 1855, Jay Co., IN, d/o James and Martha (Thomas) Jackson
(2) John Finch, b. c1785, MD, (?1850 Frederick Co., MD census)
(3) Thomas Finch, Jr.
(4) Adam Finch, b. c1790, MD
    m. 29 Jul 1823, Columbiana Co., OH, Susanah Atterholt
(5) Samuel Finch, b. c1796
    m. 9 Feb 1820, Columbiana Co., OH, Hannah Williams

The 1790 Maryland heads of households shows on page 70 a Thomas Finch with a profile of 4M<16, 1M>16, 1F and 5 slaves. On page 62 of the same there is a John Finch with a similar profile. The 1800 Maryland census does not list any Finch families. The 1820 Maryland census lists a T. Finch in Frederick County while the 1830 Maryland census lists only a John Finch in Frederick County.

From the birth locations in later censuses of some of the Finch children, it appears that Thomas Finch moved his family to Virginia some time around 1808. They most likely moved to somewhere in the Shenandoah Valley. There is a William Finch in 1810 in Faquier County so they may have been there. Some time around 1818-1820, our Finch family moved to Columbiana County, Ohio. It is not known when or where the father Thomas Finch died but it was probably before 1820.

The 1820 Ohio census for Columbiana County shows:
pg. 43 William Finch, 3M<10, 1M26-45, 2F<10, 1F26-45
pg. 74, Saml Finch, 1M<10, 1M18-26, 1F<10, 1F26-45
pg. 77, Thomas Finch, 1M16-18, 2M18-26, 1M45+, 1F16-25, 1F45+

The 1830 Columbiana County, Ohio census lists:
William Finch, 1M<5, 1M5-10, 2 M10-15, 1M40-50, 1F<5, 2F5-10, 1F10-15, 1F15-20 and 1F40-50
Adam Finch, 1M30-40,3F<5, 1F5-10, 1F20-30
Sam Finch, 2M<5, 2M5-10, 1 M10-15, 1M30-40, 1F20-30
Dawson Finch, 2M<5, 1M5-10, 1M30-40, 1F<5, 1F20-30

Then in 1837, William Finch moved his family to Jefferson Township of Jay County, Indiana. Apparently, not all of William's brothers moved with him since several of his brothers still appear in the 1840 Columbiana County census.

The 1840 Columbiana County, Ohio census shows 4 Finch families still residing there, Joshua Finch, age 60-70, Joseph Finch, age 15-20, Adam Finch, age 50-60, and Samuel Finch, age 40-50. The 60-70 year old Joshua Finch may be an uncle of our William Finch and he apparently migrated to Ohio much later than the rest of the family.

The 1840 Indiana census lists for Jay County:
William Finch, 1M<5, 1M5-10, 1M15-20, 2M20-30, 1M50-60, 1F<5, 1F5-10, 1F10-15, 1F15-20, 1F40-50
Mandeville Finch, 2M<5, 1M30-40, 1F<5, 1F5-10, 1F20-30

Family records say that William Finch married Amelia Jackson, the daughter of James and Martha (Thomas) Jackson about 1809, probably in Virginia. No marriage record has been found to confirm this.

William and Amelia (Jackson) Finch had these children:
(1) Mandeville Finch, b. 1810, VA, d. 1846
(2) Adelaide Finch, b. 1811, VA
    m. 5 Mar 1840, Jay Co., IN, William Nixon
(3) William Finch, Jr., b. 1814, VA, d. 1894
    m. 29 Jun 1848, Randolph Co., IN, Sarah Ann Shoemaker
    m. 2nd Mary Ann Atkinson, b. 1828, d. 1908
(4) John Finch, b. 1816, VA
    m. Melinda ?
(5) Elizabeth Finch, b. 1819
    m. 5 Mar 1840, Jay Co., IN, Jacob Nixon
(6) Harriet Finch*, b. 16 Mar 1821, d. 2 Aug 1884
    m. 3 Nov 1839, Jay Co., IN, Joseph Collins
(7) Martha Finch, b. 1823, OH
    m. 4 Jun 1840, Jay Co., IN, Jacob Kerns
(8) James Finch, b. 1825, OH, d. 28 Sep 1899, Jay Co., IN
    m. 1847, Ruth A. Carley
(9) Catherine Finch, b. 1827, OH
(10) Leander Finch, b. 1832, OH, d. 17 Apr 1903, Jay Co., IN
(11) Joseph Finch, b. 1834, OH

Mandeville died in 1846 but some of his descendants later moved to Missouri.

William Finch, Jr. married first to Sarah Ann Shoemaker on 29 Jun 1848 in Randolph County and they had one child Edgar born 1849 who apparently died young. Sarah apparently died shortly after the 1850 census because William later married Mary Ann Atkinson. William Finch, Jr. and Mary Ann Atkinson had a large family of:

(1) Margaret Ellen Finch, b. 1852, m. Higgenlathem
(2) Elizabeth Amelia Finch, b. 1855
(3) Sarah Ann Finch, b. 1857, m. ? McDow
(4) Thomas Finch, b. 1859
(5) Martha Finch, b. 1860, d. 1948
    m. 1882, Clousa Co., CA, John McMartin
(6) William Finch, b. 1862, d. 1931
    m. Anna Latimer
(7) Ulysses Grant Finch, b. 1864, d. 1882
(8) Elzora Finch, b. 1867, d. 1874
(9) Lincoln Ellsworth Finch, b. 1871
    m. 1896, Harriet Appers

William and Mary Ann Finch moved their family to Glenn County, California, in the 1880s.

The 1850 Jay County, Indiana census lists:
pg. 248 William Finch, 65, farmer, MD
Amelia Finch, 59, VA
Catherine Finch, 23, OH
Leander Finch, 18, OH
J. Thomas Finch, 16, OH

pg. 352 James Finch, 25, OH
Ruth A. Finch, 21, OH
Clavinda Finch, 2, IN
William M. Finch, 1, IN

pg. 353 William Finch, Jr. 36, VA
Sarah A. Finch, OH
Edgar Finch, 1, IN

pg. 353 John Finch, 34, VA
Melanda Finch, 30, VA

Harriet Finch married Joseph Collins about two years after they moved from Ohio to Jay County, Indiana. The Collins family was earlier in Warren County, Ohio, but there is no evidence that they were associated with the Finch family before moving to Indiana.

Joseph Collins died on 25 Feb 1873 and Harriet (Finch) Collins died in 1884. They are both buried in Bost (also called Flesher) Cemetery, located in Jefferson Township of Jay County, Indiana. Joseph's gravestone was toppled and in need of repair when the cemetery was last visited.

Harriet (Finch) Collins' parents, William and Amelia (Jackson) Finch, are buried in Wentz Cemetery in Jay County, Indiana

There are still a few Finch families which live in Jay and Randolph Counties, Indiana.

The Morris Family

Elizabeth Morris is the maternal grandmother of Hilda Irene Garringer. She was born on 25 Sep 1845 in Clinton County, Ohio, and married Elijah Oliver Hammers on 1 Oct 1864 in Randolph County, Indiana. Elizabeth "Libby" Morris was the daughter of George and Anceline (Grove) Morris. Elijah Oliver and Elizabeth (Morris) Hammers had four children, Arthur Leroy Hammers, Bertha Achsah Hammers*, William Blane Hammers and Lucy Irene Hammers. The name Irene may have come from Lucy Irene Hammers who married William Huston and was an aunt to Hilda Irene Garringer. Elijah Hammers died on 10 May 1920 and Elizabeth (Morris) Hammers died two years later on 7 Jun 1922. They are buried in the Woodlawn Cemetery at Maxville, Randolph County, Indiana.

Janet M. Morris of Bluffton, Indiana, researched the Morris family and wrote the Morris family history in 1977 and most of the following summary is from her book. In her book she relates that the family name Morris comes from Welsh "Mawr-rwyce" meaning "strong or brave in battle."

The earliest that we can trace our Morris line is to a John Morris who was born on 3 Mar 1680. It is unclear who his parents were but they may have been a John and Elizabeth Morris. There are at least two records of Morris families who came to America before 1680. In 1660, a John Morris and two brothers, Caleb and Phineas, emigrated from Wales to North America and settled in the counties of Pasquotank and Perquimans, in northeast North Carolina. One of these brothers might be our John Morris' father. Another Morris line, also a John Morris (born about 1595) migrated from England aboard the ship *Bona Nova* in November 1619 to Jamestown, Virginia. Some stories say this John Morris was driven out of Virginia for religious reasons and later moved to the Perquimans/Pasquotank area of North Carolina.

Our John Morris was born in 1680, probably in Virginia, and married 4 Sep 1703, Mary Symons, the daughter of Thomas and

Rebecca (White) Symons. Mary Symons was born on 4 Dec 1687 in either Virginia or North Carolina. Thomas Symons was born about 1648 and married Rebecca White, the daughter of Henry and Rebecca (Arnold) White.

Henry White originally lived in James City County, Virginia, but he later moved to Albemarle County, North Carolina, about 1664 due to persecution from the church in Virginia. He acquired a large land grant in North Carolina and died there about 1669.

John and Mary (Symons) Morris had the following children:
(1) Aaron Morris, b. 14 Jul 1704, d. 10 Sep 1770
    m. Jul 1724, Mary Pritchard
(2) Elizabeth Morris, b. 6 Sep 1707
    m. ? William Symons
(3) Joseph Morris, b. 4 Dec 1709
    m. 2 Oct 1730, Elizabeth Pritchard
(4) Sarah Morris, b. 6 Sep 1712
    m. Samuel Moore
(5) John Morris, b. 21 Dec 1716, nfi
(6) Mary Morris, b. 11 Nov 1719, d. 1760
    m. 3 Jan 1738, John Robinson
(7) Zachariah Morris*, b. 23 Sep 1722, d. 2 Mar 1809
    m. 2 Sep 1752, Anne Williams
(8) Hannah Morris, b. 23 Dec 1726
    m. 6 Oct 1750, William Bundy
(9) Isaac Morris, d. 13 Feb 1762, nfi

John Morris died at the age of 59 on 30 Sep 1739 in Pasquotank County, North Carolina. His will was probated on 18 Nov 1739 and lists his wife Mary as Executrix and lists his sons John, Zachariah, Isaac, Aaron and Joseph and daughters Hannah and Sarah. Evidently, his son John inherited the manor plantation.

Zachariah Morris, son of John and Mary (Symons) Morris

Our Morris line descends from Zachariah Morris who was born 23 Sep 1722 in Perquinmans/Pasquotank County, North Carolina. These two counties are in the northeastern corner of North Carolina and the Morris family is recorded in both counties so it is not clear exactly in which county Zachariah was born.

Zachariah Morris married Anne Williams on 1 Nov 1752 in Perquimans County. Anne was born on 12 Dec 1727 to John and Sarah (Sutton) Williams. The Morris family was of the Quaker religion, and Zachariah is listed as being chosen an overseer on 4 Feb 1762 in the Perquimans Monthly Meeting. In 1776, Zachariah moved his family to Wayne County, North Carolina, probably because of the opening up of new lands. Wayne County is in the east central part of North Carolina and contains the city of Goldsboro.

Zachariah and Anne (Williams) Morris are thought to have the following children:
(1) Isaac Morris*, b. NC, d. c1825, Grayson Co., VA
    m. 14 Sep 1788, Wayne Co., NC, Millicent Bundy
(2) Jeremiah Morris
    m. 22 Feb 1789, Wayne Co., NC, Margaret Charles
(3) Thomas Morris
    m. 19 Nov 1789, Wayne Co., NC, Sarah Musgreave
(4) Zachariah Morris, Jr.
(5) Mary Morris, b. c1753, d. 13 Dec 1799
    m. 20 Jun 1779, Wayne Co., NC, Richard Davis

Anne (Williams) Morris died on 28 Apr 1795 at the age of 67. Zachariah Morris died 2 Mar 1809 in Wayne County at the age of 86.

Isaac Morris, son of Zachariah and Anne (Williams) Morris

The first record of Isaac Morris, our direct line descendant, is his marriage to Millicent Bundy on 14 Sep 1788 recorded at the Contentney Meeting House in Wayne County, North Carolina. Isaac Morris moved his family west to Surry County, North Carolina, by 1799 where they show up in the Westfield Monthly Meeting records. By 1801, they had moved again a short distance northwest over the state line into Grayson County, Virginia, where they are recorded in the Mount Pleasant Monthly Meeting.

Isaac and Millicent (Bundy) Morris had the following children:
(1) Zachariah Morris, b. 21 Aug 1789, NC (veteran of the War of 1812)
(2) Demsey Morris, b. 15 Mar 1791, NC
(3) Nathan Morris, b. 24 Sep 1792, d. 11 Mar 1793

(4) Jeremiah Morris, b. 25 Jan 1794, NC, d. 15 Sep 1826
(5) David Morris*, b. 10 Jan 1796, NC, d. 17 Sep 1879, Fayette Co., OH
    m. 1819, Highland Co., OH, Nancy Cooper
    m. 2nd c1838, Sarah Moore
(6) John Morris, b. 19 Dec 1797, d. 29 Aug 1886
    m. Ruth Stanley
    m. 2nd Mary Stanley
(7) Zadok Morris, b. 29 Aug 1800, VA, d. 4 Sep 1888
    m. Lydia Barnett
    m. 2nd Ruth (Cary) McPherson
(8) Isaac Morris, b. 8 Oct 1802, Grayson Co., VA, d. 15 Nov 1862, Highland Co., OH
    m. Marie Cooper
    m. 2nd Millicent Johnson
(9) James Morris, b. c1804, VA, d. 8 May 1878, OH
    m. Elizabeth Hanes
    m. 2nd Hannah Whinery
    m. 3rd Hannah G. Ladd
(10) Nancy Morris
    m. Fayette Co., OH, Elisha Sexton
(11) Sarah Morris
    m. Phillip Beamer
(12) daughter, m. Pleasant Haynes

Isaac Morris's last home was located on a mountain top about halfway between Hillsville and Fancy Gap in Grayson County, Virginia. Isaac Morris died in 1825 or 1826 in Grayson County and is thought to be buried on his homesite. Millicent (Bundy) Morris outlived her husband and moved with some of her children to Ohio. According to one source, Millicent (Bundy) Morris is buried in the Sharon Church Cemetery at Kingman, Chester Township, Clinton County, Ohio.

Five of the sons of Isaac Morris migrated to Ohio. John and Zadok Morris first came to Clinton County about 1818 but returned to Virginia within a year. John later settled in Highland County then later moved to near Waynesville, Ohio. Zadok Morris moved to Fayette County about 1820, and his brother Isaac also moved about 1823 to land nearby in Fayette County. In 1830, Isaac was shown to be in nearby Paint Township of Highland County. Son James Morris also moved to Clinton

County and settled on land about one mile south of Memphis. After James's death in 1878, his widow and a son moved west to Kansas.

David Morris, son of Isaac and Millicent (Bundy) Morris

Our direct line ancestor is son David Morris who was born 10 Jan 1796 in North Carolina but grew up in Grayson County, Virginia. David migrated to Highland County, Ohio, about 1818 and he married Nancy Cooper in 1819 in that county.

David and Nancy (Cooper) Morris had the following children:
(1) Isaac Morris, b. 29 Aug 1820, OH, d. 8 Oct 1901, Randolph Co., IN, bur. Woodlawn Cem., Randolph Co., IN
   m. 20 Jul 1844, Clinton Co., OH, Jane Martin
   m. 2nd 3 Jul 1851, Clinton Co., OH, Rachel Luckey
(2) Elkanah Morris, b. 28 Feb 1822, OH, d. 1 Oct 1902, Randolph Co., IN, bur. Woodlawn Cem., Randolph Co., IN
   m. 8 Jun 1843, Fayette or Clinton Co., OH, Keziah McVey
(3) George Morris*, b. 17 Mar 1824, Fayette Co., OH, d. 11 Jul 1901, near Panora, Guthrie Co., IA
   m. 28 Jan 1845, Clinton Co., OH, Anceline Grove, b. 23 Jun 1828, d. 2 Mar 1864
   m. 2nd 21 Aug 1864, Randolph Co., IN, Mrs. Martha Wesley
(4) Cooper Morris, b. 30 Oct 1825, Fayette Co., OH, d. 12 Sep 1905, Farmland, Randolph Co., IN, bur. Woodlawn Cem., Randolph Co., IN
   m. 30 Jun 1849, Fayette Co., OH, Susan Roberts
(5) Jeremiah Morris, b. 14 Oct 1827, OH, d. 27 Aug 1828, OH
(6) Nancy Morris, b. 27 Jul 1829, OH, d. 15 Jun 1911, Randolph Co., IN, bur. Woodlawn Cem., Randolph Co., IN
   m. 15 Apr 1858, Fayette Co., OH, John F. Myers
   m. 2nd 7 Sep 1871, Jonathan Thornburg
(7) Mary Morris, b. 7 May 1831, OH, d. 4 Mar 1847, Fayette Co., OH
(8) Millicent M. Morris, b. 3 Jul 1833, OH, d. 22 Apr 1919, Randolph Co., IN, bur. Fountain Park Cem., Winchester, IN
   m. 4 Sep 1852, Fayette Co., OH, John Van Pelt

Nancy (Cooper) Morris died on 3 Dec 1835 in Fayette County at the age of 34. David Morris then married second Sarah Moore on 28 Nov 1838 in Fayette County.

David and his second wife Sarah Moore had the following children:

(9) David Morris, Jr., b. 17 Sep 1839, Fayette Co., OH, d. 21 Jan 1920, Randolph Co., IN, bur. Woodlawn Cem., Randolph Co., IN

m. 12 Oct 1862, Highland Co., OH, Charilla Ann Holmes

(10) Lydia Morris, b. 19 Jul 1841, OH, d. 4 Oct 1844, Fayette Co., OH

(11) Elizabeth H. Morris, b. 30 Jun 1844, OH, d. 19 Mar 1930, Randolph Co., IN

m. 13 Sep 1866, Randolph Co., IN, William Bailey

(12) Keziah Morris, b. 31 Jul 1846, OH, d. 4 Feb 1929, Farmland, IN

m. 23 Aug 1871, Farmland, IN, William James

(13) Sarah Morris, b. 12 Oct 1848, OH, d. 17 Jul 1926, Farmland, IN, bur. Woodlawn Cem., Randolph Co., IN

m. 18 Oct 1866, Fayette Co., OH, Benjamin Franklin Hill

(14) Lavina Morris, b. 9 Mar 1851, d. 9 Mar 1920, Sweetwater, TN

m. 18 Jun 1870, Fayette Co., OH, Sylvester Decker

(15) William Morris, b. 12 May 1853, OH, d. 11 Jul 1864, Fayette Co., OH

(16) Lucinda Morris, b. 31 Dec 1855, OH, d. 5 Oct 1922, Highland Co., OH

m. 22 May 1877, Fayette Co., OH, Thomas Achor

Although several of his children moved further west to Indiana, David Morris remained in Ohio and died there on 17 Sep 1879 at the age of 83. David is buried at the Old Fairfield Cemetery, south of Leesburg. His second wife, Sarah, died earlier on 25 Mar 1866 and is buried beside her husband. Their gravestones, although very weathered, can still be read.

Almost all of the sons and several of the daughters of David Morris that survived to adulthood moved to Randolph County, Indiana. The two youngest daughters, Lavina and Lucinda, married in Fayette County and did not make the westward trek. Son Cooper may have been the first to move in about 1851 but sons Isaac, Elkanah and George all appear to also have moved to Randolph County by 1856. The older children of David Morris by his second wife Sarah Moore moved to Randolph County in the 1860s.

The sons of David Morris settled in Monroe Township of Randolph County. The 1865 Plat Map of Randolph County shows land owners G. Morris (section 10), I. Morris, E. Morris (section 15), C. Morris, L. Morris, J. Morris (section 2), G. Morris, K. Morris and D. Morris (section 34) in Monroe Township. The map also shows the town of Morristown which is located in the southwestern corner of Monroe Township near the county border with Delaware County.

The town of Morristown was named for the Morris family but few details are known about why it was. Tucker's 1882 *History of Randolph County* says the town was first recorded in Nov 1851 and lists three proprietors, William E. Harris, Joseph Lewis and Allen W. Lewis. Another addition was added in 1857 by John Jones. The history also gives the merchants over the years, but again no Morris is listed. It is referred to in the 1882 history as Morristown, Parker Post Office. The 1865 Randolph County map shows no properties in the town owned by a Morris. There are several Morris farms one to two miles to the east of Morristown. The 1876 Plat Map still lists the town as Morristown and there is a steam saw mill on the eastern edge of the town owned by a J. Morris. The 1909 *Randolph County Atlas* lists only the name Parker. The city is currently referred to as Parker City.

A John Morris is listed in the Tucker's 1882 *History of Randolph County* as having served in the 57th Indiana Infantry during the Civil War and dying at Louisville, Kentucky on 7 Jul 1864. Also a William Morris served in the same regiment and died 7 Oct 1863 in Knoxville, Tennessee.

Three of the four oldest sons of David Morris, Isaac, Elkanah and Cooper, all remained in Randolph County where they raised their families and each is buried with his wife in Woodlawn Cemetery.

George Morris, son of David and Nancy (Cooper) Morris

Our direct line ancestor is George Morris who was born in Fayette County, Ohio, on 17 Mar 1824. He married Anceline Grove, daughter of Abraham and Elizabeth (Reed) Grove on 20 Jan 1845 in Clinton County, Ohio. George moved his family to Randolph County, Indiana, about 1852 and bought land in section 34 of Monroe Township. Anceline (Grove) Morris died on 2 Mar 1864. George then married on 21 Aug 1864 to Mrs. Martha Wesley.

George and Anceline (Grove) Morris had the following children:
(1) Elizabeth Morris*, b. 25 Sep 1845, OH, d. 7 Jun 1922,
     Farmland, IN, bur. Woodlawn Cem., Randolph Co., IN
     m. 1 Oct 1864, Randolph Co., IN, Elijah Oliver Hammers
(2) Achsah Morris, b. 26 Feb 1847, d. 1926, Randolph Co., IN,
     bur. Woodlawn Cem., Randolph Co., IN
     m. 26 Sep 1863, Randolph Co., IN, Hiram Milton Taylor
(3) William Henry Morris, b. 12 Jun 1849, Clinton Co., OH
     m. 26 May 1870, Randolph Co., IN, Eliza McCamey
(4) Catherine Morris, b. 31 May 1851, Clinton Co., OH, d. 30 Jun
     1930, bur. Rockwell City, IA
     m. 28 Dec 1871, Panora, IA, William Newton Haltom
(5) David Abraham Morris, b. 16 Oct 1853, Randolph Co., IN,
     dnm, bur. East Cem., Panora, IA
(6) Millicent "Malissa" Morris, b. 21 Sep 1855, Randolph Co., IN,
     d. 7 Mar 1936, Green Co., IA
     m. 19 Dec 1878, David Henry Secrist
(7) John Hamilton Morris, b. 17 Apr 1858, Randolph Co., IN, d.
     25 Jan 1916, Panora, IA
     m. 25 Nov 1880, Guthrie Co., IA, Armadilla Syrentya
     McLaren
(8) Anceline Morris, b. 25 Jan 1864, Randolph Co., IN, d. c1932,
     MN
     m. William LeFevre

George Morris moved his family to Iowa about 1870 and settled in Guthrie County near the town of Panora, which is located about 50 miles west of Des Moines. His two oldest daughters had married before then and remained in Randolph County.

The oldest daughter, Elizabeth, married Elijah Oliver Hammers on 1 Oct 1864 in Randolph County. They had two sons, Arthur Leroy and William Blaine, and two daughters, Bertha Achsah and Lucy Irene. When Hilda Irene Garringer was born, her mother, Bertha, was sick for a long time so her grandparents "Lige" and "Libby" Hammers cared for her for her first year. Elijah was a farmer in Monroe Township for all of his adult life and died in 1920. Elizabeth died two years later in 1922, and both are buried in the Woodlawn Cemetery.

The Grove(s) Family

Anceline Groves is a maternal great grandmother of Hilda Irene Garringer through marriage into the Morris family and later into the Hammers family. Anceline Groves was born in 1828 in Virginia and migrated with her parents Abraham and Elizabeth (Reed) Groves to Clinton County, Ohio, in about 1834. Anceline married in 1845 in Clinton County to George Morris when she was only 16. By the 1850 census when she was 21, she already had three children, Elizabeth, age 4, Achsah, age 3 and William H., age 1. In 1865, Elizabeth Morris married Elijah Oliver Hammers and is Hilda Irene Garringer's maternal grandmother.

The family name Grove or Groves is spelled both ways with and without the "s." There often appears to be no preference for which way it is spelled. The Grove or Groves name sounds English in origin but it has been spelled other ways, such as Graf, Graff, Groff or Grovez. There were some German and Swiss families which spelled it Graff and later anglicized it to Grove(s). The first names most often found in the families appear to be English but some data say that the origin of our Grove(s) is probably German/Swiss.

Our Grove family can be traced to Frederick County, Virginia, where there was a large concentration of Grove and Groves starting before 1770. The earliest Grove ancestor appears to be a Jacob Grove who was born about 1730 and lived between Martinsburg and the Cacapon River. We know that Jacob had one son John from which our line descends. There were two other sons listed in his will and there were probably others but they have not been found or identified. This Jacob Grove wrote his will on 26 Jul 1794 and it was probated on 2 Dec 1794. In the will it mentions his wife Margaret and three sons: John, James and D. Vance.

There are other Grove(s) families in Frederick County, Virginia, but how or whether they are related to our Jacob Grove has not been determined.

One of the Groves that is listed in Frederick County records is an Abraham Grove, born 1 Mar 1762, who was listed as a Revolutionary War soldier. Abraham Grove later married Rosanna Wetzel and lived in Frederick County until he died on 31 Dec 1847. Abraham and Rosanna Grove had at least one son, John W. Grove, who was born in 1791, lived in Stephens City, Virginia, all of his life and died there in 1873. The name Abraham later appears in our descendant line so this may be a related family.

A will recorded in 1782 in Frederick County for a Mathias Grove listed children: John, Mary (m. Pfeifer), George, Abraham (1762-1847), Jacob, Michael (1766-1841), Daniel and Mary. Mathias is apparently the father of the Abraham discussed above. Son Jacob is probably the Jacob who married Elizabeth Kaile in 1797 in Frederick County.

An earlier will dated 1760 of a Matthew Grove listed a widow Ester and children: William, Elizabeth, Michael, Ester and Matthew.

Our line descends from John Grove who was born in 1750 to Jacob and Margaret Grove. John and his wife Mary, maiden name unknown, had the following children:
(1) Jacob Grove*, b. 1774, Frederick Co., VA, d. 11 Nov 1860, Clinton Co., OH
    m. 13 Oct 1795, Frederick Co., VA, Catherine Lonas, b. 1775, VA, d. 2 Dec 1862, Clinton Co., OH
(2) Adam Grove,
    m. 6 Aug 1795, Frederick Co., VA, Eve Shiner
(3) Henry Grove
    m. 22 Nov 1788, Frederick Co., VA, Mary Lawyer
(4) John Grove, m. Eleanor ?
(5) Samuel Grove, m. Elizabeth ?
(6) Peter Grove, m. Mary ?
(7) Margaret Grove, m. 2 May 1804, Jacob Gibbens
(8) Rachel Grove, m. George Shiner

The following marriages are also recorded in Frederick County around the time that our Jacob Grove married Catherine Lonas on 13 Oct 1795:

Elizabeth Grove m. Abraham Mason, 11 Dec 1786
Ann Groves m. Nicholas Karns, 23 Sep 1788
Elizabeth Groves m. Michael Pierce, 30 Aug 1790
Catherine Grove m. Matthias Hite, 29 Oct 1792
Daniel Grove m. Eve Samsel, 14 Nov 1792
Michael Grove m. Elizabeth Butler, 14 May 1793
Henry Grove m. Susannah Kline, 27 Sep 1795
Sarah Grove m. John Nicewanger, 8 Oct 1795
Mary Grove m. John Lester, 29 Jan 1797
Jacob Grove m. Elizabeth Kaile, 28 Feb 1797
Anna Groves m. John Samsell, 28 Sep 1797
Solomon Grove m. Fanny Marquis, 10 May 1798
Peter Grove m. Phebe Arnold, 21 Jun 1798
William Grove m. Mary Ann Thompson, 30 Dec 1802
Susannah Groves m. Henry Oldacre, 12 Jan 1803

Most or at least several of these Groves are probably related to our Jacob Grove.

The 1790 Virginia census listed only three Grove families in Frederick County: Abraham, Jacob and John with this John probably being the father of our Jacob. The Abraham Grove is probably the son of Mathias who was born in 1762 and fought in the Revolutionary War. There were also some Groves recorded in Shenandoah County which borders on Frederick County and even more recorded in Augusta County which borders on that county. All these Groves may be related since the male first names seem common among the families.

Jacob and Catherine (Lonas) Grove had the following identified children:

(1) John Groves, b. 9 Feb 1797, d. 1858, IA
    m. 17 Mar 1825, Nancy Waln, m. 2nd 30 Jun 1845, Mary (Waln) Keedick
(2) Henry Lonas Groves, b. 1800, Frederick Co., VA
(3) Abraham Groves*, b. 1804, Frederick Co., VA, d. 29 Sep 1876, Randolph Co., IN
    m. 8 Apr 1826, Frederick County, Co., VA, Elizabeth Reed
(4) David Groves, b. c1807, VA, m. Mary ?
(5) Mary Groves

(6) George Groves, b. c1818, VA, m. Mary Babb

The 1810 Frederick County census lists the following household heads:
John Grove*, age 45+
Henry Grove, age 45+
Peter Grove, age 45+
John Grove, age 45+
Adam Groves, age 26-45
Daniel Grove, age 26-45
Ezra Grove, age 26-45
Betsey Grove, age 26-45
Henry Grove, age 26-45
Jacob Grove, age 26-45
William Grove, age 26-45
David Grove, age 18-26
John Grove, age 18-26

The 1820 Frederick County, Virginia census lists 19 Grove or Groves families headed by: Abraham (2), Adam, Daniel, David, Henry (2), Henry Jr., Isaac, Jacob (2), James, John Sr., John Jr., John W., Peter, William H., Elijah and Mary.

The 1830 Frederick County, Virginia, census lists 23 households headed by Grove, Groves or Grovez. All are in the East District and tend to be listed in two page groupings so it can be assumed that they are also related in some way. An Abraham Grovez is listed on page 59 of the census as age 20-30 with wife age 20-30, 1 female, age 10-15, 1 female age < 5 (Anciline, b. 1828), 1 male age <5 (David). This description closely fits what we know about our Abraham's family.

Anceline Groves' father, Abraham Groves, was born in Virginia in 1804 according to later census data. On 8 Apr 1826, he married Elizabeth Reed according to Frederick County records. Sometime between the 1830 census and 1834, several Groves families left Virginia and migrated to Clinton County, Ohio.

The 1840 Clinton County, Ohio, census lists Adam Grove (age 30-40), another Adam Grove (age 30-40), David Grove (age 30-40), Henry L. Grove (age 40-50), Jacob Grove (age 60-70), and John Grove in Wayne Township. Jacob Grove (age 30-40) was listed in Green Township and William Grove (age 30-40) was also listed in Union Township. No Abraham Groves was found but perhaps he was listed as one of the Adams. One Adam has his family listed as 1M30-40, 1F 20-30, 1F10-15 (Anciline), 1M 10-15 (David), 1F5-10, 2F<5 (Rebecca,?) and 1 M<5 (William). This profile does not exactly fit our Abraham but is very close.

Clinton County, Ohio, marriages involving Grove or Groves during this period were:
Adam L. Grove m. Rachel Antrim, 9 Jan 1834
Jacob Grove m. Hannah Carter, 6 Jan 1836
George Grove m. Martha Babb
Henry Grove m. Margaret Ann Goffs, 1 Jul 1841
Abraham Grove m. Elizabeth A. Canter
Susan Ann Groves m. Avery Griffith, 12 Jan 1852
David Grove m. Susan Hill, 31 Aug 1854

The 1850 Clinton County, Ohio, census lists in Wayne Township:
George Morris*, 22, Farmer, b. OH
Ansaline*, 21, VA
Elizabeth*, 4, OH
Aschsah, 3, OH
William H., 1 OH

Abraham Groves, 46,VA
Elizabeth, 35, VA
William, 16, OH
Rebecca, 14, OH
Alfred, 9, OH
Elizabeth, 7, OH
Isaac, 9/12, OH

David Groves, 43, VA
Mary, 42?,VA
Susan, 20, VA
Abraham, 17, KY
Sophiah, 14, OH
Elizabeth, 8, OH
Charles, 6, OH
Hannah, 3, OH

Jacob Groves, 76, VA

Catherine, 75, VA
Henry L. Groves, 50, VA
Catherine, 47, VA

George Groves, 32, VA
Martha, 30, TN
Elizabeth Babb, 66, TN
Malinda Babb, 24, TN

Jacob and Catherine Groves' assumed children since they were living so close together were Henry L. (b. 1800), Abraham (b. 1804), David (b. 1808), and George (b. 1818) and possible others unknown. Jacob and evidently most of his children migrated to Ohio between 1830 and 1834. His son John Grove apparently did not migrate to Ohio and later migrated to Iowa, apparently with some of his wife's family.

From census data and a few available biographies, we know that Abraham and Elizabeth (Reed) Groves had the following children:
(1) Anceline Grove*, b. 1828, VA. d. 1864, IN
    m. George Morris
(2) David Grove, b. 1831, VA
    m. 31 Aug 1854, Clinton Co., OH, Susan Hill
(3) William R. Grove, b. 27 Mar 1834, Clinton Co., OH
    m. Mary Smith
(4) Rebecca Grove, b. 1836, OH
(5) Alfred Hance Grove, b. 6 Aug 1841, Clinton Co., OH
    m. 8 Jul 1865, Louisa Morris
(6) Elizabeth Grove, b. 1843, Clinton Co., OH
(7) Isaac Grove, b. 1849, Clinton Co., OH
    m. Eliza Samantha Stump
(8) Mary E. Grove, b. 1852, Clinton Co., OH

Abraham Groves moved his family to Randolph County, Indiana, some time between 1855 and 1860 when he appears in the 1860 census. Apparently, none of the rest of the Groves families moved to Indiana at this time according to the census data. In the 1860 census, William Grove, age 26 is listed as a farm laborer in the household of George and Anceline Morris.

Abraham Groves farmed in Monroe Township until his death on 29 Sep 1876. He was buried in Rehobeth Cemetery in Monroe Township. When that cemetery was visited in 1978, his gravestone was loose and propped up against another but was still very readable.

Abraham Groves gravestone at Rehobeth Cemetery, 1978

Anceline (Grove) Morris died at age of 35 on 2 Mar 1864 in Randolph Co., Indiana. She is buried in Rehobeth Cemetery.

According to a biography in the 1912 Smith and Driver *History of Randolph County, Indiana:* William R. Groves, a son of Abraham and Elizabeth (Reed) Groves, spent his first 25 years in Ohio before migrating to Randolph County, Indiana. In April 1863, he married Mary Smith, daughter of Benjamin and Margaret (McDonald) Smith. They had three children: Irene, who married William B. Hammers; Minnie; and Benjamin (b. 22 Feb 1905) who married Minnie Anderson. After William's wife Mary died on 30 May 1872, he married Sarah Jones on 28 Apr 1874. William farmed in Green Township until his death on 28 January 1877. He is buried in Rehobeth Cemetery. In the 1910 Indiana census Sarah Grove, age 68, is listed in Monroe Township with step grandsons, Arthur Groves, age 17; Garfield, age 16; and Willard, age 13; evidently sons of Benjamin Groves.

Son David Grove married Susan A. Hill on 13 Aug 1854 in Clinton County, Ohio, and they had eight children, including Daniel Webster (b. c1857, d. 1930, bur. Woodlawn Cem., m. 14 Dec 1878, Martha E. Hupp); son Charles Edward (b. 1886, d. 1968, m. Mary Hafkemlier); Alfred M. (b. c1882, d. 4 Jun 1900, m. 13 Jun 1891, Hattie B. Williams); and John B. (b. c1859). David Groves initially bought a farm between Parker and Farmland but later moved to a farm in Monroe Township. Susan (Hill) Grove died on 3 Jan 1878 and is buried in Rehobeth Cemetery. David Grove died in 1901.

Son Alfred Hance Groves married in Randolph County on 8 Jul 1865 to Louisa Morris, the daughter of Elkanah and Keziah (McVey) Morris. Alfred and Louisa (Morris) Groves moved about 1882 to Harvey County, Kansas, and later to Newton, Kansas. They had seven children: Bennett (b. c1867), Logan (b. 1868), Milroy Elbert (b. 1870), Rilla Ann (b. 1873), Orville (b. 1875), William Henry (b. 1877) and Ethel.

Son Isaac Groves married Eliza Samantha Stump about 1875, and they had at least four children.

The Reed Family

The Reed family is connected to the Grove family by the marriage of Elizabeth Reed to Abraham Grove which occurred 8 Apr 1826 in Frederick County, Virginia. They were married by Jacob Grove, probably the father of Abraham. There were several Reed families in Frederick County and it has not been possible to identify their origin and relationships. Some members of the Reed family must have made the move west, first to Clinton County, Ohio, and then to Randolph County, Indiana. In the 1860 Indiana census, a John Reed, age 24, born Ohio, was farming and living in the household of Abraham and Elizabeth Grove.

Migration Routes

One of the goals of my research has been to find out the nationality and migrations paths for our ancestors. The families on our maternal side seem to be mostly German with some English families. On our paternal side, the families are mainly Scotch and Scotch-Irish and some English.

For most of the families we only have a general idea of when they migrated from the "old" country or some legal reference that first records their presence in America.

These families took several different routes to Randolph County. The main routes were Virginia to Ohio to Indiana or Pennsylvania to Ohio to Indiana. None of the families came from further north than Pennsylvania. The Capps were down in South Carolina for a while and the Morris family was in North Carolina before moving back to Virginia.

The following tables are a chronological listing of the families with the names of our direct line ancestors and their family locations as they can best be determined.

Family Name — Timeline: 1750 1760 1770 1780 1790 1800 1810 1820 1830 1840 1850 1860 1870 1880 1890

BOGGS *(to Indiana 1906)*
Pennsylvania → Greenbrier Co., West Virginia
1864 Noah Edward "Ed" ———— 1932
1893
1828 John A. ———— 1876
c1722 Francis, Jr ———— 1795
1702 Francis ———— 1763

KINCAID
Virginia → Greenbrier Co., West Virginia
(married Noah Edward Boggs)
1870 Clora Jane ———— 1955
1844 William Samuel ———— 1882
aft 1880
1816 James ———— 1866
1788 Samuel Kincaid
1760 Andrew Kincaid
?

CARDER
Culpepper Co., VA → Taylor Co., West Virginia
(married John A. Boggs)
1828 Phoebe E. ———— 1899
c1852
1791 Joseph ———— c1850
1767 John

KNIGHT
Greenbrier Co., West Virginia
(married William Samuel Kincaid)
1847 Rachel Ellen ———— 1930
1889
1804 Andrew ———— 1855
c1780 James
1741 James, Sr. ———— 1794

MCMILLION
Greenbrier Co., West Virginia
(married Andrew Knight)
1807 Rebecca ———— 1884
c1771 John ———— c1845

McCLUNG
Greenbrier Co., West Virginia
(married Samuel Kincaid)
1788 Katharine ———— 1874
James ———— 1790

222

Family Name

GARRINGER

Pennsylvania .... Highland Co., Ohio .... Randolph Co., Indiana

(Hilda Irene Garringer married Samuel Plummer Boggs)

1874 Isaac Luther ----1940
----1895

1838 David C. ----
----1870

1812 Isaac Jacob
----1812

1772 David, Jr

1735 David, Sr ----

HAMMERS

Pennsylvania .... Licking Co., OH .... Randolph Co., Indiana

(married Isaac Luther Garringer)

1877 Bertha Achsah ----1918
----1920

1845 Elijah Oliver ----
----1894

1817 Abraham
----1838

c1786 Peter Jr. ----1838

1757 Peter ----

COLLINS

Virginia .... Highland Co., Ohio .... Jay Co., Indiana

(married David C. Garringer)

1844 Amelia ----1908

1809 Joseph ----1873

BOOTS

Pennsylvania .... Highland Co., Ohio .... Randolph Co., Indiana

(married Isaac Garringer)

1815 Sarah ----1882

1765 Garrett ----1819

1733 Adam ----1803

HARBOUR

Virginia .... Fayette Co., Ohio .... Randolph Co., Indiana

(married Abraham Hammers)

1822 Nancy ----1892

1788 Elijah ----1872

1765 David ----1854

1750 1760 1770 1780 1790 1800 1810 1820 1830 1840 1850 1860 1870 1880 1890

223

Family Name | 1750 | 1760 | 1770 | 1780 | 1790 | 1800 | 1810 | 1820 | 1830 | 1840 | 1850 | 1860 | 1870 | 1880 | 1890

MORRIS

Randolph Co., Indiana

North Carolina

Fayette Co., Ohio

Virginia

c1760 Isaac

1796 David ----- 1825

1824 George ----- 1879

1845 Elizabeth ----- 1922
(married Elijah Hammers) ----- 1901

GROVE

Randolph Co., Indiana

Fayette Co., Ohio

Virginia

1774 Jacob

1804 Abraham ----- after 1850 ----- 1876

1828 Anceline ----- 1864
(married George Morris)

FINCH

Jay Co., Indiana

Ohio

Virginia

Maryland

Thomas ----- ?

1785 William ----- 1863

1821 Harriet ----- 1884
(married Joseph Collins)

CAPPS

Fayette Co., Ohio

South Carolina

1760 Dempsey ----- 1839

1788 Rhoda ----- 1870
(married Elijah Harbour)

224

Descendants Lists

I have included descendants lists on six of the families covered in this book. These are presented starting with a key ancestor and contain all the information I currently have on that ancestor's descendants. They are numbered as generations from the beginning ancestor so it is quite easy to identify how many generations each descendant is from the patriarch. The letter refers to the earliest ancestor with which the list begins and each subsequent dash and number refers to the order of the children in the next generation. Children are numbered in order of birth if that is known. A ? indicates that I believe this relationship to be the correct one but there is still some uncertainty.

I present this data in this form since it would be extremely difficult to present it as prose form and retain an overall grasp of the relationships. I present it to help others understand the family relationships. There are probably errors but it represents the best information currently available.

Descendants of James Boggs of Ireland

James Boggs, b. c1667, Londonderry, Ireland, immigrated to America about 1724, d. c1736 (will dated 9 Feb 1736/7)

B-1 John Boggs, b. 1700, Ireland, d. 1751, Chester Co., PA
   m. Margaret Ogelbay
B-2 Francis Boggs*, b. 1702, Londonderry, Ireland, d. 1763, Chester Co., PA
   m. c1720, Agnes ?
B-2-1 William Boggs, b. c1721, Londonderry
B-2-2 Robert Boggs, b. c1723, Londonderry
B-2-3 James Charles Boggs, b. c1725, New Castle Co., DE, d. c1805 (will written 10 Jul 1803, probated Feb 1806)
   m. 25 Jan 1751, Wilmington, DE, Margaret Jane Sharp
B-2-3-1 William Boggs, b. c1751/2, d. 31 Mar 1849
   m. Ann Clendenin
   m. 2nd. 7 Mar 1801 Elizabeth Lawson
B-2-3-2 Francis Boggs, Jr., b. 1754, Chester Co., b. PA, d. 1837, Braxton, Co., VA
   m. c1776, Mary Clendenin
B-2-3-2-1 James Clendenin Boggs, b. 20 Feb 1778, VA, d. c1846, Braxton Co., VA
   m. 11 Jun 1799, Kanawha Co., VA, Mary "Polly" Lemaster, b. 21 Sep 1782
B-2-3-2-1-5 Benjamin Lemasters Boggs, b. 29 Apr 1810, Kanawha Co., VA, d. 10 Sep 1881, Braxton Co., WV
   m. 22 Mar 1829, VA, Jane Cutlip
B-2-3-2-1-5-1 Mary C. Boggs, b. 28 Mar 1830, m. Abel Cunningham
B-2-3-2-1-5-2 Susan Boggs, b. 29 Mar 1832, m. Samuel Fox
B-2-3-2-1-5-3 Rebecca Boggs, b. 2 Apr 1834, m. Allen Corley
B-2-3-2-1-5-4 Caroline Boggs, b. 1837, m. John Cunningham
B-2-3-2-1-5-5 Henry Boggs, b. 1840
B-2-3-2-1-5-6 William Newlon Boggs, b. Mar 1843, Braxton Co., VA, d. 1914, Braxton Co., WV
   m. 1865, Delilah Ann Mollohan, m. 2nd 26 Oct 1872, Braxton Co., WV, Sarah Boone
B-2-3-2-1-5-6-1 James A. Boggs, b. c1866, WV
B-2-3-2-1-5-6-2 Benjamin F. Boggs, b. c1868, WV
B-2-3-2-1-5-6-3 William R. Boggs, b. c1869, WV
B-2-3-2-1-5-6-4 John Henry Boggs, b. 12 Sep 1870, WV, d. 7 Apr 1945, IN
   m. 3 Sep 1893, Braxton Co., WV, Larame McMorrow

B-2-3-2-1-5-6-4-1 Ethel Boggs, b. Jul 1894, WV
B-2-3-2-1-5-6-4-2 Loman G. Boggs, b. May 1896, WV
B-2-3-2-1-5-6-4-3 Stella A. Boggs, b. Sep 1898, WV
   m. 5 Apr 1921, Randolph Co., IN, Elvin Bennett
B-2-3-2-1-5-6-4-4 Burke Boggs, b. c1902, WV
   m. 5 Mar 1928, Randolph Co., IN, Bertha Spitler
B-2-3-2-1-5-6-4-5 Stanley Boggs, b. c1906, WV
B-2-3-2-1-5-6-4-6 Gladys Boggs, b. c1907, WV
B-2-3-2-1-5-6-4-7 Sophia Boggs, b. c1910, WV
B-2-3-2-1-5-6-4-8 Pauline Boggs, b. c1912, WV
B-2-3-2-1-5-6-4-9 Maxene Boggs, b. 24 Apr 1914, IN
B-2-3-2-1-5-6-4-10 James Boggs, b. 31 Mar 1916, IN
B-2-3-2-1-5-6-5 Benton Boggs, b. c1875, WV
B-2-3-2-1-5-6-6 Rebecca H. Boggs, b. c1876, WV
B-2-3-2-1-5-6-7 Sarah A. Boggs, b. c1879, WV
B-2-3-2-1-5-6-8 Charles Reynolds Boggs, b. 4 Sep 1882, Braxton Co., WV,
   d. 26 Sep 1964, Summit Co., OH
   m. 16 Apr 1906, Upshur Co., WV, Flora Bernice Davis
B-2-3-2-1-5-6-8-1 Bernice Pauline Boggs, b. 28 May 1919, Philadelphia,
   PA
   m. 22 Dec 1940, Summit Co., OH, Melvin Clarence Miller
B-2-3-2-1-5-7 Perry Boggs, b. 1845
B-2-3-2-1-5-8 Virginia Boggs, b. 28 Dec 1848, m. Benjamin Fox
B-2-3-2-1-5-9 Harriet E. Boggs, b. 19 Jun 1857, m. William Mollohan
B-2-3-2-2 John Boggs, b. 16 Feb 1780, d. 17 Jul 1842, Braxton Co., VA
   m. 19 Feb 1801, Anna Lemasters
B-2-3-2-3 Rebecca Boggs, b. 1781, d. 1821, Braxton Co., VA
   m. 1801, James Frame
B-2-3-2-4 Mary Boggs, b. 1784, d. bef. 1837
   m. 19 Mar 1804, James E. Sparks
B-2-3-2-5 Charles C. Boggs, b. 27 May 1787, d. 27 Sep 1873, Roane Co.,
   WV
   m. 12 Feb 1809, Kanawha Co., VA, Jane Lemasters
B-2-3-2-6 Jane Boggs, b. 1791, d. 1836, Braxton Co., VA
   m. 7 Aug 1818, Nicholas Co., VA, John Stewart
B-2-3-2-7 William N. Boggs, b. 1792, d. 7 May 1868, Gilmer Co., WV
   m. 30 Dec 1812, Harrison Co., VA
   m. 2nd 12 May 1865, Gilmer Co., WV, Louisa Griffith
B-2-3-2-8 Andrew Boggs, b. 1795, d. 12 Nov 1859, Braxton Co., VA
   m. 1813, Christina Shock
B-2-3-2-9 Elizabeth Boggs, b. 1798, d. Sep 1873, Braxton Co., WV
   m. 1819, Lewis Kyer
B-2-3-2-10 Margaret Boggs, b. 1799, d. 1831, Braxton Co., VA
   m. John L. Davis
B-2-3-2-11 Miriam Boggs, b. 1809, d. aft. 1880, Roane Co., WV
   m. 8 May 1832, Hugh Griffith

B-2-3-3 James Boggs, Jr., b. c1756, d. 10 Apr 1809, Gallia Co., OH
m. Jane Watts

B-2-3-4 Elizabeth Boggs, b. c1758
m. c1780 William Glackin

B-2-3-5 Ezekial Boggs, b. c1760, d. after 1830 Greenbrier Co., VA
m. 10 Dec 1788, (B-2-4-1) Margaret Boggs

B-2-3-5-1 Francis Boggs, b. 1790

B-2-3-5-2 Martha E. Boggs, b. 1795

B-2-3-5-3 James Boggs, b. c1798, Greenbrier Co., VA, d. c1831,
Greenbrier Co., VA
m. Feb 1821, Greenbrier Co., VA, Jane White, b. c1805

B-2-3-5-3-1 William M. Boggs, b. c1827, VA, m. Sarah ?

B-2-3-5-3-1-1 James Boggs, b. c1850

B-2-3-5-3-1-2 George Boggs, b. c1852

B-2-3-5-3-2 Mary J. Boggs, b. c1828, VA

B-2-3-5-3-3 Martha M. Boggs, b. c1831, VA

B-2-3-5-4 Stephen Boggs, b. c1799, Greenbrier Co., VA
m. 1 Sep 1825 Greenbrier Co., VA, Jane Reynolds

B-2-3-5-4-1 John Boggs, b. c1827, VA
m. ? 23 Jan 1858, Susan Mustarn

B-2-3-5-4-2 Elizabeth Boggs, b. c1829, VA

B-2-3-5-4-3 H. (daughter) Boggs, b. c1833, VA

B-2-3-5-4-4 Anderson Boggs, b. c1835, VA

B-2-3-5-4-5 Daniel Boggs, b. c1838, VA

B-2-3-5-4-6 Jane Boggs, b. c1842, VA

B-2-3-5-5 Ezekiel Boggs Jr., B. c1800, Greenbrier Co., VA
m. March 21, 1839, Pocahontas Co., VA, Sarah McCarty

B-2-3-5-5-1 Margaret Boggs, b. c1840

B-2-3-5-5-2 Jno. Boggs, b. c1843

B-2-3-5-5-3 Eli Boggs, b. c1845

B-2-3-5-6 Margaret P. Boggs, b. c1802, Greenbrier Co., VA
m. 14 Feb, 1822 Greenbrier Co., VA, Henry Copenhaven

B-2-3-5-7 William Boggs, b. May 1805, Greenbrier Co., VA, d. 2 Sep
1874, Greenbrier Co., WV

B-2-3-5-8 Fielding Boggs, b. c1809, Greenbrier Co., VA
m. 24 Jan 1839, Pocahontas Co., WV, Sarah Casebolt

B-2-3-5-8-1 Abitha V. Boggs, b. Apr 1840, VA
m. 12 Sep 1866, Mary C. Cutlip

B-2-3-5-8-1-1 Mary F. Boggs, b. c1869

B-2-3-5-8-1-2 George P. Boggs, b. c1875

B-2-3-5-8-1-3 son, b. c1877

B-2-3-5-8-1-4 Lizzie L. Boggs, b. Sep 1880

B-2-3-5-8-1-5 Ezekial Boggs, b. Sep 1882

B-2-3-5-9 Jeheil Boggs, b. c1815 Greenbrier Co., VA, d. 27 Apr 1882,
Greenbrier Co., WV

m. Amanda ?, m. 2nd, July 2, 1855 in Greenbrier Co., VA, Jane E. Hume

B-2-3-5-9-1 James R. Boggs, b. Sep 1857
   m. 30 Apr 1884, Sallie F. Hanna, b. 1860
B-2-3-5-9-1-1 Adp. Albert Crouse, b. c1890
B-2-3-5-9-1-2 Adp. Vesie R. Boggs, b. c1897
B-2-3-5-9-2 Andrew Mayberry Boggs, b. Apr 1860, Greenbrier Co., VA
   m. 5 Apr 1883, N. V. Hayslitt
B-2-3-5-9-2-1 George H. Boggs, b. c1884
B-2-3-5-9-2-2 Gurdie Boggs, b. c1886
B-2-3-5-9-2-3 Sarah F. Boggs, b. c1887
B-2-3-6 John Boggs, b. 14 Feb 1763, d. 1861 Roane Co., VA
   m. 25 Apr 1786, Greenbrier Co., VA, Susan Drennin
B-2-3-6-1 Margaret Boggs
B-2-3-6-2 Sally Boggs
B-2-3-6-3 Nancy Boggs
B-2-3-6-4 Lawrence Boggs, b. 25 Apr 1795, d. 23 Apr 1867, OR
   m. Elizabeth Newsome
B-2-3-6-5 Thomas "Old Tommy" Boggs, b. c1799, d. 1880, Roane Co., WV
B-2-3-6-6 William Boggs, b. c1801, d. c1865, Greenbrier Co., WV
B-2-3-6-7 Avaline Bebmount Boggs
B-2-3-6-8 Malinda Boggs
B-2-3-6-9 Ruth Boggs
B-2-3-6-10 Jane Boggs, b. c1814, dnm
B-2-3-7 Samuel Boggs, b. 1765, d. 1832 Gallia Co.
   m. Ellen Watts
B-2-3-8 "Andrew" Elliott Boggs, b. 1767, Augusta Co. (now Bath Co.), VA, d. 27 Jan 1854, Kosciusko Co., IN, bur. Leesburg Cem., Plain Twp., Kosciusko Co., IN
   m. 5 Mar 1791, Greenbrier Co., VA, Susannah Bowen, b. 1776, Greenbrier Co., VA, d. 4 May 1834, Henry Co., IN
B-2-3-8-1 Anthony Bowen Boggs, b. 12 Aug 1793, Greenbrier Co., VA, d. 1873, Sonoma Co., CA
B-2-3-8-2 Sarah Boggs, b. c1794, Greenbrier Co., VA, d. 1829, Jackson Co., OH
   m. 16 Jul 1816, Gallia Co., OH, William McCarley
B-2-3-8-3 Jane Sharp Boggs, b. 10 May 1798, Greenbrier Co., VA, d. 26 Sep 1839, Kosciusko Co., IN
   m. 18 Feb 1817, Jackson Co., OH, Joel L. Long
B-2-3-8-4 Alice Boggs, b. 7 Nov 1799, Greenbrier Co., VA, d. 11 Apr 1870, Greene Co., OH
   m. 19 Nov 1820, Jackson Co., OH, James Long
B-2-3-8-5 Mary Boggs, b. 12 Apr 1802, Greenbrier Co., VA, d. 1849, Cincinnati, OH
   m. 3 Feb 1825, Henry Co., IN, Matthew Williams

B-2-3-8-6 Cynthia Boggs, b. 26 Oct 1803, Gallia Co., OH, d. 22 May 1857, Kosciusko Co., IN

m. 25 Oct 1824, Jackson Co., OH, James Hale

B-2-3-8-7 James Boggs, b. 19 Feb 1807, Gallia Co., OH, d. 7 Nov 1842, Kosciusko Co., IN

m. 1 Jul 1827, Henry Co., IN, Martha H. StinsonzB-2-3-8-8 Hannah Boggs, b. 25 Feb 1809, Gallia Co., OH, d. 7 Mar 1888, Greene Co., OH

m. 6 Nov 1826, Greene Co., OH, Joseph Dean

B-2-3-8-9 William Bowen Boggs, b. 25 Dec 1812, Gallia Co., OH, d. 22 Mar 1906, Kosciusko Co., IN

m. 6 Jul 1837, Kosciusko Co., IN, Lydia Groves

m. 2nd Oct 1851, Kosciusko Co., IN, Sarah (Yisley) Mingel

B-2-3-8-10 Mahala Boggs, b. 5 Mar 1814, Gallia Co., OH, d. 10 Jun 1901, Marshall Co., IN

m. 12 Nov 1829, Wayne Co., IN, Obed Swain

m. 2nd 24 Oct 1841, Wayne Co., IN, Col. Thomas Sumner

B-2-3-8-11 Lewis Boggs, b. 16 Jun 1816, Gallia Co., OH, d. 16 May 1888, Marshall Co., IN

m. 20 Feb 1840, Kosciusko Co., IN, Sarah Devault

B-2-3-8-12 Julia Ann Boggs, b. 12 Nov 1818, Jackson Co., OH, d. 20 Feb 1910, Marshall Co., IN

m. 3 Mar 1836, Wayne Co., IN, Benoni Jordan

B-2-3-8-13 Andrew Hamilton Boggs, b. 7 Mar 1821, Jackson Co., OH, d. 7 Mar 1917, Kosciusko Co., IN

m. 14 Dec 1843, Kosciusko Co., IN, Martha Ann Thomas

B-2-3-8-13 m. 2nd 18 Sep 1889, Kosciusko Co., IN, Abbie (Silver) Shoup

B-2-3-8 m. 2nd 23 Apr 1836, Delaware Co., IN, Elizabeth (Peragin) Friend

B-2-3-9 Alexander Boggs, b. 1770, d. aft 1816 Gallia Co., OH

m. 6 Apr 1795, Agnes "Nancy" Boggs

B-2-4 Francis Boggs, Jr.*, b. 1726/32, New Castle Co., DE, d. soon after 31 Jan 1797, Greenbrier Co., VA

m. before 1773, Prob. Chester Co., PA, Martha Elliott, d. c1818, Gallia Co., OH, will 24 Feb 1818

B-2-4-1 Margaret Boggs, b. c1762, d. after 1830

m. 10 Dec 1788, Ezekial Boggs (B-2-3-5)

B-2-4-2 Andrew Elliott Boggs, b. 1768, d. c1840, Gallia Co., OH

m. 6 Jan 1794, Greenbrier Co., VA, Hannah Bowen

B-2-4-3 James Boggs, b. 1772, d. Gallia Co., OH

m. 16 Aug 1797, Bath Co., VA, Isabelle Wadell

B-2-4-4 Agnes "Nancy" Boggs, b. c1775

m. 6 Apr 1795, Alexander Boggs (B-2-3-9)

B-2-4-5 Elizabeth Boggs, c1782, York Co., PA, d. Sep 1855 dnm

B-2-4-6 Francis Boggs, III, b. 27 May 1786, d. 20 Jan 1853, Warren Co., IN

m. 23 Jul 1809, Greenbrier Co., VA, Jane Blair

m. 2nd 19 Sep 1844, Warren Co., IN, Nancy Clark

m. 3rd 2 Oct 1850, Warren Co., IN, Violette Toliver

B-2-4-6-1 Elliott Boggs, b. c1808

B-2-4-7 Alexander Boggs*, b. c1793, d. 5 Mar 1876, Greenbrier Co., WV

m. Elizabeth ?, b. c1794, VA, d. 1876/1880

B-2-4-7-1 Benjamin Franklin Boggs, b. c1820, VA, d. 15 Jul 1882

m. 27 Nov 1857, Sarah F. Cochran, b. 1837, VA, d. after 1910

B-2-4-7-1-1 Robert Samuel Boggs, b. 25 Sep 1858, d. before 1870 census

B-2-4-7-1-2 Martin L. Boggs, b. 28 Feb 1860

B-2-4-7-1-3 Emily J. Boggs, b. c1861

m. 10 Nov 1886, Greenbrier Co., WV, George W. Winden

B-2-4-7-1-4 John G. Boggs, b. May 1864

m. 13 May 1891, Greenbrier Co., WV, Sarah C. Gabbert, b. 1874

B-2-4-7-1-4-1 Tracey Boggs, b. c1893

B-2-4-7-1-4-2 Lizzie Boggs, b. c1896

B-2-4-7-1-4-3 Laura Boggs, b. c1896

B-2-4-7-1-4-4 William H. Boggs, b. c1899

B-2-4-7-1-4-5 Twinkee Boggs, b. c1906

B-2-4-7-1-4-6 Harry T. Boggs, b. c1909

B-2-4-7-1-5 Elizabeth N. Boggs, b. c1867

B-2-4-7-1-6 Medora M. Boggs, b. c1870

B-2-4-7-1-7 Washington L. Boggs, b. 28 May 1872

m. 22 Jun 1898, Luella McLaughlin, b. 1878

B-2-4-7-1-7-1 Roy Boggs, b. c1900

B-2-4-7-1-7-2 Mary Boggs, b. c1902

B-2-4-7-1-7-3 Cyrus Boggs, b. c1903

B-2-4-7-1-7-4 John Boggs, b. c1906

B-2-4-7-1-7-5 Daisy Boggs, b. c1908

B-2-4-7-1-7-6 Samuel Boggs, b. c1910

B-2-4-7-1-8 William L. Boggs, b. 28 May 1872

B-2-4-7-1-9 Mary F. Boggs, b. 10 Jun 1875, d. young

B-2-4-7-1-10 Charles W. Boggs, b. 26 Mar 1877

B-2-4-7-2 Sarah Boggs, b. c1822, VA, dnm, d. after 1860 census

B-2-4-7-3 Ruhanna Ann Boggs, b. c1823

m. 1 Sep 1842, Greenbrier Co., VA, Jacob McCarty

B-2-4-7-3-1 Samuel A. McCarty, b. c1844, Greenbrier Co., VA

m. Elizabeth J. ?

B-2-4-7-3-1-1 Columbus J. McCarty, b. c1868, WV

B-2-4-7-3-1-2 Thomas M. McCarty, b. c1871, WV

B-2-4-7-3-1-3 Samuel E. McCarty, b. c1873, WV

B-2-4-7-3-1-4 Margaret R. McCarty, b. c1874, WV

B-2-4-7-3-1-5 James H. McCarty, b. c1877, WV

B-2-4-7-3-1-6 Emma S. McCarty, b. Jul 1879, WV

B-2-4-7-3-2 Elizabeth J. McCarty, b. c1846

B-2-4-7-3-3 Mahala M. McCarty, b. c1848

B-2-4-7-3-4 Melissa Rachel McCarty, b. 1850

B-2-4-7-3-5 Julia A. McCarty, b. c1852

B-2-4-7-3-6 Nancy E. McCarty, b. c1858

B-2-4-7-3-7 George McCarty, b. c1861

B-2-4-7-4 John A. Boggs*, b. 5 Sep 1828, Greenbrier Co., VA, d. 26 Nov 1893, Greenbrier Co., WV
m. 9 Sep 1851, Taylor Co., VA, Phoebe E. Carder, b. 7 Aug 1828, Taylor Co., VA, d. 9 Jan 1899

B-2-4-7-4-1 Joseph A. Boggs, b. 26 Jun 1852, d. 6 Jan 1863

B-2-4-7-4-2 Cornelius Carter Boggs, b. 19 Mar 1854, Greenbrier Co., VA, d. 1909, WV
m. 12 Jan 1881, Greenbrier Co., WV, Luellin Alderman, b. c1860

B-2-4-7-4-2-1 Maggie Boggs, b. c1882, d. 18 Dec 1884

B-2-4-7-4-2-2 James R. Boggs, b. Feb 1884

B-2-4-7-4-2-3 Lydie J. Boggs, b. Mar 1889, d. 31 Mar 1891

B-2-4-7-4-2-4 Joseph Boggs, b. Feb 1895

B-2-4-7-4-3 Elizabeth Rebecca Boggs, b. 29 Oct 1856, d. aft 1920, prob. Delaware Co., IN
m. 10 Sep 1877, Greenbrier Co., WV, Marion D. McMillion

B-2-4-7-4-3-1 Albert R. McMillion, b. 4 Jun 1878, Greenbrier Co., WV

B-2-4-7-4-3-2 Dennis C. McMillion, b. Apr 1888, Greenbrier Co., WV

B-2-4-7-4-4 Thomas G. Boggs, b. 8 May 1859, d. aft. 1920, poss. CA
m. 28 Aug 1884, Mary Etta Peers, b. Jul 1860, VA

B-2-4-7-4-4-1 Herman J. Boggs, b. May 1885, WV

B-2-4-7-4-4-2 Nila Marguerite Boggs, b. Jun 1896, IN

B-2-4-7-4-4-3 Lizzie V. "Irene" Boggs, b. Jan 1898, IN

B-2-4-7-4-4-4 Florence Boggs, b. 5 Mar 1900, IN, d. 8 Sep 1900

B-2-4-7-4-5 George H. B. Boggs, b. 9 Oct 1862, d. 23 Jan 1863

B-2-4-7-4-6 Noah Edward "Ed" Boggs*, b. 10 Nov 1864, d. Nov 1932, Randolph Co., IN, bur. Redkey, IN
m. 11 Mar 1891, Clora Jane Kincaid, b. 2 Nov 1870, Greenbrier Co., WV, d. 18 Jan 1955, Farmland, IN

B-2-4-7-4-6-1 Daughter, b. 6 Mar 1892, d. 6 Mar 1892

B-2-4-7-4-6-2 Samuel Plummer Boggs*, b. 2 Apr 1893, Greenbrier Co., WV, d. 9 Apr 1965, Selma, IN, bur. Woodlawn Cem., Randolph Co., IN
m. 11 Jan 1919, Hilda Irene Garringer*, b. 28 Mar 1898, Randolph Co., IN, d. 26 Dec 1983, Parker City, IN, bur. Woodlawn Cem., Randolph Co., IN

B-2-4-7-4-6-2-1 Lloyd Keith Boggs, b. 2 Apr 1920, Farmland, IN
m. 26 Jun 1941, Cowan, IN, Marie Elizabeth Creviston, b. 31 Aug 1919, d. 29 Sep 1993, bur. Mount Tabor Cem., Delaware Co., IN

B-2-4-7-4-6-2-1-1 Rachel Ellen Boggs, b. 25 Jun 1949, Muncie, IN
m. 16 Jun 1969, Allan Kaufman, b. 19 Dec 1948, div.

B-2-4-7-4-6-2-1-1-1 Lisa Beth Kaufman, b. 27 Dec 1969, Richmond, IN

B-2-4-7-4-6-2-1-1-2 Joshua Allan Kaufman, b. 18 Nov 1974, Ann Arbor, MI

B-2-4-7-4-6-2-1-2 Martha "Marty" Elizabeth Boggs, b. 14 Dec 1951, Muncie, IN
m. 28 Feb 1982, Arlington, TX, George Dodson Howell, b. 2 Aug 1947, Tucson, AZ
B-2-4-7-4-6-2-1-2-1 Adam Christopher Howell, b. 7 May 1985, Arlington, TX
B-2-4-7-4-6-2-1-3 Mary Ann Boggs, b. 23 Nov 1956, Muncie, IN
m. 14 Feb 1980, Indianapolis, IN, John Lowther, b. 23 Sep 1953, Waterloo, IA
B-2-4-7-4-6-2-1-3-1 John Keith Lowther, b. 1 Oct 1983, Phoenix, AZ
B-2-4-7-4-6-2-1-3-2 Max Conrad Lowther, b. 23 Dec 1988, Phoenix, AZ
B-2-4-7-4-6-2-2 Frances Louise Boggs, b. 17 Jun 1922, Farmland, IN
m. 24 May 1946, Cowan, IN, Leo Vern Addington, b. 10 Apr 1923
B-2-4-7-4-6-2-2-1 Ann Frances Addington, b. 11 Jun 1947, Winchester, IN
m. 24 Apr 1971, Grissom AFB, IN, Richard Abel, b. 11 Feb 1938, Newark, NJ
B-2-4-7-4-6-2-2-1-1 Amy Louise Abel, b. 6 Mar 1978, Kokomo, IN
B-2-4-7-4-6-2-2-2 David Vern Addington, b. 4 Aug 1948, Winchester, IN
m. 29 Dec 1979, Richardson, TX, Dixie Carol Behr, b. 30 Jul 1952, Detroit, MI
B-2-4-7-4-6-2-2-2-1 Ashley Lynn Addington, b. 20 Nov 1982, Dallas, TX
B-2-4-7-4-6-2-2-2-2 Carmen Elizabeth Addington, b. 1 Nov 1985, Dallas, TX
B-2-4-7-4-6-2-2-3 Dale Lee Addington, b. 5 Dec 1950, Winchester, IN
m. 10 Jun 1972, West Lafayette, IN, Tammi Carson, b. 29 Jun 1951
B-2-4-7-4-6-2-2-3-1 Stephen Carson Addington, b. 16 May 1982, Findlay, OH
B-2-4-7-4-6-2-2-3-2 James Michael Addington, b. 28 Aug 1984, Findlay, OH
B-2-4-7-4-6-2-3 James Edwin Boggs, b. 16 Mar 1924, Farmland, IN
m. 27 May 1944, Muncie, IN, June Berry, b. 28 Oct 1924, Muncie, IN
B-2-4-7-4-6-2-3-1 Susan Boggs, b. 22 Feb 1945, Muncie, IN
m. 2 Jun 1968, Muncie, IN, Dennis Bruce Latour, b. 21 Nov 1945, Providence, RI
B-2-4-7-4-6-2-3-1-1 Jennifer Susan Latour, b. 27 May 1972, Indianapolis, IN
B-2-4-7-4-6-2-3-1-2 Jeffrey Allen Latour, b. 15 Sep 1976, Indianapolis, IN
B-2-4-7-4-6-2-3-2 Stephen Edwin Boggs, b. 3 May 1947, Muncie, IN
m. 18 Aug 1968, Martinsville, IN, Letha Mae Knerr, b. 8 Aug 1948
B-2-4-7-4-6-2-3-3 Dianna June Boggs, b. 2 Jun 1950, Muncie, IN
m. 7 Mar 1970, Muncie, IN, Jerry Richard Eiler, b. 15 Aug 1951, Muncie, IN
B-2-4-7-4-6-2-3-3-1 Lora Diane Eiler, b. 8 Oct 1971, Muncie, IN
B-2-4-7-4-6-2-3-3-2 Christy Elizabeth Eiler, b. 12 Feb 1974, Muncie, IN

m. 3 Apr 1999, Muncie, IN, Joseph Michael Knight, b. 9 Nov 1968, Huntington, IN

B-2-4-7-4-6-2-3-4 Charles Hamilton Boggs, b. 21 Nov 1951, Muncie, IN
m. 20 Oct 1972, Muncie, IN, Pam Caldwell Hammer, b. 27 Dec 1949, div 1994

B-2-4-7-4-6-2-3-4-1 Anna Stasha Boggs, b. 17 Sep 1974, Muncie, IN
m. 20 May 2000, Muncie, IN, Eric Scott Baker

B-2-4-7-4-6-2-3-4-2 Charles Edwin Boggs, b. 13 Jul 1976, Muncie, IN
m. 27 Feb 1999, Stormie Ann Morgan, b. 9 Oct 1975

B-2-4-7-4-6-2-3-4-2-1 Courtlinn Kileigh Boggs, b. 15 Oct 1996, Muncie, IN

B-2-4-7-4-6-2-3-4-2-2 Carlie Braielle Boggs, b. 13 Jul 2000

B-2-4-7-4-6-2-3-4-3 Adp. Michlynn Hammer Boggs, b. 16 Jun 1970

B-2-4-7-4-6-2-4 Robert Eugene Boggs, b. 15 Apr 1926, Farmland, IN
m. 4 Mar 1955, near Muncie, IN, Helen Roberta Wright, b. 17 Dec 1932, near Muncie, IN

B-2-4-7-4-6-2-4-1 William Robert Boggs, b. 6 Feb 1956, Muncie, IN

B-2-4-7-4-6-2-4-2 Debra Lea Boggs, b. 17 Dec 1957, Muncie, IN
m. 20 Jun 1981, Muncie, IN, Mark Charles Ladendorf, b. 17 Jun 1955, Hammond, IN

B-2-4-7-4-6-2-4-2-1 Lance Robert Ladendorf, b. 27 Apr 1986, Indianapolis, IN

B-2-4-7-4-6-2-4-2-2 Luke Mark Ladendorf, b. 9 May 1989, Indianapolis, IN

B-2-4-7-4-6-2-4-2-3 Hannah Lea Ladendorf, b. 23 Jul 1993, Indianapolis, IN

B-2-4-7-4-6-2-4-3 Rodney Eugene Boggs, b. 6 Dec 1961, Muncie, IN
m. Indianapolis, IN, Lisa Marie Burwell, b. 6 May 1966, St. Marys, OH

B-2-4-7-4-6-2-4-3-1 Bryant Eugene Boggs, b. 24 Jan 1989, Indianapolis, IN

B-2-4-7-4-6-2-4-3-2 Elizabeth Marie Boggs, b. 26 Oct 1990, Indianapolis, IN

B-2-4-7-4-6-2-5 Philip Alan Boggs, b. 4 Nov 1928, Farmland, IN
m. 23 Nov 1947, Muncie, IN, Jean Ann Gowin, b. 2 Mar 1928, Grant Co., IN

B-2-4-7-4-6-2-5-1 Catherine Ann Boggs, b. 22 Sep 1948, Muncie, IN
m. 26 Feb 1972, Muncie, IN, David Hearld, div. Sep 1986

B-2-4-7-4-6-2-5-1-1 Angela Jane Hearld, b. 29 Sep 1972, Muncie, IN

B-2-4-7-4-6-2-5-1-2 Jason Ray Hearld, b. 19 Apr 1974, Muncie, IN

B-2-4-7-4-6-2-5-2 Rebecca Jane Boggs, b. 11 Nov 1952, Muncie, IN
m. 13 Aug 1972, John Morris, div. 1975
m. 2nd 17 Jun 1978, Tom Mench, b. 14 Sep 1952

B-2-4-7-4-6-2-5-2-1 Michael Thomas Mench, b. 29 Jun 1979, Richmond, IN

B-2-4-7-4-6-2-5-2-2 Andrea Elizabeth Mench, b. 7 Dec 1984, Cincinnati, OH

B-2-4-7-4-6-2-5-3 Philip Patrick Boggs, b. 30 Jul 1955, Selma, IN
m. 26 Jan 1979, Joyce Lowe

B-2-4-7-4-6-2-5-3-1 Michelle Leann Boggs, b. 8 Dec 1980

B-2-4-7-4-6-2-5-3-2 adp Adrian Deann (Lowe) Boggs, b. 24 Apr 1976

B-2-4-7-4-6-3 Lottie Ellen Boggs, b. 30 Sep 1895, Greenbrier Co., WV, d. 5 Mar 1989, Randolph Co., IN
m. Roscoe Sumner, b. 1890, d. Apr 1939

B-2-4-7-4-6-4 Virdie Ora Boggs, b. 3 Apr 1897, Greenbrier Co., WV, d. 17 Feb 1991, Parker City, IN, bur. Woodlawn Cem., Maxville, Randolph Co., IN
m. 30 May 1918, Revillo W. Gilmore, b. 1898, d. 17 Feb 1972, bur. Woodlawn Cem., Maxville, Randolph Co., IN

B-2-4-7-4-6-4-1 Jacquelyn Sue Gilmore, b. 13 May 1928
m. Edwin Hodgin

B-2-4-7-4-6-4-1-1 Kurt Gilmore Hodgin, b. 27 May 1966

B-2-4-7-4-6-5 Mattie Opal Boggs, b. 9 Oct 1900, d. 28 Aug 1974
m. Jan 1918, Harold Worden, b. 1900, d. 1972, div.

B-2-4-7-4-6-5-1 Fancheon Madonna Worden, b. 3 Aug 1918, Albany, IN, d. 27 Nov 1999, Anderson, IN, bur. Elwood City Cem., Elwood, IN
m. 1 Aug 1941, Harold E. Hodson, b. 10 Jan 1920

B-2-4-7-4-6-5-1-1 Pamela Hodson, b. 22 Jan 1947, Elwood, IN
m. 26 Apr 1969, Thomas Vincent, b. 13 Jan 1947

B-2-4-7-4-6-5-1-1-1 Andrew Vincent, b. 25 May 1975, Danville, IL

B-2-4-7-4-6-5-1-1-2 Bryan Vincent, b. 19 Apr 1978, Danville, IL

B-2-4-7-4-6-6 James Boggs, b. 22 Apr 1909, d. 22 Apr 1909

B-2-4-7-4-7 Mary F. J. Boggs, b. 25 Jun 1868, d. 3 Feb 1871

B-2-4-7-5 Elizabeth Boggs, b. c1828, d. Mar 1854, bur. Old Stone Church Cem., Lewisburg, WV

B-2-4-7-6 Almira (or Alcinda) "Jane" Boggs, b. c1833
m. 27 Sep 1852, Greenbrier Co., VA, Mathew V. Peers

B-2-4-7-6-1 Martha E. Peers, b. c1856

B-2-4-7-6-2 Thomas E. Peers, b. c1858

B-2-4-7-7 daughter, b. 1815/20 (implied from census data)

B-2-4-7-8 daughter, b. 1815/20 (implied from census data)

B-2-5 Ezekial Boggs, b. c1734, d. 7 Jun 1815, St. Clairsville, OH, m. 1756, Jane Johnson,

B-2-5-1 Ezekial Boggs, Jr., b. c1770, Ohio Co., VA
m. 20 Nov 1782, Fort Henry, Ohio Co., VA, Eve Catherine Haney

B-2-5-2 Alexander Boggs, m. Hannah Martin

B-2-5-2-1 Francis Boggs, b. 17 May 1807, Belmont Co., OH
m. Evelina Martin

B-2-5-3 Francis Boggs, nfi

B-2-6 Agnes Boggs
m. 15 Aug 1762, Philadelphia, PA, Davidson Filson

B-2-7 Samuel Boggs, d. c1815, Mason Co., KY

B-3 James Boggs, Jr., b. 1704, Ireland, d. c1779, Augusta Co., VA
m. 1726, New Castle Co., DE, Elizabeth Bryan

B-3-1 Robert Boggs

B-3-2 James Boggs

B-3-3 Henry Boggs

B-3-4 Thomas Boggs

B-3-5 Jennat Boggs

B-3-6 Alexander Boggs

B-3-7 John Boggs

B-4 Mary Boggs, b. c1710, Ireland, d. aft 1763, Chester Co., PA
m. Francis Morris

B-5 Robert Boggs, b. 1712, d. 2 Apr 1804, New Castle Co., DE
m. 3 Mar 1741, Margaret Robinson, b. 1721, d. 1804

B-5-1 James Boggs, b. 16 Jan 1742, d. young

B-5-2 Robert Boggs, Jr., b. 9 Sep 1746
m. 5 Apr 1782, Greenbrier Co., VA, Sarah McCreary Huston

B-5-3 William Boggs, b. 9 Sep 1746, d. Revolutionary War

B-5-4 James Boggs, b. 10 Sep 1747, d. 1820, KY
m. Sallie Wynn, b. 1747

B-5-5 Agnes Boggs, b. 4 Feb 1749, d. young

B-5-6 Elizabeth Boggs, b. 11 Feb 1751, nfi

B-5-7 Benjamin Boggs, b. 12 Mar 1753, d. Revolutionary War

B-5-8 Moses Boggs, b. 12 Nov 1756, d. 22 Feb 1833, Muskingham Co.,
OH
m. 16 Dec 1788, Margaret Donnell Moore

B-5-9 John Boggs, b. 11 Jan 1759, d. 5 Apr 1847, Kentucky

B-5-10 Joseph Boggs, b. 2 Jan 1761, d. 13 Jul 1843, Madison Co.,
Kentucky
m. 8 Sep 1807, Elizabeth Plew

B-6 Rebecca Boggs, b. 1714, dnm, d. after 1763, Chester Co., PA

B-7 William Boggs, b. 1716, d. c1790, Chester Co., PA
m. 1733, New Castle Co., DE, Jane Stein,

B-8 Alexander Boggs, b. 1719
m. 1759 Elizabeth Lloyd, Philadelphia, PA

B-9 Ezekial Boggs, b. c1719, Ireland, d. c1756 New Castle Co., migrated
to Delaware after 1737
m. c1736, Strabane Co., Tyrone, Ulster, Ireland, Elizabeth Baird

B-9-1 Rebecca Boggs, b. 1738, d. 1790, m. Charles Risk

B-9-2 James Boggs, b. 22 Jan 1740, d. 8 Jul 1830, Halifax, Nova Scotia
m. c1765, Mary Morris

Descendants of David Gerringer, Sr.

G David Gerringer, Sr., b. 5 Nov 1735, Edenkoben Pfalz, Germany, d. 1812, Berkeley Co., VA David Gerringer, Sr. was the son of Emig "Emich" Gerringer, born 26 Nov 1682, Edenkoben Pfalz, Germany, d. 16 Feb 1737, Edenkoben Pfalz, Germany and his wife, Anna Marie Neu. Emig Gerringer was the son of Georg Diether Gerringer, born c1651, and his wife Clara, born c1653
   m. c1765, Ann Barbara ?, b. Germany, d. 15 Mar 1814, Berkeley Co., VA

G-1 Anne Marie "Mary" Garringer, b. 8 Feb 1766, Frederick Co., MD, d. 1836, Morgan Co., VA
   m. c1784, John Culp (also spelled as Kolp), d. 1829, Morgan Co., VA
G-1-1 Frederick Culp, b. c1786, Frederick Co., MD
   m. Jun 1806, Hagerstown, MD, Catharine Coaler
G-1-1-1 Mary Ann Culp, b. 1807, Morgan Co., VA, d. 22 Aug 1864, Hancock Co., OH
   m. 1823, Ambrose Clark Pewters
G-1-1-2 John Culp, b. 17 Aug 1808, Morgan Co., VA, d. 23 Sep 1892, Morgan Co., VA
   m. 17 Feb 1831, Morgan Co., VA, Mary Bechtol
G-2 Elizabeth Garringer, b. c1768, Frederick Co., MD
   m. c1792, Matthis Zenas
G-2-1 Anna Maria Zenas, b. 26 Dec 1794
G-3 Magdalena Garringer, b. c1770, Frederick Co., MD, m. Miller
G-4 David Garringer, Jr.*, b. 12 Oct 1772, Frederick Co., MD, d. 11 Nov 1865, Fayette Co., OH, bur. Cochran Cem., Fayette Co., OH
   m. 27 Oct 1795, Berkeley Co., VA, Elizabeth Smith, b. Dec 1771, Frederick Co., VA, d. Sep 1848, Randolph Co., IN, bur. Garringer Homestead Cem., Randolph Co., IN
G-4-1 John Garringer, b. 14 Aug 1796, Berkeley Co., VA, d. 14 Jul 1852, Howard Co., IN
   m. 23 May 1823, Fayette Co., OH, Elizabeth Johnson
G-4-1-1 Eliza Garringer, b. 23 May 1824, Fayette Co., OH, d. 10 Mar 1874, Delaware Co., IN, bur. Bethel M. E. Church Cem.
   m. 17 Oct 1843, Jay Co., IN, Joshua F. Maitlen
G-4-1-2 Margaret Garringer, b. c1826, Fayette Co., OH, d. c1862
   m. 20 Apr 1848, Howard Co., IN, Oliver Tyre
G-4-1-3 Elizabeth Garringer, b. c1829, Fayette Co., OH
   m. 14 Apr 1849, Howard Co., IN, Edmond Mannen
   m. 2nd 29 Nov 1866, Howard Co., IN, John G. Hochstedler

G-4-1-4 Drucilla Garringer, b. c1831, Fayette Co., OH, d. c1875, Putnam Co., MO

 m. 13 Jul 1848 Howard Co., IN, (G-4-2-2) David Garringer

G-4-1-5 Nancy Garringer, b. c1832, Fayette Co., OH, d. aft. 1853

 m. 4 May 1850, Howard Co., IN, Elijah Tyre

G-4-1-6 Jacob Garringer, b. c1834, Randolph Co., IN, d. c1869

 m. 10 Mar 1858, Howard Co., IN, Margaret Rich

G-4-1-6-1 Mary Ellen Garringer, b. 4 Jan 1861, Howard Co., IN

 m. 18 Mar 1878, Jerry Phipps

G-4-1-7 Rhoda Ann Garringer, b. 25 Dec 1835, Randolph Co., IN, d. 22 Feb 1914, Cloud Co., KS

 m. 11 Dec 1853, Delaware Co., IN, William B. Maitlen

 m. 2nd 2 Jun 1871, Jesse McDowell

G-4-1-8 Amanda Garringer, b. c1836, Jay Co., IN

 m. 15 Oct 1856, Howard Co., IN, Richard Bodle

 m. 2nd 17 Aug 1865, Howard Co., IN, Oliver Tyre

G-4-1-9 John Garringer, b. 18 Oct 1838, Randolph Co., IN, d. 28 Jul 1902, White Co., IN

 m. 6 Mar 1864, Howard Co., IN, Martha Jane Travis (Jane 1900 census White Co., IN)

G-4-1-9-1 Ella Garringer, b. c1865, Howard Co., IN

G-4-1-9-2 Margaret Garringer, b. c1867, Howard Co., IN

G-4-1-9-3 Etta Garringer, b. c1868, Howard Co., IN

 m. 4 Jan 1891, Stephens Co., IN, James Stephens

G-4-1-9-4 William Garringer, b. 1871 (1900 White Co., IN)

 m. 23 Apr 1895, White Co., IN, Louisa Hinshaw

G-4-1-9-4-1 Fay Garringer, b. c1897, IN

G-4-1-9-5 Infant Garringer, b. 2 Aug 1874

G-4-1-9-6 Julia Garringer, b. c1876

G-4-1-9-7 Minnie Garringer, b. 1880, White Co., IN

 m. 18 Feb 1899, White Co., IN, George W. Custer

G-4-1-9-8 Pearl Garringer, b. Apr 1883, White Co., IN

 m. 10 Apr 1901, White Co., IN, Stephen Bose

G-4-1-9-9 Francis M. Garringer, b. Aug 1884, White Co., IN

G-4-1-10 James E. Garringer, b. 8 Oct 1842, Howard Co., IN, d. 28 Sep 1865, Delaware Co., IN, bur. Bethel M. E. Cem. (member Co. E, 11th Indiana Vol. Cavalry)

G-4-1-10-1 Mary Garringer, b. c1859, IN

G-4-2 Alexander Garringer, b. 25 Feb 1800, Berkeley Co., VA, d. Jun 1849, Howard Co., IN

 m. 13 Aug 1818, Fayette Co., OH, Mary Ellen Boots, b. 1 Sep 1798, Hardy Co., VA

G-4-2-1 Mary Garringer, b. c1819, Fayette Co., OH

 m. 14 Nov 1842, Randolph Co., IN, Thomas Love

G-4-2-2 David Garringer, b. c1821, Fayette, OH, d. Putnam Co., MO

 m. 13 Jul 1848, Howard Co., IN, (G-4-1-4) Drucilla Garringer

G-4-2-2-1 Mary E. Garringer, b. c1849, Howard Co., IN
G-4-2-2-1-1 son Joshua ?, b. c1895
G-4-2-2-2 Solomon Garringer, b. c1851, Howard Co., IN
G-4-2-2-3 John W. Garringer, b. c1855, Putnam Co., MO
G-4-2-2-4 Isaac Garringer, b. c1857, Putnam Co., MO
   m. 1 Sep 1877, Putnam Co., MO, (G-4-2-3-4) Mary Etta Garringer
G-4-2-2-4-1 Sarah Garringer, m. Alfred Martin
G-4-2-2-4-2 Albert Garringer, m. 2nd Ersa Feltner
G-4-2-2-4-3 William Garringer
G-4-2-2-4-4 John Garringer
G-4-2-2-4-5 Ida Garringer
G-4-2-2-4-6 Luvina Garringer
G-4-2-2-4-7 Grace Garringer
G-4-2-2-4-8 Riley Garringer
G-4-2-2-4-9 Charles Garringer
G-4-2-2-5 Rhoda Ann Garringer, b. c1860, MO
G-4-2-2-6 William Garringer, b. c1864, MO
G-4-2-3 Isaac Garringer, b. 12 Jan 1824, Fayette Co., OH, d. 4 Aug 1902,
   bur. Mitchell Cem., Putnam Co., MO
   m. 2 Sep 1849, Howard Co., IN, Mary Louisa Martin
G-4-2-3-1 Jessie Garringer, b. Aug 1850, IN
G-4-2-3-2 Simon Garringer
G-4-2-3-3 Joseph Garringer, b. 1854, MO
G-4-2-3-4 Mary Etta Garringer, b. 14 Feb 1862, Putnam Co., MO, d. 21
   Mar 1947, NE
   m. 1 Sep 1877, Putnam Co., MO, (G-4-2-2-4) Isaac Garringer
G-4-2-3-5 Sarah Jane Garringer, b. 1852, IN
G-4-2-3-6 Samuel Garringer, b. 1856, MO
G-4-2-3-7 Phoebe Garringer, b. 1858, MO
G-4-2-3-8 Isaac Lane Garringer, b. 1866, MO
G-4-2-3 m. 2nd Sarah Jane Davis
G-4-2-3-9 James Riley Garringer, b. 3 Jul 1873, Putnam Co., MO, d. 23
   Jan 1922, Iowa Co., IA
   m. Anna Lue Treacey Kelly
G-4-2-3-10 Minnie Garringer, b. 1875, m. William Peckinpaugh
G-4-2-4 Sarah Jane Garringer, b. Aug 1825, Fayette Co., OH
   m. William H. Good
G-4-2-5 Alexander Garringer, b. Oct 1827, Fayette Co., OH
   m. 10 Oct 1849, Phebe Betson
   m. 2nd 25 Jan 1854, Rebecca Simons
G-4-2-5-1 Thomas B. Garringer, b. 1854, IA
G-4-2-5-2 Rhoda Garringer, b. 1857, IA
G-4-2-5-3 Mary J. Garringer, b. 1858, IA
G-4-2-5-4 Sarah Garringer, b. c1860, IA, m. Daniel Hochstedler
G-4-2-5-5 James Garringer, b. c1863, IA
G-4-2-5-6 Margaret Garringer, b. c1865, IA

G-4-2-6 Absolom Garringer, b. 12 Jan 1829, Fayette Co., OH, d. 25 Nov 1887, Harper Co., KS
m. 15 Apr 1850, Howard Co., IN, Delila Ann Martin
G-4-2-6-1 William Henry Garringer, b. 14 Mar 1851, IN, d. 17 Mar 1929, Freeport, KS
m. Hannah Frances Richardson
G-4-2-6-1-1 Daniel Riley Garringer, b. 22 Jul 1870, TN
m. 20 Aug 1891, Angie Belle Joseph
G-4-2-6-2 Maryetta Garringer, b. 2 Jan 1853, IN, d. 9 Jun 1938
m. John Henry Swope
G-4-2-6-3 John W. Garringer, b. 30 Mar 1855, Putnam Co., MO (1920 census Randolph Co., IN)
m. 2 Oct 1880, Nancy Ann Canann
G-4-2-6-3-1 Leonard Garringer, b. c1904, IN
G-4-2-6-4 Elizabeth Eleanor Garringer, b. 27 Apr, 1857, Putnam Co., MO, d. 9 Nov 1867
G-4-2-6-5 A. Lincoln Garringer, b. 25 Aug 1859, Putnam Co., MO
m. 20 Apr 1890, Martha A. Dull
G-4-2-7 Samuel Garringer, b. 26 Mar 1831, Fayette Co., OH, d. 10 Feb 1909 (1880, 1900 censuses Putnam Co., MO) m. Frances Neighbors
G-4-2-7-1 Samuel Garringer, b. Jun 1851, IN (1900 census Putnam Co., MO)
G-4-2-7-2 Frances Garringer, b. 1858, MO
G-4-2-7-3 Elizabeth Garringer, b. c1859, MO
G-4-2-7-4 Martha J. Garringer, b. c1861, MO
G-4-2-7-5 Sherma Garringer, b. Aug 1865, MO
G-4-2-7-6 Madison S. Garringer, b. c1866, MO
G-4-2-7-7 William G. Garringer, b. c1867, MO
G-4-2-7-8 Grant Garringer, b. c1868, MO
G-4-2-7-9 Alexander Garringer, b. c1870, MO
G-4-2-7-10 John N. Garringer, b. c1873, MO
G-4-2-7-11 John Garringer, b. c1876, MO
G-4-2-7-12 Saluda Garringer, b. c1877, MO
G-4-2-7-13 Celestia Garringer, b. c1879, MO
G-4-2-8 Elizabeth Rebecca Garringer, b. c1833, Randolph Co., IN, d. Feb 1864, Putnam CO., MO
m. 14 May 1853, Howard Co., IN, Joseph U. Martin
G-4-2-9 Solomon Garringer, b. 10 Apr 1835, Randolph Co., IN, d. 20 Jan 1919, MO
m. 29 Dec 1857, Permilla Dollard, m. 2nd Emiline Minks Crockett
G-4-2-10 William Henry Garringer, b. 16 Aug 1840, Jay Co., IN, d. 19 Jan 1921, Putnam Co., MO, no issue
m. 10 Aug 1861, Lydia E. Gastrage, m. 2nd 26 Oct 1865, Louisa J. Forbes, m. 3rd 26 Jun 1906, Nancy Berry
G-4-3 David Garringer, b. 12 Oct 1802, Berkeley Co., VA, d. 17 Sep 1869, Fayette Co., OH

m. 12 Sep 1825, Fayette Co., OH, Cyrene Yeoman, b. 6 Apr 1806, NY, d. 21 Oct 1888, Fayette Co., OH

G-4-3-1 Sarah Jane Garringer, b. 19 Oct 1826, Fayette Co., OH, d. 4 Jun 1914

m. 10 Aug 1845, Fayette Co., OH, Henton Hoppes

G-4-3-2 Angeline Garinger, b. 19 Nov 1828, Fayette Co., OH, d. 3 Jan 1915

m. 27 Feb 1848, Fayette Co., OH, Abraham Booco

G-4-3-3 Amanda Melvina Garinger, b. 3 Sep 1828, d. 13 Feb 1904

m. 24 Jan 1847, Fayette Co., OH, James Stokesbury

G-4-3-4 Albert Garinger, b. 21 Mar 1834, d. 6 Sep 1923

m. 31 Oct 1858, Fayette Co., OH, Angeline Little

G-4-3-5 Samantha Garinger, b. 7 Aug 1836, d. 15 Sep 1916

m. 22 Oct 1857, Fayette Co., OH, Arthemas Hendrickson

G-4-3-6 Osee Garinger, b. 7 Jun 1839, d. 9 Dec 1916

m. 15 May 1859, Fayette Co., OH, John Weller

G-4-3-7 Thomas Benton Garinger, b. 14 Oct 1841, d. 14 Sep 1921

m. 22 Oct 1872, Fayette Co., OH, Malissa Ann Catherine Parrett

G-4-3-8 Stephen Garinger, b. 17 Apr 1844, d. 8 Feb 1923

m. 22 Mar 1865, Clinton Co., OH, Rebecca Ann Borton

G-4-3-9 Ira James Garinger, b. 1 Jan 1848, Fayette Co., OH, d. 24 Oct 1925

m. 18 Dec 1871, Highland Co., OH, Lucy Ellen Smith,

G-4-4 Elizabeth Garringer, b. 17 Feb 1806, Berkeley Co., VA, d. 20 Mar 1848

m. 14 Aug 1831, Fayette Co., OH, Acquilla Jones, b. 14 Aug 1831, d. 17 Oct 1882, Fayette Co., OH

G-4-5 Mary "Polly" Garringer, b. 27 Jan 1810, OH, d. 27 Jan 1886

m. 1 Jul 1830, Fayette Co., OH, Elias Brakefield, b. 31 Aug 1806, Berkeley Co., VA, d. 30 Mar 1893, Fayette Co., OH

G-4-6 Isaac Jacob Garringer*, b. 7 Mar 1812, Fairfield Co., OH, d. 16 Jan 1870, Randolph Co., IN, bur. Garringer Homestead Cem., Randolph Co., IN

m. 16 Mar 1834, Delaware Co., IN, Sarah "Sally" Boots, b. 23 Mar 1814, Ross Co., OH, d. 8 Aug 1882, Randolph Co., IN, bur. Garringer Homestead Cem., Randolph Co., IN

G-4-6-1 Simon Garringer, b. 7 Sep 1835, Randolph Co., IN, d. 9 May 1863, dnm, bur. Garringer Homestead Cem., Randolph Co., IN

G-4-6-2 Delilah Garringer, b. 13 Jan 1837, Randolph Co., IN, d. 17 Jun 1872, Randolph Co., IN, bur. Garringer Homestead Cem.

m. 24 May 1860, Randolph Co., IN, Henry Dull

G-4-6-2-1 Alice Dull (adopted by Ziegler), b. 17 Nov 1862, Randolph Co., IN

m. 24 Jun 1882, Charles Ford

G-4-6-2-1-1 Clessie Herman Ford, b. 15 Nov 1892

G-4-6-2-1-2 Clarence E. Ford

G-4-6-2-1-3 William Ford

G-4-6-2-1-4 Carsie Ford, b. c1892, d. 1971, m. Sarah E. Gilbert

G-4-6-2-1-5 Myrtle Ford, m. Munnich

G-4-6-2-1-6 Mary Mildred Ford, b. 5 Sep 1900, Randolph Co., IN, m. Carl Flesher

G-4-6-2-1-7 Ethel "Etta" Ford, b. 22 Jan 1901, Chicago, IL, m. Enos Francis McCartney

G-4-6-2 m. 2nd 25 Aug 1866, Randolph Co., IN, Christian Ziegler

G-4-6-2-2 Isaac L. Ziegler, b. c1867, IN, d. c1930, bur. Hopewell Cem., m. Alma Moon

G-4-6-2-3 Riley O. Ziegler, b. c1868, IN, d. c1920, bur. Hopewell Cem., m. Louisa Stilwell

G-4-6-3 David Carson Garringer*, b. 4 Aug 1838, Randolph Co., IN, d. 10 Dec 1895, Randolph Co., IN, bur. Hopewell Cem., Randolph Co., IN
m. 6 Mar 1871, Jay Co., IN, Amelia Alisa Collins, b. 30 Jun 1844, Jay Co., IN, d. 9 Jun 1908, bur. Hopewell Cem.

G-4-6-3-1 James Milton Garringer, b. 17 Nov 1872, Randolph Co., IN, d. 4 Aug 1931, Randolph Co., IN, bur. Tomlinson Cem., Delaware Co., IN, no issue
m. 18 Feb 1897, Delaware Co., IN, Addie Pearl Heath, b. 8 May 1876, IN, d. 27 Dec 1945, bur. Tomlinson Cem., Delaware Co., IN

G-4-6-3-2 Isaac Luther Garringer*, b. 15 Jun 1874, Randolph Co., IN, d. 2 Jun 1940, Delaware Co., IN, bur. 4 Jun 1940, Woodlawn Cem.
m. 10 Aug 1895, Randolph Co., IN, Bertha Achsah Hammers, b. 30 Jan 1877, d. 29 Oct 1918, bur. Woodlawn Cem.
m. 2nd 1 Sep 1925, Charity Belle Marquis Clements, b. 25 Oct 1878, d. Jan 1973, bur. 23 Jan 1973, Woodlawn Cem.

G-4-6-3-2-1 Helen Marie Garringer, b. 18 Jun 1896, Randolph Co., IN, d. 29 Oct 1969, Marion Co., IN, bur. Williamsburg Cem., Wayne Co., IN
m. 18 Jan 1922, Covington, KY, Paul M. Williams, b. 29 Feb 1892, Williamsburg, Wayne Co., IN

G-4-6-3-2-1-1 Mildred Jane Williams, b. 25 Nov 1924, Williamsburg, IN
m. ? Tuke, AZ, div.

G-4-6-3-2-1-1-1 Margaret Tuke

G-4-6-3-2-1-2 Sarah Ann Williams, b. 5 Sep 1928, Indianapolis, IN, d. 5 Feb 1929, bur. Williamsburg, IN

G-4-6-3-2-2 Hilda Irene Garringer*, b. 28 Mar 1898, Randolph Co., IN, d. 26 Dec 1983, Parker City, IN, bur. Woodlawn Cem., Randolph Co., IN
m. 11 Jan 1919, Samuel Plummer Boggs*, b. 2 Apr 1893, Greenbrier Co., WV, d. 9 Apr 1965, Selma, IN, bur. Woodlawn Cem., Randolph Co., IN
(see Boggs Descendants List, B-2-4-7-4-6-2)

G-4-6-3-2-3 Mildred Martha Garringer, b. 14 Dec 1903, Farmland, Randolph Co., IN, d. 9 Apr 1999, Hollywood, FL, no issue

m. 1 Jan 1927, Ralph Raymond Gilpin, b. 27 Aug 1902, d. 16 Nov 1977, bur. Hollywood, Florida

G-4-6-3-2-4 Lloyd Milton Garringer, b. 12 Sep 1910, Randolph Co., IN, d. 18 Jan 1979, FL, bur. Nokomis, FL

m. 17 Nov 1942, Indianapolis, IN, June Ellen Hawk, b. 11 Jul 1918, Fort Wayne, IN

G-4-6-3-2-4-1 Kay Ellen Garringer, b. 11 Jul 1943, Muncie, IN

m. 3 Sep 1966, Lake Luzerne, NY, Earnest J. Quinto, b. 29 Jun 1941

G-4-6-3-2-4-1-1 Matthew David Qunito, b. 4 Jul 1971

G-4-6-3-2-4-1-2 Mark Lloyd Quinto, b. 26 Oct 1975

G-4-6-3-3 Sarah Melissa Garringer, b. 10 Oct 1875, Randolph Co., IN, d. 1 Apr 1958, Muncie, IN, bur. Hopewell Cem., Randolph Co., IN

m. 24 Dec 1890, Randolph Co., IN, William B. Life, b. 1868, d. 1954

G-4-6-3-3-1 Bessie May Life, b. 1892, Randolph Co., IN, d. 2 Apr 1962, Muncie, IN

m. Charles Filler, d. 1961

G-4-6-3-3-1-1 Harold Edwin Filler, d. 1955

G-4-6-3-3-1-1-1 Eddie Filler

G-4-6-3-3-1-1-2 Darlene Filler

G-4-6-3-3-1-1-3 Carolyn Filler

G-4-6-3-3-1-2 Max Filler

G-4-6-3-3-2 David Martin Life, b. 8 Sep 1894, Randolph Co., IN, d. 21 Jan 1982, Jay Co., IN, m. Pauline Craig

G-4-6-3-3-2-1 Phyllis Life, b. 1916, m. Howard Spurgeon Bowen

G-4-6-3-3-2-1-1 Michael Bowen, b. 1940, m. Margie McKinley

G-4-6-3-3-2-1-1-1 Lori Ann Bowen, b. 1964

G-4-6-3-3-2-1-2 Bette Louise Bowen, b. 1946, m. Bernard Winship

G-4-6-3-3-2-1-2-1 Barbara Lynn Winship, b. 1969

G-4-6-3-3-2-1-2-2 Mary Ann Winship, b. 1971

G-4-6-3-3-2-2 Janyce Life, b. 1918, m. William J. Bousman

G-4-6-3-3-2-2-1 Billy J. Bousman, b. 1936, m. 1956, Sue Ritchie

G-4-6-3-3-2-2-1-1 Larry David Bousman, b. 1958

G-4-6-3-3-2-2-1-2 Keith Alan Bousman, b. 1961

G-4-6-3-3-2-2-1-3 Connie Beth Bousman, b. 1968

G-4-6-3-3-2-2-1-4 Craig Ritchie Bousman, b. 1969

G-4-6-3-3-2-2-2 Larry Martin Bousman, b. 1937, m. 1958, Joycelyn Harkema

G-4-6-3-3-2-2-2-1 Deborah Jean Bousman, b. 1960

G-4-6-3-3-2-2-2-2 Wendy Jo Bousman, b. 1968

G-4-6-3-3-2-2-3 Deborah Bousman, b. 1939, m. 1965, Gordon Haddock

G-4-6-3-3-2-2-3-1 Janice Marie Haddock, b. 1967

G-4-6-3-3-2-2-3-2 Andrea Lynn Haddock, b. 1969

G-4-6-3-3-2-2-4 Sue Ann Bousman, b. 1941, m. Carl Cabbiness

G-4-6-3-3-2-2-4-1 Carl O. Cabbiness, II, b. 1966

G-4-6-3-3-2-2-4-2 Christopher Cabbiness, b. 1968

G-4-6-3-3-2-3 Norma Jean Life, b. 1920, m. Joseph William Reynard, b. 1920, d. 1968

G-4-6-3-3-2-3-1 Joyce A. Reynard, b. 1939, m. Robert Marks

G-4-6-3-3-2-3-1-1 Susan Joyce Marks, b. 1959

G-4-6-3-3-2-3-1-2 Robert Kent Marks, b. 1963

G-4-6-3-3-2-3-2 Jackie Joe Reynard, b. 1941, m. Doris Jean Crouch

G-4-6-3-3-2-3-2-1 Julie Lynn Reynard, b. 1961

G-4-6-3-3-2-3-3 Jerald William Reynard, b. 1944, m. Judith Marlene Greg

G-4-6-3-3-2-3-3-1 Amy Joe Reynard, b. 1965

G-4-6-3-3-2-3-3-2 Joseph William Reynard, b. 1970

G-4-6-3-3-2-3 m. 2nd John M. Selvey

G-4-6-3-3-3 Ethel Amelia Life, b. 1896, Randolph Co., IN, m. Calvin Ralston

G-4-6-3-3-3-1 Calvin Ralston, Jr., b. 1927, m. Marilyn Sanderson

G-4-6-3-3-3-1-1 William Ralston, b. 1949

G-4-6-3-3-3-1-2 Debra Ralston, b. 1953

G-4-6-3-3-3-1-3 Diane Ralston, b. 1953

G-4-6-3-3-3-1-4 Sara Elizabeth Ralston, b. 1966

G-4-6-3-3-3-2 Phama Ralston, b. 1920, m. Clarence Hudson

G-4-6-3-3-3-2-1 John Hudson, b. 1949

G-4-6-3-3-4 Lottie Crystal Life, b. 25 Sep 1898, d. 1919, m. Charles Fuller

G-4-6-3-3-4-1 child, d. at birth

G-4-6-3-3-5 Carlos Arthur Life, b. 1901, Randolph Co., IN, d. 16 May 1984

m. 1928, Margaret Van Norman, m. 2nd Frances ?

G-4-6-3-3-5-1 Richard Arthur Life, b. 1930, d. 4 Dec 1978, m. 1951, Dorothy Mort

G-4-6-3-3-5-1-1 Linda Dianne Life, b. 1953, VA

G-4-6-3-3-5-1-2 Susan Ann Life, b. 1956, Peru, IN

G-4-6-3-3-5-1-3 William Arthur Life, b. 1960, Peru, IN

G-4-6-3-3-5-2 Dorothea Joan Life, b. 1932, m. 1954, Jack B. Jackson

G-4-6-3-3-5-2-1 Jeffrey Brian Jackson, b. 1958

G-4-6-3-3-5-2-2 Michael Jonathon Jackson, b. 1960

G-4-6-3-3-5-2-3 Timothy James Jackson, b. 1963

G-4-6-3-3-5-2-4 Julie Beth Jackson, b. 1971

G-4-6-3-3-5-3 Lois Ann Life, b. 1940, m. Dr. George Michael Ball

G-4-6-3-3-5-3-1 Thomas Michael Ball, b. 1967

G-4-6-3-3-5-3-2 Karen Diane Ball, b. 1968

G-4-6-3-3-5-3-3 Deborah Joan Ball, b. 1970

G-4-6-3-3-6 Homer Lawrence Life, b. 1904, Randolph Co., IN, d. 17 Jul 1992, Delaware Co., IN, m. Mary Banks

G-4-6-3-3-6-1 Judith Life, b. 1936, m. Stanley O. Ikenberry

G-4-6-3-3-6-1-1 David Lawrence Ikenberry, b. 1960, Lansing, MI

G-4-6-3-3-6-1-2 Steven Oliver Ikenberry, b. 1963, Morgantown, WV

G-4-6-3-3-6-1-3 John Paul Ikenberry, b. 1968, Morgantown, WV

G-4-6-3-3-7 Hershel W. Life, b. 1907, d. Sep 1976, m. Nixola Scranton

G-4-6-3-3-7-1 Larry Life, b. 1943

G-4-6-3-3-7-2 Sara Lynn Life, b. 1948, m. Jerry Hoege

G-4-6-3-3-7-2-1 Amy Lynn Hoege, b. 1972

G-4-6-3-3-7-3 David Life, b. 1949

G-4-6-3-3-8 Clara Estella Life, b. 1910, Green Twp., Randolph Co., IN, d.
19 Mar 1999, Woodlands, Muncie, IN, m. 1934, Ralph York, d. 1973

G-4-6-3-3-8-1 Rebecca York, d. bef 1999, m. David Ross Miller

G-4-6-3-3-8-1-1 Stacey Lee Miller, b. 1967

G-4-6-3-3-8-1-2 Bradley David Miller, b. 1968

G-4-6-3-3-8-1-3 Mark Miller

G-4-6-3-3-9 Buelah Lavina Life, b. 1912, d. bef. 1999, m. Everett Smith, d.
1949

G-4-6-3-3-9-1 Douglas Smith, b. 1934, m. Nancy Porter

G-4-6-3-3-9-1-1 Julie Ann Smith, b. 1960

G-4-6-3-3-9-1-2 Stephen Smith, b. 1962

G-4-6-3-3-9-2 Phyllis Smith, b. 1939, m. Paul Anthony Welter

G-4-6-3-3-9-2-1 Eric Anthony Welter, b. 1966

G-4-6-3-3-9-2-2 Darren Douglas Welter, b. 1969

G-4-6-3-3-9 m. 2nd Stewart Shaffer

G-4-6-3-3-10 Geraldine Life, b. 1915, d. aft 1998, m. Leo Heaton

G-4-6-3-3-10-1 Lewis Edward Heaton, m. Judith Ann Harris

G-4-6-3-3-10-1-1 Beverly Sue Heaton, b. 1956

G-4-6-3-3-10-1-2 Brenda Kay Heaton, b. 1958

G-4-6-3-3-10-1-3 Deborah Ann Heaton, b. 1962

G-4-6-3-3-10-1-4 Lewis Edward Heaton, b. 1964

G-4-6-3-4 David Arthur Garringer, b. 25 Apr 1881, Randolph Co., IN, d.
1 Jun 1940, Delaware Co., IN, bur. Desoto Cem., Delaware Co., IN
m. 27 Jun 1903, Delaware Co., IN, Iva Perle Pittenger, b. 3 Sep 1882, d.
11 May 1979, IN, bur. Desoto Cem., Delaware Co., IN

G-4-6-3-4-1 Clarence Carson Garringer, b. 31 May 1904, d. 15 Mar 1920,
dnm

G-4-6-3-4-2 Thelma Marie Garringer, b. 25 Sep 1905, Desoto, Delaware
Co., IN, d. 12 Aug 1985, bur. Beech Grove Cem., Muncie, IN
m. 1 Apr 1932, George W. Masing

G-4-6-3-4-2-1 Thomas Masing

G-4-6-3-4-2-2 James Masing

G-4-6-3-4-2-3 Milton Masing

G-4-6-3-4-2-4 Sally Masing, m. Sam Waggoner

G-4-6-3-4-3 Margaret Alisa Garringer, b. 22 Feb 1909, Delaware Co., IN
m. 1st ? Masing, m. 2nd 10 May 1930, Nicholas J. Grannan

G-4-6-3-4-4 Harriet Ethel Garringer, b. 6 Oct 1913, Delaware Co., IN, d.
31 Jul 1986, Delaware Co., IN, m. 13 Sep 1935, Clifford L. Swift

G-4-6-3-4-5 Sarah Frances Garringer, b. 30 Jan 1916, Delaware Co., IN
m. 17 Aug 1935, Forrest Keely, m. 2nd 1 Nov 1941, Kenneth M. Ritter

G-4-6-3-4-6 Rosella Maude Garringer, b. 28 Apr 1918, Randolph Co., IN,
d. 19 Jun 1928, Mohave Co., AZ, m. 12 Jun 1938, Albert Haber

G-4-6-3-4-7 Isaac Milton Garringer, b. 30 Sep 1920, Randolph Co., IN, d. 12 Feb 1982, Clark Co., NV, m. 31 Aug 1946, Mary K. Herdering

G-4-6-3-4-8 Betty Louise Garringer, b. 11 Feb 1924, d. 11 Feb 1924

G-4-6-3-4-9 Iva Jean Garringer, b. 28 Mar 1926, Randolph Co., IN m. 28 Mar 1946, Harold E. Plank

G-4-6-3-5 Elizabeth Catherine "Katie" Garringer, b. 20 Jan 1887, d. 1 Mar 1888, bur. Hopewell Cem., Randolph Co., IN

G-4-6-4 Samuel Garringer, b. 31 Aug 1840, Randolph Co., IN, d. 13 May 1912, bur. Hopewell Cem.
m. 21 Dec 1861, Randolph Co., IN, Susannah Troyer, b. 31 Apr 1844, Darke Co., OH, d. 24 Feb 1926, Randolph Co., IN

G-4-6-4-1 Katie Garringer

G-4-6-4-2 Melissa Garringer, b. 12 Dec 1862, d. 25 Apr 1866, bur. Garringer Family Homestead

G-4-6-4-3 William Lewis Garringer, b. 30 Apr 1865, IN, Randolph Co., IN, d. 1 Mar 1942, bur. Hopewell Cem., Randolph Co., IN, dnm

G-4-6-4-4 Eddie Garringer, b. c1865, IN, d. ? young after 1870

G-4-6-4-5 Rosa Armina Garringer, b. Oct 1870, d. 18 Apr 1910, m. 23 Apr 1891, Henry Wise

G-4-6-4-6 Elmer L. Garringer, b. 15 Jul 1875, Randolph Co., IN, d. 6 Nov 1880, bur. Hopewell Cem., Randolph Co., IN, dnm

G-4-6-4-7 Cora Elmetta Garringer, b. 20 Nov 1877, d. 3 May 1950, bur. Hopewell Cem., Randolph Co., IN, dnm

G-4-6-5 Phoebe Garringer, b. 23 Nov 1842, Randolph Co., IN, d. 20 Nov 1923
m. 18 Aug 1861, Randolph Co., IN, William Bales

G-4-6-6 Isaac B. Garringer, b. 25 Nov 1844, Randolph Co., IN, d. 8 Nov 1924, bur. Hopewell Cem., Randolph Co., IN
m. 3 Oct 1868, Randolph Co., IN, Sarah Catherine Godwin, b. 10 Sep 1848, d. 11 Nov 1933

G-4-6-6-1 Albert Weldon Garringer, b. 9 Sep 1869, Randolph Co., IN, d. 3 Dec 1869

G-4-6-6-2 Mazana Belle Garringer, b. 7 Jan 1871, Randolph Co., IN, d. 5 Feb 1957
m. 9 Feb 1889, Randolph Co., IN, Jacob Woodard

G-4-6-6-2-1 Charles Woodard, b. 5 Jun 1890, d. aft 5 Jun 1890

G-4-6-6-2-2 Della W. Woodard, b. 30 Jul 1891, d. 3 Jan 1970
m. Joe "Bert" Baker, m. 2nd Joe Anderson

G-4-6-6-2-3 Carl Woodard, b. 13 May 1894, Randolph Co., IN, d. May 1954, Jay Co., IN
m. Dolly Cleota "Tot" Miller

G-4-6-6-2-4 Lola Woodard, b. 1 Nov 1897, d. 23 Nov 1900

G-4-6-6-2-5 Clessie Woodard, b. 6 Nov 1899, d. 23 Mar 1910

G-4-6-6-2-6 Olah May Woodard, b. 7 Oct 1903, d. 29 Jun 1990
m. 7 Aug 1920, Jay Co., IN, William Keith Bost, b. 6 Aug 1899, d. 13 May 1973

G-4-6-6-2-6-1 Weldon Leo Bost, b. 27 Jul 1921, Jay Co., IN, d. 23 Jun 1930, Jay Co., IN

G-4-6-6-2-6-2 Joseph Franklin Bost, b. 7 May 1923, Jay Co., IN, d. 17 Nov 1997, Jay Co., IN
m. 26 May 1945, Jay Co., IN, Mildred Irene Prescott

G-4-6-6-2-6-3 Arlene Marie Bost, b. 18 Jul 1925, Jay Co., IN
m. 24 Oct 1948, Jay Co., IN, Charles Angus Hambrock, b. 24 Jul 1917, Jay Co., IN, d. 22 Jul 1961, Allen Co., IN

G-4-6-6-2-6-3 m. 2nd Apr 1963, Robert Keith Owens

G-4-6-6-2-6-3-1 Robert Dale Hambrock, b. 29 Sep 1949, Jay Co., IN

G-4-6-6-2-6-3-2 James Leroy Hambrock, b. 5 Jan 1951, Jay Co., IN

G-4-6-6-2-6-3-3 Marylyn Sue Hambrock, b. 22 Aug 1952, Jay Co., IN, m. John David Cox, m. 2nd Steven Leroy Garinger

G-4-6-6-2-6-3-4 Glenn Richard "Rick" Hambrock, b. 29 Sep 1954, Jay Co., IN
m. 27 Aug 1982, Jay Co., IN, Janet Lee Gilbert, b. 13 Mar 1949, KY

G-4-6-6-2-6-3-5 Cathy Jo Hambrock, b. 6 Feb 1957, Jay Co., IN
m. James Ronald Garringer

G-4-6-6-2-6-3-6 Charles Thomas Hambrock, b. 19 Jan 1960, Jay Co., IN, m. Teresa Ann Sears

G-4-6-6-2-6-4 Victor Verl Bost, b. 8 Jul 1927, Jay Co., IN, d. 23 Jun 1930, Jay Co., IN

G-4-6-6-2-6-5 Arlie Cleon Bost, b. 15 Jul 1928, Jay Co., IN, d. 17 Dec 1981, Delaware Co., IN

G-4-6-6-2-6-6 Betty Maxine Bost, b. 5 Jan 1932, Jay Co., IN

G-4-6-6-2-6-7 Glen Dwaine Bost, b. 31 Jan 1936, Jay Co., IN

G-4-6-6-2-6-8 Cletis Jay Bost, b. 20 Jun 1938, Jay Co., IN, d. 20 Dec 1984, Jay Co., IN

G-4-6-6-2-6-9 Clinis Ray Bost, b. 20 Jun 1938, Jay Co., IN

G-4-6-6-2-6-10 Wanda Joanne Bost, b. 26 May 1940, Jay Co., IN

G-4-6-6-2-6-11 Marvin Berl Bost, b. 20 Jan 1943, Jay Co., IN

G-4-6-6-2-7 Larkin Woodard, b. 2 Jun 1906, d. 4 Nov 1980, m. Elsie Yost

G-4-6-6-2-8 Lester Woodard, b. 6 Jun 1909, d. 20 Apr 1997, m. Hanora Elizabeth Haley

G-4-6-6-2-9 Evylene Woodard, b. 14 May 1914, d. 1930

G-4-6-6-3 John Lewis Garringer, b. 24 Nov 1872, IN, d. 1 Mar 1952, bur. Hopewell Cem., Randolph Co., IN,
m. 31 Aug 1893, Janie "Rachel" Bales, b. 1870, d. 1915, ni

G-4-6-6-4 Dorotha Ann Garringer, b. 15 Jan 1875, IN, d. 1945, bur. Hopewell Cem., Randolph Co., IN
m. Jul 1893, Thomas Orville Moon

G-4-6-6-5 Milla Elma "Mille" Garringer, b. 28 Mar 1878, IN, d. 17 Jan 1969
m. 5 Sep 1900, Randolph Co., IN, Albert Luther Stephens

G-4-6-6-6 Sarah Samantha Garringer, b. 17 May 1880, IN, d. 21 Oct 1946, bur Woodlawn Cem., Randolph Co., IN

m. 20 Aug 1900, Benjamin Dytmire

G-4-6-6-7 Isaac Jacob Garringer, b. 28 Aug 1882, IN, d. 2 Mar 1963

G-4-6-6-8 David Oscar Garringer, b. 11 Oct 1884, IN, d. 21 Jan 1973, bur. Hopewell Cem. Randolph Co., IN

m. Sep 1907, Iva L. Day, b. 7 Feb 1886, d. 21 Jun 1973, bur. Hopewell Cem., Randolph Co., IN

G-4-6-6-8-1 Roy "Leroy" Verlin Garringer, b. 30 Aug 1909, d. 5 Aug 1981
  m. Nellie L. Addington, b. 1912

G-4-6-6-8-1-1 Roy Garringer

G-4-6-6-8-1-2 Mark Garringer

G-4-6-6-8-1-3 Lee Garringer

G-4-6-6-8-2 Dollie Floy Garringer, b. 12 Apr 1913, IN
  m. 5 Jun 1933, Glenn Friar, b. 1912, d. 1972, bur. Woodlawn Cem., Randolph Co., IN

G-4-6-6-9 William Mahlon Garringer, b. 16 Nov 1886, Randolph Co., IN, d. 25 May 1948, m. Louise E. Gantz, b. 29 Jun 1889, d. 4 Aug 1964

G-4-6-6-9-1 Cecil Leottus Garringer, b. 3 Dec 1909, Randolph Co., IN, d. Apr 1981, IN, m. Freda Smith

G-4-6-6-9-1-1 Amalie Ann Garringer, b. 26 Sep 1933, m. Raymond Dale Green

G-4-6-6-9-1-2 Ronald Garringer, b. 1936

G-4-6-6-9-1-3 Donald Eugene Garringer, b. 19 Sep 1938, Delaware Co., IN
  m. 1961, Janis Kay Washburn

G-4-6-6-9-1-3-1 Pamela Kay Garringer, b. Jan 1962, m. James Jeffers

G-4-6-6-9-1-3-2 Marcy Ann Garringer, b. May 1964, m. Kent Marks

G-4-6-6-9-1-3-3 Jodon Garringer, b. 19 Nov 1970, m. Marcie Flannery

G-4-6-6-9-1-4 Sharon Kay Garringer, b. 29 Oct 1943
  m. Douglas Dwaine Stanley

G-4-6-6-9-2 Mildred Garringer, b. 4 Sep 1914, m. Hubert Stauffer

G-4-6-6-9-3 Acel Garringer, d. 5 Apr 1994, m. Martha V. Vinson

G-4-6-6-9-3-1 Judy Garringer, m. Rick Sayre

G-4-6-6-9-3-2 Barbara Garringer

G-4-6-6-9-4 Esteil (son) Garringer

G-4-6-6-10 Joseph Linus Garringer, b. 18 Aug 1888, d. 13 Apr 1970, IN
  m. Lillie H. Sumner, b. c1888, IN

G-4-6-6-10-1 Thelma Garringer, b. 2 Oct 1909, d. 17 Mar 1911

G-4-6-6-10-2 Pauline Madonna Garringer, b. 16 Jun 1912, Randolph Co., IN, m. George Bales

G-4-6-6-10-3 Charles Leander Garringer, b. 25 Feb 1914, IN
  m. 8 Jun 1938, Jay Co., IN, Mary Imogene Hoth

G-4-6-6-10-4 Robert E. Garringer, b. 15 Apr 1916, IN, d. 9 Apr 1967, IN
  m. 27 Jul 1938, Jay Co., IN, Rachael Margaret Priest

G-4-6-6-10-5 Wilma Delight Garringer, b. 12 May 1918, IN
  m. Charles Oscar Orr

G-4-6-6-10-6 Joseph Richard Garringer, b. 23 May 1920, d. 27 Oct 1962, m. Marie ?

G-4-6-6-10-7 Lily May Garringer, b. 29 Sep 1923, m. Robert Donald Koontz

G-4-6-6-10-8 Lee Edward Garringer, b. 11 Jun 1926, d. 8 Apr 1968, Delaware Co., IN, m. in Austria, Elfriede Sollfrank

G-4-6-6-10-9 Richard Duane Garringer, b. 9 Aug 1929, Indianapolis, IN, d. Mar 1984, Hopewell, VA, m. Reba Hensley

G-4-6-6-10-10 Bernard Rex Garringer, b. 29 Jan 1932, m. Shirley McPherson

G-4-6-6-10 m. 2nd 24 Dec 1937, Jay Co., IN, Stella Eastep

G-4-6-6-11 Lafayette Garringer, b. 6 Jun 1891, d. at birth

G-4-6-6-12 Iva Ina Garringer, b. 18 Aug 1893, d. 29 Dec 1893

G-4-6-7 Lewis Garringer, b. 19 Jan 1847, Randolph Co., IN, d. 31 Oct 1916, Pulaski Co., AR, bur. Bluff Point Cem., Jay Co., IN
m. 31 Dec 1871, Randolph Co., IN, Ann Bartlette, d. bef 1876
m. 2nd 20 Feb 1876, Randolph Co., IN, (G-7-7-1) Hannah Ella Garringer, b. 2 Feb 1857, Jay Co., IN, d. 4 May 1926, Jay Co., IN

G-4-6-7-1 Sarah Garringer, b. 7 Jul 1877, Jay Co., IN, d. 9 Jul 1877

G-4-6-7-2 Mary Garringer, b. 14 Jul 1878, Jay Co., IN, d. 17 Sep 1878

G-4-6-7-3 John (Twin) Garringer, b. 13 May 1882, Jay Co., IN, d. 6 Jul 1882

G-4-6-7-4 Nancy (Twin) Garringer, b. 13 May 1882, Jay Co., IN, d. 6 Jul 1882

G-4-6-7-5 Lewis Garringer, b. 1 Mar 1886, IN, d. 21 May 1979, Dunkirk, IN

G-4-6-7-6 Henry Garringer, b. 23 Jul 1888, Jay Co., IN, d. 10 Oct 1961, Delaware Co., IN
m. 11 Dec 1908, Jay Co., IN, Josephine Friedline

G-4-6-7-6-1 Lewis Samuel Garringer, b. 14 May 1910, Jay Co., IN, d. 5 Dec 1986, Jay Co., IN, m. 15 Mar 1930, Frances Ethel Kaugher, b. 17 Jan 1912, d. 9 Jun 1983

G-4-6-7-6-1-1 Floyd Everett Garringer, b. 13 Jun 1934, Randolph Co., IN m. Joyce Elsie Clousey

G-4-6-7-6-1-1-1 Walter Evert Garringer, b. 5 Feb 1961, Randolph Co., IN m. Michele Denise Holcomb

G-4-6-7-6-1-1-1-1 Ashley Ronielle Garringer, b. 16 Oct 1983

G-4-6-7-6-1-1-1-2 Amanda Mary Garringer, b. 24 Apr 1987

G-4-6-7-6-1-1-1-3 Angela Rose Garringer, b. 9 Sep 1989

G-4-6-7-6-1-2 Joseph Lewis Garringer, b. 10 Jun 1937
m. Wilda Diann Dunmoyer

G-4-6-7-6-1-2-1 Scott Duane Garringer

G-4-6-7-6-1-2 m. 2nd Norma

G-4-6-7-6-1-2-2 Terri Jo Garringer, b. 22 Oct 1966, m. Mike Roop

G-4-6-7-6-1-3 Jerry Thomas Garringer, b. 7 Mar 1943
m. 6 Jun 1954, Maxine L. Masters, d. 13 Aug 1994, Jay Co., IN

G-4-6-7-6-1-3-1 Gregory B. Garringer

G-4-6-7-6-1-3-2 Shawn Garringer

G-4-6-7-6-1-3-3 Shannon Garringer

G-4-6-7-6-1-3-4 Bradley Garringer

G-4-6-7-6-1-4 Nancy Louise Garringer, b. 15 Apr 1950, m. Oliver Robert Earehart

G-4-6-7-6-1-5 Susan Kay Garringer, b. 29 Oct 1951, m. George York

G-4-6-7-6-1-6 David Lee Garringer, b. 25 Dec 1954, m. Judy Ellen Keller

G-4-6-7-6-1-6-1 Tiffany Garringer, b. 5 Mar 1982

G-4-6-7-6-1-6-2 Dusty Lee Garringer, b. 4 Jan 1989

G-4-6-7-6-1-6-3 Jackie Kay Garringer, b. 12 Feb 1991

G-4-6-7-6-2 William H. Garringer, b. 18 Mar 1912, Jay Co., IN
m. 14 Sep 1932, Mary Galbreath

G-4-6-7-6 m. 2nd 10 Jan 1920, Mina Booher

G-4-6-7-6-3 Lester Dwight Garringer, b. 12 Apr 1924, m. Minnie Marie Mondy

G-4-6-7-7 Ida Elizabeth Garringer, b. 21 Dec 1890, Jay Co., IN, d. 23 Dec 1976, Jay Co., IN
m. 3 Mar 1910, Martin Henry Eley

G-4-6-7-8 David Garringer, b. 9 Sep 1893, Jay Co., IN, d. 27 Dec 1970, Portland, IN
m. 30 Nov 1918, Jay Co., IN, Faye Money, b. 24 Aug 1899, d. 22 Jul 1985, IN

G-4-6-7-8-1 Leo Levon Garringer, b. 23 Jul 1919, Jay Co., IN, m. Clara Wanda Hicks

G-4-6-7-8-2 David Garringer, Jr., b. 27 Sep 1922, Jay Co., IN, d. 11 Nov 1996
m. 6 Jun 1947, Genevieve Jill Pease

G-4-6-7-8-3 Betty Louise Garringer, b. 24 Nov 1924, Jay Co., IN, m. Clarence Edward Mann

G-4-6-7-8-4 Arthur Willis Garringer, b. 21 Oct 1927, Jay Co., IN
m. 23 Nov 1946, Jay Co., IN, Edna Helen Loy

G-4-6-7-8-4-1 Michael Duane Garringer, b. 6 Mar 1949

G-4-6-7-8-4-2 Mark Edward Garringer, b. 22 Mar 1953

G-4-6-7-8-4-3 Matthew John Garringer, b. 17 Sep 1955

G-4-6-7-8-4-4 Martin Andrew Garringer, b. 26 Dec 1957

G-4-6-7-8-4-5 Francis Eugene Garringer, b. 27 Dec 1958

G-4-6-7-8-4-6 Andrew James Garringer, b. 31 Jul 1961

G-4-6-7-8-5 Robert Edward Garringer, b. 10 Oct 1929, Jay Co., IN
m. 16 Oct 1949, Jay Co., IN, Mary Irene Brock

G-4-6-7-8-5-1 Deloris Jean Garringer, b. 22 Apr 1950

G-4-6-7-8-5-2 Robert Eugene Garringer, b. 22 Mar 1953

G-4-6-7-8-5-3 Sonia Christine Garringer, b. 19 Jan 1955

G-4-6-7-8-6 Donald Wayne Garringer, b. 28 Jul 1931, Jay Co., IN, m. Nancy Elliott

G-4-6-7-8-6-1 Donna Cornelia Garringer, b. 25 Jun 1970

G-4-6-7-9 Isaac Jacob "Dyke" Garringer, b. 21 Nov 1897, Jay Co., IN, d. 2 May 1972, Madison Co., IN
m. 19 Feb 1919, Jay Co., IN, Mabel Edna Manor
G-4-6-7-9-1 Richard Lee Garringer, b. 27 Sep 1919, Jay Co., IN, d. 11 Dec 1994, Anderson, IN
G-4-6-7-9-2 David Garringer, Jr., b. 27 Sep 1922, Jay Co., IN
G-4-6-7-9-3 Betty Louise Garringer, b. c1924, Jay Co., IN
G-4-6-7-9-4 Arthur Willis Garringer, b. 31 Oct 1927, Jay Co., IN
G-4-6-7-9-5 Robert Edward Garringer, b. 10 Oct 1929, Jay Co., IN
G-4-6-7-9-6 Donald Wayne Garringer, b. 28 Jul 1931, Jay Co., IN
G-4-6-8 John Garringer, b. 7 Feb 1849, Randolph Co., IN, d. 4 Nov 1914, bur. Woodlawn Cem., Randolph Co., IN
m. 8 Aug 1874, (G-7-3-11) Louisa Merriah Garringer, b. 9 Feb 1852, d. 12 Aug 1918, bur. Woodlawn Cem., Randolph Co., IN
G-4-6-8-1 Uriah N. Garringer, b. 4 May 1875, IN, d. Aug 1945, bur. 19 Aug 1945, Woodlawn Cem., Maxville, Randolph Co., IN
m. Myrtle Alice Moon, b. c1880, IN
G-4-6-8-1-1 Donald Garringer, b. 27 Nov 1902
G-4-6-8-1-2 Harold C. Garringer, b. 18 Nov 1905, Randolph Co., IN, d. Jan 1980, CA
G-4-6-8-1-3 Marcele Fredda Garringer, b. 3 Nov 1908, IN
G-4-6-8-1-4 Roger G. Garringer, b. c1912, IN
G-4-6-8-1-5 Virgie Juanita Garringer, b. 15 Jan 1913, IN
G-4-6-8-2 Nettie Harriet Garringer, b. 22 Aug 1878, IN, d. 6 Jun 1899 ae 22-9-12, bur. Woodlawn Cem., Randolph Co., IN
G-4-6-8-3 Manuel H. Garringer, b. 1878, IN, d. 4 Nov 1939, bur. Woodlawn Cem., Randolph Co., IN
m. 1st Lena Moon, m. 2nd Mabel Johnson, b. 1884, d. 1963, bur. Woodlawn Cem., Randolph Co., IN
G-4-6-8-3-1 Paul Victor Garringer
G-4-6-8-4 Arlington Earl Garringer, b. 1880, Randolph Co., IN, d. 1938, bur. 25 Aug 1938, Woodlawn Cem., Randolph Co., IN
m. Lola Manor, b. 25 May 1883, d. 12 Oct 1967, bur. 14 Oct 1967, Woodlawn Cem., Randolph Co., IN
G-4-6-8-4-1 Modjeska Waveline (dau.) Garringer, b. 12 Aug 1908, IN
m. Ward Richard Slaughter
G-4-6-8-4-2 Manor Leo Garringer, b. 14 Apr 1911, Randolph Co., IN, d. 10 Dec 1997, m. Conchita Grooms
G-4-6-8-4-2-1 Billie Joe Garringer
G-4-6-8-4-2-2 Kitty Ann Garringer, m. ? Myer
G-4-6-8-5 John B. Garringer, b. 1 May 1886, IN, d. 1947, bur. Hopewell Cem., Randolph Co., IN
m. Lottie E. Wood
G-4-6-8-6 Opal Ella Garringer, b. 7 Dec 1888, IN, d. 20 Dec 1949, m. Charles Raymond Clevenger
G-4-6-8-7 Bonnie Hazel Garringer, b. 1891, IN, m. Robert Rohlfing

G-4-6-9 George W. Garringer, b. 21 Apr 1851, Randolph Co., IN, d. 15
May 1931, bur. Woodlawn Cem., Randolph Co., IN
m. 13 Feb 1886, Martha Ann Cox, b. 3 Nov 1866, d. 7 Mar 1945, bur.
Woodlawn Cem., Randolph Co., IN
G-4-6-9-1 Bertha Garringer, b. 25 Dec 1886, Randolph Co., IN
m. 24 Jun 1905, Robert Lawrence
G-4-6-9-2 Tessie B. Garringer, b. 25 Dec 1888, m. 25 Dec 1905, Herman
Grooms
G-4-6-9-3 child, b. 5 Aug 1890, IN, d. ?young
G-4-6-9-4 Dallas Corwin Garringer, b. 7 Jun 1892, Randolph Co., IN, d.
2 Apr 1971, bur. Colville, WA, m. 21 Dec 1916, Thelma Marie Newlee
G-4-6-9-4-1 Robert Keith Garringer, b. 28 Sep 1918, IN
G-4-6-9-4-2 Frederick Garringer, b. 10 Oct 1920, Delaware Co., IN
G-4-6-9-5 Goldie Marie Garringer, b. 25 Oct 1897, IN, d. 1971,
Bellefontaine, OH, bur. Woodlawn Cem., Randolph Co., IN
m. 1917, Samuel A. Coldwell, b. 1893, d. 1946, bur. Woodlawn Cem.,
Randolph Co., IN
G-4-6-10 Uriah Garringer, b. 14 Mar 1853, Randolph Co., IN, d. 18 Jul
1920, bur. Hopewell Cem., m. 1 Nov 1877, Randolph Co., IN, Mary
Elizabeth Godwin, b. 1857, d. 1934
G-4-6-10-1 Mary Ona Garringer, b. 17 Jul 1884, d. 1969, m. Robert
Stephens
G-4-6-10-2 daughter, b. 28 Jun 1887, d. ? young (not in 1900 census)
G-4-6-10-3 Russell J. Garringer, b. c1888, IN, d. 7 Jan 1938, bur.
Hopewell Cem., Randolph Co., IN
m. Bertha E. Shaffer b. 1889, IN, d. 1966, bur. Hopewell Cem.,
Randolph Co., IN
G-4-6-10-3-1 Farrell Carnell Garringer, b. 6 Aug 1910, IN
G-4-6-10-3-2 Merriet "Max" L. Garringer, b. Jul 1914, IN
G-4-6-10-3-3 Rex Garringer
G-4-6-10-3-4 Richard Keith Garringer
G-4-6-11 Sarah Ellen Garringer, b. 29 Jan 1855, Randolph Co., IN, d. 31
Jan 1936, bur. Hopewell Cem., Randolph Co., IN
m. 12 Dec 1872, Randolph Co., IN, William Harrison Collins, b. c1849,
d. 2 Apr 1930, bur. Hopewell Cem., Randolph Co., IN
G-4-6-11-1 Harriet Collins, b. c1874, m. Dick Mills
G-4-6-11-2 Amelia V. Collins, b. c1876, m. Jesse Oran
G-4-6-11-3 Melissa Alice Collins, b. c1878, m. Melvin C. Craig
G-4-6-11-4 Samuel Collins, b. c1882, m. Julia Sommerville
G-4-6-11-5 David Harrison Collins, b. c1884, m. Ola Woods
G-4-6-11-6 John Isaac Weldon Collins, b. 1886, m. Chloris Loyd
G-4-6-11-7 Herbert Louis Collins, b. 1888, m. Opal Harrison Jones
G-4-6-11-8 Henry Arlington Collins, b. c1891, m. Iva E. Sumner
G-4-6-11-9 Ida Collins, b. c1895, m. Chester King
G-4-6-11-10 Grace Phoebe Collins, b. 1899, m. Garth Halstead

G-4-6-12 Henry Garringer, b. 23 Jan 1857, Randolph Co., IN, d. 25 Feb 1930, bur. Woodlawn Cem., Randolph Co., IN
m. 19 Aug 1879, Ida A. Moore, d. 28 Apr 1904, bur. Woodlawn Cem.
G-4-6-12-1 Emma Pearl Garringer, b. May 1880, m. Chaney Thornburg
G-4-6-12-2 Jessie Garringer, b. 30 Jan 1883, m. Marshall Wood
G-4-6-12-3 Albert Wesley Garringer, b. 18 Jul 1891, IN, d. Apr 1962, bur. 5 Apr 1962, bur. Woodlawn Cem., Randolph Co., IN
m. Margaret M. Karns, b. 1893, IN, d. Oct 1935, bur. 4 Oct 1935, Woodlawn Cem., Randolph Co., IN
m. 2nd Goldie Lemon
G-4-6-12-3-1 Madonna Garringer, b. 1904, d. ? young
G-4-6-12-3-2 Yvonne Garringer, d. ? young
G-4-6-12-3-3 Jana Garringer, d. ? young
G-4-6-12-3-4 Glendo Carroll (son) Garringer, b. 7 Jul 1911, IN
G-4-6-12-3-5 Nellie M. Garringer, b. c1914, IN
G-4-6-12-2-6 Byran L. Garringer, b. 16 Jan 1918, IN, d. 26 Apr 1985
G-4-6-12 m. 2nd c1906, Martha Moore, bur. 29 Jul 1956, Woodlawn Cem., Randolph Co., IN
G-4-6-13 Sarah Garringer, b. c1858, IN (12 in 1870 census, not in 1860 census)
G-5 John J. Garringer, b. 13 Aug 1777, Frederick Co., MD, d. 9 May 1861, Fulton Co., OH
m. c1803, Elizabeth Bowersmith, b. c1783, MD, d. 9 Oct 1854, Fulton Co., OH
G-5-1 Benjamin Geringer, b. c1804
m. 4 May 1824, Wayne Co., OH, Mary Ann Rouse
G-5-2 Nancy Geringer, b. c1806, m. 19 Aug 1833, Holmes Co., OH, John McConkey
G-5-3 Sarah Geringer, b. c1808, m. 20 Oct 1836, Holmes Co., OH, Isaac Darnell
G-5-4 Elizabeth Geringer, b. 4 Aug 1819, Holmes Co., OH
m. 20 Jun 1841, Lucas Co., OH, John Warner
G-5-5 John Jacob Geringer, b. 23 Jan 1828, Holmes Co., OH, d. 13 Jul 1916, Ringgold Co., IA, m. Dorothy Ayers
G-5-5-1 Albert W. Garringer, b. 3 May 1855, Fulton Co., OH
m. 15 Sep 1877, Ringgold Co., IA, Eunice Warner
G-5-5-1-1 Eve Garringer, b. c1876, IA
G-5-5-1-2 John Garringer, b. c1877, IA
G-5-5-1-3 Caroline Garringer, b. c1879, IA
G-5-5-2 Harvey D. Garringer, b. c1857, OH
G-5-5-3 Amos Garringer, b. c1859, OH
G-5-5-4 John E. Garringer, b. c1862, OH
G-5-5-5 Eli Abraham Garringer, b. 1 Jan 1865, Ringgold Co., IA, d. 11 Jul 1942
G-5-5-6 Dorothy Emma Garringer, b. 12 Feb 1869, IA, m. Newman
G-5-5-7 Byron Napoleon Garringer, b. 30 Apr 1872, IA

G-5-5-8 Anna Dell Garringer, b. 13 Jan 1876, m. Billington
G-5-5-9 George C. Garringer, b. 16 Apr 1878, IA
G-5-5-10 William Garringer, b. 15 Feb 1885, IA
G-6 Sevil Garringer, b. c1782, Frederick Co., MD, d. Sep 1869
    m. 31 Oct 1809, Berkeley Co., VA, Thomas Y. Canby, b. Mar 1850,
    Berkeley Co., VA
G-6-1 John Canby, dnm
G-6-2 David Canby, m. 14 Nov 1835, Susanna Weddle
G-6-3 Nancy Canby, m. George Deck, Jr.
G-6-4 Beulah Margaret Canby, m. 4 Nov 1843, Jacob Siler
G-7 Jacob Garringer, b. c1784, Frederick Co., MD, d. Pontiac, IL
    m. 19 Nov 1806, Berkeley Co., VA, Martha Patsy Moore
G-7-1 David Van Garringer, b. c1807, Berkeley Co., VA, d. 18 Feb 1863,
    Jay Co., IN
    m. Tamara Adams, d. ? bef. 1860 census
G-7-1-1 Martha Garringer, b. 27 Aug 1831, OH, d. 21 Sep 1894, Jay Co.,
    IN
    m. 25 Mar 1852, Jay Co., IN, Gilbert Patterson
G-7-1-2 Mary B. Garringer, b. c1832, Delaware Co., OH
    m. 17 Dec 1854, Jay Co., IN, Gideon Rathbun
G-7-1-3 John Jeffreys Garringer, b. 24 Nov 1834, Delaware Co., OH, d.
    24 Feb 1905, Jay Co., IN, age 71
    m. 27 May 1860, Jay Co., IN, Harriet Beckoven, b. 2 May 1841,
    Delaware Co., OH, d. 24 May 1894, Polk Co., NE
G-7-1-3-1 Elmer Franklin Garringer (twin), b. 24 May 1861, IN, d. 15
    May 1923, Modesto, CA
G-7-1-3-2 Emma Frances Garringer (twin), b. 24 May 1861, IN, d. 1953,
    m. John E. Davis, m. 2nd Angus Ray
G-7-1-3-3 Lewis Irving Garringer, b. 7 Mar 1864, Jay Co., IN
G-7-1-3-4 Victor Orrington Garringer, b. 9 Jun 1869, Jay Co., IN, d. 30
    May 1871, Jay Co., IN
G-7-1-3-5 Albert Garringer, b. 22 Feb 1875, IN, m. 1 May 1900, Annette
    Burns
G-7-1-4 James Wesley Garringer, b. 11 Aug 1836, Delaware Co., OH, d.
    28 Apr 1914, Jay Co., IN, age 77
    m. 28 Feb 1861, Randolph Co., IN, Serepta Flood, b. 11 Jan 1843, OH,
    d. 18 Mar 1917, Jay Co., IN, age 72
G-7-1-4-1 David "Edward" Garringer, b. Dec 1861, IN, d. 1929, Jay Co.,
    IN
    m. 24 Nov 1888, Jay Co., IN, Ester McDonald (Hall)
G-7-1-4-1-1 Edward Garringer, b. 29 Nov 1890
G-7-1-4-1-2 Leroy Evert Garringer, b. 16 Dec 1893, d. 19 Jul 1936, Wayne
    Co., IN
    m. 7 Aug 1914, Nelle Josephine Stephen
G-7-1-4-1-2-1 Mabel L. Garringer, b. 18 May 1917, Jay Co., IN
G-7-1-4-1-2-2 Todd L. Garringer, b. 25 Mar 1920, Jay Co., IN

G-7-1-4-1-3 Oma Garringer, b. 16 Jun 1895, IN, m. 25 May 1914, Jay Co., IN, Joseph Bishop

G-7-1-4-1-4 James Herbert Garringer, b. 18 Apr 1889, IN, m. 10 Jun 1939, Edna Mae Osborn

G-7-1-4-1-5 Floyd Thomas Garringer, b. 1901, Jay Co., IN, d. 27 Nov 1927, m. 12 Jun 1926, Wretha Murel Mock

G-7-1-4-2 Isaac Joshua Garringer, b. 28 Dec 1864, Jay Co. IN (1900&1920 censuses Monroe Co., IN)
m. 12 Sep 1890, Monroe Co., IN, Emma Amelia Stine

G-7-1-4-2-1 Nora Faye Garringer, b. 13 Jun 1891, Monroe Co., IN, m. 3 Mar 1910, Franklin Snooks

G-7-1-4-2-2 Jessie Mae Garringer, b. 2 Oct 1894, Monroe Co., IN
m. 25 Jun 1910, Monroe Co., IN, Hugh A. Martin

G-7-1-4-2-3 Mary Hazel Garringer, b. 30 Nov 1897, Monroe Co., IN, m. 22 Nov 1914, Fred Dutton

G-7-1-4-3 Demeis (dau.) Victoria Garringer, c1867, IN
m. 15 Oct 1884, Jay Co., IN, Isaac H. Landess

G-7-1-4-4 George W. Garringer

G-7-1-4-5 Nancy Jane Garringer, b. c1873, IN
m. 24 Dec 1892, Jay Co., IN, Francis Coulter

G-7-1-4-6 Della A. Garringer, b. 11 Mar 1878, Jay Co., IN
m. 10 Jun 1899, Jay Co., IN, Benjamin Sutton

G-7-1-5 Tamar Garringer, b. c1838, Delaware Co., IN
m. 11 Jul 1859, Jay Co., IN, George Rathbun

G-7-1-6 David V. "Van" Garringer, b. 26 Sep 1840, Delaware Co., IN, d. 16 Mar 1916, Jay Co., IN age 75
m. 2 Dec 1866, Jay Co., IN, Mary Catharine Whitneck, b. Jul 1849, d. 25 Aug 1914

G-7-1-6-1 Warren E. Garringer, b. 13 Feb 1868

G-7-1-6-2 Charles E. Garringer, b. 25 May 1870, Jay Co., IN, d. 8 Sep 1946, Jay Co., IN
m. 24 Dec 1908, Mary C. Kronsbeine

G-7-1-6-3 Rosa A. Garringer, b. 31 Jan 1872

G-7-1-6-4 William Irvin Garringer, b. 19 Jul 1874

G-7-1-6-5 Archa Elbert Garringer, b. 14 Feb 1882, Jay Co., IN, d. 6 May 1941, bur. Bluff Point Cem., Pike Twp., Jay Co., IN
m. 1 Oct 1902, Jay Co., IN, Grace Elvina Cook

G-7-1-6-5-1 Celia Aurena Garringer, b. 13 Aug 1903, Jay Co., IN, m. 1920, Ira E. Ervin

G-7-1-6-5-2 Franklin Elsworth Garringer, b. 21 Mar 1905, Jay Co., IN, d. 30 May 1973
m. 4 Mar 1948, Thelma Cummins

G-7-1-6-5-3 Sherman Paul Garringer, b. 17 Oct 1906, Jay Co., IN, d. 28 Oct 1951, Jay Co., IN
m. 9 Nov 1929, Maggie Kelly

G-7-1-6-5-4 William Howard Garringer, b. 1 Nov 1909, Jay Co., IN, d. 31 May 1981, FL, m. 9 Dec 1932, Dorothy Cook

G-7-1-6-5-5 Leroy Edward "Barney" Garringer, b. 31 Mar 1911, d. 17 Aug 1986, Blackford Co., IN
m. 16 Dec 1939, Jay Co., IN, Ethel May Ireland

G-7-1-6-5-6 Arance Etole Garringer, b. 1 Nov 1913
m. 29 Sep 1934, Jay Co., IN, William Spade

G-7-1-6-5-7 Russell Morton Garringer, b. 18 Sep 1915, Jay Co., IN
m. 6 Oct 1938, Estell Moystner

G-7-1-6-5-8 Mary Emma Garringer, b. 18 Jan 1918, m. 28 Mar 1937, Oscar Arnold

G-7-1-6-5-9 James Harold Garringer, b. 19 Jan 1920, Jay Co., IN, dnm, d. 17 Apr 1942, HI

G-7-1-6-5-10 Della Opal Garringer, b. 11 Dec 1922, d. 25 May 1991, Allen Co., IN
m. Mar 1938, Charles Albert Spade, m. 2nd 22 May 1948, Lawrence Farris

G-7-1-6-5-11 Marie Ellen Garringer, b. 15 Feb 1924, m. 1940, Charles Burke

G-7-1-6-5-12 Orla Archa Garringer, b. 13 Apr 1931, m. Aug 1951, Tokyo, Japan, Harue Shirota

G-7-1-7 Elizabeth Garinger, b. c1842, IN, m. William Robinson

G-7-1-8 Sarah Garringer, b. c1844, Jay Co., IN
m. Charles Lumas, m. 2nd William Fisher

G-7-1-9 Isaac E. Garringer, b. c1845, Jay Co., IN, d. 7 Jul 1865, Greensboro, NC, in 8th Indiana Cavalry

G-7-1-10 Rebecca Jane Garringer, b. c1847, Jay Co., IN, m. 19 Nov 1863, Jay Co., IN, Charles Rider

G-7-2 John Garringer, b. 18 Mar 1809, Berkeley Co., VA, d. 27 Feb 1833, Delaware Co., OH
m. Anne ?, m. 2nd Esther Adams

G-7-2-1 Vashti Garringer, b. c1832

G-7-3 Jacob "Snortin Jake" Garringer, Jr., b. 3 Feb 1812, Berkeley Co., VA, d. 13 Sep 1904, Jay Co., IN, age 92
m. 22 Apr 1837, Delaware Co., OH, Margaret Felkey

G-7-3-1 Amos Garringer, b. 10 Dec 1837, OH, d. 1837

G-7-3-2 Laura Garringer, b. 20 May 1839, Livingston Co., IL, d. 1840

G-7-3-3 Jane Garringer, b. 16 Sep 1840, Livingston Co., IL
m. 6 Aug 1855, Jay Co., IN, Elijah McCartney

G-7-3-4 John W. Garringer, b. 21 Apr 1843, d. 1848

G-7-3-5 Royal Garringer, b. 13 Jan 1845, d. young

G-7-3-6 Martha Garringer, b. 8 Sep 1845, Delaware Co., OH, d. 1847

G-7-3-7 Mary L. Garringer, b. 8 Sep 1845, d. 30 Mar 1914, m. 6 Jul 1866, Jay Co., IN, Benjamin Bisel, m. 2nd Alonzo C. Davis

G-7-3 m. 2nd 2 Dec 1846, Delaware Co., OH, Harriet Lewis, d. 6 Oct 1901, Jay Co., IN

G-7-3-8 Charles Garringer, b. 17 Sep 1847, d. 5 Jun 1848

G-7-3-9 John Lewis Garringer, b. 22 Nov 1848, OH, d. 29 Jul 1922, Randolph Co., IN, bur. Hopewell Cem., Randolph Co., IN
m. 6 Aug 1864, Jay Co., IN, Kathryn C. Collins

G-7-3-9-1 William H. Garringer, b. 29 Jan 1870, Randolph Co., IN, d. 1 Dec 1958, Delaware Co., IN, bur. Hopewell Cem., Randolph Co., IN
m. 25 Jan 1890, Jay Co., IN, Louisa Imel

G-7-3-9-1-1 Ora A. Garringer, b. 1890, Jay Co., IN

G-7-3-9-1-2 Fay Garringer, b. 6 Dec 1894, IN

G-7-3-9-1 m. 2nd 6 Apr 1897, Estella Maud Taylor

G-7-3-9-1-3 Russell B. Garringer, b. 15 Feb 1898, Pulaski Co., IN, d. 3 Jan 1976, Delaware Co., IN, bur. Hopewell Cem., Randolph Co., IN, m. Phoebe Booher

G-7-3-9-1-4 Olive C. Garringer, b. c1902, IN, m. Orval Ullom

G-7-3-9-1-5 Henry L. Garringer, b. c1910, IN

G-7-3-9-2 Jacob Ulyses Garringer, b. 1 Oct 1872, Jay Co., IN, d. 1966
m. 5 Jun 1920, Delaware Co., IN, Florence Daisy Dixon

G-7-3-9-3 Sarah Adeline Garringer, b. 26 Mar 1876, d. Nov 1967
m. Francis William Craigmile

G-7-3-10 Annetta Garringer, b. 7 Jul 1851, Delaware Co., OH, d. 1 Feb 1940, Randolph Co., IN
m. Adam Almonrode, m. 2nd Henry Gibbs, m. 3rd 30 Sep 1869, Jay Co., IN, Jonathan Bisel, m. 4th 19 Oct 1899, Jay Co., IN, John Huber

G-7-3-11 Louisa Merriah Garringer, b. 8 Feb 1852, Delaware Co., IN, d. 12 Aug 1916, bur. Woodlawn Cem., Randolph Co., IN
m. 8 Aug 1874, Randolph Co., IN, (G-4-6-8) John Garringer

G-7-3-12 Ophelia Garringer, b. 4 Oct 1853, Jay Co., IN, d. 28 Nov 1944, Jay Co., IN
m. 20 Apr 1874, Jacob Woodring

G-7-3-13 Harriet "Hattie" Garringer, b. 14 May 1855, Jay Co., IN
m. 5 Nov 1872, Jay Co., IN, William Cummings

G-7-3-14 Martha Ellen Garringer, b. 1 Jan 1857, IN, d. 2 Jun 1936, Jay Co., IN
m. 21 Aug 1879, Isaac Whitneck

G-7-3-15 Sara Garringer, b. 20 Nov 1858, Jay Co., IN, d. 1945
m. 21 Aug 1879, Jay Co., IN, Andrew Hamilton Hines

G-7-3-16 Benjamin A. "Quaker Ben" Garringer, b. 9 Sep 1860, d. 1927, Jay Co., IN
m. 19 Apr 1883, Randolph Co., IN, Eliza Jennie Lewellen

G-7-3-16-1 Bertha Mae Garringer, b. 3 Nov 1884, Jay Co., IN, d. 30 Jan 1973, Jay Co., IN, m. 11 Oct 1907, Jay Co., IN, Clifford Budp, b. 30 Oct 1882, d. 2 May 1937

G-7-3-16-2 Walter F. Garringer, b. 27 Nov 1895, Jay Co., IN
m. 20 May 1917, Gertrude Vivian Albright

G-7-3-17 Rebecca Elizabeth Garringer, b. 28 Apr 1862, Jay Co., IN, d. infancy

G-7-3-18 Ruth Garringer, b. 24 Aug 1864, Jay Co., IN, d. 17 Sep 1888
m. 14 Oct 1883, William Hines (1st wife)

G-7-3-19 Lurinda Garringer, b. 26 Mar 1866, d. 1884, m. George W.
Confer

G-7-3-20 Lucinda Garringer, b. 26 Mar 1866, IN, d. 30 Mar 1948
m. 12 Apr 1890, Randolph Co., IN, William Hines (2nd wife)

G-7-3-20-1 George Hines, b. c1891, IN

G-7-3-20-2 Charles Hines, b. c1893, IN

G-7-3-20-3 Benjamin Hines, b. c1894, IN

G-7-3-20-4 Jacob Hines, b. c1896, IN

G-7-3-20-5 Ruth Hines, b. c1897, IN

G-7-3-20-6 Lewis Hines, b. c1899, IN

G-7-3-21 Emma Garringer, b. 7 Nov 1868, d. 4 Nov 1888, Jay Co., IN

G-7-4 Mary Ann Garringer, b. c1815, Berkeley Co., VA, d. 1859, Jay Co.,
IN
m. c1838, Rueben Warren Lewis

G-7-5 Benjamin Garringer, b. 1820, Fairfield Co., OH, d. 1884, Jay Co.,
IN
m. 17 May 1841, Jay Co., IN, Sarah McCartney, b. 1823, VA

G-7-5-1 John Andrew Garringer, b. 11 Nov 1843, Bluff Point, Jay Co.,
IN, d. 24 Dec 1891
m. 27 Dec 1865, Jay Co., IN, Nancy West, b. 26 Oct 1842, d. 28 Jan
1921

G-7-5-1-1 Lucy Ann or Leaha (Samantha in 1870 census) Garringer, b. 9
May 1867, Jay Co., IN, d. 13 Feb 1942, Jay Co., IN
m. 22 Sep 1890, Delaware Co., IN, John Lake

G-7-5-1-2 Benjamin Alexander Garringer, b. 25 Jan 1869, Jay Co., IN, d.
30 Nov 1953, bur. Weimer Cem., Randolph Co., IN
m. 21 Nov 1903, Jay Co., IN, Bessie Miller, b. 10 Mar 1884, Jay Co.,
IN, d. 20 Mar 1976

G-7-5-1-2-1 son, b. 2 Jan 1906, Jay Co., IN, d. in infancy

G-7-5-1-2-2 Everett Samuel Garringer, b. 17 Aug 1907, d. 22 Feb 1995,
bur. Gravel Hill Cem., Jay Co., IN
m. 14 Mar 1936, Jay Co., IN, Lelia Tucker

G-7-5-1-2-3 Merritt Charles Garringer, b. 14 Feb 1911
m. 27 Nov 1937, Jay Co., IN, Vera Tucker

G-7-5-1-2-4 Thurman Edward Garringer, b. 28 May 1916, Randolph Co.,
IN, d. 6 Mar 1981, Delaware Co., IN
m. 4 Jan 1941, Lorene Harris

G-7-5-1-2-5 Irene Mary Garringer, b. 12 Aug 1918, m. 27 Feb 1940, Isom
Harris

G-7-5-1-2-6 Evelyn Garringer, b. 18 Mar 1921, d. 8 Sep 1946
m. 1 Jun 1940, Jay Co., IN, Otto Heath

G-7-5-1-2-7 Melba Ethelyn Garringer, b. 10 Feb 1924, d. 20 Feb 1924

G-7-5-1-2-8 Roberta Eileen Garringer, b. 12 Feb 1926, m. 1 Oct 1945, Jay
Co., IN, Daniel P. Wallace

G-7-5-1-3 Isaac William Lewis Garringer, b. 28 Apr 1871, Jay Co., IN, d. 14 Dec 1958, Petoskey, MI
m. 7 Nov 1915, Olive Elizabeth Niles

G-7-5-1-4 David Levi Stanton Garringer, b. 16 Jun 1873, d. 17 Aug 1949, Randolph Co., IN
m. 25 Mar 1899, Jay Co., IN, Ella Lucy Steed

G-7-5-1-4-1 Fay Marie Garringer, b. 16 Mar 1900, Jay Co., IN, d. 6 Aug 1980, Jay Co., IN
m. 12 Oct 1918, Jay Co., IN, Edson Kelly

G-7-5-1-4-2 David Carl Garringer (twin), b. 8 Mar 1902, d. 1990, Mercer Co., OH
m. 13 Oct 1923, Lula Emma Arnold

G-7-5-1-4-3 Stanton Earl Garringer (twin), b. 8 Mar 1902, d. 28 Mar 1919

G-7-5-1-4-4 Mary Helen Garringer, b. 24 Jul 1906, Jay Co., IN, d. 28 Mar 1919, m. Jesse Pearson

G-7-5-1-4-5 James Kenneth Garringer, b. 22 Dec 1909, Jay Co., IN, d. 1912

G-7-5-1-5 Martha Ellen "Rebecca Jane" Garringer, b. 19 Feb 1875, Randolph Co., IN, d. 22 May 1949
m. 1899, Robert Waltz

G-7-5-1-6 John Morton Garringer, b. 7 May 1878, d. 17 Aug 1885

G-7-5-1-7 Infant son, b. & d., 27 Apr 1880

G-7-5-1-8 Lillie Rosetta Garringer, b. 20 Aug 1881, d. 20 Mar 1889

G-7-5-1-9 Infant son, b. & d., 13 Aug 1883

G-7-5-1-10 Samuel Wesley Garringer, b. 19 May 1886, d. 14 Nov 1954
m. Johannah Beck

G-7-5-2 Jacob Delaughter Garringer, b. 21 Oct 1847, IN, d. 18 May 1910, Jay Co., IN
m. Sarah E. Whitneck, d. 17 Apr 1920, Jay Co., IN, age 71

G-7-5-2-1 David Morton Garringer, b. 23 Aug 1869, IN, d. 20 Nov 1945
m. 7 Mar 1891, Jay Co., IN, Mary E. Harford

G-7-5-2-1-1 Zanna Alice Garringer, b. 29 May 1892, Jay Co., IN

G-7-5-2-1-2 Lucretia Garringer, b. 17 Nov 1894, Jay Co., IN

G-7-5-2-2 Benjamin Garringer, b. 4 Aug 1872, Jay Co., IN, 17 Mar 1949, Jay Co., IN
m. 16 Feb 1901, Jay Co., IN, Susan Warren

G-7-5-2-2-1 Hazel Garringer, b. 22 Dec 1903, Jay Co., IN, d. 23 Sep 1905

G-7-5-2-2-2 Sarah Esther Garringer, b. 24 Jul 1906, Jay Co., IN, d. c1951
m. Percy "Tiny" Robb

G-7-5-2-2-3 Ethel P. Garringer, b. 5 Dec 1908, Jay Co., IN
m. Bert Jordan, m. 2nd Dale Bouse

G-7-5-2-2-4 Kenneth Isaac Garringer, b. 19 Feb 1912, Jay Co., IN, d. 5 Aug 1986, IN
m. 12 Jun 1937, Jay Co., IN, Maxine Lucille Shaw, m. 2nd Cynthia Vincent

G-7-5-2-2-5 Roy Thurman Garringer, b. 19 Mar 1915, Jay Co., IN, d. 14 Feb 1988, Allen Co., IN
  m. 28 May 1938, Jay Co., IN, Cora Belle Fowler
G-7-5-2-2-6 Sherman Tilden Garringer, b. 21 Dec 1918, Jay Co., IN, d. 9 Mar 1986, Jay Co., IN
  m. 5 Mar 1942, Jay Co., IN, Vernadine Janice Green
G-7-5-2-2-7 Velma Addeline Garringer, b. 8 Jan 1922, Jay Co., IN
  m. 14 Jun 1942, Delaware Co., IN, Charles Everard Henry
G-7-5-2-2-8 Lucy Frances Garringer, b. 3 Nov 1924, d. 26 Mar 1940
G-7-5-2-3 Isaac Garringer, b. 4 Aug 1872, IN, d. 6 Jan 1921, Jay Co., IN
  m. 23 Dec 1899, Jay Co., IN, age 23, Martha Alice Harford
G-7-5-2-3-1 Ezra W. Garringer, b. 1901, IN
G-7-5-2-3-2 son, b. 17 Feb 1904, Jay Co., IN, d. bef. 1910
G-7-5-2-3-3 Alta E. Garringer, b. 2 Sep 1913, Jay Co., IN
G-7-5-2-3-4 Isaac Benjamin Garringer, b. 15 Dec 1917, Russel Co., IN
  m. 9 May 1949, Jay Co., IN, Velma Mae Dillavou
G-7-5-2-4 Mary Iona Garringer, b. c1875, IN, d. 20 Mar 1938
  m. 14 Apr 1894, Jay Co., IN, Willis A. Martin
G-7-5-2-5 Silas Garringer, b. 28 Feb 1878, Jay Co., IN
  m. 15 Oct 1906, Jay Co., IN, Mae Bailey
G-7-5-2-5-1 Mabel Garringer, b. c1910, IN
G-7-5-2-6 Louisa Marie Garringer, b. 17 Dec 1879, IN
  m. 18 Sep 1897, Jay Co., IN, Henry Potter
G-7-5-2-7 James Sherman Garringer, b. 20 May 1882, Jay Co., IN, d. Aug 1966, IN
  m. 7 Feb 1906, Jay Co., IN, Emeline Bonnell
G-7-5-2-7-1 Adrain Garringer, b. c1907, IN, d. ? young
G-7-5-2-7-2 Arthur Garringer, b. c1911, IN, d. 16 Dec 1991, Randolph Co., IN
  m. 30 Dec 1934, Vonia Agnes Brinkerhoff
G-7-5-2-7 m. 2nd 29 Oct 1921, Jay Co., IN, Martha Alice Harford
G-7-5-2-7-3 Viola Iona Garringer, b. 30 Sep 1922, m. 22 Jun 1941, Jay Co., IN, Ezra Elbert Byrum
G-7-5-2-7-4 Morton Robert Garringer, b. 28 Jun 1924, Jay Co., IN
  m. 24 Sep 1946, Jay Co., IN, Violet Maxine Coats
G-7-5-2-7-5 James A. Garringer, b. 1 Feb 1926, m. 30 Jun 1945, Jay Co., IN, Carol Olive Warren
G-7-5-3 Sarah Ellen Garringer, b. 27 Jan 1849, IN, d. 17 Apr 1920, Jay Co., IN
  m. 1 Oct 1868, Jay Co., IN, William Rathbun
G-7-5-4 David Elijah Garringer, b. 4 Mar 1852, IN, d. c1876
  m. 8 Apr 1875, Jay Co., IN, Sarah Mariah Rantz
G-7-5-4-1 Eugene David Morton Garringer, b. 25 Aug 1875, Jay Co., IN, d. 12 Aug 1940
  m. 31 Aug 1895, Jay Co., IN, Eva Bockren

G-7-5-4-1-1 Glee Agnes Garringer, b. 25 Jan 1896, Jay Co., IN, d. 13 May 1974, Delaware Co., IN
m. 24 Sep 1914, Jay Co., IN, Leroy Clayton Knisely

G-7-5-4-1-2 Leo E. Garringer, b. Mar 1897, IN, m. Edith Haines

G-7-5-4-1-3 Orville Jasper Garringer, b. 9 Jan 1899, IN, d. 23 Jan 1977, Dayton, OH
m. 3 Sep 1921, Jay Co., IN, Helen Orletta Nash

G-7-5-4-1-4 Ralph M. Garringer, b. 2 Mar 1901, Jay Co., IN
m. 31 Jan 1915, Jay Co., IN, Mabel Kober

G-7-5-4-1-5 Lelia M. Garringer, b. 15 May 1903, Jay Co., IN, d. 14 Aug 1983, Montgomery Co., OH
m. c1923, Ralph Black

G-7-5-4-1-6 Doris E. Garringer, b. 4 Jun 1910, Jay Co., IN, m. Fran Farlow

G-7-5-5 Benjamin Alexander Garringer, b. c1853, d. young

G-7-5-6 Isaac W. Garringer, b. 24 Apr 1854, d. 9 Sep 1858

G-7-5-7 infant, b. 22 Jul 1856, d. 22 Jul 1856

G-7-5-8 Harriet Garringer, b. 4 Jul 1857, IN, d. 1944, Jay Co., IN, m. Peter Brosher

G-7-5-9 Johnson Levi Garringer, b. 9 Mar 1860, IN, d. c1877

G-7-5-10 Martha "Mattie" Isabelle Garringer, b. 6 Jan 1862, IN
m. 23 Apr 1885, Jay Co., IN, James H. Stout

G-7-5-11 Mary Arminta Garringer, b. 13 Aug 1863, Jay Co., IN, d. 2 Mar 1942, Jay Co., IN
m. 22 May 1885, Jay Co., IN, John Robert Steed

G-7-5 m. 2nd 9 May 1869, Jay Co., IN, Mary Ann Harford, d. ?? 1884, Jay Co., IN

G-7-5-12 George Henry Garringer, b. 21 May 1870, IN, d. 15 Sep 1924, bur. Bluff Point Cem., Jay Co., IN
m. 27 Feb 1892, Jay Co., IN, Emma Whitnack, b. 30 Jan 1874, IN, d. 15 Mar 1919

G-7-5-12-1 Oliver Ronald Garringer, b. 7 Jan 1893, IN, d. 31 Dec 1944, Edmund, OK
m. Arana Shireling, m. 2nd Hallie Miller, m. 3rd 10 Oct 1928, Fay Harrow

G-7-5-12-2 Icey Mabel (dau.) Garringer, b. 22 Sep 1894, IN, d. 9 Aug 1986, Delaware Co., IN, m. Joseph Lester Baughman

G-7-5-12-3 Cyrus Franklin Garringer, b. 9 Mar 1896, d. 22 Jul 1897

G-7-5-12-4 Cora Iona Garringer, b. 27 Nov 1897, IN, d. 14 Mar 1980, Mt. Pleasant, MI
m. 23 Jan 1918, Charles Newton Steed

G-7-5-12-5 Mary Ann Garringer, b. 15 May 1900, Jay Co., IN, d. 2 Sep 1993, Wakarusa, IN, m. Ozro Paul Shireling

G-7-5-12-6 Silas Matthew Garringer, b. 6 Dec 1902, Jay Co., IN, d. 25 Jul 1993, Huntington Co., IN, m. Cleo Inez Brouse

G-7-5-12-7 Cynthia Mae Garringer, b. 9 Feb 1905, Jay Co., IN, m. Carl Raymond Sipe

G-7-5-12-8 Lucy Viola Garringer, b. 6 Jul 1907, Jay Co., IN
m. Harold Magley, m. 2nd Charles Blackford, m. 3rd Glen Burns

G-7-5-12-9 Luther Albert Garringer, b. 8 Jun 1914, IN, m. Fairy Belle Johnson

G-7-5-13 Robert M. Garringer, b. c1873, Jay Co., IN

G-7-5-14 Benjamin Cyrus Garringer, b. 5 May 1876, IN, d. 22 Jan 1907, Jay Co., IN
m. 20 Jan 1900, Jay Co., IN, Mattie Bisel

G-7-5-14-1 William H. Garringer, b. 24 Nov 1900, Jay Co., IN
m. Doris Wagner, m. 2nd Della Williams

G-7-5-14-2 Walter Franklin Garringer, b. 15 Jan 1904, Jay Co., IN

G-7-5-14-3 Ethel Marie Garringer, b. c1907, IN

G-7-5-15 Silas Franklin Garringer, b. 28 Feb 1878, IN, d. 1941
m. 16 Oct 1906, May Bailey

G-7-5-16 Rebecca Jane Garringer, d. at 3 weeks

G-7-6 Isaac Garringer, b. c1822, OH, d. c1865, IA
m. 18 Mar 1843, Marion Co., OH, Rachel Biggerstaff

G-7-6-1 Thomas Garringer, b. c1848, ?

G-7-6-2 Isaac Garringer, b. c1856, ?

G-7-7 Alexander Garringer, b. 25 Jan 1824, Columbus, Delaware Co., OH, d. 27 Aug 1901, Jay Co., IN
m. 24 Nov 1850, Jay Co., IN, Elizabeth "Betsy" Bonnell, b. 24 Sep 1827, PA, d. 20 Nov 1899, Jay Co., IN

G-7-7-1 Hannah Ella Garringer, b. 2 Feb 1857, Jay Co., IN, d. 4 May 1926, Jay Co., IN
m. (G-4-6-7) Lewis Garringer, b. 1847, d. 1916

G-7-7-2 Mary Lamb Garringer, b. c1859, IN, d. 1935
m. 20 Mar 1890, Jay Co., IN, Otto Lamburn

G-7-7-3 George Alexander Garringer, b. 29 Apr 1863, Pike Twp., Jay Co., IN, d. 31 Oct 1943, Jay Co., IN
m. 18 Jun 1885, Jay Co., IN, Amelia Esther Finch, b. 8 Sep 1865, Jay Co., IN, d. 14 Nov 1929, Jay Co., IN

G-7-7-3-1 Sarah Elizabeth "Betsey" Garringer, b. 5 Apr 1886, IN, d. 21 Oct 1951,
m. 22 Apr 1922, Jay Co., IN, James Moneysmith

G-7-7-3-1-1 Florence Moneysmith

G-7-7-3-1-2 Adrian Moneysmith

G-7-7-3-2 Alexander "Dick" Garringer, b. 6 May 1887, Jay Co., IN, d. 2 Jun 1963

G-7-7-3-3 George Garringer, b. 13 Jan 1889, IN, d. 23 Jan 1901, Jay Co., IN, age 12

G-7-7-3-4 Grover C. Garringer, b. 6 Sep 1893, Jay Co., IN, d. 12 Jul 1963, IN
m. 5 Oct 1932, Jay Co., IN, Mabel Shaneyfelt

G-7-7-3-5 James M. Garringer, b. 15 Feb 1896, Jay Co., IN, d. 1918, in W
  W I in France with 323rd Field Artillery Signal Battalion

G-7-7-3-6 Ruth Ann Garringer, b. 31 Aug 1898, IN, d. 28 Feb 1961
  m. 30 Dec 1918, Delaware Co., IN, Toney Becktell

G-7-7-3-7 Mertal Marcele Garringer, b. 25 Oct 1901, Jay Co., IN, d. 9 Jan
  1982, Jay Co., IN
  m. 1922, Frank Hughes

G-7-7-3-8 Devaly "Ivory" Garringer, b. 25 Oct 1901, Jay Co., IN, d. 26
  Sep 1980, Wells Co., IN, m. Harold Edmundson

G-7-7-3-9 Pauline Hannah Garringer, b. 25 Jun 1907, IN
  m. 3 Jul 1929, Jay Co., IN, Paul Earnest Albertson

G-7-7-4 Sarah Garringer, b. c1868, Jay Co., IN

G-7-7-5 Ida Garringer, b. Apr 1870, IN (1900 census Jay Co., IN) dnm

G-7-8 Martha Garringer, b. c1828, OH, d. 1863, Randolph Co., IN
  m. 20 Sep 1849, Jay Co., IN, William M. Sutton

G-7-8-1 Nancy E. Sutton, b. c1850, IN

G-7-8-2 Benjamin A. Sutton, b. c1853, IN

G-7-8-3 Phebe A. Sutton, b. c1855, IN

G-7-8-4 Margaret J. Sutton, b. c1858, IN

The Garringers of Elkhart County, Indiana
(It has not been determined whether this family is related to the above
Garringer family.)

GD   David Garringer, b. 1799, OH? (1850 census Whitley Co., IN
   census) m. Margaret ?, b. Germany
GD-1 Samuel Garringer, b. c1836, OH
GD-2 Solomon Garringer, b. c1837, OH
GD-3 Sarah Garringer, b. c1838, OH
GD-4 Catherine Garringer, b. c1840, OH
GD-5 David Garringer, b. c1842, OH
GD-6 Jacob Garringer, b. c1844, OH, m. Susan ?, b. 1845, PA
GD-6-1 Samuel Garringer, b. c1868, IN
GD-6-2 Jacob Garringer, b. c1870, IN, d. 3 Mar 1902, Elkhart Co., IN,
   age 31
GD-6-3 Daniel Garringer, b. 27 Aug 1872, IN (1900,1920 censuses
   Elkhart Co., IN)
   m. ?2nd 27 Oct 1918, Elkhart Co., IN, Sadie R. Knapp
GD-6-3-1 Bernice Garringer, b. c1904, IN
GD-6-3-2 Virginia Garringer, b. c1909, IN
GD-6-4 Minnie Garringer, b. c1876, IN, m. 20 Jul 1895, Elkhart Co., IN,
   Philip J. Mabin
GD-6-5 Charles A. Garringer, b. 27 Sep 1877, IN,
   m. 27 Nov 1911, Elkhart Co., IN, Louise Cutshaw
GD-6-5-1 Charles E. Garringer, b. 25 Dec 1912, IN, d. Mar 1979, IN
GD-6-5-2 Robert L. Garringer, b. c1918, IN
GD-7 John Garringer, b. c1846, IN (1880 census White Co., IN, 1900
   census Pulaski Co., IN)
   m. Jane ?
GD-7-1 Ella Garringer
GD-7-2 Margaret Garringer
GD-7-3 Etta Garringer, d. 20 Dec 1910, Elkhart Co., IN, age 36
GD-7-4 William Garringer
GD-7-5 Juli Garringer
GD-8 George Garringer, b. c1849, IN (1880 census Kosciusko Co., IN)
   m. Sarah ?, b. 1850
GD-8-1 Loren Garringer, b. 1880, IN

The Johann Adam Geringer Family with Descendants in Randolph
County, Indiana

GJ **Johann Adam Geringer**, b. c1721, Germany, d. c1791, Northampton
Co., PA
   m. Anna Catherine ?, b. c1751, PA (This Geringer family is not
known to be related to the Hilda Irene Garringer family but some
descendants did reside in Jay and Randolph Co., IN)
GJ-1 Anna Elizabeth Geringer, vc. c1753, m. Andrew Schwitzer
GJ-2 Johannes Adam Geringer, b. 1756, Easton, PA, d. Jan 1796,
   Northampton Co., PA
   m. c1774, PA, Anna Maria Elizabeth
GJ-2-1 Catherine Maria Geringer, b. 29 Aug 1775
GJ-2-2 Anna Elizabeth Geringer, b. 18 Nov 1777
GJ-2-3 Anna Maria Geringer, b. 31 Mar 1780
GJ-2-4 Margaret Geringer, b. 9 Jan 1783
GJ-2-5 John J. Geringer, b. 1 Aug 1785, Northampton Co., PA
GJ-2-6 Susanna Geringer, b. 20 May 1788
GJ-2-7 Johann Adam Geringer, b. 16 Aug 1790
GJ-2-8 Thomas Geringer, b. 12 Apr 1794, Northampton Co., PA
GJ-2-9 Daniel Geringer, b. 12 Apr 1794, Northampton Co., PA, d. 18
   Sep 1871, Jay Co., IN
   m. 1815, Northampton Co., PA, Elizabeth ?
GJ-2-9-1 Lucinda Frederic Garinger, b. 1816
GJ-2-9-2 Unknown Garinger, b. 1822
GJ-2-9-3 Eliza Ann Garinger, b. 16 Apr 1826, Luzerne Co., PA
GJ-2-9-4 John Garinger, b. 4 Jul 1834, Luzerne Co., PA, d. aft 1900 (1870
   Jay Co., Madison Twp., 1900 White Co., IN)
   m. Margaret E. Maggert, b. c1841, OH
GJ-2-9-4-1 Daniel Webster Garinger, b. c1858, OH
   m. Ellen Short
GJ-2-9-4-1-1 Pearl Garinger
GJ-2-9-4-1-2 Elva F. Garinger, b. 3 Oct 1884, Blackford Co., IN
   m. Lena Thomas
GJ-2-9-4-1-2-1 Effie Garinger, b. c1904, IN
GJ-2-9-4-1-2-2 Cecil Garinger, b. c1908, IN
GJ-2-9-4-1-3 Violet Garinger
GJ-2-9-4-2 Mary "Molly" Garinger, b. c1860, OH
GJ-2-9-4-3 Nancy Jane "Fanny" Garinger, b. c1861, OH
GJ-2-9-4-4 Amanda Garinger, b. c1863, OH
GJ-2-9-4-5 George Washington Garinger, b. 29 Jan 1867, Randolph Co.,
   IN (? 1900 census Randolph Co., Jackson Twp.)
   m. 1 Sep 1888, Sarah Ellen Ruckweed
   m. 2nd 2 Apr 1892, Augusta Jane "Jennie" Loy
GJ-2-9-4-5-1 Clarence Garinger, b. 12 Sep 1889, Jay Co., IN
GJ-2-9-4-5-2 Asa Waldo Garinger, b. Sep 1892, IN

GJ-2-9-4-5-3 Lola E. Garinger, b. 15 Dec 1894, IN
GJ-2-9-4-5-4 Noah Abe Garinger, b. Oct 1896, IN
GJ-2-9-4-5-5 Virgil L. Garinger, b. Sep 1898, IN
GJ-2-9-4-5-6 Orla E. "Skeet" Garinger, b. 25 Jul 1901, Randolph Co., IN
GJ-2-9-4-5-6 Brandt Robert Garinger, b. 1908, Randolph Co., IN
GJ-2-9-4-6 William Schnepp Garinger, b. 18 Apr 1868, Jay Co., IN
GJ-2-9-4-7 John Wesley Garinger, b. 24 Oct 1871, Jay Co., IN
  m. Nancy Ellen Key
GJ-2-9-4-7-1 Alma May Garinger, b. 6 Dec 1894
GJ-2-9-4-7-2 Cora Garinger, b. c1896
GJ-2-9-4-7-3 Leonard Garinger, b. c1902

Descendants of Peter Hammer

Peter Hammer*, b. 19 Aug 1757, Bucks Co., PA, d. 18 Apr 1838, Monongalia Co., VA

m. 1779, York Co., PA, Elizabeth White Bonser (b. Elizabeth White), b. c1755, York Co., PA, d. c1797, Allegheny Co., PA

H-1 Joseph Hammers, b. 6 Apr 1780, near Little York, PA, d. 27 Feb 1863, Woodford Co., IL, bur. Hammers Cem., Panther Creek, Panola, IL

m. May 1803, Fayette Co., PA, Elizabeth Hanna, b. 22 Sep 1781, d. 15 May 1851

H-1-1 Jesse Hammer, b. 7 May 1804, Fayette Co., PA, d. 3 Sep 1881

m. 7 May 1831, Greene Co., PA, Eleanor Buckingham

H-1-1-1 Isaac Buckingham Hammers, b. 17 May 1832, PA, d. 5 Nov 1854, IL

H-1-1-2 Joseph S. Hammers, b. 3 Sep 1833, PA, d. 4 Jan 1861

m. 4 Jan 1861, IL, Mary Bailey

H-1-1-2-1 Isaac Hammers

H-1-1-2-2 Jesse Hammers

H-1-1-2-3 Laura Hammers

H-1-1-3 Elizabeth Hammers, b. 7 May 1836, IL, d. 2 Nov 1855, IL

H-1-1-4 Morgan Hammers, b. 11 Jul 1838, IL

m. 12 Feb 1861, Rose Gibson

H-1-1-5 James A. Hammers, b. 9 May 1840, IL

m. 28 Jun 1866, Juella Bayne

H-1-1-6 William Hammers, b. 22 Sep 1842, IL, m. Julia Bayne

H-1-1 m. 2nd Ruth (Garrison) Buckingham

H-1-1-7 George Hammers, b. 20 Apr 1852, IL, d. 9 Dec 1852

H-1-1-8 Ruth Eleanor Hammers, b. 24 Nov 1853, IL, d. 28 May 1854

H-1-1-9 Mary Hammers, b. 1 Jul 1859, IL, d. 29 Jan 1862

H-1-2 James Hammers, b. c1805, Greene Co., PA, d. 2 Sep 1879

m. Laurie Minor, m. 2nd Alice Carrington

H-1-3 Mary Hammers, b. 23 Sep 1807, d. 1 Jan 1883,

m. 1827, Greene Co., PA, Ayres Myers

H-1-4 Elizabeth Hammers, b. 16 Feb 1809, d. 4 Feb 1899, m. Samuel Hartley

H-1-5 Sarah Hammers, b. c1811, d. 1818

H-1-6 Joseph Hammers, b. 16 Mar 1814, Greene Co., PA, d. 22 Dec 1901

m. 21 Apr 1835, Green Co., PA, Phebe Tyler Evans

H-1-6-1 George Hammers, b. 9 Oct 1835, Greene Co., PA

H-1-6-2 Mary Hammers, b. c1844, PA

H-1-6-3 Joseph Hammers, b. c1846, PA

H-1-6-4 Phebe Hammers, b. c1848, PA

H-1-6-5 Benjamin Hammers, b. c1851, IL

H-1-6-6 Jennie Hammers, b. c1858, IL

H-1-7 Samuel Hammers, b. 14 Nov 1816, d. 5 Jan 1892
   m. Melissa Hopkins Skinner
H-1-8 Rebecca Hammers, b. 10 Apr 1819, d. 1847, m. John D. Whittaker
H-2 Agnes Hammers, b. 15 Jun 1782, York Co., PA, d. 16 Jul 1829
   m. 16 May 1805, James Woodmansey (1820, 1830, 1840 Jackson Co.,
   IN censuses)
H-3 Elizabeth Hammers, b. c1784, York Co., PA
   m. Joseph Hanna (1820, 1830 Jackson Co., IN census)
H-4 Peter Hammers*, b. c1786, York Co., PA, d. 1838, Licking Co., OH
   m. c1808, Mary Fry (or Frye), d. 1838, Licking Co., OH (data on
   children from Lola Mae Wood via Rosa Bartlett Strong and a Mrs.
   Lambert)
H-4-1 Samuel Hammers, b. ? c1810, PA, m. Elizabeth ?, b. c1809, OH
   (1850 Licking Co., OH census)
H-4-1-1 Jafford Hammer, b. c1837, OH
H-4-1-2 Mary C. Hammer, b. c1839, OH
H-4-1-3 Angeline Hammer, b. c1842, OH
H-4-1-4 Robert Hammer, b. c1846, OH
H-4-1-5 Martha Hammer, b. c1848, OH
H-4-1-6 Samuel Hammer, b. c1850, OH
H-4-2 probably James Hammers, b. c1810, PA (Peter Hammers sold 60
   acres of land in Licking Co., OH on 28 Dec 1835 to a James Hammers,
   presumably a son)
(There is a James Hamer (or Hanna), age 49 with family in the 1860
   Licking Co., OH census which may be this son)
   (? Randolph Co., IN, 27 Oct 1842 James Hammers married Sarah
   Walker, unknown James Hammers)
H-4-3 Catherine Hammers, b. c1813, PA
   m. Samuel Mesarvey (1850 census Randolph Co., IN)
H-4-3-1 George Mesarvey, b. c1830, OH
H-4-3-2 Samuel Mesarvey, b. c1834, OH
H-4-3-3 Janet Mesarvey, b. c1835, OH, m. John Q. Adams
H-4-3-3-1 Abraham Henry Adams, m. Flora Wood
H-4-3-3-2 William Loring Adams, m. Stella Wood
H-4-3-3-3 Millicent Adams, m. James Nixon
H-4-3-3-4 Nancy Jane Adams, m. William Ray
H-4-3-3-5 Cora Belle Adams, m. Charles Jackson
H-4-3-3-6 Charles Adam
H-4-3-3-7 Lula Adams m. Orla Keener
H-4-3-4 Abraham Mesarvey, b. c1840, IN
H-4-3-5 Nancy E. Mesarvey, b. c1846, IN, m. ? Meeks
H-4-4 Anna "Amy" Hammers, b. 4 Aug 1816, Greene Co., PA, d. 7 Sep
   1899, Randolph Co., IN, bur. Woodlawn Cem., Randolph Co., IN
   m. Licking Co., OH, Alfred McCamy, b. 1 May 1813, OH, d. 13 Apr
   1895, Randolph Co., IN, bur. Woodlawn Cem., Randolph Co., IN

H-4-4-1 Daniel Webster McCamy, b. c1840, IN, d.1863 during Civil War, bur. National Cem., Franklin, TN

H-4-4-2 John Wesley McCamy, b. c1842, IN, m. Rebecca Fletcher, div.

H-4-4-2-1 Orpha McCamy

H-4-4-2 m. 2nd Serepta ?

H-4-4-2-2 Daisy McCamy

H-4-4-2 m. 3rd Catherine ?

H-4-4-2-3 Maude McCamy

H-4-4-2-4 Eva McCamy

H-4-4-2-5 Lillie McCamy

H-4-4-2-6 Rose McCamy

H-4-4-2-7 Bert McCamy

H-4-4-2-8 Jesse McCamy

H-4-4-2-9 Elmer McCamy

H-4-4-2-10 Ben McCamy

H-4-4-3 Sarah Elizabeth McCamy, b. 8 Mar 1844, Randolph Co., IN, d. 13 Jan 1930
m. 31 Oct 1870, Delaware Co., IN, John Bartlett

H-4-4-3-1 Melda McCamy, m. Edgar Barnes

H-4-4-3-2 Orla (or Arla) McCamy, d. young

H-4-4-3-3 Bertha McCamy, m. Walter Morris

H-4-4-3-4 Ina McCamy, m. Otis Jacobs

H-4-4-3-4-1 Mildred Jacobs, m. Thornburg

H-4-4-3-4-2 Wayman Jacobs

H-4-4-3-5 infant, d. young 1886

H-4-4-4 Mary Ann McCamy, b. c1846, IN, m. 1 Oct 1864, Stroder Craig

H-4-4-4-1 Hattie Craig, m. James Stanley

H-4-4-4-2 Laura Craig, m. Frank Hoover

H-4-4-4-3 Ira Craig, m. Nora Hupp

H-4-4-4-4 Oscar Craig, m. Gussie Davis

H-4-4-4-5 Rosa Craig, m. John M. Strong

H-4-4-4-6 Cora Craig, m. Curtis Huston

H-4-4-5 Eliza Jane McCamy, b. c1848, IN, d. 29 Jan 1884, (ae 35y-11m) bur. Woodlawn Cem., Randolph Co., IN
m. William Henry Morris

H-4-4-5-1 Myrtle Morris

H-4-4-5-2 Ada Anceline Morris, b. 24 May 1875, Randolph Co., IN, d. 25 Jul 1956, Fresno, CA, m. 12 Apr 1894, James Andrew Willis

H-4-4-5-3 Lettie Morris, m. Frank David Barnett

H-4-4-6 James A. McCamy, b. 25 Dec 1850, Randolph Co., IN, d. 30 Dec 1936, bur. Woodlawn Cem., Randolph Co., IN
m. 30 May 1879, Anna Grooms, b. 1859, d. 1916, bur. Woodlawn Cem., Randolph Co., IN

H-4-4-6-1 Hattie McCamy, bur. Woodlawn Cem., Randolph Co., IN

H-4-4-6-2 Ethel McCamy, d. 1900, bur Woodlawn Cem., Randolph Co., IN

H-4-4-6-3 Walter Raymond McCamy

H-4-4-6-4 Robert McCamy

H-4-4-6-5 Ermal McCamy, m. George Flora

H-4-4-6-6 Esther McCamy, m. Clifford Lambert

H-4-4-6-7 Mary McCamy, m. Milter Main

H-4-4-6-8 Birdie McCamy, m. Fred Woodbury

H-4-4-6-9 Ruth McCamy, m. Frank Getz

H-4-4-7 Nancy McCamy, b. 21 Oct 1852, d. 15 Jan 1879, m. Riley Spillers

H-4-4-7-1 Ernest Spillers

H-4-4-8 Cassa Emeline McCamy, b. 19 Sep 1854, Randolph Co., IN
m. Cyrus C. Calhoun

H-4-4-8-1 Claude Alfred Calhoun, b. 19 Nov 1883, m. Nilah Glee Wood

H-4-4-8-2 Jesse Wilbert Calhoun, b. 13 Jul 1886, d. 26 Oct 1970, m. Anna
Belle Taylor

H-4-4-8-3 Lola Edna Calhoun, b. 2 Feb 1889, d. 4 Nov 1908

H-4-4-8-4 infant daughter, b. 6 Oct 1891, d. 29 Nov 1891

H-4-4-8-5 Arlie Hobert Calhoun, b. 3 May 1894, Randolph Co., IN, d. 20
Jan 1957, Pinellas Co., FL
m. 14 Nov 1914, Randolph Co., IN, Dora Mae Reed, b. 19 May 1895,
Clinton Co., IN, d. 12 Feb 1992, Delaware Co., IN, bur Hopewell
Cem., Randolph Co., IN

H-4-5 Abraham Hammers*, b. 14 Nov 1817, PA, d. 7 Aug 1894, bur.
Woodlawn Cem.
m. 19 Nov 1839, Randolph Co., IN, Nancy Harbour, b. c1822, OH, d.
24 Apr 1892, bur. Woodlawn Cem., Randolph Co., IN

H-4-5-1 Elijah Oliver Hammers*, b. 10 Jun 1845, d. 10 May 1920, bur.
Woodlawn Cem., Randolph Co., IN
m. 1 Oct 1864, Randolph Co., IN, Elizabeth Morris, b. 25 Sep 1845, d.
7 Jun 1922, bur. Woodlawn Cem., Randolph Co., IN

H-4-5-1-1 Arthur Leroy Hammers, b. 7 Feb 1865, d. 3 Apr 1879, bur.
Rehobeth Cem., Randolph Co., IN

H-4-5-1-2 Bertha Achsah Hammers*, b. 30 Jan 1877, Randolph Co., IN,
d. 29 Oct 1918, bur. Woodlawn Cem., Randolph Co., IN
m. 10 Aug 1895, Randolph Co., IN, Isaac Luther Garringer
(see Garringer Descendants G-4-6-3-2)

H-4-5-1-3 William Blaine Hammers (twin), b. 4 Aug 1885, d. 1950, bur. 5
Oct 1950, Woodlawn Cem., Randolph Co., IN
m. 28 Jun 1911, Opal McGuire, b. 28 Aug 1891, d. 1972, bur. 26 Dec
1972, Woodlawn Cem., Randolph Co., IN

H-4-5-1-3-1 John Oliver Hammers, b. 15 Oct 1914, d. 1970, bur. 26 Apr
1970, Woodlawn Cem., Randolph Co., IN

H-4-5-1-3-2 Margaret Helen Hammers, b. 13 Feb 1916, d. Feb 1976, bur.
Webster, IN
m. 24 Dec 1939, Maurice Cammack Jordan

H-4-5-1-3-2-1 James David Jordan, b. 16 Mar 1942

H-4-5-1-3-2-2 Richard Jordan

H-4-5-1-4 Lucy Irene Hammers (twin), b. 4 Aug 1885, d. 29 Jan 1961, bur. Woodlawn Cem., Randolph Co., IN

m. 19 Feb 1910, William Hervet Huston, b. 26 Aug 1886, d. 11 Dec 1961, bur. Woodlawn Cem., Randolph Co., IN

H-4-5-1-4-1 William Hervet Huston Jr., b. 1 Aug 1916, d. 31 Jul 1971, bur. Hollywood, Florida

m. Mary Jane Everett

H-4-5-1-4-1-1 William Earl Huston

H-4-5-2 Mary Elizabeth Hammers, b. 10 Jun 1845, d. bef 1894

m. 2 Aug 1866, Randolph Co., IN, James Richwine, b. c1846

H-4-5-2-1 Wesley Richwine, b. c1868

H-4-5-2-2 Viola Richwine, b. c1871

H-4-5-2-3 Benjamin Richwine, b. c1877

H-4-5-2-4 Egbert Richwine, b. Aug 1879

H-4-5-3 Abraham Preston Hammers, b. c1852, d. after 1920 (1920 Randolph Co., IN)

m. 1st Laura A. Sommerville, b. c1857

m. 2nd 6 Feb 1875, Ann E. Odle

H-4-5-3-1 William Alvin Hammers, b. 31 Dec 1875

m. Julianna Flood, b. 5 May 1879, d. 3 Jan 1905, bur. Fairview Cem., Randolph Co., IN

H-4-5-3-1-1 Preston E. Hammers, b. 7 Nov 1898, Randolph Co., IN, d. 2 Mar 1899, Randolph Co., IN

H-4-5-3-1-2 Marcecia Hammers, b. 9 Sep 1902, Randolph Co., IN

H-4-5-3-1 ? m. 2nd ? Anderson, b. c1888, IN

H-4-5-3-1-3 Mabel Marjorene Hammers, b. 25 Sep 1906, Randolph Co., IN

H-4-5-3 m. 3rd c1885, Lydia J. Booher, b. 1860, IN, d. aft 1920

H-4-5-3-2 A. (son) Hammers, b. 11 Nov 1886, d. 25 Jan 1888, Randolph Co., IN

H-4-5-3-3 George Ray Hammers, b. 17 Feb 1889, Randolph Co., IN (1920 census Green Twp., Randolph Co., IN)

m. 11 Jun 1909, Bessie May Craig, b. 21 Feb 1891

H-4-5-3-3-1 Hollis C. Hammers, b. c1911, IN

m. Myrtle Younce

H-4-5-3-3-1-1 son, b. 5 Nov 1934, Randolph Co., IN

H-4-5-3-4 Jesse L. Hammers, b. c1896, IN (1920 census Randolph Co., IN)

m. Dorothy Harres

H-4-5-3-4-1 daughter, b. 18 Dec 1926, Randolph Co., IN

H-4-5-3 m. 4th 27 Feb 1906, Mary Edna Anderson

H-4-5-4 William Blane Hammers, b. 8 Aug 1858, d. 1891, ae 35-11-13, bur. 3 Sep 1891, Woodlawn Cem., Randolph Co., IN

m. Irene Groves, b. 6 Jul 1866, IN, d. 28 May 1916, Pasadena, CA

H-4-5-4-1 Margaret "Maud" Hammers, b. 19 Oct 1887, d. 27 Jun 1954, bur. Woodlawn Cem., Randolph Co., IN

m. Frederick W. Fox, b. 1879, d. 1961, bur. Woodlawn Cem., Randolph Co., IN

H-4-5-5 Nancy J. Hammers, b. c1860, IN, d. 6 Oct 1911, bur. Woodlawn Cem., Randolph Co., IN
m. c1879, Hamilton Pursley, b. 1857, d. Nov 1935

H-4-5-5-1 Luther Pursley

H-4-5-5-2 Charles Pursley

H-4-5-5-3 Atlee ("Roy"?) Pursley

H-4-5-5-4 Hammers Pursley

H-4-6 Mary Hammer, b. c1820
m. 16 Jan 1840, Randolph Co., IN, William Sinclair Page

H-4-6-1 Sinclair John Page

H-4-6-1-1 Mary "Mollie" Page, c1867, IN (living with H-4-3 Joseph Hammers in 1880 Randolph Co., IN census)
m. John Life, m. 2nd Carey Ross

H-4-6-2 Nancy Page

H-4-7 Sarah Hammers, b. c1821, Greene Co., PA, d. 1899, IN, (1850, 1860 censuses Randolph Co., IN), bur. Rehobeth Cem., Randolph Co., IN but not listed in records or gravestone noted
m. 4 Feb 1840, Randolph Co., IN, Henry G. Hulderman, d. 3 Jun 1863, (ae 53-10-20), bur. Rehobeth Cem., Randolph Co., IN

H-4-7-1 Marietta Hulderman, b. c1841, IN, m. Henry Jones

H-4-7-2 Nancy Hulderman, b. c1843, IN, m. Sam Myers

H-4-7-3 James W. Hulderman, b. c1845, IN

H-4-7-4 Lewis E. Hulderman, b. c1848, IN, dnm

H-4-7-5 Catharine M. Hulderman, b. c1851, IN,

H-4-7-6 Abraham R. Hulderman, b. c1856, IN, m. Etta Nixon

H-4-7-6-1 Ada Hulderman, dnm

H-4-7-6-2 Alice Hulderman, m. William Mosier

H-4-7-6-3 Morris Hulderman, dnm

H-4-7-7 Joseph Hulderman, b. c1857, IN, m. Ella Harris

H-4-7-8 Silas Hulderman, m. Alice Silvers

H-4-7 m. 2nd Daniel Booker

H-4-8 Joseph Hammers, b. Sep 1829, OH, d. Aug 1903, bur. Woodlawn Cem., Randolph Co., IN (1880, 1900 Randolph Co., IN censuses)
m. 22 Mar 1853, Randolph Co., IN, Achsah Jane Howery, b. 1835, IN, d. 16 Jan 1917, bur. Woodlawn Cem., Randolph Co., IN

H-4-8-1 Sarah Ann Hammers, d. 18 Jan 1856, 25 days, bur. Rehobeth Cem., Randolph Co., IN

H-4-8-2 Mary L. Hammers, d. 28 Aug 1862, Randolph Co., IN, bur. Rehobeth Cem., Randolph Co., IN

H-4-8-3 Laura Hammers, d. 31 Aug 1862, Randolph Co., IN, bur. Rehobeth Cem., Randolph Co., IN

H-4-8 raised niece but did not adopt (H-4-6-1) Mary Page, b. c1867, IN

H-5 Anna Hammers, b. c1788, York Co., PA
m. 1st Samuel Hanna, m. 2nd Joseph McDonald

H-6 Mary Hammers, b. c1791, Fayette Co., PA
m. William Carothers, d. before 1857, IN
H-7 John Hammers, b. c1792, Fayette Co., PA (there is a John Hamer (or
Hames) in the 1820 Greene Co., PA census with family which might
be this John Hammers)
went south and probably died there according to one story
H-8 Phebe Hammers, b. c1794, Fayette Co., PA, d. before 1857, IN ?
m. ? Stevens ? m. 2nd Okey McCabe
H m. 2nd 12 Sep 1812, Monongalia Co., VA, Sarah Pierce, b. c1792, VA
(Sarah m. 2nd Isaac Rice)
H-9 Delilah Hammers, b. Oct 1813, Monongalia Co., VA, d. 27 Sep 1874
(1850, 1860 Marion Co., VA censuses)
m. John Martin Fleming
H-9-1 William Colston Fleming, b. c1837, VA
H-9-2 Allison Fleming, b. c1839, VA
H-9-3 Sarah E. Fleming, b. c1841, VA
H-9-4 Mary E. Fleming, b. c1843, VA
H-9-5 Charles P. Fleming, b. c1846, VA
H-9-6 Anna Almeda Fleming, b. c1849, VA
H-9-7 Thomas Fleming, b. c1852, VA
H-10 Augustus Hammers, b. 1817, Monongalia Co., VA
m. Nancy ?, m. 2nd Caroline ?
H-10-1 Rebecca Hammers, b. c1844, OH
H-10-2 Franklin Hammers, b. c1853, IL
H-10-3 Ektelbert Hammers, b. c1855, VA
H-10-4 Sanford Hammers, b. c1855, VA
H-10-5 Charles Hammers, b. 1859, VA
H-11 Rebecca Hammers, b. c1819, Monongalia Co., VA
H-12 Permala Hammers, b. c1821, Monongalia Co., VA (1850 census
Marion Co., VA shows an Amelia Hammers, age, 19 living with
Rebecca Hammers, age 30)

HJF-Immigrant Johann Frantz Hammer, b. 1725, Palatinate, Germany, d. 1802, m. 13 Jun 1749, York Co., PA

HJF-4 John Michael Hammer, b. 1760, d. 1842, m. Margaret ?

HJF-4-3 Michael Hammer, Jr., b. 1793, d. 1872, m. Anna Slick

HJF-4-3-1 John Abraham Hammers, b. May 1825, PA (moved from PA to IN in 1862, 1880 Randolph Co., IN census, apparently unrelated to the above Hammer line but lived in Randolph Co.)
m. 2nd 13 Jan 1856, Blair Co., PA, Elizabeth Andrews (or Anders), b. Oct 1836, PA, (1920 census Randolph Co., IN age 86, PA), d. 6 Dec 1921, Randolph Co., IN, bur. Union Cem., Randolph Co., IN

HJF-4-3-1-1 Jacob Hammer, b. Oct 1857, Bedford Co., PA, d. 15 Jan 1932, bur. Woodlawn Cem., m. Emma Thornburg, b. Jan 1865, IN, d. 1934, bur. 18 Aug 1834, Woodlawn Cem.

HJF-4-3-1-1-1 Girtie Nina Hammer, b. 20 Aug 1882, Randolph Co., IN

HJF-4-3-1-1-2 Fred Hammer, b. 8 May 1885, Randolph Co., IN, d. 1929, bur. Woodlawn Cem., Randolph Co., IN

HJF-4-3-1-1-3 Ray A. Hammer, b. 1888, d. 1924, bur. 14 May 1924, Woodlawn Cem., Randolph Co., IN

HJF-4-3-1-1-4 Tilo? Hammer, b. 24 Aug 1890, Randolph Co., IN

HJF-4-3-1-1-5 Gail Hammer, b. Nov 1893, IN

HJF-4-3-1-2 James Calvin Hammers, b. c1860, PA, d. 1941, bur. 15 Mar 1941, Woodlawn Cem., Randolph Co., IN
m. 1st 16 Dec 1884, Delaware Co., IN, Orie Kegeries, b. 1868, d. 4 Dec 1892, bur. Windsor Cem., Randolph Co., IN

HJF-4-3-1-2-1 Dosey Hammers, b. c1885, IN (1900 Delaware Co., IN)
m. 26 Feb 1902, Delaware Co., IN

HJF-4-3-1-2-2 Ollie Hammers, b. c1889, d. 8 Apr 1891, bur. Windsor Cem., Randolph Co., IN

HJF-4-3-1-2-3 Dick Hammers, b. 7 Jul 1890, IN
m. 26 Mar 1910, Delaware Co., IN, Ollie Dudley

HJF-4-3-1-2 m. 2nd Minnie E. Thornburg, b. 1869, IN, d. 1952, bur. 13 Feb 1952, Woodlawn Cem., Randolph Co., IN

HJF-4-3-1-2-4 Beatrice N. Hammers, b. c1904, IN

HJF-4-3-1-3 Catherine Hammer, b. c1862, PA

HJF-4-3-1-4 William A. Hammer, b. c1866, IN (1920 census Stoney Creek Twp., Randolph Co., IN)
m. 27 Sep 1890, Flora Sutton, b. c1871, IN

HJF-4-3-1-4-1 daughter, d. 25 Sep 1891, Windsor, IN

HJF-4-3-1-4-2 Cressie Hammers, d. 25 Aug 1893, Windsor, IN

HJF-4-3-1-4-3 Jason Hammers, b. 25 Jan 1895, Randolph Co., IN

HJF-4-3-1-4-4 Fay Hammers, b. 13 Oct 1898, Randolph Co., IN

HJF-4-3-1-4-5 John A. Hammers, b. 1901, d. 1969, bur. 4 Dec 1969, Woodlawn Cem., Randolph Co., IN
m. Lela Rouch, b. 1903, d. 1965, bur. Woodlawn Cem.

HJF-4-3-1-4-5-1 John Howard Hammers, b. 1 May 1925, d. 1967, bur. 3 Jul 1967, Woodlawn Cem.

HJF-4-3-1-4-6 Dortha Elizabeth Hammers, b. 22 Nov 1903, Randolph Co., IN

HJF-4-3-1-4-7 Russell Hammers, b. c1906, IN

HJF-4-3-1-4-8 Glee Winifred Hammers, b. 1907, IN

HJF-4-3-1-5 Franklin Hammer, b. c1873, IN, d. 1956, bur. 25 May 1956, Woodlawn Cem., Randolph Co., IN
m. Alfaretta Wright, b. c1876, IN, bur. 29 Apr 1956, Woodlawn Cem., Randolph Co., IN

HJF-4-3-1-5-1 Wilbur C. Hammers, b. c1897, IN, m. Eula R. ?

HJF-4-3-1-5-2 Sheldon P. Hammers, b. 21 Jun 1899, IN
m. Evea Rust, b. 1904, IN

HJF-4-3-1-5-2-1 Rexford Eugene Hammers, b. 6 Apr 1921, Randolph Co., IN, d. 1925, bur. 30 Jul 1925, Woodlawn Cem.

HJF-4-3-1-5-3 Charles Franklin Hammers, b. 10 Aug 1911, IN

HD David Hammer, b. c1767, NC, d. 26 Dec 1845, IA (moved into Randolph Co., IN by 1820, apparently unrelated to the Peter Hammer line above, later moved to IA)
m. 1789, Newberry Co., SC, Charlotte Jay

HD-1 Margaret Hammer, b. 1792

HD-2 Rachael Hammer, b. 1797

HD-3 David Hammer, b. 1801, m. Mary Lewellen

HD-4 Ann Hammer, b. 1804, m. Edward Thornburg

HD-5 William Hammer, b. c1807

HD-6 Mary Hammer, b. c1809

Descendants of John Collins

C John Collins, Sr., b. c1715, Ireland, d. shortly bef. 1795, Stoney Run, Hackers Creek, Harrison Co., VA, immigrated to Philadelphia in 1745, moved to Frederick Co., VA shortly thereafter, wife's name unknown

C-1 Thomas Collins, b. c1743, d. 1820, Hampshire Co., VA
   m. c1774, Elizabeth Spriggs Cresap
C-1-1 Charity Collins, b. 1776, m. Abraham Johnston
C-1-2 Daniel Collins
C-1-3 John Collins
C-1-4 Thomas Collins, b. 1779, m. Elizabeth Tomlinson
C-1-5 Jenny Collins, m. Jones
C-1-6 Cassandra Collins, m. Callahan

C-2 John Collins*, Jr., b. c1748, Frederick Co., VA, d. c1835, Warren Co., OH
   m. c1770, Monongalia Co., VA, Hannah Cozad, b. Mt. Oliver, Morris Co., NJ, d/o Jacob Cozad and Elizabeth (Sutton) Cozad. Elizabeth was the daughter of David Sutton who was b. c1727, Somerset, NJ. John and Hannah (Cozad) Collins moved back to NJ shortly after their marriage and their first children were born there. John Collins, Jr. moved to Hampshire Co., VA about 1764 and lived there until 1785 when he moved to Harrison Co., VA. About 1806, he moved to Bath Co., VA and then about 1816 moved to Warren Co., OH.
C-2-1 Cornelius Collins, b. 1768 (according to 1850 census) NJ, d. after 1850 (Will of Cornelius Collins in 1863 in Wabash Co., IN but that would make him 95 at death, probably different Cornelius) (from census data 1810, Harrison Co., VA, 1820, Clark Co., OH, 1830, Champaign Co., OH, 1840 and 1850, Jay Co., IN)
   m. 1 Oct 1794 or 1798, Harrison Co., VA, Eleanor Richards
C-2-1-1 Cornelius Collins, Jr., b. c1796, d. 21 Jan 1830, Miami Co., OH
   m. Nancy Keith, d. 4 Jun 1866, age 79y, 3m, 8 d
C-2-1-1-1 Samuel G. Collins
C-2-1-2 ? George Collins, b. 1798/1800, VA (1830 Champaign Co., OH with Cornelius, Sr.)
C-2-1-3 ? James Collins, b. c1800, VA
   m. 3 Jul 1825, Warren Co., OH, Nancy Everhart, b. c1800, PA
C-2-1-3-1 Williams Collins, b. c1833
C-2-1-3-2 Sally A. Collins, b. c1834
C-2-1-3-3 Rachel Collins, b. c1835
C-2-1-3-4 Melissa Collins, b. c1836
C-2-1-3-5 John Collins, b. c1838

C-2-1-3-6 David Collins, b. c1839

C-2-1-4 ? David Collins, b. 1813, OH (1850 census Jay Co., IN)

C-2-2 Jacob Collins, b. 11 Sep 1773, NJ, d. 7 Mar 1837, Warren Co., OH
m. 25 Mar 1795, Harrison Co., VA, Mary Elsworth, b. c1776, d. 1821
Warren Co., OH

C-2-2-1 Mercy Collins, b. Dec 1795, Harrison Co., VA
m. John Keith, d. bef 1837

C-2-2-2 Elizabeth Collins, b. c1797, Harrison Co., VA
m. 27 Jun 1816, Warren Co., OH, Joseph Jones

C-2-2-3 Levi Collins, b. 11 Nov 1799, Lewis Co., WV, d. 6 Jan 1852,
Shelby Co., IN
m. 25 Jan 1818, Warren Co., OH, Elizabeth Snell, d. 1830, Miami Co.,
OH

C-2-2-3-1 Samuel Snell Collins, b. 26 Jun 1819, Warren Co., OH, d. aft
1888
m. 7 Mar 1844, Jane M. Cairns, d. Aug 1850

C-2-2-3-2 Edmund Robert Collins, b. 6 Apr 1822, Miami Co., OH, d. 14
Apr 1877, Macon Co., IL
m. 25 Oct 1844, Shelby Co., IN, Emily Melvina Dulton, d. 2 May 1856,
ae 32y, 1m, 3d

C-2-2-3-2-1 Frances Collins, b. 1846, Shelby Co., IN

C-2-2-3-2-2 Ollie Parthina Collins, b. 20 Feb 1848, Shelby Co., IN

C-2-2-3-2-3 Margaret Collins, b. 9 Feb 1851, Shelby Co., IN

C-2-2-3-2-4 Sarah Louise Collins, b. c1852, Shelby Co., IN

C-2-2-3-2 m. 2nd 16 Jan 1859, Shelby Co., IN, Eliza Conner, b. 14 Apr
1841, Randolph Co., IN

C-2-2-3-2-5 Luman Jones Collins, b. 25 Apr 1860

C-2-2-3-2-6 Edmund Robert Collins, b. 12 Nov 1863, Shelby Co., IN

C-2-2-3-2-7 Chas. L. Collins, b. 20 Jul 1870, Macon Co., IL

C-2-2-3-2-8 Emma J. Collins, b. 6 Oct 1874, Macon Co., IL

C-2-2-3-3 Catherine Collins, b. 26 Sep 1826, Shelby Co., IN, m. ? Ford

C-2-2-3-4 Lydia Ann Collins, b. 1829, Shelby Co., IN

C-2-2-3 m. 2nd 28 Dec 1830, Nancy Sleeth, d. 1 Dec 1850, Shelby Co., IN

C-2-2-3-5 Amelia "Millie" Collins, b. 1833, Shelby Co., IN

C-2-2-3-6 Leander Milton Collins, d. 10 Aug 1863, Murfeesboro, PA, Co.
F, 70th Ind. Inf.·

C-2-2-3-7 Sarah Jane Collins, m. ? Barker, d. aft. 1888 (1888, Boggstown,
IN)

C-2-2-3-8 James Levi Collins, d. aft 1888

C-2-2-3-9 Nancy Elizabeth Collins, b. 8 Aug 1847, d. Aug 1864

C-2-2-3-10 Mary Josephine Collins, b. 5 Jul 1848, Shelby Co., IN, d. 29
Aug 1869
m. J. R. Fleming

C-2-2-4 Lydia Collins, b. c1799, VA (moved to Kosciusko Co., IN, later
to NE)
m. 10 Nov 1825, William Cummins

C-2-2-5 Hannah Collins, b. c1801, Lewis Co., VA, d. bef. 1837
m. 4 Nov 1819, Warren Co., OH, Edmund Collins (NH Collins)

C-2-2-6 Jacob Collins, Jr., b. 16 Sep 1811, Lewis Co., VA, d. 24 Dec 1885,
Auburn, NE m. 1836, Shelby Co., IN, Ann Davis

C-2-2-6-1 John D. Collins, b. 7 Jan 1837, Shelby Co., IN, d. 1 Apr 1893

C-2-2-7 Joseph B. Collins, b. 9 Dec 1814, Warren Co., OH, d. 18 Aug
1867, Hancock Co., IN
m. 26 Nov 1835, Shelby Co., IN, Lucinda David, d. 1838
m. 2nd 20 Jun 1839, Annie Engle

C-2-2-7-1 Joshua Collins, b. 20 Jan 1840, d. 19 Feb 1866

C-2-2-7-2 Tabitha Collins, b. 20 Jul 1843, d. 20 Aug 1872,
m. David Stage
m. 2nd Isaac David

C-2-2-7-3 Samuel Engle Collins, b. 6 Aug 1845, d. 8 Jan 1921,
Indianapolis, IN

C-2-2-7-4 Alpheus Collins, b. 16 Jul 1848, d. 4 May 1865, Newbern, NC

C-2-2-7-5 Hannah L. Collins, b. 31 May 1852, d. 2 May 1856

C-2-2-7-6 Lydia Ann Collins, b. 21 May 1855, d. 6 Sep 1868, m. ? Horton

C-2-2-7-7 Emma Bell Collins, b. 1 Jun 1860, d. 8 Feb 1880, m. ? Horton

C-2-2-7-8 ? Collins

C-2-2-8 Jesse Collins, b. c1818, Warren Co., OH

C-2-2-9 Alphious Collins, b. c1820, Warren Co., OH

C-2-2-10 Amos Mix Collins, b. 3 Jul 1826, Warren Co., OH, d. 23 Jun
1903, Ross Co., OH
m. 7 May 1846, Warren Co., OH, Elizabeth Swigert

C-2-2 m. 2nd 17 May 1825, Lewis Co., VA, Cleranda Beemna

C-2-3 George Collins, b. c1775, NJ, d. 7 Mar 1830, Warren Co., OH
m. 1 Oct 1798, Harrison Co., VA, Abigail Smith
m. ? 2nd 23 Sep 1819, Harrison Co., VA, Elizabeth Crossan

C-2-4 Mary Collins, b. c1777, m. 21 Jan 1793, Harrison Co., VA,
Abraham Bennett

C-2-4-? Abigail Bennett, b. c1803, VA, d. 1878
m. 10 Dec 1819, Warren Co., OH, Amos Collins (NH Collins)

C-2-5 John Collins*, Jr., b. 5 Jan 1782, VA (prob. Hampshire Co.), d. 13
Sep 1838, Jay Co., IN, bur. Bost Cem., Jefferson Twp., Jay Co., IN
m. 1800/1805, prob. Harrison Co., VA, Elizabeth Liggett, d. 30 Aug
1838, Jay Co., IN

C-2-5-1 Mary Collins (stayed in OH)
m. ? Watkins

C-2-5-2 Joseph Collins*, b. 1 Dec 1810, VA, d. 25 Feb 1873, Jay Co., IN,
bur. Bost Cem., Jefferson Twp., Jay Co., IN
m. 1st c1834, OH, Susan ?, d. 19 May 1838, Jay Co., IN, bur. Bost
Cem., Jefferson Twp., Jay Co., IN

C-2-5-2-1 Mary Collins, b. c1835, OH

C-2-5-2-2 Martin Collins, b. c1837, OH

C-2-5-2 m. 2nd 7 Nov 1839, Jay Co., IN, Harriet Finch*, b. 16 Mar 1821, OH, d. 2 Aug 1884, Jay Co., IN

C-2-5-2-3 Susan Collins, b. c1841, IN

C-2-5-2-4 Elizabeth Collins, b. c1842, IN

C-2-5-2-5 Amelia Alisa Collins*, b. 30 Jun 1844, IN, d. 9 Jun 1908, Randolph Co., IN, bur. Hopewell Cem., Randolph Co., IN
m. 6 Mar 1871, Jay Co., IN, David C. Garringer (see Garringer descendants list G-4-6-3)

C-2-5-2-6 Catherine Collins, b. c1846, IN

C-2-5-2-7 Joseph Collins, b. c1848, IN

C-2-5-2-8 William Harrison Collins, b. c1849, IN, d. 2 Apr 1930, bur. Hopewell Cem.
m. 12 Dec 1872, Randolph Co., IN, (G-4-6-11) Sarah Ellen Garringer, b. 29 Jan 1855, d. 31 Jan 1936, bur. Hopewell Cem., Randolph Co., IN

C-2-5-2-9 Melissa Collins, b. c1852, IN

C-2-5-2-10 John Collins, b. c1854, IN

C-2-5-3 Jesse C. Collins, b. c1811, OH
m. Eliza Cook, d/o John and Mary Cook

C-2-5-3-1 Mary Collins, b. 1839, m. M. House

C-2-5-3-2 Julia A Collins, b. 1841, m. W. Kidder

C-2-5-3-3 Prudence Collins, b. 1843

C-2-5-3-4 John Elliott Collins, b. 25 April 1845, Warren Co., OH

C-2-5-3-5 Jesse Collins

C-2-5-3-6 Lucinda Collins, m. J. Hastings, m. 2nd ? Jackson

C-2-5-3-7 James W. Collins

C-2-5-3-8 Edith Collins, m. D. Orcutt

C-2-5-3-9 Joseph L. Collins

C-2-5-4 Prudence Collins, m. Samuel Blazer

C-2-5-5 Elliott Collins

C-2-5-6 Elizabeth Collins, m. Joseph Kidder

C-2-5-7 George Collins, b. ?? 1802/1810, d. bef. 1840

C-2-5-7-1 Mary Melinda Collins
m. Jacob Ozborn

C-2-5-8 Hannah Collins, d. bef. 1840
m. Elias Jackson

C-2-5-8-1 Elizabeth Jackson, m. James Whitaker

C-2-5-8-2 William Jackson, b. aft. 1819

C-2-5-8-3 Sarah Ellen Jackson, b. aft. 1819

C-2-5-8-4 Jemima Jackson, b. aft. 1819

C-2-5-9 John Collins, b. 1802/10, d. bef. 1840

C-2-5-9-1 Elizabeth Collins, b. aft. 1819

C-2-5-10 Susan Collins, d. bef. 1840, m. Henry Williams

C-2-5-10-1 John Williams

C-2-5-11 Harrison Collins, d. 1839/40 (minor in Feb 1840 legal document)

C-2-6 Abigail Collins, b. 1785, NJ

m. 1802, Joseph Bennett

C-2-7 Elizabeth Collins, b. c1786, Fayette Co., PA
m. 15 Apr 1801, Harrison Co., VA, John B. Burnsides

C-2-8 Benjamin Collins, b. 3 Mar 1787, Harrison Co., VA, d. 16 Feb 1871, Union Co., IN
m. Hannah Emory, b. 5 Jun 1787

C-2-9 Isaac S. Collins, b. 1792, Harrison Co., VA, d. 11 Dec 1871, Calhoun Co., WV
m. 6 Oct 1812, Harrison Co., VA, Rachel Cunningham

C-2-10 Hannah Collins, b. Sep 1795, d. 4 May 1874, Liberty, IN
m. 22 Dec 1814, Warren Co., OH, Joseph Liggett

C-3 George Collins, b. c1755, Hampshire Co., VA, d. 4 Sep 1833, Lewis Co., VA
m. 12 Mar 1791, Harrison Co., VA, Mary Richard
m. 2nd 8 Oct 1798, Abigail Smith

C-3-1 William Collins, b. c1793, m. Elizabeth Wiant, m. 2nd Sarah Norman

C-3-2 Sarah Collins, m. Henry Stallman, m. 2nd Aaron Schoolcraft

Descendants of Jacob Grove

GR Jacob Grove, b. c1730, d. 1794, Frederick Co., VA (lived betw. Martinsburg and the Cacapon River, VA[WV]), m. Margaret ?

GR-1 John Grove*, b. 1750, d. 1828, wife's name unknown

GR-1-1 Jacob Grove*, b. 1774, Frederick Co., VA, d. aft 1850
m. 13 Oct 1795, Frederick Co., VA, Catherine Lonas, b. 1775, VA, d. aft 1850, Prob. OH

GR-1-1-1 John Grove, b. 9 Feb 1797, d. 1858, IA
m. 17 Mar 1825, Nancy Waln, m. 2nd 30 Jun 1845, Mary (Waln) Keedick

GR-1-1-1-1 Jacob Grove, b. 29 Dec 1825, Frederick Co., VA

GR-1-1-1-2 Mary Ann Grove, b. 19 Jul 1827

GR-1-1-1-3 Joseph Grove, b. 6 Sep 1828

GR-1-1-1-4 Joshua B. Grove, b. 2 Apr 1830, d. 29 May 1906, Ames, IA

GR-1-1-1-5 Susan Grove

GR-1-1-1-6 John Grove, b. 21 May 1834, m. Barbara

GR-1-1-2 Henry Lonas Grove, b. 1800, Frederick Co., VA

GR-1-1-3 Abraham Groves*, b. 1804, Frederick Co., VA, d. 29 Sep 1876, Randolph Co., IN, bur. Hopewell Cem., Randolph Co., IN
m. 8 Apr 1826, Frederick Co., VA, Elizabeth Reed

GR-1-1-3-1 Anceline Groves*, b. 1828 VA, prob. Frederick Co., d. 2 Mar 1864, Randolph Co., IN
m. 1845, Clinton Co., OH, George Morris

GR-1-1-3-1-1 Elizabeth Morris*, b. 25 Sep 1845, d. 7 Jun 1922, Randolph Co., IN, bur. Woodlawn Cem., Randolph Co., IN
m. 1 Oct 1864, Elijah Oliver Hammers, (see Hammer Descendants List H-4-5-1)

GR-1-1-3-1-2 Achsah Morris, b. 26 Feb 1847, bur. 22 May 1926, Woodlawn Cem., Randolph Co., IN
m. 26 Sep 1863, Hiram Milton Taylor, b. 1842, d. 1937, bur. Woodlawn Cem., Randolph Co., IN

GR-1-1-3-1-3 William Henry Morris, b. 12 Jun 1849, m. 26 May 1870, Eliza McCamey

GR-1-1-3-1-4 Catherine Morris, b. 31 May 1851, d. 30 Jan 1930
m. 28 Dec 1871, William Newton Haltom

GR-1-1-3-1-5 David Abraham Morris, b. 16 Oct 1853

GR-1-1-3-1-6 Millicent Morris, b. 21 Sep 1855, Randolph Co., IN, d. 7 May 1930, IA
m. 19 Dec 1878, David Secrist

GR-1-1-3-1-7 John Hamilton Morris, b. 17 Apr 1858, Farmland, IN, d. 25
Jan 1916, IA
m. 25 Nov 1880, Armadilla McLaren
GR-1-1-3-1-8 Anceline Morris, b. 25 Jan 1864, d. 1932
m. William LeFevre
GR-1-1-3-2 David Groves, b. Dec 1832, VA, bur. 1 Nov 1901, Woodlawn
Cem., Randolph Co., IN
m. Susan A. Hill, d. bef. 1880
GR-1-1-3-2-1 Daniel Webster Grove, b. 6 Sep 1857, d. 31 Jan 1929, bur.
Woodlawn Cem., Randolph Co., IN
m. 14 Dec 1878, Randolph Co., IN, Martha Hupp, b. 1862, d. 1948,
bur. Woodlawn Cem., Randolph Co., IN
GR-1-1-3-2-1-1 Henry Grove (twin), b. 1879, IN, d. ?infancy
GR-1-1-3-2-1-2 Earl C. Groves (twin), b. Oct 1879, IN
GR-1-1-3-2-1-3 Herbert Groves, b. Apr 1881, IN
GR-1-1-3-2-1-4 Charles Edward Groves, b. Nov 1886, d. 1968, bur.
Woodlawn Cem., Randolph Co., IN
m. Mary Hafkemlier, d. 12 Feb 1928, bur. Woodlawn Cem.,
Randolph Co., IN
GR-1-1-3-2-1-5 Opel Grove, b. Apr 1888, IN,
GR-1-1-3-2-1-6 David H. Groves, b. Nov 1889, IN
GR-1-1-3-2-1-7 Morris H. Groves, b. Sep 1891, IN, m. Nevajoy ?
GR-1-1-3-2-1-7-1 Neomia Joy Groves, d. 3 Feb 1916, age 2 mo.
GR-1-1-3-2-1-8 Lawrence Groves, b. Apr 1896, IN
GR-1-1-3-2-2 John B. Groves, b. c1860, IN
GR-1-1-3-2-3 Alfred M. Groves, b. Feb 1861, IN, d. 4 Jun 1900, bur.
Woodlawn Cem., Randolph Co., IN
m. 13 Jun 1891, Randolph Co., IN, Hattie B. Williams, b. Nov 1871, IN
GR-1-1-3-2-4 Marietta Groves, b. c1870, IN
GR-1-1-3-2 m. 2nd Ruth Craig, b. Jun 1844, IN, bur. 12 Aug 1929,
Woodlawn Cem.
GR-1-1-3-3 William R. Groves, b. 27 Mar 1834, d. 28 Jan 1877, age
42-10-1
m. April 1863, OH, Mary Smith, d. before 1870
GR-1-1-3-3-1 Irene Groves, b. c1865, IN
m. William B. Hammers (see Hammers descendants list H-4-5-4)
GR-1-1-3-3-2 Minnie Groves, b. c1867, IN
GR-1-1-3-3-3 Benjamin Groves, b. Nov 1868, IN, d. 22 Feb 1905, bur.
Woodlawn Cem., Randolph Co., IN
m. Minnie Anderson, b. 1871, d. 12 Nov 1900, Randolph Co., IN, bur.
Woodlawn Cem., Randolph Co., IN
GR-1-1-3-3-3-1 daughter, b. 6 Apr 1891
GR-1-1-3-3-3-2 Arthur Groves, b. 17 Aug 1892
GR-1-1-3-3-3-3 Garfield Groves, b. c1894, IN
GR-1-1-3-3-3-4 Willard Groves, b. 5 Mar 1897

GR-1-1-3-3-3-5 Ralph V. Groves, b. 10 Dec 1898, d. 23 Nov 1907, bur.
    Woodlawn Cem., Randolph Co., IN
GR-1-1-3-3 m. 2nd Sarah Jones, b. c1852
GR-1-1-3-3-4 ? son Groves, b. c1866, IN
GR-1-1-3-3-5 ? infant Groves, b. c1869, IN
GR-1-1-3-4 Rebecca Groves, b. 1836
GR-1-1-3-5 Alfred H. Groves, b. 1841, OH, d. 4 Jun 1900
    m. 8 Jul 1865, Randolph Co., IN, Louise A. Morris, b. c1849, OH
GR-1-1-3-5-1 Dennis Bennett Groves, b. c1867, IN
GR-1-1-3-5-2 Logen Groves, b. c1868, IN
GR-1-1-3-5-3 Milroy Groves, b. c1870, IN
GR-1-1-3-5-4 Rilla Groves, b. c1873, IN
GR-1-1-3-5-5 Orville Groves, b. c1875, IN
GR-1-1-3-5-6 Wm H. Groves, b. c1877, IN
GR-1-1-3-6 Elizabeth Groves, b. 1843
GR-1-1-3-7 Isaac W. Groves, b. 1849, OH
    m. Eliza Samantha Stump
GR-1-1-3-7-1 Martin V. Groves, b. c1876, IN
GR-1-1-3-7-2 William L. Groves, b. c1878, IN
GR-1-1-3-7-3 Sarah Alice Groves, b. 31 Aug 1883
GR-1-1-3-7-4 daughter, b. 26 Aug 1886, Randolph Co., IN
GR-1-1-3-8 Mary E. Groves, b. 1852
GR-1-1-4 David Groves, b. c1807, VA, m. Mary ?
GR-1-1-5 Mary Groves
GR-1-1-6 George Grove, b. c1818, VA, m. Mary Babb
GR-1-2 Adam Grove, m. 6 Aug 1795, Frederick Co., VA, Eve Shiner
GR-1-3 Henry Grove, m. 22 Nov 1797, Frederick Co., VA, Mary Lawyer
GR-1-4 John Grove, m. Eleanor
GR-1-5 Samuel Grove, m. Eliz
GR-1-6 Peter Grove, m. Mary
GR-1-7 Margaret Grove, m. 2 May 1804, Jacob Gibbens
GR-1-8 Rachel Grove, m. George Shiner
GR-2 James Grove (listed in Jacob's will)
GR-3 D. Vance Grove (listed in Jacob's will)

Kincaid Descendants

The following is a proposed descendant's list for the Greenbrier Kincaids who descended from Alexander, David and Thomas Kincaid of Scotland. It has been assembled from the genealogy by Dr. Herbert Clarke Kincaid, Greenbrier County records, census records and records of the author. The number scheme has been made consistent with that used in the book *Our Families* by Larry Shuck.

K-1* James Kincaid (son of James), Laird of-that-ilk, Scotland

K-1-1 child, name unknown

K-1-2 Alexander Kincaid of Scotland, b. c1670, (pharmacist in Edinburgh)

K-1-2-1 Samuel Kincaid, Sr., b. c1710, (emigrated in 1746 with at least two sons Samuel and George, settled at Beverly Manor, Augusta Co., VA) d. 1780, Falling Spring, Jackson's River, Allegheny Co., VA
m. ? wife's name unknown

K-1-2-1-1 Alexander, died young

K-1-2-1-2 Samuel Kincaid, Jr., b. 1734, Scotland, d. 23 Jan 1819, Greenbrier Co., VA
m. c1776, Margaret Clarke, b. 1740, d. 1834

K-1-2-1-2-1 Samuel Kincaid, b. 15 May 1782, Greenbrier Co., VA, d. 7 Mar 1853, Greenbrier Co., VA
m. 15 Feb 1827, Sarah Ann "Sallie" Kester

K-1-2-1-2-1-1 Elizabeth Jane Kincaid, b. c1829
m. 11 Jan 1852, James Hull, m. 2nd William H. Mockbee

K-1-2-1-2-1-2 Margaret Kincaid, b. c1830, m. Henry Hefner

K-1-2-1-2-1-2 Sarah A. Kincaid, b. c1832, m. Matthew Mays

K-1-2-1-2-1-3 Harriet Frances Kincaid, b. c1834, m. Lance Scott

K-1-2-1-2-1-4 Virginia Kincaid, b. c1836, d. 4 Nov 1873, m. Joseph Scott

K-1-2-1-2-1-5 Mary Catherine Kincaid, b. c1838, d. 1874
m. Franklin Renick Holyman

K-1-2-1-2-1-6 George Kincaid, b. c1840, d. 1908, m. Margaret White

K-1-2-1-2-1-7 Phoebe Kincaid, b. c1842
m. Charles Hagen, m. 2nd Otto Ruckman

K-1-2-1-2-1-8 William Kincaid, b. c1848, d. bef. 1860

K-1-2-1-2-1-3 Margaret Susan Kincaid, b. 27 Jan 1820, d. 25 Apr 1888
m. ? McCallister

K-1-2-1-2-1-4 Frances Jane Kincaid, b. 7 Mar 1822, d. 8 May 1893
m. Michael Gillilan

K-1-2-1-2-1-5 Agnes Letitia Kincaid, b. 19 Jan 1824
m. Josiah Lowry

K-1-2-1-2-1-6 Susan Rebecca Kincaid, b. 25 Oct 1825, d. 7 Aug 1826
K-1-2-1-2-1-7 Mary Louisa Kincaid, b. 31 May 1827, d. 7 Apr 1849
   m. ? Dean
K-1-2-1-2-1-8 Avalina Lovinia Kincaid, b. 22 Apr 1829, d. 6 Feb 1837
K-1-2-1-2-2 George Kincaid, m. Susie Remley moved west
K-1-2-1-2-3 James Kincaid, b. 15 May 1782, d. 9 Jul 1838
   m. 26 Mar 1816, Phebe Kincaid (K-1-2-1-3-9), b. 1795, d. 1858
K-1-2-1-2-3-1 Elizabeth Ann Kincaid, b. 3 Jan 1817, d. 8 May 1842, dnm
K-1-2-1-2-3-2 Alexander Clarke Kincaid, b. 27 Feb 1818, Greenbrier Co.,
   VA, d. 6 Dec 1893, Frankford, Greenbrier Co., WV
   m. 31 Oct 1847, Nicholas Co., VA, Maria Louisa Hamilton
K-1-2-1-2-3-2-1 Robert Alexander Kincaid, b. 1 Jun 1852, Pocahontas
   Co., VA, d. 25 Jan 1926, Richmond, WV
   m. 25 May 1880, New Orleans, LA, Mary Thomas Patton
K-1-2-1-2-3-2-1-1 Phala Hamilton Kincaid, b. 1 Apr 1881, Summersville,
   WV
   m. William Baltzer Moore
K-1-2-1-2-3-2-1-2 Herbert Clarke Kincaid, b. 16 Oct 1883, d. after 1951
   m. 4 Dec 1912, Weston, WV, Bess Lucille Rollyson
K-1-2-1-2-3-2-1-3 Wallace Patton Kincaid, b. 2 Feb 1886
K-1-2-1-2-3-2-1-4 Robert Truslow Kincaid, b. 11 Oct 1888, d. 23 Sep 1892
K-1-2-1-2-3-2-1-5 Mary Louise Kincaid, b. c1891
K-1-2-1-2-3-2-1-6 James Baldwin Kincaid, b. 10 Jul 1895,
K-1-2-1-2-3-2-1-7 Ralph Templeton Kincaid, b. 29 May 1898, m.
   Katherine Leo Boggs
K-1-2-1-2-3-2-2 James Renick Kincaid, b. 22 Mar 1854, d. 12 Jan 1922, m.
   Alice White
K-1-2-1-2-3-2-3 Fannie Bell Kincaid, b. 25 Aug 1856, d. 22 Feb 1863
K-1-2-1-2-3-2-4 Phebe Caroline Kincaid, b. 27 May 1857, d. 9 Aug 1933
   m. Robert Woodward
K-1-2-1-2-3-2-5 Laura Margaret Kincaid, b. 19 Oct 1858, m. Cal. Levisay
K-1-2-1-2-3-2-6 Mary Agnes Kincaid, b. 2 Feb 1864, d. 28 Jan 1873
K-1-2-1-2-3-2-7 Lucy Hamilton Kincaid, b. 8 Apr 1869,
   m. William A. Jameson
K-1-2-1-2-3-3 Frances Jane Kincaid, b. 7 Mar 1822, d. 8 May 1893, m.
   Michael Gillilan
K-1-2-1-2-3-4 Agnes Letitia Kincaid, b. 19 Jan 1824, m. Josiah Lowry
K-1-2-1-2-3-5 Sarah Rebecca Kincaid, b. 25 Oct 1825, d. 7 Aug 1826
K-1-2-1-2-3-6 Mary Louisa Kincaid, b. 31 May 1827, d. 7 Apr 1849, m.
   Dean
K-1-2-1-2-3-7 Avalina Lovinia Kincaid, b. 22 Jan 1829, d. 6 Feb 1837
K-1-2-1-2-3-8 William Renick Kincaid, b. 19 Jan 1831, d. Aug 1884
   m. Mary Ann Bell
K-1-2-1-2-3-8-1 Emily Kincaid, b. c1852
K-1-2-1-2-3-8-2 Thomas Alexander Bell Kincaid, b. 14 Mar 1854,
   Greenbrier Co., VA, d. Huntington, WV aft. 1936

K-1-2-1-2-3-8-3 James Alexander Kincaid, b. 2 Dec 1855, Greenbrier Co., VA

K-1-2-1-2-3-8-4 Michael Kincaid, b. c1857

K-1-2-1-2-3-8-5 Mary S. Kincaid, b. 14 Nov 1858, Greenbrier Co., VA

K-1-2-1-2-3-8-6 Eliza Kincaid, b. c1860, Greenbrier Co.

K-1-2-1-2-4 Sally Kincaid, m. 1804, William Brown

K-1-2-1-2-5 Elizabeth "Betty" Kincaid, b. 1787, m. John Brown

K-1-2-1-2-6 Ann Kincaid, b. 30 Aug 1791
  m. 12 Sep 1810, (K-1-2-3-1-1) Andrew Kincaid

K-1-2-1-2-7 Harriet Frances Kincaid, m. Lanty Scott

K-1-2-1-2-8 Thomas Kincaid, b. ?? (listed in will)

K-1-2-1-2-9 David Kincaid, b. ?? (listed in will)

K-1-2-1-2-10 Susannah Kincaid, b. ?? (listed in will)

K-1-2-1-3 George Kincaid, b. 1730/40, prob. in Scotland, d. Greenbrier Co., WV
  m. c1770, Margaret "Peggy" Renick, b. c1751

K-1-2-1-3-1 Samuel Kincaid, m 18 Jun 1801, Greenbrier Co., VA, Mary Allison, later moved to IL

K-1-2-1-3-2 Thomas Kincaid, m. Jemima Allison, later moved to IL

K-1-2-1-3-3 Margaret Kincaid, b. 1785, m. 1804, Daniel Allison, later moved to Gallia Co., OH

K-1-2-1-3-4 Andrew Kincaid

K-1-2-1-3-5 John Kincaid

K-1-2-1-3-6 Renick Kincaid

K-1-2-1-3-7 William Kincaid

K-1-2-1-3-8 Hugh Kincaid, b. 25 Apr 1795, m. Maria Brooks in IL

K-1-2-1-3-9 Phebe Kincaid, b. 15 Apr 1795, d. 16 Jan 1858, bur. Neola, WV
  m. 26 Mar 1816, Greenbrier Co., VA, (K-1-2-1-2-3) James Kincaid

K-1-2-1-4 James Kincaid, moved to KY about 1800

K-1-2-1-5 Ann Kincaid, m. 11 Feb 1782, (K-1-2-3-1) Andrew Kincaid

K-1-2-1-6 Robert Kincaid, b. 1735/50 (had 95 acres adjoining "Renick" in 1782), nfi

K-1-2-1-7 Hugh Kincaid, b. 1735/50 (had 95 acres in Greenbrier Co. in 1782), nfi

K-1-2-1-8 William Kincaid, b. 1735/50 (had 400 acres near Greenbrier River recorded 20 Jun 1782), nfi

K-1-2-2 George Kincaid, d. 25 Jun 1756, killed by Indians, (settled in now Allegheny Co., VA, John Dean was executor of George's estate)

K-1-2-2-1 Samuel Kincaid, m. Elizabeth Wilson

K-1-2-3 Robert Kincaid, b. Scotland, m. Anna Helena

K-1-2-3-1 Andrew Kincaid, b. bef. 1750
  m. 11 Feb 1782, Ann Kincaid (K-1-2-1-5)

K-1-2-3-1-1 Andrew Kincaid, b. 24 Mar 1783, Greenbrier Co., VA
  m. 12 Sep 1810, Greenbrier Co., VA, (K-1-2-1-2-6) Ann Kincaid

K-1-2-3-1-1-1 John Clarke Kincaid, b. 10 Feb 1818

K-1-2-3-2 John Kincaid, b. c1746, d. 11 Aug 1835
m. 25 Jul 1787, Alice Dean
K-1-2-3-3 James Kincaid, b. Bath Co., VA
m. 30 Oct 1786, Elizabeth Dean
K-1-2-3-3-1 Nancy Kincaid, b. 9 Aug 1791, d. 27 Feb 1867, m. 16 Jul
1826, Charles Ford
K-1-2-3-3-2 Jane Kincaid, b. 1793, m. Samuel McClung
K-1-2-3-3-3 John Dean Kincaid, b. 15 Mar 1795, d. 13 Feb 1843, m. 21 Oct
1816, Mary "Polly" Hyde
K-1-2-3-3-4 Andrew Kincaid, b. 1797, Greenbrier Co., VA,
m. 1 Aug 1839, Elizabeth Knapp
K-1-2-3-3-4-1 Charles Andrew Kincaid, m. Clarinda Taylor Lewis
K-1-2-3-3-5 Sarah Kincaid, b. 1802, d. 22 Feb 1845, m. 6 Sep 1825, John
Fulwider
K-1-2-3-3-6 William McClanchan Kincaid, b. 18 Sep 1805, d. 6 Jul 1877,
m. 18 Sep 1828, Sarah Hutzenpiller, m. 2nd 4 Apr 1861, Mary
Elizabeth Waggoner
K-1-2-3-3-6-1 Mary Kincaid, b. c1865, Gilmer Co., WV
K-1-2-3-3-6-2 Martha Kincaid, b. 1867, Gilmer Co., WV
K-1-2-3-3-7 Adam Dean Kincaid, b. 17 Nov 1807
m. Mary Bubger or Bunger, b. 1816, VA
K-1-2-3-3-7-1 Margaret E. Kincaid, b. Nov 1834
K-1-2-3-3-7-2 Sarah Jane Kincaid, b. Nov 1836
K-1-2-3-3-7-3 Mary V. Kincaid, b. & d. 1838
K-1-2-3-3-7-4 William H. Kincaid, b. & d. 1839
K-1-2-3-3-7-5 James Dickinson Kincaid, II, b. 14 Mar 1840, d. 16 Nov
1861 (Civil War)
m. 23 Aug 1860, Elizabeth Andrews
K-1-2-3-3-7-5-1 Kate Dickinson Kincaid
K-1-2-3-3-7-6 Michael Kincaid, b. 1844, d. 1844
K-1-2-3-3-7-7 Joseph Renick Kincaid, b. 4 Mar 1847, d. 5 Dec 1911
m. Agnes ?, b. 1845
K-1-2-3-3-7-7-1 Mary Kincaid, b. c1876
K-1-2-3-3-7-7-2 Newman Kincaid, b. c1880
K-1-2-3-3-7-7-3 Nannie Kincaid, b. c1882
K-1-2-3-3-7-7-4 Lula Kincaid, b. c1884
K-1-2-3-3-7-7-5 Laura Kincaid, b. c1885
K-1-2-3-3-7-7-6 Meggie Kincaid, b. c1889
K-1-2-3-3-7-7-7 Anname (son) Kincaid, b. c1898
K-1-2-3-3-7-8 Lewis George Kincaid, b. 1849, d. 1851
K-1-2-3-3-7-9 Mary Susan Kincaid, b. 16 Sep 1856? (?c1853)
K-1-2-3-3-7-10 Davidson Kincaid, b. 1861, d. 1864
K-1-2-3-3-7-11 Caroline Kincaid, b. 4 Nov 1856
K-1-2-3-3-7-12 Addie Davidson Kincaid, b. 2 Sep 1861
K-1-2-3-3-8 James Dickinson Kincaid, b. c1813, d. 3 May 1881,
Greenbrier Co., VA

m. 20 Aug 1839, Nancy Bunger

K-1-2-3-3-8-1 Susan A. Kincaid, b. c1841

K-1-2-3-3-8-2 Ally Kincaid, b. c1842

K-1-2-3-3-8-3 Anthony Kincaid, b. c1844

K-1-2-3-3-8-4 Manuel Kincaid, b. c1849

K-1-2-3-3-8-5 Harvey Albert Kincaid, b. 2 Aug 1854, Greenbrier Co., VA

K-1-2-3-3-8-6 Mary A. Kincaid, b. c1858
    m. A. H. Wolfenbarger

K-1-2-3-3-9 Harriet Kincaid, m. 24 Sep 1829, Henry Fulwider, b. 4 Jan 1896

K-1-2-3-4 Robert Kincaid, m. 1786, Botetourt Co., VA, Becky Wright

K-1-2-4 James Kincaid (moved south according to Dr. Herbert Clarke Kincaid genealogy, another record says buried St. Henlena, Lees Co., KY)

K-1-2-5 Alexander Kincaid, did not emigrate, a printer in Edinburgh

K-1-3 David Kincaid, b. c1680/1700, Scotland, came to America in 1715, first to Spotsylvania Co., VA, later to Albemarle Co., then Augusta Co., died in Bath Co., VA

K-1-3-1 David Kincaid, Jr., m. Winifred (maiden name unknown)

K-1-3-2 John "the weaver" Kincaid, m. Elizabeth (Maiden name unknown)

K-1-3-2-1 Andrew Kincaid, m. Jean (maiden name unknown)

K-1-3-2-2 Mathew Kincaid, m. Elizabeth ?

K-1-3-2-3 James Kincaid

K-1-3-2-4 John Kincaid, went to KY by 1784

K-1-3-3 poss. Joseph Kincaid

K-1-3-4 poss. Borough Kincaid

K-1-3-5 Elizabeth Kincaid

K-1-3-6 Hobson Kincaid

K-1-3-7 poss. James Kincaid

K-1-4 William Kincaid, came to America in 1715, nfi

K-1-5 Thomas Kincaid*, b. c1704, Scotland, d. 1750, Augusta Co., VA, m. Margaret ? (maiden name unknown), came to America by 1715 to Lancaster Co., PA, purchased land in Augusta Co., VA, in 1747

K-1-5-1 William Kincaid, b. c1735, d. 1823 Augusta Co., VA
    m. Eleanor Gay

K-1-5-2 prob. Thomas Kincaid, b. c1737, d. betw. 13 Sep 1817 and 3 Aug 1818, Greenbrier Co., VA (This connection is the one stated in Larry Shuck's book Our Families. According to another researcher, Richard Bradley, the father of the Thomas who married Hannah Tincher, was a John Kincaid. Which John Kincaid and where he fits is uncertain)
    m. c1760, Hannah Tincher

K-1-5-2-1 John Kincaid, b. c1760, Augusta Co., VA, d. 1830s
    m. 11 Feb 1782, Greenbrier Co., VA, Elizabeth Gillespie

K-1-5-2-2 Margaret "Peggy" Kincaid, b. c1761, Augusta Co., VA, m. Charles Harra

K-1-5-2-3 Samuel Kincaid, b. 1765, Augusta Co., VA, d. betw. Sep 1847 and Jun 1849
m. 21 Jun 1785, Mary Tincher, m. 2nd 13 Mar 1802, Hulda Osborne, m. 3rd Diana Ewing
K-1-5-2-3-1 William "Moccasin Bill" Kincaid, b. 1787, m. 22 Nov 1812, Greenbrier Co., VA, Virginia Jane Kincaid
K-1-5-2-3-2 Mathew Kincaid, went to MO
K-1-5-2-3-3 John Kincaid, went west
K-1-5-2-3-4 Thomas "Mountain Tim" Kincaid, b. c1795, d. 7 May 1875, Lewis Co., WV
m. Mary "Polly" Withrow
K-1-5-2-4 Elizabeth Kincaid, b. 1766, Augusta Co., VA, m. Daniel Harra
K-1-5-2-5 Sarah Kincaid, m. 23 Dec 1789, Thomas Terry
K-1-5-2-6 Thomas Kincaid, Jr., b. c1770, Augusta Co., VA, d. Madison Co., IN
m. 22 Nov 1791, Greenbrier Co., VA, Hanney Viney
m. 2nd Elizabeth Murdock
K-1-5-2-6-1 prob. Viney Kincaid, m. 2 Apr 1812, Mary Kincaid
K-1-5-2-6-2 prob. Francis Kincaid
K-1-5-2-6-3 prob. Hannah Kincaid
K-1-5-2-6-4 Prob. James Kincaid
K-1-5-2-6-5 Elizabeth Kincaid, m. Thomas Frazer
K-1-5-2-6-6 Thomas Kincaid
K-1-5-2-6-7 John Kincaid, m. Mary ?
K-1-5-2-6-8 Samuel Kincaid, m. Martha
K-1-5-2-6-9 Margaret Kincaid, m. A. Van Gorder
K-1-5-2-6-10 Andrew Kincaid
K-1-5-2-6-11 Sarah Kincaid, m. M. Whitecotton
K-1-5-2-7 George Kincaid, m. Johanna Baldwin
K-1-5-2-8 Francis Kincaid, m. Nancy Murdock
K-1-5-2-9 William Kincaid, b. 1777, m. 18 May 1802, Greenbrier Co., VA, Mary Ann Tincher
K-1-5-2-10 poss. Hannah Kincaid, m. 13 Dec 1798, Greenbrier Co., VA, James Walker
K-1-5-3 John Kincaid, b. c1740, Augusta Co., VA, d. c1810 Greenbrier Co., VA
m. c1765, Augusta Co., VA, Anne Graham, d. c1848
K-1-5-3-1 Elizabeth Kincaid, b. 1768/70, m. 10 Dec 1788, Greenbrier Co., VA, William Hopkins
K-1-5-3-2 Lanty Kincaid, b. 1770/80, d. 1850 Monroe (now Summers) Co., VA
m. 6 Feb 1798, Greenbrier Co., VA, Catharine Scott, b. c1775, Greenbrier Co., VA, d. ? 5 Jun 1774, Greenbrier Co., VA
K-1-5-3-2-1 Mathew Kincaid, b. c1797, d. 2 Apr 1828, Greenbrier Co., VA, m. Elizabeth Harrah

K-1-5-3-2-2 John Kincaid, b. c1798, d. Dec 1862, Greenbrier Co., VA, m.
Leah Withrow
K-1-5-3-2-2-1 Charles Kincaid, b. c1894
K-1-5-3-2-2-2 Lewis Kincaid, d. c1890
K-1-5-3-2-2-3 Octavia Kincaid, b. St. Clair Burdette
K-1-5-3-2-3 Julia Kincaid, b. 7 Aug 1814, Greenbrier Co., VA, d. 1 Oct
1887
m. 12 Sep 1833, Samuel McCorkle, Jr., b. 11 Jun 1814, Greenbrier Co.,
VA, d. 28 Dec 1856, Monroe Co., VA
K-1-5-3-2-3-1 Catherine McCorkle
K-1-5-3-2-3-2 Stuart McCling McCorkle
K-1-5-3-2-3-3 Elizabeth H. McCorkle
K-1-5-3-2-3-4 William Graham McCorkle
K-1-5-3-2-3-5 Charles Madison McCorkle
K-1-5-3-2-3-6 Rebecca Ann McCorkle
K-1-5-3-2-3-7 Isabel Jane McCorkle
K-1-5-3-2-3-8 Mason Clay McCorkle, b. 3 Sep 1853, d. 3 Mar 1932
m. 19 Jul 1879, Rhoda Cannady McCorkle
K-1-5-3-2-3-8-1 Merton R. McCorkle, b. 2 May 1880, m. Margaret
Kennedy McCorkle
K-1-5-3-2-4 Nancy Kincaid, m. ? Heffmer
K-1-5-3-2-5 Lanty Kincaid, Jr., b. c1808 (Lanty 42 in 1850 Greenbrier
census)
m. Agnes Holcomb
K-1-5-3-2-5-1 Frances Kincaid, b. c1832
K-1-5-3-2-5-2 Madeline Kincaid, b. c1834
K-1-5-3-2-5-3 Alex Kincaid, b. c1836
K-1-5-3-2-5-4 Wallace Kincaid, b. c1838
K-1-5-3-2-5-5 Sarah Kincaid, b. c1840
K-1-5-3-2-5-6 Nancy S. Kincaid, b. c1842
K-1-5-3-2-5-7 Lanty Kincaid, III, b. c1842
m. 6 Dec 1871, Mary Margaret Hogshead
K-1-5-3-2-5-7-1 William F. Kincaid, b. c1872
K-1-5-3-2-5-7-2 Nancy E. Kincaid, b. c1874
K-1-5-3-2-5-7-3 Charles A. Kincaid, b. c1876
K-1-5-3-2-5-7-4 Walter L. Kincaid, b. c1878
K-1-5-3-2-6 Rebecca Kincaid
m. 13 Feb 1835, William Graham, Jr.
K-1-5-3-2-6-1 James Lanty Graham
K-1-5-3-2-6-2 Catherine Scott Graham
K-1-5-3-2-6-3 Julia Elizabeth Graham
K-1-5-3-2-6 m. 2nd John Miller
K-1-5-3-2-7 Catherine (Katy) Kincaid, m. William Heffmer
K-1-5-3-2-8 Octavia Kincaid, m. George St. Clair Burdett
K-1-5-3-2-9 Cynthia Kincaid, m. Samuel Tincher

K-1-5-3-3 Mathew Kincaid, b. 1772, d. 1860, Summer Co., WV (1 son, 9 daughters)
m. 24 Jul 1804, Bath Co., VA, Elizabeth Scott, b. c1780
K-1-5-3-3-1 Katy Kincaid
K-1-5-3-3-2 Ann Graham Kincaid
K-1-5-3-3-3 Jane Kincaid, m. Moses Hedrick
K-1-5-3-3-4 Lanty Graham Kincaid (apparently moved to Summers Co., VA, later to IL where he died after 1865)
m. Eliza Keller
K-1-5-3-3-4-1 John Kincaid, lived and died on Lick Creek in Sommers Co., VA
K-1-5-3-3-4-1-1 Charley Kincaid, d. c1905
K-1-5-3-3-4-1-2 Lewis Kincaid, d. c1905
K-1-5-3-3-4-2 William Kincaid, m. Emma Lively (later moved to OR)
K-1-5-3-3-5 Sarah Kincaid, b. Samuel Humphreys
K-1-5-3-3-6 Florence Graham Kincaid, m. Isaac Tincher, m. 2nd Thomas Holstein
K-1-5-3-3-7 Nancy Kincaid, m. Richard Meadows
K-1-5-3-3-8 Rebecca Kincaid, m. Harry Karns
K-1-5-3-3-9 Elizabeth Kincaid
K-1-5-3-3-10 Susan Kincaid, m. Griffith Meadows
K-1-5-3-4 prob. Sally Kincaid, b, c1776, m. 6 Feb 1796, James Thompson
K-1-5-4 Andrew Kincaid*, b. 1740, d. 1810, Greenbrier Co., VA
m. Mary (?Kincaid or Caldwell)
K-1-5-4-1 Andrew Kincaid*, b. c1760, d. after 1812
m. Rebecca (family name unknown)
K-1-5-4-1-1 Samuel Kincaid*, b. 15 Mar 1788, VA, d. 28 Dec 1866
m. 20 Jun 1812, Greenbrier Co., VA, Katherine McClung, b. 5 Oct 1788, d. 5 Jun 1874
K-1-5-4-1-1-1 Joseph Kincaid, b. c1813, Greenbrier Co., VA, d. aft 1860 nfi (in 1860 census, age 47 unmarried, but not found in any later census)
K-1-5-4-1-1-2 James Kincaid*, b. c1816, Greenbrier Co., VA, d. after 1880
m. Mary Jane Wallace, b. 1829, WV, d. 1870/80
K-1-5-4-1-1-2-1 William Samuel Kincaid*, b. 10 Dec 1844, d. 27 Feb 1882
m. 21 Oct 1869, Greenbrier Co., WV, Rachel Ellen Knight
K-1-5-4-1-1-2-1-1 Clora Jane Kincaid*, b. 2 Nov 1870, Greenbrier Co., WV, d. 18 Jun 1955, Randolph Co., IN, bur. Redkey, IN
m. 11 Mar 1891, Greenbrier Co., WV, Noah Edward "Ed" Boggs, b. 10 Nov 1864, Greenbrier Co., WV, d. Nov 1932, IN, bur. Redkey, IN
(see Boggs descendants, B-2-4-7-4-6)
K-1-5-4-1-1-2-1-2 Della Rebecca Kincaid, b. 28 Sep 1872, d. 26 Feb 1958
m. 13 Mar 1895, Greenbrier Co., WV, Edgar Huff
K-1-5-4-1-1-2-1-2-1 Clayton O. Huff, b. 19 Jun 1897
K-1-5-4-1-1-2-1-2-2 Lister L. Huff, b. 10 Jan 1899
K-1-5-4-1-1-2-1-3 Mary Uginia Kincaid, b. 18 May 1874, d. 22 May 1908

m. 5 Sep 1894, Greenbrier Co., WV, Michael Marion Burr

K-1-5-4-1-1-2-1-4 James Andrew Kincaid, b. 6 Oct 1875, d. 7 May 1944 (in 1910 McLeans Co., IL census)
m. 25 Jun 1903, Annie Catherine Sward

K-1-5-4-1-1-2-1-4-1 James C. Kincaid, b. c1907, IL

K-1-5-4-1-1-2-1-4-2 Helen Kincaid, b. 21 May 1910, Bloomington, IL

K-1-5-4-1-1-2-1-5 Mattie Ora Kincaid, b. 22 Sep 1877, d. 9 Mar 1957
m. 2 Oct 1901, Mason Knapp

K-1-5-4-1-1-2-1-6 George Robert "Buzz" Kincaid, b. 10 Sep 1879
m. Lillian ?

K-1-5-4-1-1-2-1-7 Samuel Alexander Kincaid, b. 13 Mar 1882 (1910 McLeans Co., IL census)
m. 20 Jul 1905, Emma C. Sward, b. 1882, IL

K-1-5-4-1-1-2-1-7-1 Lloyd Kincaid, b. c1908, IL

K-1-5-4-1-1-2-2 George Robert Kincaid, b. c1846, d. 4 Dec 1869

K-1-5-4-1-1-2-3 Mary C. Kincaid, b. 1 Mar 1855, Greenbrier Co., VA,

K-1-5-4-1-1-2-4 Margaret L. Kincaid, b. 11 Dec 1859

K-1-5-4-1-1-2-5 Elizabeth N. Kincaid, b. c1867

K-1-5-4-1-1-3 Samuel Kincaid, b. c1819
m. 26 Nov 1840, Greenbrier Co., VA, Catharine Hawver

K-1-5-4-1-1-3-1 Henry Kincaid, b. c1843

K-1-5-4-1-1-3-2 Rebecca J. Kincaid, b. c1845

K-1-5-4-1-1-3-3 Mary E. Kincaid, b. c1848

K-1-5-4-1-1-4 daughter, name unknown, b. c1820/1 (5-10 in 1830 census, not listed in 1840 census)

K-1-5-4-1-1-5 Hugh Kincaid, b. c1827, Greenbrier Co., VA, d. after 1880
m. 16 Mar 1870, Greenbrier Co., WV, Jemima McMillion

K-1-5-4-1-1-5-1 Robert H. Kincaid, b. 1871, WV

K-1-5-4-1-1-5-2 Catharine A. Kincaid, b. 23 Dec 1872, WV

K-1-5-4-1-1-6 Robert Kincaid, b. c1829, d. 1853/60
m. c1848, Margaret ?, b. c1829, VA

K-1-5-4-1-1-6-1 Virginia C. Kincaid, b. Jun 1849
m. 4 Oct 1871, Hiram S. McMillion

K-1-5-4-1-1-6-1-1 Oakie McMillion, b. 1872, d. 1947, Bloomington, IL

K-1-5-4-1-1-6-1-2 Mary L. McMillion, b. c1874

K-1-5-4-1-1-6-1-3 Robert D. McMillion, b. Jan 1876, d. 1934

K-1-5-4-1-1-6-1-4 Harry McMillion, b. 1878, d. 9 Jul 1881

K-1-5-4-1-1-6-1-5 Katherine H. McMillion, b. 1881, d. 1950, Bloomington, IL, m. Halstead

K-1-5-4-1-1-6-1-4 Clyde S. McMillion, b. Mar 1884, d. Jan 1926, Phoenix, AZ

K-1-5-4-1-1-6-2 Samuel D. Kincaid, b. c1851

K-1-5-4-1-1-6-3 Robert Kincaid, b. c1852

K-1-5-4-2 John Kincaid

K-1-5-4-3 Robert Kincaid

K-1-5-4-4 James Kincaid

K-1-5-4-5 Thomas Kincaid

K-1-5-4-6 Sarah Kincaid, m. 3 Mar 1788, Kincaid Caldwell

K-1-5-4-7 Elizabeth Kincaid, m. Miller

K-1-5-4-8 Ann Kincaid, m. 2 Aug 1792, Richard Gartner

K-1-5-4-9 Mary Kincaid, m. Wyatt

K-1-5-4-10 Margaret Kincaid
   m. 20 Apr 1802, Greenbrier Co., WV, William Slone

Abbreviations and Numbering

aft	-	after
adp.	-	adopted
b.	-	born
bef	-	before
betw.	-	between
c	-	circa, about the time of (c often used with census data to indicate the year of birth)
Co.	-	County
d.	-	died
dnm	-	did not marry
m.	-	married
nfi	-	no further information
ni	-	no issue, children
prob.	-	probably
Twp	-	Township
?	-	Indicates probable connection but some uncertainty in information
??	-	Indicates speculation on the information
*	-	Indicates direct line ancestor

Ancestral Chart, Numbering System - Father's name is always twice number of the offspring. Mother's name is twice the offspring's number plus one. Therefore fathers' numbers are always even and mothers' numbers are always odd.

Descendant's List, Numbering System - Letter refers to the earliest ancestor with which the list begins. Each subsequent dash indicates the next generation and the number refers to the order of the children in the next generation. Children are numbered in order of birth if that is known.

The US Postal Service two letter abbreviations for the states are used when any state is abbreviated.

Bibliography

1. Tucker, Ebenezer, *History of Randolph County, Indiana with Illustrations and Biographical Sketches*, A. L. Kingman, Chicago, 1882.

2. Bowen, A. W. and Company, *A Portrait and Biographical Record of Delaware and Randolph Counties*, Chicago, 1894.

3. Smith and Driver, *Past and Present of Randolph County, Indiana*, 1914.

4. Randolph County Historical and Genealogical Society, *Randolph County, Indiana*, 1990.

5. Helm, Thomas B., *History of Delaware County, Indiana*, 1881.

6. Kemper, G. W. H., *History of Delaware County, Vol. II*, 1908, Lewis Publishing, Chicago.

7. Rice, Otis K., *A History of Greenbrier County*, McClain Printing, Parsons, West Virginia, 1986.

8. U. S. Federal census records, 1790-1920.

9. Randolph County, Indiana, marriage, birth and death records.

10. Greenbrier County, West Virginia, marriage, birth and death records.

11. Grady, Mrs. Alice, Editor, *Boggs Newsletter*, 1971-1979.

12. Woodyard, Edward L., *James Boggs from Londonderry, Ireland to New Castle Co., Delaware*, Boggs Newsletter, Vol. 10 (1&2) Jan-June 1987, pg. 2.

13. Boggs, William E., *Ruminations About the Origin(s) of the Name Boggs and the Livingstone Tradition*, Boggs Family History Quarterly, Vol. 12(3), Fall, 1998, pg. 84.

14. Simons, Mary Louise Williams *et al*, *Descendants of James Boggs*, 1998, privately published.

15. Harlow, Benjamin Franklin, *The Renicks of Greenbrier*, Appendix on Kincaids by Herbert Clarke Kincaid, 1951, FHL Film 1697747, Salt Lake City.

16. Carder, Robert W., *et al*, *Carder family genealogical collection*, FHL Films 1421642 and 1421643, Salt Lake City.

17. Carder, W. Ashley, *Carder, An American Family, A History of the Carder Family Originally of Culpeper County, Virginia*, 1993.

18. McClung, *History of the Cavendish Family*, ca.1750-1920, FHL Film 1320634, Salt Lake City.

19. McClung, Rev. William, *The McClung Genealogy*, McClung Printing Co., Pittsburgh, 1904, FHL Film 981925, Salt Lake City.

20. Shaper, M. Caroline, *Unpuzzling One David Geringer/Gerringer/Garinger/Garringer*, Boswell Printing, 1992, privately published.

21. Boots, Clyde S., *Descendants of Adam Boots : born Hans Adam Stieffel - 1733 and related families*, FHL Film 897035, Salt Lake City.

22. Boots, Clyde S., *Descendants of Adam Boots, b. 1733, d. 1803*, FHL Film 1036425, Salt Lake City.

23. Boots, Cylde S., *Petersen (Biedert) Family Records*, FHL Film 1036370, Salt Lake City.

24. Boots, Jack Robert, *A Heritage of Eli and Eunice Boots*, FHL Film 1015837, Salt Lake City.

25. Couper, William, *The Couper Family of Longforgan Scotland and Norfolk, Virginia,* Virginia Magazine of History and Biography, Vol. 59 (1951).

26. Williams, Louis J., *The Harbours in America,* 1982, Harbour-Harbor-Harber Family Association, Lubbock, Texas.

27. Freeborg, Rebecca, *Lonas is my Line,* FHL Film 1035912, Salt Lake City.

28. Parker, Wayne V., *The Hammers Genealogy, Descendants of Peter Hammer 1757-1838,* 1972.

29. Morris, Janet M., *Morris Family History, 1977,* Bluffton, Indiana, published privately.

30. Groves, George N., *Genealogy of the Grove and Groves Family,* 1941, FHL Fiche 6048063, Salt Lake City.

31. Life, Carlos A., *A History of the Life Family,* Peru, Indiana, 1972, FHL Film 908243, Salt Lake City.

32. Hambrock, Rick, *Garringer Descendants Lists,* private communications, 1999, Portland, Indiana.

33. Williams, Helen Knight, *Knight Papers,* private communications, 2000, Annapolis, Maryland.

Index

Carder, John Anderson 71, 111
Carder, John Jr. 113
Carder, Joseph 38, 61, 71,
111, 112, 113
Carder, Josina 111
Carder, Lucinda 113
Carder, Mahalia 113
Carder, Mary Day 111, 114
Carder, Mary Rinker 71
Carder, Mont 64
Carder, Phoebe E. 38, 58, 61,
73, 111, 232
Carder, Plummer 1, 111, 112
Carder, Rebecca 111
Carder, Rebecca Wiseman 111
Carder, Rebecca Wiseman 61,
111, 112
Carder, Thomas 113, 114
Carder, W. Ashley 114
Carley, Ruth A. 201
Carothers, William 156, 158
Carr, Conrad 171
Carrell, Margaret 107
Carrenger, David 123
Carson, Tammi 18, 233
Carter, Hannah 217
Cavendish, Andrew 104
Cavendish, Jane 103
Cavendish, Joseph 103
Cavendish, Margaret 40, 102, 103
Cavendish, Mary Polly 103
Cavendish, Rebecca 104
Cavendish, William 103
Cavendish, William Hunter 33, 41,
102, 103
Cavendish, Jane Murphy 102
Caylor, Samuel 174
Charles, Margaret 206
Churchill, Armstead 108
Clara, Maria 116
Clark, Nancy 54
Clarke, James 80
Clarke, Margaret 80
Clements, Charity Belle Marquis 242
Clements, Charity Marquis 137, 142
Clendenin, Ann 48
Clendenin, James 76
Clendenin, Mary 48, 50, 53
Clendenin, William 49
Cochran, Sarah F. 58, 60
Collins, Abigail 193, 196
Collins, Amelia Alisa 118, 133,
137, 191, 197, 242, 279
Collins, Amos 195, 196
Collins, Benjamin 193, 196

Collins, Catherine 196, 197
Collins, Cornelius 193, 195,
196, 197
Collins, David 197
Collins, Elisha 196
Collins, Elizabeth 193, 195,
196, 197
Collins, Elizabeth J. 197
Collins, Elizabeth Liggett 194
Collins, Elliott 195
Collins, George 192, 193, 194,
195, 196
Collins, Hannah 193, 195
Collins, Hannah Cozad 193
Collins, Harriet 194, 196
Collins, Harriet Finch 203
Collins, Harrison 195
Collins, Isaac S. 193
Collins, Jacob 193
Collins, James 196
Collins, Jesse 195
Collins, Jesse C. 195
Collins, John 118, 191, 192,
194, 195, 196, 197, 278
Collins, John G. 196
Collins, John III 118, 193, 194
Collins, John Jr. 118, 192, 193, 276
Collins, John Sr. 276
Collins, Joseph 118, 195, 196,
197, 199, 201, 203, 278
Collins, Joseph B. 196
Collins, Joseph Coltmus 137
Collins, Joseph H. 194
Collins, Martin 196, 197
Collins, Mary 193, 194, 196, 197
Collins, Melissa 196, 197
Collins, Mildred 196
Collins, Nancy 196
Collins, Oceanna 196
Collins, Prudence 194, 195
Collins, Rachel 196
Collins, Robert 196
Collins, Sally A. 196
Collins, Sarah 196
Collins, Sarah E. 197
Collins, Susan 195, 196, 197
Collins, Susan Ann 194
Collins, Thomas 192
Collins, William 196
Collins, William H. 196
Collins, William Harrison 134,
197, 279
Collins, William T. 196
Comer, Martin 26
Constantine, Patrick 107

Cook, Eliza 195
Cook, John 195
Cook, Mary 195
Cooper, Marie 207
Cooper, Nancy 122, 207, 208
Cornwallis, General 189
Couper, Colonel William 184
Court, C. B. 126
Cox, Frances 185
Cox, Martha A. 134
Cozad, Elizabeth Sutton 192
Cozad, Hannah 118, 192, 276
Cozad, Jacob 276
Cozad, Rev. Jacob 118, 191, 192
Cresap, Col. Daniel 192
Cresap, Elizabeth 192
Cresap, Ruth Swearingen 192
Creviston, Marie 5
Creviston, Marie Elizabeth 15, 232
Cross, John 113
Crossan, Elizabeth 193
Culp, Frederick 126
Culp, John 125, 126
Culp, John Jr. 127
Culp, John Sr. 127
Culp, Mary 126, 127
Culver, Daniel 173, 174
Cunningham, Rachel 193
Current, Harriet Jane 175
Current, John 73

D

Dalton, Ann Nancy 183
Dalton, Charlotte Gallihue 183
Darnell, Isaac 127
Davids, Andrew 179
Davis, John L. 54
Davis, Martha 145, 146
Davis, Richard 206
Davis, Susannah 179, 180
Dawley, Dennis 185
Day, Mary 38
Dean, Alice 79
Dean, Elizabeth 79
Dean, Joseph 52
Decker, Sylvester 209
Devault, Sarah 52
Dickenson, Col. 40, 88
Dickenson, Nancy 40, 87, 88
Dickson, Abigail 87
Dieter, George 118
Dieter, Rosina 118, 172
Dillman, Daniel 175
Dillon, Rhoda Strong 175

Dixon, Joseph 88
Doudel, Michael 154
Draper, John 179
Draper, Mary Ann 41, 106
Draper, Wesley 179
Drennin, Susan 50
Driver, Lee 145
Dull, Henry 133
Dunmore, Lord 112

E

Edward, Charles 220
Eiler, Christy 19
Eiler, Christy Elizabeth 18, 233
Eiler, Jerry Richard 18, 233
Eiler, Lora Diane 18, 19, 233
Elliott, Andrew 38
Elliott, Martha 38, 48, 49,
    54, 230
Elsworth, Mary 193
Emory, Hannah 193
Ewing, James 108

F

Fairfax, Thomas Lord 191
Felkey, Margaret 128
Filson, Davidson 48
Finch, Adam 200, 201
Finch, Adelaide 201
Finch, Alice Stevens 199
Finch, Amelia 202
Finch, Amelia Jackson 199
Finch, Anna Marie 199
Finch, Catherine 201, 202
Finch, Clavinda 202
Finch, Dawson 200
Finch, Edgar 202
Finch, Elizabeth 201
Finch, Elizabeth Amelia 202
Finch, Elzora 202
Finch, Ethel 198
Finch, Francis 199
Finch, Harriet 118, 137, 195, 197,
    199, 201, 203, 279
Finch, J. Thomas 202
Finch, James 201, 202
Finch, Johann 199
Finch, John 199, 200, 201, 203
Finch, Joseph 201
Finch, Joshua 201
Finch, Leander 201, 202
Finch, Lincoln Ellsworth 202
Finch, Mandeville 201, 202

Finch, Margaret Ellen 202
Finch, Martha 201, 202
Finch, Mary Ann 202
Finch, Matthis 199
Finch, Melanda 203
Finch, Ruth A. 202
Finch, Sam 200
Finch, Saml 200
Finch, Samuel 200, 201
Finch, Sarah A. 202
Finch, Sarah Ann 202
Finch, Thomas 118, 199, 200, 202
Finch, Thomas Jr. 200
Finch, Ulysses Grant 202
Finch, Vianna 199
Finch, William 118, 199, 200,
    201, 202, 203
Finch, William Jr. 201, 202
Finch, William M. 202
Fleming, John Martin 157
Flowers, Thomas 181, 182
Fountain, Anne Land 185
Fowler, William M. 139
Frame, James 53
Frances, Harriet 81
Franklin, Benjamin 57
French, Clifford 68
French, Ralph 68
Friend, Elizabeth Peragin 49, 52
Friend, Mary 51
Friend, Nicholas 51
Fry, John 159
Fry, Mary 119, 156, 158, 159, 268
Fry, Peter 159

G

Gabbert, Sarah C. 60
Gantz, Ida Taylor 145
Garinger, Barbara 125
Garinger, David 125
Garinger, Henry 124
Garinger, John 151
Garner, Mrs. Clyde 110
Garringer, Absolum 132
Garringer, Albert 129
Garringer, Alexander 25, 128, 129,
    130, 132, 133, 135, 173, 175
Garringer, Amanda 129, 131
Garringer, Amelia 141
Garringer, Amelia Collins 139,
    140, 198
Garringer, Angeline 129
Garringer, Arthur 140
Garringer, Barbara 125, 128

Garringer, Barbary 126
Garringer, Benjamin 128
Garringer, Bertha 9, 13, 145, 150
Garringer, Bertha Achsah 148
Garringer, Bertha Hammers 28
Garringer, Charity 142
Garringer, Clarence 138
Garringer, Cyrene Yeoman 130
Garringer, Daniel 151
Garringer, David 116, 124, 125,
    126, 128, 129, 130, 131, 132,
    133, 134, 136, 139, 151
Garringer, David A. 139
Garringer, David Arthur 137,
    138, 245
Garringer, David C. 116, 133,
    137, 139, 140, 141, 197,
    198, 279
Garringer, David Carson 136,
    191, 197, 242
Garringer, David Jr. 125, 128, 237
Garringer, David V. 137
Garringer, Delilah 133, 134
Garringer, Drucilla 131, 132
Garringer, Eliza 131
Garringer, Elizabeth 125, 127,
    129, 131
Garringer, Elizabeth Betsey 133
Garringer, Elizabeth Boots 133
Garringer, Elizabeth Catherine 138
Garringer, Elizabeth Johnson 132
Garringer, Elizabeth Rebecca 133
Garringer, Elizabeth Smith 131, 133
Garringer, Fred 152
Garringer, George 136
Garringer, George W. 134
Garringer, Hannah E. 134
Garringer, Harriet 138
Garringer, Helen 12, 13, 143,
    144, 146, 148, 149
Garringer, Helen Marie 1, 141,
    142, 149, 242
Garringer, Henry 134, 136
Garringer, Hilda 2, 9, 143, 144,
    145, 146, 148, 149, 150
Garringer, Hilda Irene 1, 4, 23,
    25, 46, 69, 70, 149, 153,
    169, 178, 184, 197, 199,
    204, 212, 213, 232, 242
Garringer, Ike 12, 13
Garringer, Ira James 130
Garringer, Isaac 128, 132, 133,
    135, 136, 139, 143, 169
Garringer, Isaac B. 134
Garringer, Isaac Jacob 116, 129,

302

Groves, Adam 216, 217
Groves, Alex 108
Groves, Alfred 217
Groves, Alfred Hance 220
Groves, Alfred M. 220
Groves, Anceline 213, 281
Groves, Ann 215
Groves, Anna 215
Groves, Arthur 219
Groves, Benjamin 219
Groves, Bennett 220
Groves, Catherine 218
Groves, Charles 217
Groves, David 215, 217, 218
Groves, Elizabeth 217
Groves, Elizabeth Reed 213, 218
Groves, Ethel 220
Groves, Garfield 219
Groves, George 216, 218
Groves, Hannah 217
Groves, Henry L. 218
Groves, Henry Lonas 215
Groves, Irene 164
Groves, Isaac 217, 220
Groves, Jacob 217, 218
Groves, John 215
Groves, John B. 220
Groves, John Grove 218
Groves, Logan 220
Groves, Lydia 52
Groves, Martha 218
Groves, Mary 215, 217
Groves, Milroy Elbert 220
Groves, Minnie 219
Groves, Orville 220
Groves, Rebecca 217
Groves, Rilla Ann 220
Groves, Sophiah 217
Groves, Susan 217
Groves, Susan Ann 217
Groves, Susannah 215
Groves, Willard 219
Groves, William 217
Groves, William Henry 220
Groves, William R. 219
Grovez, Abraham 216

H

Hafkemlier, Mary 220
Hagler, Leonard 171
Hagler, Sebastian 170
Hale, James 52
Haltom, William Newton 211
Hamer, James 161

Hamilton, William 80
Hammer, Agnes 157, 158
Hammer, Ann 163
Hammer, Anna Slick 163
Hammer, David 163
Hammer, Elizabeth 157, 158
Hammer, James 161
Hammer, Johann Frantz 163
Hammer, John 158
Hammer, John Abraham 163
Hammer, John P. 153, 155, 157
Hammer, John Peter 153, 157
Hammer, Joseph 157, 158, 159
Hammer, Margaret 163
Hammer, Mary 158, 160, 163
Hammer, Mary Fry 161
Hammer, Pam Caldwell 234
Hammer, Peter 119, 153, 154,
    155, 156, 157, 158, 267
Hammer, Phebe 157
Hammer, Rachael 163
Hammer, Rebecca Eisen 163
Hammer, Samuel 160
Hammer, William 163
Hammers, Abraham 28, 119,
    161, 162, 164, 165, 166,
    178, 179, 270
Hammers, Abraham Preston 164, 165
Hammers, Abram 161
Hammers, Achsah 163, 167
Hammers, Agnes 156
Hammers, Angeline 160
Hammers, Anna 156, 161
Hammers, Anna Amy 160
Hammers, Arthur Leroy 166, 168,
    204, 212, 270
Hammers, Augustus 157
Hammers, Bertha 142
Hammers, Bertha Achsah 1, 115,
    119, 137, 141, 153, 163, 166,
    167, 204, 212, 242, 270
Hammers, Catherine 160
Hammers, Daniel 160
Hammers, Delilah 157
Hammers, Elijah 165, 167, 168
Hammers, Elijah O. 165, 167
Hammers, Elijah Oliver 28, 119,
    164, 166, 204, 211, 212, 213,
    270, 281
Hammers, Elizabeth 156, 160
Hammers, Elizabeth Morris 28,
    167, 168
Hammers, James 159, 160, 161
Hammers, Janet 162
Hammers, Jappard 160

Hammers, Jarrel 160
Hammers, Jim 161
Hammers, John 156, 159
Hammers, John Oliver 168
Hammers, Joseph 156, 160,
    161, 162, 163, 267
Hammers, Katy 161
Hammers, Laura 163
Hammers, Lucy Irene 167, 168,
    204, 212, 271
Hammers, Margaret Helen 168
Hammers, Martha 160
Hammers, Mary 156, 160,
    162, 163
Hammers, Mary Elizabeth 164
Hammers, Mary Fry 160, 164
Hammers, Maud 165
Hammers, Nancy 166
Hammers, Nancy Harbour 28,
    162, 165
Hammers, Nancy J. 164
Hammers, Pam Caldwell 19
Hammers, Permela 157
Hammers, Peter 159, 160,
    162, 164, 268
Hammers, Peter Jr. 119, 156,
    158, 160
Hammers, Phebe 156
Hammers, Rebecca 157
Hammers, Robert 160
Hammers, Samuel 160
Hammers, Sarah 160, 161, 162
Hammers, Sarah Ann 163
Hammers, Saul 161
Hammers, William B. 165, 219
Hammers, William Blaine 212, 270
Hammers, William Blane 164, 166,
    168, 204
Hammery, Katherine 159
Hammet, James 161
Hamrick, Benjamin 107
Hanes, Elizabeth 207
Hanna, Calvin Huston 84
Hanna, Elizabeth 156, 158
Hanna, Francis Clark 84
Hanna, Joseph 156, 158
Hanna, Mary 158
Hanna, Robert 158
Hanna, Samuel 156
Hanna, William 176
Hannah, James W. 108
Hannah, Jane 107, 108
Hannah, Eliza 108
Harbour, Abner 182
Harbour, Adonijah 183

304

www.ingramcontent.com/pod-product-compliance
Lightning Source LLC
Chambersburg PA
CBHW070558270326
41926CB00013B/2361

* 9 7 8 0 7 8 8 4 1 7 2 5 2 *